A Traveller in Time

**The Critical Practice
of Maureen Kincaid Speller**

Edited and with an introduction
by Nina Allan

Foreword © Paul Kincaid 2023
Introduction © Nina Allan 2023
Articles © Maureen Kincaid Speller 2023
Maureen © Jonathan McCalmont 2023
Afterword © Aishwarya Subramanian and Dan Hartland 2023
Cover Design 'Path' © Iain Clark 2023
Maureen's picture #1 © Leigh Kennedy

The right of Maureen Kincaid Speller to be identified as the Author of the articles has been asserted by her in accordance with the Copyright, Designs and Patents Act 1988.

First published by Luna Press Publishing, Edinburgh, 2023

A Traveller in Time - The Critical Practice of Maureen Kincaid Speller © 2023. All rights reserved. No part of this publication may be reproduced, stored in a retrieval system, or transmitted in any form or by any means, electronic, mechanical, photocopy, recording or otherwise, without prior written permission of the copyright owners. Nor can it be circulated in any form of binding or cover other than that in which it is published and without similar condition including this condition being imposed on a subsequent purchaser.

www.lunapresspublishing.com

ISBN-13: 978-1-915556-20-2

Maureen Kincaid Speller
1959 - 2022

Contents

A Common Reader: a foreword by Paul Kincaid	1
Maureen Kincaid Speller: a critical life. An Introduction by Nina Allan	4
ASTONISHED BY SCIENCE FICTION	11
{and then} – a writing life beyond reviews	12
All right, have it your way – you saw a man with a raygun!	18
Reading Margaret Atwood's *In Other Worlds: science fiction and the human imagination*	25
A Judge's Summary of the Clarke Award	29
On wanting to be astonished by science fiction	35
We Need to Talk About Dragons: John Mullan, George R.R. Martin, *Game of Thrones* and the triumph of fantasy fiction	39
Making an Emotional Investment – surviving the announcement of the Hugo Awards shortlists	46
WRITING IN THE MARGINS	51
Daughters of Earth, edited by Justine Larbalestier	52
Women's Weird 2: More Strange Stories by Women 1891 – 1937, edited by Melissa Edmundson	56
Galactic Suburbia: Recovering Women's Science Fiction by Lisa Yaszek	66
James Tiptree Jr.: The Double Life of Alice B. Sheldon by Julie Phillips	70
Love Beyond Body, Space & Time edited by Hope Nicholson	73
They Are Not Ghosts: on the representation of the indigenous peoples of North America in science fiction and fantasy	77
Reading *Mothership: Tales from Afrofuturism and Beyond* edited by Bill Campbell and Edward Austin Hall, and *We See a Different Frontier* edited by Fabio Fernandes and Djibril al-Ayad	82
AfroSF: Science Fiction by African Writers edited by Ivor W. Hartmann	87
AfroSF Volume 2 edited by Ivor W. Hartmann	89
LOST LANDSCAPES AND NEW HORIZONS	93
Quis Est Iste Qui Venit	94
England's Redemption: an examination of Richard Cowper's Corlay Sequence	102
The Owl Service TV series adapted for the screen by Alan Garner, directed by Peter Plummer	111
'Fusion with a land rescued me': landscape and presence in the writings of Alan Garner	112
Boneland by Alan Garner: preliminary notes	117
First Light: A Celebration of Alan Garner edited by Erica Wagner and *The Beauty Things* by Mark Edmonds and Alan Garner	125

The Critic and the Clue: tracking Alan Garner's *Treacle Walker*	132
A Field Guide to Reality — Joanna Kavenna	144
Walking with Tolkien and Macfarlane	149
Review: *Mothlight* by Adam Scovell	153

READING FOR THE FUTURE 161

Reading for the Future	162
The Children of Green Knowe and *A Traveller in Time* – a tale of two novels	167
'We were all monsters and bastards and we were beautiful' – Rachel Hartman's *Seraphina*	173
Reading *Diana Wynne Jones: Children's Literature and the Fantastic Tradition* by Farah Mendlesohn	179
More Than This by Patrick Ness	182

SEEING STARS 185

'Recordings alone aren't sufficient' – speaking *Arrival*	186
The view from G21: watching *Star Wars: The Force Awakens*	193
'he had a remarkable gentleness and courtesy in his dealings with women' – the *Sherlock* Christmas special	199
The Hobbit, or Madly in All Directions	208
Watching *Hamlet*	214

THE STORIES THAT SHAPE US 222

Reading van Vogt's *Slan*	223
The Weird – *The Dunwich Horror* – by H.P. Lovecraft	228
Embassytown – China Miéville	233
Osama – Lavie Tidhar	237
Azanian Bridges – Nick Wood	239
The Book of Phoenix by Nnedi Okorafor	244
The Testament of Jessie Lamb – Jane Rogers	246
Gods Without Men by Hari Kunzru	250
By Light Alone – Adam Roberts	254
Zone One – Colson Whitehead	257
Reading *Elysium* by Jennifer Marie Brissett	263
Europe in Autumn – Dave Hutchinson	271
The Stone Boatmen by Sarah Tolmie	277

AFTERWORD 283

Maureen by Jonathan McCalmont	284
Afterword by Aishwarya Subramanian and Dan Hartland	288
Acknowledgements	294
Reference List	295

A Common Reader: a foreword by Paul Kincaid

Years ago, when some enterprising manufacturer produced a range of mugs designed like the iconic covers of original Penguin paperbacks, Maureen and I decided that as a bookish couple we really should own one apiece.

Now, in that first set of mugs at least, I don't think there was any title that I felt instinctively I must own. So I picked one more or less at random, because it amused me: *Man And Superman* by George Bernard Shaw (or, as both the mug and the original paperback would have it, simply Bernard Shaw). But Maureen knew exactly what she wanted: *The Common Reader* by Virginia Woolf.

The Common Reader and *The Second Common Reader*, in secondhand American paperback editions, have been sitting on our shelves forever. I've dipped into them, and I'm pretty sure that Maureen read them both. But if so, it was a long time ago; she never re-read them. It wasn't for the book itself that she wanted that particular mug, but for the symbolism of the title. A common reader: that, I'm sure, was how she saw herself, and it was certainly how she saw the role and duty of the critic. The job of the critic is not to laud a book or to eviscerate it, but to act as a bridge between book and reader in the ongoing, unending conversation that is literature.

When we first met, we seemed to spend all of our time in long, intricate conversations about books. It wasn't long before I found myself saying that she really ought to write some of this down. And since I was, at the time, reviews editor for *Vector*, I suggested that she should do some reviews for me. Her immediate response was: no, I can't, I've not read enough, I've not read the right books. The depth and range of our discussions before this point was ample evidence that she was wrong, but it took a while to persuade her of that. Nobody can read 'enough', and despite what some people claim, there is no set canon of science fiction that must be read if we are to claim to understand the genre as a whole. Every time we read a new book for review, we are starting from scratch all over again; science fiction or fantasy or crime fiction or mainstream literature or whatever is being reinvented anew as we turn each page of the book. It was this notion, I think, this sense that everything we read is part of an ongoing and unending exploration, that convinced her to start reviewing. It was certainly the guiding principle behind the criticism she did write.

Everything she wrote was part of her report on that exploration, a way of connecting with those of us who followed, or those of us who were cutting through the jungle on a parallel track. The world is too big for any one critic to encapsulate all of it; but each report added more to the picture, more to our understanding. And that was how she saw criticism: building our understanding in order to provide a platform upon which others might add their own insights.

Her reviews were never meant to be the last word on any book. That's why you so rarely find the lazy judgementalism that most of us have fallen back on at one time or another, no familiar variations on 'buy this book!' or 'cast this abomination into outer darkness!' None of that was what criticism was for in her view: none of that served the author, or the critic, or, least of all, the reader. Instead she was the common reader, putting herself in the place of any other reader approaching the work in question. She would say: this is how the book spoke to me, or this is why it didn't speak to me. She would say: this is what I found interesting about the book, or this is why I found it uninteresting. She would say: these are ideas that shouted out to me from the book, or this is why it seems to have nothing to say. And always there was the implied, unstated question: how did it speak to you, what did you find interesting, what ideas did you glean.

The critic does not tell you how to read a book, but rather suggests approaches you might or might not find fruitful. The book is not the end of criticism, but merely the trigger for a wider conversation. And for Maureen the job of the critic was simply to engage in that conversation.

And she engaged with wit. She could be a very funny writer when she wanted to be, though more often she employed the sort of wit that catches you unawares, that makes you stop later and turn back and ask yourself: did she really say that? And yes she did, though rarely just for the sake of being funny. She used wit as a tool, as a way of sharpening your perception, as a way of pointing out absurdity, as a way of making profound thoughts slip by in a palatable and attractive way. It is what makes so much of her work so readable.

It was a tool that she used liberally, not just in her popular reviews but in her more serious writing also. There is a contribution to a collection of academic essays; her piece is a study of the Native American playwright, Guillermo Verdecchia. The essay, '"Some Borders Are More Easily Crossed Than Others": Negotiating Guillermo Verdecchia's *Fronteras Americanas*' (in *Parallel Encounters: Culture at the Canada-US Border* edited by Gillian Roberts and David Stirrup, 2013), takes as its central metaphor the absurdity of the idea of borders. The fact that one might fly deep into the heart of a country (I'm sure she was thinking of a flight we had made to Atlanta) and yet, in the airport, an arbitrary line on the floor somehow acts as the border. What landscape can you possibly be occupying in the moment before you step across that line? For all its depth (and she could be a very deep writer) that essay is as readable as any of her more comic pieces.

Yet it would be wrong to think that this easy wit, this friendly engagement in the literary conversation, meant that she gave any writer an easy pass. Far from it: the more she valued an author the more she demanded of them. Like any of us, she had many favourite writers: the American essayist, John McPhee; the science fiction writers Ian McDonald and Sarah Tolmie; the nature writer, Richard Fortey. And she was constantly adding to that list. In the weeks before she died she had discovered, with evident pleasure, the novels of the mid-twentieth-century writer, Jocelyn Brooke. But the writer who was probably most enduringly and most intimately a part of her intellectual life was Alan Garner. His first book, *The Weirdstone of Brisingamen*, was published the year after she was born; his latest (last?), *Treacle Walker*, was shortlisted for the Booker Prize in the year that she died. In between, she read, avidly, everything he wrote, including relatively obscure works like *Holly from the Bongs*, *The Guizer*, and *The Lad of the Gad*. She walked the landscape of *Thursbitch*, she bought hefty tomes about the history of Alderley Edge, she once drove from Folkestone to Cheltenham and returned the same night simply to hear Garner give a talk. She was a fan. Yet she held him to account. She highlighted colonialist tendencies in his work, something that made her a rather controversial figure in Garner-related discussion groups. She pointed to inconsistencies in the stories he told about his life and his accumulation of objects. The last piece of writing she published was a review of *Treacle Walker* that explored how much of the novel depended on familiarity with tropes he had used throughout his career.

It is a matter of great regret, among those of us who know and love Maureen's writing, that she never got to write the book about Garner that would have showcased the intense and intimate engagement his work is clearly crying out for. The closest we can now come to that is the collection of reviews and essays gathered here. And they come escorted by other pieces, some familiar, some, perhaps, less so, but all of which allow us to rejoin that conversation about literature that she maintained so well for so long.

When I was putting together photographs of Maureen to be shown at her funeral, I was struck by how many of them showed her laughing. I remember her as a very serious person, but there is no contradiction between laughter and seriousness. And I think she would be laughing now at the joy of being, once again and for always, a common reader.

Maureen Kincaid Speller: a critical life

An Introduction by Nina Allan

The last time I saw Maureen was on Zoom, moderating a British Science Fiction Association panel discussion to celebrate the 50th anniversary of the Science Fiction Foundation. The four of us—Chris and I, Paul and Maureen—met up for a Zoom coffee not long before that, and had exchanged emails since. We spoke of the lockdowns and their effects, the books we were reading, the various writing projects we were engaged in. We had high hopes that Maureen and Paul would be able to visit us in Scotland in the spring, a trip that had been long postponed due to the pandemic.

There is nothing that can adequately prepare you for bad news, and the shock of hearing about Maureen's illness, early in 2022, is one that is still reverberating through the lives of all who knew her. As with many of my closest friends, I knew Maureen through her writing before we ever met. I'd read her reviews in *Vector*, knew that she had been a Clarke judge. As a writer who is also a critic, I love the company of critics. I gravitate naturally towards those who enjoy not only reading books but discussing books in a robust manner, teasing out an author's intention or capacity for experiment, bemoaning 'the state of the field' or celebrating the shortlisting of a favourite novel for a literary prize. I relish the conversation, in other words, and Maureen Kincaid Speller was a champion at it. Since her death in September 2022, many have spoken of Maureen's kindness, her unique sense of humour, her camaraderie and I can attest to all three. I warmed to her on sight. Our friendship over ten or so years is something I feel privileged to have experienced.

I treasure especially the time we spent together on the Shadow Clarke jury in 2017, when for the duration of several months we were in constant daily contact, exchanging ideas, expressing frustrations, having a laugh. Our commitment to the project was serious, but there was much, much laughter. It does not feel like a coincidence to me that it was then, within the context of work, of writing, that I feel I truly came to know Maureen well, to appreciate what she was about. There is joy in that knowledge, as there is joy in time shared, no matter that such time turned out to be shorter than any of us could have wished for or have known.

*

My original hope and intention for this volume was that I would have time to consult with Maureen about which of her essays she would personally like to be included. More importantly even than that, I wanted to sit down with her and simply talk—about her life in science fiction, her early experiences as a reader, her ideas about the nature and purpose of criticism. Time moved against us, alas, and in the writing of this introduction especially I am still feeling the lack of that conversation. There are past conversations, of course, and there are clues we can pick up about what might be missing—indeed, the essays in this volume will provide more than a few. We know Maureen was drawn to fantasy from a young age. We will discover that she read *The Lord of the Rings* so many times she knew parts of it by heart. We can infer that her reading tastes—indeed her bookishness generally—were not always appreciated by her family, and can only speculate about the effect this might have had upon a young, endlessly curious, and adventurous mind. We know her first marriage—to a man who did not like science fiction—was unhappy; we are gratified that she later found lifelong mutual support and happiness in her marriage to Paul Kincaid, a delight in each other's company that was obvious to anyone who knew them.

Reading her over the longer haul, we may gradually come to the conclusion that Maureen felt ambivalent about revisiting her youth, which was, as it is for many, a time of complications and contradictions, blessings that are decidedly mixed. In the essay that leads off this collection, she talks about how she would often begin a piece by describing the beginnings of her reading and writing life—in libraries, at school—only to destroy or delete these autobiographical references out of annoyance with herself for treading the same ground once too often. The irony, of course, is that in her anxiety not to repeat herself, she has left us with a far sketchier account than she probably realised. We know she grew up in Oxford, a city she loved, even as she held conflicting feelings towards it, a set of emotions she explores in some depth in what is perhaps my favourite of all her essays, the review of Joanna Kavenna's *A Field Guide to Reality* that she wrote for the Shadow Clarke project. Here is a piece in which she seems to throw doubt and caution aside in a poetical and loving tribute to her own home place. The essay makes knowing reference to Philip Pullman and Penelope Lively, two authors I wish she'd had time to write about at greater length.

We know she loved the work of certain writers especially—Alan Garner, perhaps, most of all—but such love, for Maureen, was never a matter of unequivocal adulation. Love, she intimates, begets responsibility, and as a critic Maureen never shirked the responsibility of interrogating her enthusiasms. Her ongoing dialogue with the works of Alan Garner shows how she was never afraid to question her own previous assumptions alongside those of the writer she most admired. The paper she presented as part of the academic track of the 2005 Glasgow Worldcon became controversial in certain circles for its post-colonial critique of Garner's sense of place, but Maureen found no contradiction in subjecting a beloved author's work to such critical scrutiny. 'To truly celebrate an author is to keep asking those difficult questions,' she says, and the questions her essay raises are both fascinating and worthy of notice. They do what all good criticism should do, which is to allow us to see a work reflected through a different lens. Sit with this piece for a while and its truths, however uncomfortable, begin to emerge.

It seems especially fitting that the last piece of her work Maureen saw published was her examination of the critical response to Garner's 2021 novel *Treacle Walker*. I feel tremendously happy and glad that Maureen got to read *Treacle Walker*, possibly Garner's final novel, though who knows. Maureen's commentary on his 2012 novel *Boneland* reminds us we have been wrong about this before, and, if we are lucky, may be again. I am only sorry that Maureen cannot be here to wait this one out.

*

One of the hallmarks of Maureen's criticism is her capacity for creative self-doubt. 'I am not a limpet,' she writes in "A writing life beyond reviews", 'though I can see the attraction of the limpet lifestyle. Just keep doing what you do, over and over, bedding in, digging deep. For some people, that works, perhaps because they've already reached a point where they are utterly secure in what they're doing and they can move on to polishing the skills they've painstakingly acquired. I still have too much work left to do and the groove only ever fits for a little while before it is time to move on'.

Again and again in her essays, we see Maureen backing up, taking stock, coming at the argument from a different angle. This speaks to me of intellectual curiosity, of an imagination that was restless and questioning, of the determination to more exactly reflect her thoughts and ideas. Of the perceived impossibility of achieving perfection, combined with the determination to do so. I wonder too if there might not be a certain insecurity there, an indication of the precariousness of being a woman in what was held for so long to be a man's arena. 'Women's presence as readers and as vocal fans of the genre has frequently been contentious, sometimes distinctly unwelcome,' Maureen writes in her review of Justine Larbalestier's 2006 anthology *Daughters of Earth*, 'but they have always defended their right to participate, despite the sometimes appalling responses of male fans and editors alike'. She might as well be describing her own struggle.

When Maureen first became involved with fandom in the 1980s, the climate for women writers and especially for women critics was undergoing one of its periodic ice ages. In her essay 'An Open Letter to Joanna Russ', published in the fanzine Aurora in 1986, Jeanne Gomoll writes of how a seemingly throwaway line by Bruce Sterling in his introduction to William Gibson's collection *Burning Chrome* made her realise how the progress made during the 70s towards a more inclusive science fiction was being put at risk.

'Today I sit in the audience at all-male "Fandom of the 70s" panels,' writes Gomoll, 'and so far, that's the way the panels I've witnessed have been filled, by men only, and I don't hear <u>anything</u> of the politics, the changes, the roles women played in that decade, except sometimes a little chortling aside about how it is easier now to get a date with a female fan'. This makes depressing reading, especially in the knowledge that other demographics are now having to fight exactly the same battles, against practically the same expressions of prejudice—'it's boring!' 'it's too political!' 'it's a fad!'—just a couple of decades later.

Such were the attitudes Maureen must have encountered when she first began attending conventions and BSFA meetings. It is hardly surprising then, that on asking herself why it was that she originally had such doubts about beginning work as a critic, Maureen observes that 'possibly, just possibly, I'd noticed that most of the reviews I read were written by men. Especially in the amateur genre press. I doubt I'd fully theorised any of that, but I am sure I'd already noticed that men wrote about books, not women. It had never occurred to me that anyone might be interested in my opinions'.

Such scars take a long time to heal, and sometimes they never do. I doubt there's a single woman in science fiction who has not experienced some sort of backlash, at some time, at some level. Even if not outright hostility, there is that barely concealed *un-interest*, that turning of the shoulder. It is boring and it is wearying, having to take on the work of self-justification alongside the actual work. Maureen first began to talk to me about putting together a collection of her criticism in 2017. Buoyed up by the sense of togetherness and mutual purpose generated by the Shadow Clarke project, she felt eager to consolidate her personal achievement. At the same time, she was doubtful that anyone would be interested in publishing a collection of essays by a critic who, in her own words, so few people had heard of.

This perceived lack of recognition was something I know she found both depressing and intensely enervating. Such was her resilience, her unstinting enthusiasm for the work in hand, that she never allowed these frustrations to overwhelm her. The breadth and depth of her output—the ISFDB lists more than four hundred articles—is testament not only to her lifelong engagement with the subjects that most interested her but to her fighting spirit. Her work as reviews editor at *Strange Horizons*—the most recent chapter of her critical life—revealed her commitment to opening up the field to others, to encouraging new voices from diverse communities, to promoting a more inclusive critical commentary.

*

Maureen's life in criticism was a long one. Her first review, of John Gordon's novel for young people *The Edge of the World*, appeared in Ghosts and Scholars #8 in 1986. Today, as I began putting together my notes for this introduction, I happened to read what might be the last published piece of Maureen's criticism, a review in *Vector* #296 of the British Library's 2021 reissue of Eleanor Scott's 1929 collection of ghost stories, *Randalls Round*. Anyone who knew Maureen will know she loved ghost stories. Of the antiquarian, Jamesian stripe of ghost story in particular her knowledge was deep and wide and pretty much inexhaustible. The fact that her career was bookended by reviews of ghost stories is one of those strange coincidences I think would have pleased her.

And in between those bookends, what a mighty array of accomplishments and experiences. Maureen first made contact with fandom through the Oxford University Science Fiction Group in 1979. She was nineteen years old. By 1985 she was writing for the BSFA magazine Matrix, and became its editor in 1986, a post she held until 1989, when she was elected BSFA co-ordinator. She took on the role of BSFA administrator in 1995, a title she held until the end of that decade.

The 80s and 90s were undoubtedly Maureen's most active period within fandom, a time that saw her edit and produce fanzines, help to run conventions, and oversee other fannish events. She and Paul Kincaid were both Guests of Honour at Evolution, the 1996 Eastercon, and in 1998 Maureen won a Nova Award for best fan writing. The following year saw her nominated for a Hugo in the Best Fan Writer category, and her attendance at AussieCon, the 57th World Science Fiction Convention in Melbourne in 1999 as a program participant and Hugo finalist perhaps marks the moment where her work as a critic finally began to gain some wider recognition.

By this point she had already served two separate terms as a Clarke Award judge, in 1989 and 1990 for the BSFA and in 1993 and 1994 for the Science Fiction Foundation. She also chaired the Tiptree Award in 2004. Right through the 1990s and 2000s, Maureen was a frequent program participant at a multitude of conventions, debating the art and practice of criticism alongside her particular literary interests. Her series of 2012 blog posts, The Shortlist Project, in which she reads and discusses all the shortlisted novels for both the BSFA and the Clarke Awards, together with some notable omissions, was one of the critical highlights of that year and was itself nominated for the BSFA Award in the Best Related Work category in 2013.

Maureen became assistant editor of *Foundation* in 2009 and taught the Science Fiction Foundation Masterclass in 2016. She took over as copyeditor at *Foundation* in 2013, a post she continued to hold right up until her death.

She first began writing reviews for the groundbreaking online speculative fiction magazine *Strange Horizons* in 2006, five years after it was launched. Ten years after that, she took over from Abigail Nussbaum as senior reviews editor. This was a significant milestone for Maureen, an opportunity to share ideas and knowledge with a new generation of critics, a responsibility she took extremely seriously and that will see her influence continue to percolate for many years to come.

The day before her death, Maureen became the recipient of the British Fantasy Society's Karl Edward Wagner Award for her outstanding contribution to the genre.

*

Compiling this collection has been a joy. Through the weeks and months immediately following Maureen's death, the simple act of reading her—in depth and repeatedly, across the entire spectrum of her critical life—has not only provided the kind of definite focus that is often helpful in processing loss but more than that, it has been an act of remembrance, carrying with it the sense of a conversation that is still ongoing. It has also necessitated some difficult decisions. The sheer wealth of material available has made it inevitable that not everything I wanted to include has in fact been included. My initial intention was to reprint all Maureen's essays from both The Shortlist Project and the Shadow Clarke. In practice this proved impossible, not only for reasons of space, but also because, reading through the various essays, it quickly became apparent that any attempt to reproduce them outside of their original context—the wealth of conversation, interlinked blog entries and contemporary references that were current at the time—would be to diminish their power. As a partial remedy to this, I have chosen instead some of the pieces from both projects for inclusion within those chapters of this book that best represent their themes. I would encourage anyone with a particular interest in these projects—or in British science fiction awards—to read through Maureen's entries in their entirety at the *Anglia Ruskin CSFF blog* and at *Paper Knife*.

I would also dearly have liked to include some of Maureen's collaborations with other critics and writers—her interviews with Tade Thompson and Sarah Tolmie, for example, or the roundtable discussions on Alan Garner's *Red Shift* and Kazuo Ishiguro's *The Buried Giant*. The word count gods were against me, very firmly this time, but once again I would urge readers to seek out these insightful, wide-ranging discussions at *Strange Horizons*.

Most of the pieces included here date from the last twenty years, that is, the second half of Maureen's life as a critic and the period that sees a shift away from the shorter, more concise reviews produced for fanzines and towards the longer, more discursive commentary she grew into and was still developing at the time of her death. It is no coincidence that this period also marks the shift away from a magazine culture that was largely print-based and towards an online discourse. Online venues have always offered greater flexibility in terms of word count, and the advent of a more inclusive ethos promoted by magazines such as *Strange Horizons* has encouraged critics to be more adventurous, both in terms of texts considered and styles of criticism. Maureen was enthusiastic in taking up this invitation, not least through the medium of her own blog, *Paper Knife*, the space where she perhaps felt most at home and could be entirely herself.

In choosing pieces for this volume, I have tried to concentrate attention upon the subject areas and writers that could best be considered to reflect Maureen's core interests and areas of greatest knowledge: the ghost story, classic fantasy for young people, science fiction by marginalised writers, sense of place, the state of the field and of course Alan Garner. Some pieces have been trimmed or adjusted slightly to bring them in line with their new context within this book; in all instances I have done my utmost to imagine how Maureen herself might have prepared them. There will inevitably be gaps, the ghosts of different choices. Perhaps in the future an alternative volume is still to be compiled.

How does one sum up a life? The simple answer to that is: one cannot, or at least not adequately, and especially not a life as fully lived, as multifariously engaged as that of Maureen Kincaid Speller. The best I can hope for is that this book will trigger memories—different memories for every reader of the Maureen they knew and loved to talk to and simply loved. I know I will always miss her, just as I will go on missing the writing she had still to do.

Nina Allan

Rothesay, Isle of Bute, November 2022

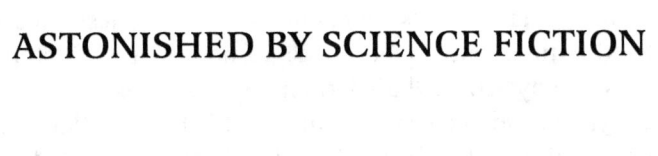

{and then} – a writing life beyond reviews

{insert obligatory introductory section detailing how I learned to read, what I read once left to my own devices, my life as a young library user, how I 'found' fantasy and science fiction and so on. Because that is how I always seem to start these 'state of me and my critical practice' articles when I write them}

Or not, because I have trained myself to delete rather than publish them. It interests me that almost invariably when I write such articles (and over the years I've begun a few) I do so by laying out my history as a reader, as a genre reader and so forth. Why do I do that? I presume I do it to establish my authority and emphasise that I am knowledgeable about the genres I review in. That is, I know what I'm talking about. I've never questioned why I do it. I barely noticed until recently. And now I've noticed I can't stop noticing it. I have binned so many articles half-written because I keep on doing the same thing. I bore myself rigid even as I'm doing it. It's become like a ritual. I can't begin anything until I do this. But still I do it. I did it with the first version of this, and then binned five hundred words. I am almost about to do it now, so let's end this paragraph and move on.

Oddly, the one thing I never seem to mention is how I came to start writing reviews and criticism (maybe I get too bored before I get to that point). That's simple. Paul Kincaid listened to me talking about books and, when I said I could never be a reviewer, gave me a book to review for *Vector*, commenting only that all I had to do was to write down the things I'd been saying. (Now you know who to blame). There was, as I recall, no theory of reviewing, no particular way to review; I just did it. I've looked at that first review fairly recently, and it's not bad. Naïve in places, and prone to making sweeping judgements and statements, and I would undoubtedly do it differently now, but it's not bad for a first attempt.

What *is* interesting at this point is why I thought I could never be a reviewer. At such a distance of time, I'm guessing, of course, but I suspect I thought one needed a university education in order to be able to review; to be better read than I was; and possibly, just possibly, I'd noticed that most of the reviews I read were written by men. Especially in the amateur genre press. I doubt I'd fully theorised any of that, but I am sure I'd already noticed that men wrote about books, not women. It had never occurred to me that anyone might be interested in my opinions. Certainly, I would not have dreamed of foisting them on anyone other than Paul Kincaid, because no one else seemed interested.

{fast forward thirty years, and several hundred reviews and pieces of criticism for venues such as *Vector, Paperback Inferno*, the Birmingham Science Fiction Group Newsletter, *Foundation, Interzone, Strange Horizons, The Zone*, and my blog, *Paper Knife*}

My dissatisfaction with my critical practice seems in part to be cyclical, in that I have often gone through periods of discontent and then got back in the groove. But each time this happens, getting back seems to get harder. Limpets, which are creatures of habit, return to the same patch of rock after their nightly perambulations; to the exact same spot, to the point where they wear a groove in the rock, into which they can then settle. You have to wonder if, after a while, they go there because that tiny patch of rock fits them better than any other patch of rock in the world, and it's just easier and more comfortable to keep going back. Does habit enslave the limpet or has the limpet just figured out what it takes to make life easy?

I am not a limpet, though I can see the attraction of the limpet lifestyle. Just keep doing what you do, over and over, bedding in, digging deep. For some people, that works, perhaps because they've already reached a point where they are utterly secure in what they're doing and they can move on to polishing the skills they've painstakingly acquired. I still have too much work left to do and the groove only ever fits for a little while before it is time to move on. And here we are again.

{skip boring recitation of dissatisfactions with current reviewing practice}

Well, not entirely, because, as Paul Kincaid pointed out the other night, it is to some extent my own fault that I spend so much of my time reviewing first novels that seem to have been ripped untimely from their literary wombs and spat out prematurely by the publishing machine to satisfy ... well, to satisfy what or who? Reviewing first novels too often feels like marking first-year undergraduate essays. Same damn mistakes, over and over. Somewhere in the back of my head lurks a template review, I'm quite sure. I suspect I keep on reviewing debuts because I long to find those first novels that, while they might be messy and unruly, at least show signs of promise and make me want to jump up and down and say 'look at this. Look. At. THIS! It's amazing. I cannot wait to read this writer's next novel, to see what they do next'. No, I don't remember me doing that too often, either.

It is much easier to write about something you don't like; in effect the review writes itself, though I flatter myself that if I write a negative review of a novel, I at least make it clear why the novel sucks rather than simply performing variations on a theme of "dear god, this novel is bad". My reviews tend to be quite heavy on the whys of awfulness.

But perhaps this is where the doubt is creeping in. Very often now, I see novels I have read and believe to be flawed being trumpeted as the best thing ever. While I naturally allow a certain latitude for taste, it nonetheless seems that everything is the best thing ever these days. I find this at best disconcerting, at worst concerning. Concerning because frequently nowadays I find myself doubting my own judgement. That is, not my judgement of novels on a book-by-book basis, but I wonder more and more if I'm not in danger of becoming like one of those people who is convinced that no decent science fiction has been written since Asimov or Clarke put the covers over their keyboards. Well, maybe not that extreme, but am I really keeping up with changing tastes? Or is an awful lot of contemporary science fiction and fantasy as flimsy and insubstantial as I think it is? Am I too demanding as a reviewer? Too fussy? Looking for things it is unreasonable of me to expect to find?

{insert digression on taste, aesthetics, and whether I should be tailoring my reviews to anyone's tastes but my own}

For some time, I have been teetering on the brink of giving up writing reviews and criticism altogether, mostly because I wasn't clear on why I should keep going. Why was I struggling to keep writing when the very thought of opening another book, any book, made me feel sick, let alone actually writing about it?

{pause to wince because that sounds like I'm asking for approbation and validation. I'm not. Actually, possibly I am, but don't indulge me or patronise me. I'm an adult, I shall work this out on my own}

The simplest answer is that I couldn't imagine not doing it. Having been been a critic, reviewer, and more latterly a blogger for thirty years, it would be hard to just walk away from my critical life. But if I were to write my reviews in a notebook, for my own personal consumption, would that be enough? Obviously not, so equally obviously there was (is?) a part of me that wants to be a public rather than a private critic. But how public is a specialist publication ('nobody reads print reviews', said an anonymous author a while ago, someone I am sure pays no attention whatsoever to print reviews of their own work) or a low-traffic blog (my stats suggest my blog exists mainly to do US students' Frankenstein homework for them). Is the simple act of consigning a piece of criticism to a blog enough?

{those are rhetorical questions, and anyway, I have switched off comments on my blog. At least for now.}

It isn't the texts that are the problem (well, some of them are, but we know I am quite capable of handling that). It's the reading culture that's changed. Or at any rate, my relationship with it.

{and now, for the second time, we are going to step around the autobiographical material I would normally insert here, save to observe that, as previously noted, for a long time my reading culture consisted of reading books, reading other people talking about books in the commercial and small presses, and talking to Paul Kincaid about books. Later, it took in various APAs (amateur press associations—like bulletin boards, but on paper), and then came the internet}

LiveJournal never really worked for me as a venue for discussing books. It ought to have done, given that I was in charge of my own journal, but I learned quite quickly that making the journal public apparently gave total strangers the right to lecture me on what content I should include, and how my journal should look. But making the journal 'friends only' brought its own difficulties. Joining reading communities revealed the exciting world of people who judged their reading prowess exclusively by how many books they could get through in a year (the thinner the better, the more the merrier) and presented me with my first ethical dilemmas (I never listed manuscripts I worked on, nor anything I read only part of—I read parts of a lot of textbooks). And then I realised I didn't like listing my year's reading anyway, because although I think it was supposed to provide hooks for conversation and discussion, it ended up looking like bragging.

Bulletin boards and discussion forums I never really mastered, in part because dial-up was expensive, and later, when I got broadband, I found it difficult to keep up with discussions I hadn't been following from the beginning. Endless scrolling back through everyone's comments, only to end up adding the not tremendously helpful 'me, too', because everything of any interest had already been said.

{I rarely engage in conversation or discussion on the internet because of this sort of thing. Also, I am not particularly good at blowing my own trumpet. However, I am a top-level lurker.}

Once I discovered client apps, Twitter has worked better for me than anything else as a forum for engaged conversation, despite the format being utterly inimical to in-depth discussion. There is nothing people love more than challenging the limitations of a format. Multi-tweet explanations are an art form in their own right, and I have been lucky enough to fall in with people who like to tweet links and recommendations. Twitter has at times been a powerhouse of suggestion-trading. It's been fun.

And yes, that is a past tense. It's not that it isn't still fun, but the dynamic seems to have changed. People's interests have shifted, and a whole slew of special-interest groups (publishers, agents, editors, authors, or people who would like to be publishers, agents, editors, authors, or something, anything in publishing) have come increasingly to dominate bookish social media.

It was the cover reveal tweets that started it. As I have never bought books according to their covers, I found this a little baffling. I did wonder, as I looked at the rebranding of the *Apex Books of World SF*, what the etiquette was when confronted with a truly ugly cover. It turns out you say what's on your mind and everyone ignores you, which is probably as it should be. But those covers really are ugly.

{we will take as read the discussion about how women do not put themselves forward, unlike men, though it probably explains why, after thirty years, comparatively few people have still ever heard of me.}

As a rule, I don't chase publishers for review copies because I write too irregularly even for my own blog, and because, bizarre though it might seem, it has never occurred to me until fairly recently that I could and probably should pitch reviews to sites rather than be content with what happens to be offered to me by the publications I have worked for.

In any event, publishers do not generally beat a path to my door to offer me unsolicited review copies. I'm not remotely surprised by this, given that I do not write user-friendly reviews that overflow with the kind of comments that make good cover blurbs. Nonetheless, the excited tweets about books received, the glitzy photos on Instagram of the latest releases often serve to remind me that I operate at a tangent to that particular reviewing community.

And yes, of course I'm sometimes envious, because though my attitudes may seem austere, I enjoy the validation of a freebie as much as the next person. But I can't help thinking that all this pandering to the publicity gods is like the online equivalent of queuing to get into a fashionable club, having dressed with scrupulous regard to that club's dress code. It's all very aspirational but I somehow have the feeling that even if I were to join that queue, the doorkeepers would still find an excuse not to let me in.

{I could at this point boast outrageously about the proof we found waiting for us when we got home from our holiday because, seriously, it is awesome … but I hope I am better than that, not least because it wasn't sent so that I would promote the book but as a thoughtful act from an old friend, and I want to retain a shred or two of integrity}

Few people ever mention the difficulties that ensue if or indeed when you allow yourself to get caught up in the New Shiny hype culture. Are you prepared to sacrifice your critical integrity to keep those free review copies coming? Given that my reading tastes are not particularly commercial, that hardly applies (though I might be persuaded to sell my soul to a couple of smaller presses that publish a lot of fiction in translation). Wading through endless identikit epic fantasies isn't really how I want to spend my time. And yet, a niggling thought persists: assuming I want people to look at my blog, how do I get them there, if not by reviewing the New Shiny?

Of course I'd like more traffic—most people want their writing to be read, and I am not immune to that—but at what cost?

It is clear that some view blogging as a step on the road to finding employment in the publishing industry: a presence on social media becomes a way of performing 'professionalism' in order to attract the attention of actual professionals. It's the dance-club queue all over again, in other words, and yes, I'm a little envious of those people too, but at the same time I am disinclined to jump through the necessary hoops of compromise to achieve popularity. I am by nature an unglamorous nitpicking copyeditor-and-proofreader type rather than a promotions and publicity sort of person, but still. Many people seem to regard being a critic as a remarkably unglamorous pursuit in any case (though when Paul Kincaid and I first became a couple, I remember someone did accuse me of trying to sleep my way to the top. Clearly, the reviews editorship of *Vector* was more highly prized than either of us had realised).

{name one famous contemporary copyeditor or proofreader. Famous for being a copyeditor or proofreader. No, I can't either}

Which gives me the answer to at least one of my questions, insofar as I now know what I don't want. It is important to me to be able to write freely: entertaining other people is an incidental benefit rather than a goal. As to what I do want? I have no idea.

All right, have it your way – you saw a man with a raygun!

I took out a subscription to the *New Yorker* in 1999, the year after I came back from my first trip to the United States. It was a way of keeping in touch with my new discovery, America!, or at any rate, with a very particular part of the US with which I had fallen in love, New York. Hindsight now tells me that this was a New York that was either entirely inaccessible to me, no matter how much I might want it, or one that had vanished long before I arrived.

But reading the *New Yorker* was also about buying into a particular style. I discovered a lot of new writers, thanks to recommendations from my US friends. Many of those writers were essayists rather than novelists, and had contributed regularly to the *New Yorker* over the years; the late Joseph Mitchell was a prime example, but I became particularly besotted with the writing of John McPhee. Possibly I subscribed to the *New Yorker* just to read his infrequent essays, though I also relish the biographical essays; and when it is in the mood, the *New Yorker* can really crank out the investigative journalism. And then there are the cartoons …

The fiction? There is a distinctive *New Yorker* style, undoubtedly. The magazine has its favourite authors, some of whom are authors I especially like, such as Louise Erdrich and Chris Adrian; others, I'm less familiar with, but I'm happy to try them out. Sometimes such experiments are successful, sometimes less so, but I try to keep an open mind. The *New Yorker* would not be the first magazine to spring to mind when thinking about science fiction, but it has flirted with it from time to time, both in its fiction and in its non-fiction. There have been Chris Adrian stories that remind me of Sylvia Townsend Warner, an excerpt from Karen Russell's first novel *Swamplandia*, an essay by Michael Chabon about Neil Gaiman, to name but a few.

And now we have the *New Yorker*'s first sci-fi issue. It is annoying that the *New Yorker* doesn't editorialise about its own content, so we will never know what their original intentions were in embarking on such a project. One can only speculate, and of course I am going to do that, as others have already done.

Let's start with the cover, the first thing people are going to see. I've already seen complaints that the magazine should have asked this artist or that artist to do a special science fiction cover. My immediate response was 'but why would they?' This is the *New Yorker* after all; the cover is situated firmly within its customary cover aesthetic, and is by one of their regular cover artists, Daniel

Clowes. Clowes is a good fit for this issue, as he has incorporated science fictional tropes into previous covers. He seems to have a taste for the gently ironic and is not averse to mocking those who make a big production number out of things that are really straightforward. I particularly like the *New Yorker* cover where a young gun is trying to design a flying car, while a middle-aged man cruises past his office window in a spacesuit rigged as a flying machine. Indeed, given that Clowes is a comics artist and cartoonist with a retrospective currently on at the Oakland Museum of California, he seems to me to be a far better choice as cover artist than, say, Bob Eggeling, one name I saw put forward by the dissenters.

The demand that the magazine should use a recognised science fiction artist already points to the assumption in certain quarters that the *New Yorker* should first of all be embracing the genre as understood by hardcore SF fans, and that secondly, if it is going to embrace the genre, it should make damn sure that everyone knows that from the outset. I'd hazard a guess this was not quite what the *New Yorker* had in mind.

But let's go back to Clowes's cover. What is going on here? At first glance we have what looks like a fairly staid party in someone's apartment. Drinks, canapés, people talking. Six people: middle-aged white woman, perhaps the hostess; middle-aged white man, with beard and glasses, looks like he might be an academic. Is it his apartment? Don't think so, not least because the bookshelves are artfully empty. I've never yet met a real academic whose bookshelves aren't stuffed solid. The man looks startled, but more taken aback than horrified. Next to him is another middle-aged woman, this time a woman of colour; she is visibly shocked by what is happening in front of her, and is that a slight hint of revulsion in her expression? In front of them is another man, a younger version of the middle-aged academic: the dress sense is the same, although he has different glasses, no beard as yet, though he carries the other badge of office of the male academic, the book under the arm.

This might easily be a faculty party. To the far right of the picture is another white man who might be the administrative head of the department, and who, like his anxious-to-please wife on the far left, is only partly in the picture. As well as framing the scene, his expression mirrors hers; their collective consternation seems directed as much at the damaged wall and books as towards the appearance of the gate-crashers at their party.

Three of these gate-crashers are bursting through the wall, but we'll set them aside for the moment. The figure I want to concentrate on first is the one we can't see. Right at the centre of the cover stands a young woman with her back to us. She is strikingly bright in comparison to the others in the room, with her yellow hair, her black sleeveless top and a string of white beads (pearls?) around her neck. Who is she? What is she doing there? Critically, what is the expression on her face?

She is the one figure in the room who appears to be staring directly at the spaceman who has burst through the bookshelves; the others look at him side-on, although the perspective of the picture makes it difficult to tell how far into the room he and his companions have actually intruded. Except that he doesn't seem to have stepped over the threshold of the hole in the wall at all, and a closer look suggests that the young woman is looking past him, to the green blob behind.

Looking even more closely, the spaceman isn't so much gazing at her as past her, towards the viewer outside the picture. The spaceman himself is young, dark-haired, more forehead, chin and teeth than seems feasible, plump-cheeked, redolent of apple pie and bubble-gum, the wholesome all-American sports jock. The epitome of 1950s comic book science fiction, yet that doesn't quite ring true, either. This spaceman is a little too young, perhaps? Less craggy Dan-Dare, more teenage boy living his dream. The blob-monster and the robot seem to be his companions rather than his adversaries. One might initially read him as the space adventurer who gets the girl, indeed who has come to rescue the girl from the dreariness of a faculty party. Although we might suspect that 'rescue' would involve marriage and a Bradburyesque existence in astronaut-suburbia, he is obviously not interested in her at all. Perhaps he wants us to admire him in his spacesuited glory with his whacking great raygun.

At this point we might begin to wonder whether this is a literal portrayal of a fantastical event or whether we should read this cover in a more metaphorical way. There is something about the way that hole in the wall seems to hang in space. Yes, it's surrounded by damaged books, but in real terms, if that is a blaster, wouldn't the books be burned rather than torn? Come to think of it, doesn't that gun look rather disproportionate? If this is not a real incursion into the ordered world of the faculty party, what is it?

I'm tempted to interpret it as a thought bubble, the collective thought bubble of a group to whom the young woman, the focus of our attention, has just revealed that she reads science fiction. The four gate-crashers represent the common perception of SF: garish, filled with aliens and astronauts with jutting chins and rayguns. This issue of the *New Yorker* then, we hope, might be offering a corrective to that old-fashioned view, with the magazine's contents representing science fiction as the young woman herself sees it. This is in turn problematic in that it might be interpreted by hardcore SF fans as a rejection of their tastes. And perhaps it is: the contents are, after all, a *New Yorker* version of science fiction. Then again, how might they have reacted if they'd picked up a *New Yorker* with a Bob Eggeling cover and found inside fiction by Jonathan Lethem, Junot Diaz, Sam Lipsyte, and Jennifer Egan. With just as much consternation as we see on this cover, I suspect. Go figure.

At which point, it is time to peruse the contents. The first fifty-seven pages consist of the usual *New Yorker* diet of listings and short pieces, the editorial being about Obama and Syria. There is a distinction made in the contents page between 'sci-fi', fiction, and several non-fiction pieces, as well as two pieces in the critical section; investigation reveals that the 'sci-fi' non-fiction comprises a series of very short memoirs by Ray Bradbury, Ursula K. Le Guin, China Miéville, Margaret Atwood, Karen Russell, and William Gibson. There is a certain flavour of 'the usual suspects' about these writers but they are, for the most part, regular contributors to the magazine, so it is not surprising that they have been called upon again.

Of the four pieces of fiction, the three by Lipsyte, Lethem, and Egan are in my view not exactly taxing pieces of contemporary SF. The Lipsyte and Egan fall into that category of experiments in form that is too easily mistaken for science fiction. There are hints in Lipsyte's 'The Republic of Empathy' that one of his characters is moving in and out of alternative versions of his life, but what is most striking about this interlocking multi-viewpoint narrative, apart from that same character being wiped out by a drone strike on his own front lawn, is the fact that Lipsyte's characters are, for the most part, aware of their own fictionality and deliberately foreground that fact. Is this science-fictional? Probably not, and I doubt *New Yorker* readers are unfamiliar with this technique. For readers who prefer their science fiction with a straight linear narrative it may be more of a problem.

Jennifer Egan's 'Black Box' was famously first published as a series of tweets, which I suppose might be perceived as science-fictional in and of itself, though it might equally be argued that the story more than adequately demonstrates the shortcomings of Twitter as a medium for fiction. The last piece of fiction I read by Egan was in fact a list, and one has a sense that she enjoys this particular form. However, while some might see 'Black Box' as being achingly, post-ironically postmodern or some such, to me it feels more old hat than anything, and having your second-person viewpoint character festooned with surveillance implants does not make the story any more science-fictional than it already is ... or indeed, isn't. Though I concede it might have a certain novelty value if one is unfamiliar with such tropes.

The same might be said of Jonathan Lethem's 'My Internet', an amusing squib about the Internet within the Internet, though this is less about the internet itself, more about social behaviour within groups. One has never needed the internet in order to form a clique.

Which leaves us with Junot Díaz's 'Monstro', which would not look out of place in any one of half a dozen more obviously science fictional publishing venues. Set in Haiti and the Dominican Republic, this is the story of a mysterious plague, La Negrura, The Blackness [*sic*], which begins to infect refugees in the relocation camps of Haiti. Which particular relocation this might be, Díaz doesn't say; one thinks immediately of the camps created after the recent earthquake, but Díaz offers sufficient detail to suggest that the story is a little further into the future. The nature of that future as such is not what interests Díaz; his focus is on what is happening in it. Our narrator is a young man, a university student, hanging out with a group of wealthy young Dominicans, marking time while his mother dies, chasing girls, one in particular, and the new disease doesn't really impinge much on his life. He has other things to do while, as he puts it, 'watching the apocalypse creep in'.

The narrator informs us that he survives the apocalypse; whatever it is that turns him into a 'time witness', the nature of the events remains unclear. The narrator describes what happens to the sufferers of La Negrura, but has little analysis to offer the reader. He is trapped in the thick of it, particularly once the island comprising Haiti and the Dominican Republic is cut off. Díaz is again using conventional SF tropes: the mysterious plague, the odd behaviour of the infected, the mass killings by the Possessed, the bombing of major population centres, the nebulous sightings of 'Them'. But while this is not precisely a cosy catastrophe in the Home Counties, neither is it exoticised by its setting or its participants. The tone of the story is perhaps best summed up in the narrator's response to stories about the nature of the mysterious attackers: 'Forty-foot-tall cannibal motherfuckers running loose on the Island? Negro, please'. The narrator, more accustomed to life in Brooklyn than in his family's homeland, is simply incredulous.

Indeed, there is a lot more to dig out of this story about othering, expectations of settings and so on, but that was not the intention of this article. There is no doubt that Díaz combines his Dominican roots and his long-standing familiarity with science fiction to produce a good solid story told by a relative outsider, trapped in an unfamiliar place. It is open to interpretation and indeed I am most intrigued to see how mainstream readers would respond to it.

If the *New Yorker* and I don't see quite eye to eye over the fiction, things get more interesting in the non-fiction section. The memoirs that make up 'sci-fi' are boxed out, almost like advertorials, which in a way is what they are: testimonies about the life-affirming properties of science fiction and how it shaped the lives of those who write it. At the same time, I can't quite shake the feeling that the boxes are also there to protect ... well, what, the rest of the magazine? The other thing that strikes me is how they historicise SF, position it as a literature of the past, a memento of childhood, even though all these writers, yes even Margaret Atwood, work with the material now (apologies here to Ursula K. Le Guin, who writes instead of the problems of trying to get a science fiction story into Playboy with a female byline).

Even Colson Whitehead's excellent 'A Psychotronic Childhood', detailing the genesis of his love of horror films and incidentally showing how one acquires critical judgement, has its face turned firmly to the past (and god forgive me, at one point I did wonder whether I wasn't in fact reading a real-life version of Pinkwater's Snarkout Boys stories. Indeed, while checking that

I hadn't muddled them with *Lizard Music*, I learned that a third Snarkout Boys novel, *I Snarked With a Zombie*, was planned but never written).

At a critical level I am, I admit, mostly blind to film, so it is interesting to read about Whitehead's education in cinema. At the same time, I found myself wondering if a secondary function of the article wasn't to demonstrate to genre readers that Whitehead is, so to speak, 'one of ours', whilst reassuring mainstream readers that it is OK to attribute his zombie novel *Zone One* to a misspent childhood.

The late Anthony Burgess's article on the genesis of *A Clockwork Orange* reaches even further into the past. Again, it's well-written, a fascinating meditation on what it means for society to intervene in the control of behaviour, but other writers have written about their fiction since 1973. On the one hand, it's good to have this article back in circulation; on the other, it seems to reinforce the notion of SF as a literary artefact.

The two critical essays focusing on science fiction take a similarly historical line. Laura Miller's piece on the physical appearance of early fictional aliens, 'The Cosmic Menagerie', is a good general overview for the uninitiated, referencing the likes of Camille Flammarion and J.H. Rosny alongside more familiar writers such as H.G. Wells, as well as mentioning a number of critics such as Brian Stableford and George Slusser (consistently referred to throughout as Slosser; so much for the much-vaunted fact-checkers of the *New Yorker*).

Emily Nussbaum's 'Fantastic Voyage' attempts to get to grips with the idea of the fan and the TV franchise, with particular reference to *Doctor Who* and *Community*. There is no doubt that she gets it in terms of discussing the intensity of that relationship, though one might argue too that she indulges in fan service, playing to the geek mentality rather than conducting a more rigorous investigation. Are television shows and their fandoms always 'so much larger when you're on the inside'? Possibly, but I would like to have seen Nussbaum thinking a little more about the dividing lines. Overall, these articles offer history rather than context; the memoirs, by contrast, offer context but the history is, inevitably, sketchy.

So let us return to where we started, to that thought-bubble spaceman and his intergalactic friends, messily intruding into an ordered world of panelled rooms, just enough books, the polite canapés and the modest glass of fizz, and to the girl who brought him into being when she cried sci-fi. If, as I suggest, he is a composite of the preconceived ideas of the five outsiders in that room about the nature of science fiction, do the contents of the *New Yorker* represent the sixth person's view of it? They present an *alternative* view, certainly, but they seem to me to be working terribly hard, maybe a little too hard, to establish a pedigree for SF beyond the standard genre sensibility. Time and again, we are assured that SF has a history, a long history; that well-known writers, even almost-Pulitzer-winning writers, care about science fiction. It is as though the *New Yorker* is telling us that it is OK to like science fiction, all sorts of science fiction, because it has made us what we are. Díaz comes closest to a true understanding, but in such a way as to satisfy those who think they don't like genre as well as those who know they do. But most of the items in this issue of the *New Yorker* are content to talk about genre without actually performing it.

As to whether that is a good thing or a bad thing? In truth, I do not think for a moment it matters. I no longer see any point in being an evangelist for the healing properties of genre, not least because there are as many ways of defining science fiction and fantasy as there are people queuing up to define it. To imagine that the *New Yorker* should be out there attempting to convert its readership to hardcore genre SF is both absurd and to make unwarranted assumptions about *New Yorker* readers. It is safe to assume that many *New Yorker* readers already know what science fiction looks like, and where they can find it. It's probably equally safe to assume that the rest had little interest to begin with and stuffing it down their throats now is unlikely to make them change their minds. At best, one might say this issue presents an idea of what SF might look like, and readers can follow it up if it takes their fancy. Of course, there is the risk that for some, this will be a diluted extract of SF, to be taken with pinched nose and a reassuring 'there, that wasn't as bad as you thought it would be, was it?' Then again, so be it. And perhaps it wouldn't hurt some genre readers to take a few steps beyond their own preconceptions about science fiction and take a look at this *New Yorker*.

Reading Margaret Atwood's *In Other Worlds: science fiction and the human imagination*

It is almost impossible to write about Margaret Atwood in relation to the science fiction and fantasy genres without reference to her now notorious 'squids in space' comment. What originated as a seemingly off-the-cuff remark on a morning TV chat show has been taken up by genre fans and commentators as the prime example of Atwood's ignorance of and lack of sympathy for contemporary science fiction. Conversely, writers who want to use genre topoi while rejecting that problematic genre label now brandish the phrase as a shield against what they regard as the wrong sort of critical attention.

In subsequent interviews, Atwood herself has repeated the phrase, or versions of it, though whether because she sincerely believes what she said, because it has become part of her 'brand', or because, as I have come to suspect, she simply likes winding up critics of genre, is not clear.

Given there is no ignoring the cephalopod in the Atwood sitting room, how then does one approach *In Other Worlds: SF and the Human Imagination*, which one might take as Atwood's definitive statement on the subject? This essay collection is comprised of three parts. First, we have the three Richard Ellmann Lectures in Modern Literature given by Atwood at Emory University, Atlanta, Georgia, in 2010. Secondly, there is a selection of reviews of and introductions to science fiction novels, written by Atwood during the 2000s, with an outlier from 1976. Lastly, there is a selection of short fictions by Atwood which she has designated (confusingly, for reasons that will become clear later) 'science fiction'.

To begin with, we should be clear that Atwood knows what science fiction is, or rather, she knows what it is she points to and calls 'science fiction'. Atwood's definition is distinguished by two things: its unusual rigidity and the fact that Atwood, as a public figure, is better placed than most to promulgate that definition. John Clute noted in his review of this book in the *Los Angeles Review of Books* that during the 'squids in space' controversy, he had argued 'that a person who had attained a public voice had a public responsibility [...] not to allow offhand comments to be understood as discourse'. Similarly, he reminded us that Ursula K. Le Guin 'made it clear that the squids-in-space bon mot was genuinely discourteous'. I see no reason to disagree with either statement. It may be that Atwood's comment was simply careless, but it is a salutary reminder to us of the power of words, and of the care that should be exercised in using them, given that even ten years on we cannot escape their effect.

I would not seek to frame this discussion in terms of an ongoing disagreement between Atwood and Le Guin (though if I were to do so, I would say here and now that my sympathy lies mainly with Le Guin, whose perception of genre is both more capacious and more nuanced than Atwood's), yet Le Guin's presence looms over every page of this collection, from the dedication to her, through Atwood's discussion of Le Guin's review of *The Year of the Flood* and *Oryx and Crake*, to Atwood's inclusion of her puzzled review of Le Guin's *The Birthday of the World and Other Stories*.

Let us begin in fact with that review, which clearly articulates Atwood's lack of ease with the term 'science fiction'. '[I]t's an awkward box: it bulges with discards from elsewhere. Into it have been crammed all those stories that don't fit comfortably into the family room of the socially realistic novel or the more formal parlour of historical fiction, or other compartmentalized genres: westerns, gothics, horrors, gothic romances, and the novels of war, crime, and spies' (p.115). And that's before Atwood goes on to list the many subdivisions of science fiction and fantasy in tones of fascinated horror. Her choice of words is interesting, too—'discards' carries with it a certain flavour of the orphan child, or the unacceptable by-blow, while 'awkward' and 'bulges' suggest a lack of neatness. All of these are clearly antithetical to the 'comfortably' that is associated with the 'family room' of the 'socially realistic novel'.

It is this last category that we should necessarily take note of. For Atwood's perception of science fiction is founded in part on her fierce need to distinguish between the social realist and the fantastical, and to make an equally fierce distinction between the novel and the romance. The novel belongs to social realism while the romance is the form associated with the fantastic. And for Atwood never the twain shall meet. In theory at least, though in practice this becomes rather more difficult, for what then is one to make of *The Handmaid's Tale*, a novel that most regard as science fiction, yet which is clothed in the trappings of the social realist novel, as defined by Atwood—texture, detail, character.

And this is where Atwood performs her great feat of legerdemain. First, she proclaims her own 'lifelong relationship' with science fiction, which she defines from the outset as 'not of this here-and-now Earth'. Yet, on the following page, Atwood admits that as of 2008 she 'didn't really grasp what the term science fiction meant any more'. Four pages later, Atwood redefines science fiction again: 'What I mean by "science fiction" is those books that descend from H.G. Wells's *The War of the Worlds* [...] whereas, for me, "speculative fiction" [Atwood's preferred term for her own SF at this point] means plots that descend from Jules Verne's books'. Neither definition of SF is objectionable in and of itself; most critics and academics are able to hold both in their heads simultaneously. Atwood, however, seems to prefer, indeed to insist on, dichotomy and thus one must have one or the other but no kind of synthesis.

Despite her own protestations to the contrary, Atwood also seems to be driven by a need to keep making definitive statements about meaning, and this brings us back to Le Guin. In 2010, the two writers took part in a public discussion, during which Atwood, by her own account, found that 'what Le Guin means by "science fiction" is what I mean by "speculative fiction", and what she means by "fantasy" would include some of what I mean by "science fiction." [...] When it comes to genres, the borders are increasingly undefended, and things slip back and forth across them with insouciance'. Again, these conclusions might seem unsurprising to scholars of genre, and with Atwood having apparently found her way to a broader understanding of the terminology, one might suppose that the matter would be finally closed.

Except that the Ellmann Lectures suggest the situation is otherwise. In 'Dire Cartographies', the third in the series, Atwood offers us yet another new perception of her 'science-fictional' works. They should now be read as 'ustopias', a word Atwood claims to have coined by joining utopia and dystopia, on the basis that in each utopia is a latent dystopia, and vice versa. Her tone does smack rather of the clever if poorly read undergraduate coming up with a brilliant new idea, without taking due regard of the considerable body of criticism and analysis of utopian literature that already exists; yet it is clear from Atwood's account of her postgraduate studies that at some point at least she was more than passingly familiar with the state of utopian studies, even if she did not keep up with her critical reading.

It is this facet of Atwood's account of her relationship with SF, or at any rate with utopian literature, that is to me the most interesting and revealing part of the lectures: here we see a young and thoughtful Atwood putting together ideas that, while they may seem familiar now, were much less so then. One can't help wondering how her storytelling might have turned out had she maintained a closer relationship with current critical thinking.

Similarly, the glimpses of the child Margaret are illuminating. We see two children (Atwood and her brother), with limited access to forms of culture we take for granted, pouring their imaginative energies into creating a race of rabbit superheroes. It is clear from Atwood's account that her early apprehension of science fiction is intensely visual, influenced as much by comic strips and film as by the drawing of the rabbits' adventures. This is reflected both in her later concern with the visual signifiers of science fiction ('if you put skin-tight black or silver clothing on a book cover along with some jetlike flames and/or colourful planets, does that make the work "science fiction"?') and also in her fascination with utopian literature, which she identifies as in part being about making lists and describing things. Indeed, it would seem that Atwood's understanding of SF is literally superficial, in that to her it is all about surface and appearance, whereas utopian or ustopian literature, despite its similar preoccupation with things, or perhaps because of its avowed interest in paraphernalia, has been transmogrified into a form of social realism after all.

Anyone who comes to this collection of writings in search of a definitive answer as to what Atwood means when she uses the words 'science fiction' is probably going to be disappointed. However, the Ellmann Lectures do provide a valuable glimpse into the foundations of Atwood's thinking on the issue. Having said that, it does seem to me that Atwood is using the academic context of the Ellmann Lectures as a means to establish a discourse in which her unusually narrow definition of science fiction is given a greater validity than I think it deserves.

The alert reader will notice that Atwood returns again and again to the same few exemplary texts in both the lectures and the reviews, texts that are now beginning to show their age. Sterling and Gibson get a mention apiece, as does Silverberg, but it's clear too that for Atwood, science fiction or utopian literature stopped dead in the 1950s, at the point when she abandoned her PhD. Similarly, looking at the selection of reviews offered here, one has the sense of Atwood constantly reploughing the same furrow. Most revealing perhaps is how little her view has shifted from her 1976 review of Marge Piercy's *Woman on the Edge of Time*, which Atwood insists is a utopia, to her most recent reviews. Certainly there is a sense of weary familiarity, as Atwood once again reaches for the set responses.

Scholars will also note the lack of a useful critical apparatus; footnotes are minimal and those that exist are often risible, as though their compiler had no sense of the audience for whom this book is intended, and there is no accompanying bibliography for those who want to read further. Indeed, the collection as a whole is not indexed, so it is difficult to track repeated mentions of particular texts unless one takes notes.

If as I suspect, the Ellman Lectures were supposed to state Atwood's position once and for all, then they have failed in their intent. I have no doubt that Margaret Atwood will continue to formulate explanations of her work that insist that certain aspects of it are not, contrary to appearance, science fiction, and elements of the science fiction community will continue to express anger and frustration at her apparent obtuseness. The point is that try as she will, Atwood cannot control the reader's response to her writing, and for many commentators *The Handmaid's Tale*, *The Year of the Flood*, *Oryx and Crake* and *Maddaddam* are as much science fiction as they are utopian, ustopian, or speculative fiction, or whatever else Atwood chooses to call them. In the end, what they are has become less interesting than Atwood's attempts to tell us what they are not.

A Judge's Summary of the Clarke Award

Like the Booker Prize, the Arthur C. Clarke Award is no stranger to controversy, though this time the recriminations have ranged louder and longer than usual. Kim Stanley Robinson was robbed, while Marge Piercy didn't deserve to win because her novel had been marketed as mainstream fiction. We'll come back to both those points later. First, let me re-introduce you to the other books on the shortlist, the ones that got lost in the uproar. I'll take them in alphabetical order by author so as to avoid the appearance of playing favourites.

Unfortunately, this means that Ian McDonald's *Hearts, Hands and Voices* is first on to the podium. Unfortunate because of all the books, this is the one with which I find myself least in sympathy. Even rereading it has not changed my opinion and I have found myself seriously at variance with one of my judging colleagues over this book. The Land is the last remaining province of a crumbling empire, separated by a river. Given the various environmental conditions, it ought to be paradise, but the province is riven by religious conflict between the Proclaimers and the Confessors—does this scenario seem familiar, given that McDonald himself lives in Belfast? In the midst of violence and bloodshed, Mathembe Files and her family become refugees, are separated, leaving Mathembe to journey through the Land in search of her lost family. The parallels with the Irish conflict are obvious, but equally the book stands as a metaphor for every war, every conflict, and the refugees they create. I prefer McDonald's lush, almost baroque style when it is penned within the confines of a short story. Left to rampage at will through a novel, I was overwhelmed by the words to the point where I was gasping for breath. There are touching vignettes throughout the story, but taken as a whole, it was too much for me.

By comparison, Richard Paul Russo's *Destroying Angel* was underwritten, to the point of carelessness in places. The book features that staple of so many private-eye novels, and a growing number of futuristic novels too: the burned-out ex-cop. Tanner is a surprisingly decent sort of man to be an ex-cop in any historical period. Like Robin Hood, he robs the rich to give to the poor, or rather he smuggles drugs, giving a percentage of his cargoes to the free hospitals which patch up the poor for next to nothing. He makes money from the cut he takes, selling drugs on the street. The police turn a blind eye, even co-operating by allowing him to use the police van. In the midst of this evocation of futuristic San Francisco lurks a serial killer. Dead bodies are discovered, with chains welded to their bodies and Taylor, you won't be surprised to learn, has a hunch and sets off after the killer.

What I liked about this novel was the general sketch of the corrupt and violent society where people, within certain parameters, can still live fairly decent lives, even in the dreaded Tenderloin. San Francisco is partitioned into sectors; depending on who and what you are, certain areas present a risk. On the other hand, the risk isn't always as great as is claimed. When sprawling megalopolises and wall-to-wall brutality are the order of the day in so many novels, this much made a refreshing change.

However, there was too much else that dissatisfied me about *Destroying Angel*. For example, it was impossible to get any sense of when this novel was set. The twenty-first century was mentioned as though it was already in the past, yet, putting aside the fact that the rich live off-world, so America must have restarted its space programme, the story could be set right here and now. There wasn't enough to convince me that this novel was what it claimed to be. And it has to be said that the story itself was feeble: a rogue military cyborg wreaking havoc by killing and tattooing its victims. The cyborg, presumably the destroying angel of the title, is rarely seen; the final confrontation between it and Taylor takes place off-page, which is hardly satisfactory. In the end, the gaudy patched skin of this novel has nothing to support it, alas.

Curiously enough, Michael Swanwick's *Stations of the Tide* has been criticised by some, not necessarily the judges, for precisely the reason I disliked Ian McDonald's novel, namely its baroque nature. I guess it's a question of degree. Swanwick is much more restrained in his descriptions of Miranda, a world about to be inundated by its own ocean, as periodically happens. It's a restricted world, denied the technology its people feel it needs, but one of its inhabitants has stolen that technology and brought it back to Miranda. The bureaucrat is sent to retrieve the items and finds himself entirely unprepared to deal with a world on the brink of cataclysmic change. His hunt for Gregorian is, in some respects, an education for the bureaucrat himself as he discovers a completely different perspective on life. The novel is also distinguished by its entirely plausible use of virtual reality technology during a long sequence in the latter part of the novel. Yet, in the end, the novel somehow fails to satisfy. It comes so close to being prize-winning material but stumbles at the final hurdle.

One (male) critic has dismissed Sue Thomas's *Correspondence* as an exercise in creative writing rather than an SF novel. I mention the gender of the critic because it is becoming clear to me that men and women, for the most part, react to this book very differently. People are also distracted by the layered structure. True, the book is a little more complicated than a straightforward narrative, but perseverance is handsomely rewarded. Apart from the complexity of the novel's structure, that of role-players exploring the story of Rosa and the woman, now more machine, who has created her, I was particularly fascinated by Thomas's exploration of the transition from human to machine, in this instance by choice. It's something of a cliché to describe a person, in the trauma of bereavement, as dying inside, but in this instance, the narrator is systematically annihilating herself as a human being, rebuilding herself as a machine, a ruthless response to the situation in which she finds herself, an ultimate withdrawal from the world. I always value a book that can withstand rereading and still offer fresh insight.

This was one such book and I regret that more of the judges didn't share my enthusiasm for it.

Lisa Tuttle's *Lost Futures* touched on another subject much in vogue in current SF writing, the quantum nature of the universe. One version of the theory suggests that there is no such thing as time travel; we cannot reach our own past or future because they don't exist. There is only the moment, the second. Every changing second opens a multitude of possibilities. For Clare Beckett, the possibilities seem to have become probabilities, as she shuttles between her many other fates, each determined by something that she decided in her 'real-time' life. Other Clares represent the successes and failures she might have been while she drifts, discontented, in her current life. So far as it went, this novel was fascinating in its attempt to portray the nature of the quantum universes, switching rapidly from one to another. In the same way, the portrayal of the Clare Beckett believed to be mad because she can recall some of her other lives was chilling in the extreme as her parents and friends struggled to cope with her condition.

Unfortunately, the thread of the novel began to break down once we met Clare Beckett from the future, Luz, who dreams her way through other lives. After this it was really no longer possible to accept the existence of quantum universes. Rather, it was as if we had strayed into Dallas country, where entire lives could be wiped out in a blink with the explanation that it had all been a dream. Beyond that, I felt that Tuttle's ending reneged on her female readers who, having worked their way through Clare's harrowing experiences, and her search to make something of her life, are then expected to accept the trite assumption that meeting the right man will be enough. I felt cheated but I still rate the novel highly for its ambitious attempt to explore the nature of life itself and through the eyes of an ordinary woman at odds with society's expectations.

Connie Willis's *Doomsday Book*, by comparison, is like the irrepressible child in class, the one who clowns around but whom no-one can quite find it in their hearts to chastise. It's set in a future Oxford, an Oxford where Kivrin, a student of medieval history, is planning to travel back to the fourteenth century. She is prepared; she's learned the languages, knows the period thoroughly, has been immunised against all the relevant diseases but, as she rapidly discovers when she arrives in fourteenth-century West Oxfordshire, is utterly unprepared for real fourteenth-century life.

Thus far, I was with this novel, and not just because it is set in my birthplace. It set up an interesting tension between history as perceived through books, texts and the actuality of being there. However, it has become almost a tradition that when any two readers of this book meet, they begin to point out its errors and inconsistencies. Future England has inexplicably returned to paper money; everyone refers to scarves as 'mufflers', an old-fashioned and regional usage in England, even now. Willis's knowledge of Oxford is, let me assure you, patchy. Likewise, her understanding of medieval Oxfordshire history is riddled with fundamental inconsistencies. I have a suspicion that Willis doesn't really care that much about this inaccuracy, such is her absorption in the real story. And the real story is of Kivrin struggling to care for the family that takes her in and which, tragically, begins to die of the Black Death.

The settings on the time machine had been false and Kivrin, far from avoiding this threat, finds herself in the middle of it. I cannot think of any description of death which is quite so moving, so harrowing as this. Juxtaposed with the flu epidemic in future Oxford, and the deaths of people unused to germs in a sanitised society, the effect of both is quite overwhelming. But is it science fiction? Yes it is, but the SF is almost incidental to Kivrin's struggle with knowledge she can't use and a complete lack of medicines. This story is about people and the will to survive; the SF content is incidental.

Whch brings us to Kim Stanley Robinson's *Red Mars* and Marge Piercy's *Body of Glass*. *Red Mars* is the first part of a trilogy about the colonisation of Mars, and concentrates on the arrival of people on Mars itself, the first hundred scientists and engineers, and their struggle to create an environment suitable for humankind. The scope of this novel is vast, encompassing every range you could think of; race, attitude, religious beliefs, environmental theories to name but a few. My biggest concern about it was the very hugeness of the subject and Robinson's attempts to cram it all in to one book. I felt there was just too much in too small a space. A myriad of issues were raised but not fully confronted, not through any cowardice on the part of the author but because the magnitude of the undertaking was simply too great for the arena in which it was being undertaken. This is not to say that I don't like the book. There is much about it which I find admirable. For example, Robinson raises moral issues about the right of Earth, for which read the United Nations, for which read whoever has the ascendancy at the time of the mission, to decide to terraform Mars. There is much discussion about this throughout the novel, but the issue is not comfortably resolved.

Although one recurring motif is that of plans having been laid by people who would never visit Mars, without taking into consideration the local conditions, I still find it difficult to believe that the basic decision wouldn't have already been taken. In fact, it is clear that despite appearances to the contrary, the mission is very poorly organised; how plausible this is, I don't know, but I can't help feeling that, for instance, the disappearance of so many personnel to form their own colonies ought to have been foreseen. Surely the authorities would have realised that for many this would be a chance to start over rather than act as puppets on behalf of the UN.

The novel raises a thousand puzzles of this sort and, in its vastness, fails to satisfy my curiosity. It is a brave attempt at describing the colonisation of Mars, the best so far, certainly the most rounded, but I was still left with an uncomfortable sense that we had already stepped too far beyond the question of whether we should colonise for the ethical issues to be raised. Likewise, I felt that Robinson hadn't entirely got control of his characters or their stories. Too many doubts were being raised in my mind for me to feel entirely comfortable with this book. It was my second choice, not my first.

And. as we all know, the judges selected Marge Piercy's *Body of Glass* as the winner. Just to clear up one minor controversy, this book was placed first by five out of the six judges, and was the second choice of the remaining judge. For some reason this is considered damning by certain critics of the decision, though I can't imagine why. The Booker Prize has, on more than one occasion, been settled by a majority vote, as indeed has the Clarke Award itself in previous years. Why it should be such a big deal this year, I can only guess.

The story centres on Shira, a square peg in the round hole of corporate culture. A computer whizz-kid, she cannot bring herself to conform to the requirements of her company and is punished with the loss of her child when her husband leaves her. Returning to her childhood home, the freetown Tikva, she finds that the life she remembers is under threat from the conglomerates and participates in the creation of an illegal cyborg to help protect the town. Piercy cuts this with the story of the Prague ghetto in 1600 and the creation of the golem to support the oppressed Jews in their struggle against the Gentiles. The stories of Yod and Joseph intertwine, the one a creature of day, the other a complex assembly of circuits and organic material. Each develops far beyond their creators' original intentions. Does each become human? How do you define human? Human because of the nature of its structure? Human because it thinks and feels, possesses emotions, can love, as each of them does?

Joseph's humanity is recognised in his acceptance of the need to unmake him, the golem. He has the strength to resist but doesn't. Yod sacrifices himself in order to save Shira and the freetown. It's been argued that as an AI he didn't have to make the sacrifice quite as he did. He could have downloaded himself and preserved his intelligence, sacrificing only his body. This criticism, I feel, misses the point about the nature of the sacrifice, made as a human rather than as a cyborg. In fact, Yod does live on, in the crystals which Shira later destroys. He leaves the choice with her and she recognises his humanity; thus the choice is doubly made.

It has also been said that this book should not have won because it was marketed as a mainstream novel, that Marge Piercy has no track record as an SF writer—in other words, that she is 'not one of us'. This overlooks both her novels *Dance the Eagle to Sleep* and *Woman on the Edge of Time*, as well as her immense popularity among science fiction readers. Quite apart from anything else, if it looks like a duck, walks like a duck, quacks like a duck, yet is labelled a hen, it is still indubitably a duck. *Body of Glass* is a science fiction novel, the equal of every other novel on the shortlist and, as the judges decided, the best of them.

On wanting to be astonished by science fiction

Those of you who have been reading my critical writing for a while will know I tend to employ a very subjective definition of science fiction and fantasy, deriving from the 'what I point to' school of thought. Or, as I sometimes term it, 'stuff Maureen likes'. It is by no means ideal, but over the years it has accommodated my preference for the kind of fiction that blurs genre boundaries and takes more pleasure in subverting or ignoring genre tropes than in reinforcing them.

Such inexact definitions can be difficult to rely on when talking to readers who are not familiar with your tastes. But neither do I want to be one of those people who defines science fiction or fantasy in excruciating taxonomic detail, working through layers of subgenre to achieve the perfect description of an individual text. It might work for classifying living organisms, but I've never been entirely convinced that applying this 'scientific' approach to a piece of fiction is remotely effective.

There might be a limited use in making the broadest distinctions in subject matter—space opera or military SF, for example—but I can't help thinking that the moment you begin categorising titles according to the minutiae of specific content, you are inevitably going to run into problems. Of course, taxonomy, classification, categorisation, call it what you will, brings with it a pleasing sense of rigour, because it is science of a sort and, as we know, science is good, and especially pertinent to science fiction. Except this is not science, but performance. This is not deep textual analysis but prescription, boundary-building, gate-keeping, exclusion, scent-marking, and so on. Indeed, I'd say there's an unsettling implication of a desire to avoid contamination. I'd go so far as to say it is a form of literary germophobia, and something far more pernicious even than the endless debate about the differences between 'literary' and 'genre' fiction. Hint: there are fewer than you think.

I'm always surprised, though frankly relieved, that no one has thus far attempted an <u>Aarne-Thompson</u>-style classification system for tropes in science fiction. Perhaps the closest we have come to such a thing is Gary K. Wolfe's *Critical Terms for Science Fiction*, listing thirty-three definitions of SF. I've read them all, but none of them seem to be entirely what I am looking for, and to come up with one of my own would be to provoke yet another round of discussion on a topic I have just devoted five paragraphs trying not to talk about. Well done, me.

It was only when I read a piece by Adam Roberts last autumn that I realised I might have been coming at the problem from the wrong angle. That there was another way of thinking about science fiction and fantasy, and it had been staring me in the face all along. Adam's essay is entitled 'How I define "science fiction"', but what it contains is more far-reaching than the title suggests.

Adam begins by discussing what he calls 'the most famous jump-cut in cinema', at the beginning of Stanley Kubrick's *2001: A Space Odyssey*. You know the one—the ape man throws the bone into the air, and as it begins its fall to earth it is replaced by a shot of a bone-shaped spacecraft. Adam says:

> ...this seems to me an extremely beautiful and affecting thing, a moment both powerful and eloquent, even though I'm not sure I could lay out, in consecutive and rational prose, precisely why I find it so powerful or precisely what it loquates.

In other words, it would appear that the beauty lies in part in the observer's inability to properly articulate what that image represents, even though the observer, here Adam Roberts, experiences the meaning at an intuitive level. The image defies interpretation even as it invites it.

I would happily argue that *2001* is full of such moments. It is visually one of the most beautiful science fiction films I know, but what further distinguishes it is how difficult it is to explain precisely what the film is 'about'. The elements most people remember are HAL's attempt to 'save' the mission and his subsequent demise, which are easily grasped, and the hyperspace sequence, which is not explained at all, only experienced. The film is infinitely open to interpretation, and therein lies its power.

I'm interested too in Adam's difficulty in laying out what that sequence means to him. Words are all he has, and are indeed his stock-in-trade, but here they are not, and perhaps can never be, quite enough to explicate that experience.

Or perhaps they are too much. Could it be that when Adam tries to explain the sequence something is lost? The image seems so right, so perfectly wrought, so replete with meaning it seems wrong to even begin to try and rationalise it.

And yet we persist. The way Adam sees it, the 'bone' image works 'not by a process of rational extrapolation, but rather *metaphorically*'. It actualises the 'vertical "leap" from the known to the unexpected that is the structure of metaphor, rather than the horizontal connection from element to logically extrapolated element that is the structure of metonymy'. For Adam, then, science fiction is 'more like a poetic image than it is a scientific proposition'.

This particularly catches my attention because of my own reading background. As a child I read fantasy rather than SF. Such science fiction as was available to me consisted primarily of Heinlein juveniles and things like the Tom Swift stories. Consequently, science fiction presented itself very strongly as being 'for boys', which probably wouldn't have concerned me as I tended to run a mile from anything presented strongly as 'for girls' (I had no interest whatsoever in the Chalet School stories, for example). But insofar as I tried most things that came my way, I'm fairly sure I read Heinlein and Tom Swift and discarded them for one very simple reason: they bored me. They tried to educate me rather than entertain me.

I definitely read some Andre Norton—*Moon of Three Rings* sticks in my memory, and I think that may be as much because it presents itself more as fantasy than hard space fiction. Slightly later, I read Wyndham but never really thought of his novels as science fiction because of the obviously terrestrial settings, then read Asimov's *Foundation* to please a friend at school, and hated it. It was only when I started reading Le Guin in my early twenties that I found science fiction that possessed what we might think of as poetry. All of which is a slightly overblown way of explaining why I've never had much truck with the idea of SF as a way of getting children into science. Take that, Hugo Gernsback. This is not to say that it might not do so as a corollary; I just don't believe that is what science fiction or fantasy is truly about.

But let us continue with Adam's notion that 'science fiction is a fundamentally metaphorical literature because it sets out to represent the world without reproducing it'. There is a part of me that wants to say, but isn't that true of all literature, in that even if it is avowedly mimetic, it cannot be fully mimetic, otherwise we'd all be lost in a Borgesian nightmare of labyrinths and forking paths. But while all fiction is to some extent mimetic, some fiction is more mimetic than it is metaphorical. Unless one wants to argue that some science fiction is mimicking other science fiction … and am I the only person stuck on this solipsistic merry-go-round? I do hope not.

But this does bring me to a genuine problem I have with science fiction, or certain strains thereof. The painstaking extrapolation from known to unknown, based on what we currently know about the world, the rivet-counting, the insistence that X cannot happen without Y, and so on. For years I thought I could only be a good science fiction critic if I assiduously read *New Scientist* every week, and for a long time I did, and watched *Horizon* (when it was still good), and even made it all the way through Stephen Hawking's *A Brief History of Time*. Which was, I think now, to miss the point somewhat. It's one thing to be a science geek, and I like to be informed about science, and am genuinely interested in the history of science, but if I can only fully appreciate science fiction by putting myself through this sort of training programme, then something is wrong. Because it doesn't matter how rigorous the science is if a science fiction novel actively sucks as fiction. And bluntly, a lot of it does, even now. A novel that would rather you fawned over the accurate use of equations rather than appreciating the quality of the storytelling is not a novel

I'm interested in reading. Neither is it the kind of science fiction I'm interested in writing about.

Large deviations from what is permissible in science fiction are, Adam suggests, more liable to bounce the reader 'out of her reading experience'. I take the point, but still I find myself thinking, well why not? Why shouldn't the experience of reading science fiction be as 'alien' as the concept of science fiction itself? Suppose we take it as given that SF invites a radical detachment from the truly mimetic. Adam invokes Coleridge's willing suspension of disbelief; it seems to me that the very notion of SF is to invite the willing suspension of disbelief, to think 'what if?' in the broadest way possible.

What does it say about readers if they don't want that? And yet, too often, I suspect they don't. Half the problem with the genre heartland is that it reinforces the status quo rather than challenging it. The city on the hill is transformed into a citadel. None shall enter, none shall leave. As Adam suggests, while 'worldbuilding is part of the system of a science fiction text […] the point of SF is not its system'. Certainly, I don't think it should be about the system.

> The point [of SF] is that it transports us—that it takes us somewhere new, that it brings us into contact with something wonderful, that it blindsides us, makes us gasp, unnerves or re-nerves us, makes us think of the world in a different way.

Where is the science fiction that is 'wonderful, or radically new, or strangely beautiful, or beautifully dislocating', Adam asks, the science fiction that is 'at least flavoured with Strange'? Not all SF is great. It's the way things are. The most rewarding novels to write about are often those that have aspired to greatness but, for whatever reason, have not quite achieved it. The gaps in the carapace are inevitably far more revealing than the shiny surface. As the oyster requires grit to make a pearl, so a critic often requires less than sublime science fiction to test their abilities. I want to be astonished by science fiction. Always. I want to be surprised by everything I read, but science fiction and fantasy more than most kinds of fiction seem to offer up that promise.

I also like the way Adam equates the idea of Sense of Wonder with the Sublime, prompting us to look back to the Romantics and their sense of awe. The concept of the Sublime has been overlooked of late and I'd love to see it come back into critical play. Good science fiction should, Adam suggests, achieve 'escape velocity'. It should achieve 'rapture'. It would, I think, be tiring if all science fiction wallowed endlessly in its Sense of Wonder, though it would be wonderful if more of it even aspired to that condition.

We Need to Talk About Dragons:
John Mullan, George R.R. Martin, *Game of Thrones* and the triumph of fantasy fiction

It was something of a surprise to find literary scholar and pundit John Mullan discussing fantasy fiction in the Guardian a week ago. A surprise because, on past accounting, Mullan and genre fiction are not comfortable bedfellows. The nature of Mullan's distaste for genre fiction is still not entirely clear to me, other than that it is not literary fiction. As I've noted elsewhere, one of the problems with this stance is Mullan's failure to recognise that literary fiction is itself a genre, with distinctive characteristics of its own, characteristics that Mullan himself has delineated in various articles.

So, what are we to make of Mullan's essay 'George RR Martin, *Game of Thrones* and the triumph of fantasy fiction'? My first response to the piece was that it was drivel, poorly constructed and poorly referenced. Some have suggested I was a bit harsh on Mullan, as his article did seem to suggest that he had changed his mind about fantasy, and was attempting some sort of rapprochement with the genre. Perhaps they were right. I decided to put the article aside for a few days and then look at it again. In the meantime, the Hugo nominations were announced, after which all previous topics of discussion were lost forever. There is little I can usefully contribute to the Hugo discussions right now that hasn't already been said elsewhere, but I can go back to Mullan's article and give it the rigorous analysis I think it deserves.

Before I begin, I should say that I've no problem with Mullan's tastes in literature. We all like different things, after all. My problem lies with his continuing predilection for writing on subjects for which he clearly has little sympathy, and little knowledge. When in 2010 Niall Harrison reported on the infamous encounter between Mullan and China Miéville at the Cheltenham Literary Festival, he noted that:

> ...it became awkwardly clear that while the discussion was going to be primarily about the absence of category SF from the Booker list, only one of the participants could and would talk fluently about fiction from all over the literary map. Mullan had almost no recent primary experience with category science fiction.

While I think Mullan makes a distinction between genre fiction and literary fiction, he fails to recognise that 'literary fiction' is as much a category as 'science fiction' or indeed 'fantasy fiction'. Mullan's article seems to make a rigidly enforced distinction between science fiction and fantasy, to the point where science fiction is not mentioned at all. He begins with a question:

> Has fantasy fiction, for decades a thriving literary genre, finally taken its place in the literary mainstream?

It's a nice, friendly sort of question. Mullan represents fantasy as a thriving genre, a literary genre even, which definitely sounds like an improvement on his previous stance. He goes on to note that fantasy does not need 'bien pensant "literary" admirers', and comments too on how fantasy fandom is characterised by 'companion volumes, analytical websites, conferences and online commentaries'. It is also a genre [category] that has 'always generated critical expertise, and fantasy novelists have long been in a dialogue with their readers that other novelists must envy'. In particular, Mullan notes Neil Gaiman's 2.2 million followers on Twitter.

This all seems unobjectionable, though by the end of the paragraph, I kept finding myself wanting to insert 'and SF' into every other sentence. It struck me also that Mullan's description of the critical activity surrounding fantasy fiction was carefully couched in terms that would resonate with a more scholarly audience. Substitute 'conventions and blogging' and the tone shifts entirely.

However, Mullan goes on to say this:

> Fantasy's devotees must feel rueful as the critics now rush to declare their addiction to HBO's *Game of Thrones* […] or record their admiration of Terry Pratchett.

And then says:

> The debt to fantasy fiction of *The Buried Giant*, the new novel by one of Britain's leading literary novelists, Kazuo Ishiguro, must seem overdue vindication of the genre.

Are we rueful about the critics rushing in? By which I guess Mullan means the critics from the mainstream press rather than the category press. I suspect many would see praise for Martin or Pratchett as vindication of their tastes rather than encroachment upon them, but perhaps this remark says more about Mullan's perception of 'fans' of fantasy fiction. By the same token, why would 'we' regard Ishiguro's *The Buried Giant* as a vindication of our tastes, particularly if, as Mullan is simultaneously proposing, we are so insular we are supposed to resent mainstream critics saying nice things about 'our' category?

Mullan seems to be suggesting that there exists some sort of cultural power struggle between fantasy fans and mainstream critics. This might have been true once, given that SF and fantasy fans have historically shown a tendency towards insularity, but fans these days welcome intelligent commentary wherever they find it.

However, I think the issue that lies at the heart of Mullan's article is the recent commotion around Kazuo Ishiguro's new novel *The Buried Giant*, which has the temerity to include such fantasy markers as ogres, elves, and dragons. To get some perspective on this so-called controversy, I will just point out that ogres, dragons, and elves are similarly mentioned in *Beowulf*, a text that is explicitly referenced in *The Buried Giant* on more than one occasion. I can't say I've ever noticed critics growing apoplectic that the unknown composer of *Beowulf* was using such figures in their fiction, so why they have been so exercised over Ishiguro, I'm not clear. I have felt embarrassed to observe one or two of fantasy's finest criticising Ishiguro for claiming his novel as fantasy, an issue that perhaps merits further discussion at some later date. For now, I will confine myself to saying that I've read Ishiguro's novel, I've read fantasy novels too, and I do not find Ishiguro's observations particularly controversial. Indeed, *The Buried Giant* is precisely the kind of fantastic writing I like best.

But Mullan won't let up on the cultural struggle he seems to think he has uncovered. 'Ishiguro has spoken in the past few weeks of how the barrier between this once disdained brand of fiction and "serious" novels is breaking down'. In the interview Mullan references, Ishiguro explains his own ground rules for writing *The Buried Giant*, describing how he is writing from within the world view of the novel's characters, a world view that admits ogres, elves, pixies, and dragons. I refer you back to that well-known work of fantasy, *Beowulf* (I'm using the Seamus Heaney version as my translation source, and he definitely says ogres, elves, and dragons).

As Mullan shifts the discussion to George R.R. Martin's *A Song of Ice and Fire* (*ASOIAF*) sequence, we learn that Martin has a 'host of fans who resent the low status accorded to their favoured genre and some distinguished admirers who rather agree'. What low status is this, I wonder, and who is according it? A moment ago, the genre was thriving and the writers and readers were happy: what happened between then and now? Mullan next invokes the 'accomplished literary novelist', John Lanchester, who likes both *ASOIAF* and *Game of Thrones*, and recently wrote an article to that effect in the *London Review of Books*. It's rather a good article—Lanchester is clearly familiar with both text and series and writes well about them. He is also clear that people who are snobbish about not reading the likes of GRRM are missing out, and he is not at all patronising about people who read a lot of fantasy.

Obviously, legions of disgruntled Martin fans will be relieved to know from Mullan that they now have the support of an 'accomplished literary novelist' alongside the support of those presumably less accomplished non-literary novelists who also like GRRM's work. Mullan refers to *ASOIAF* as a roman fleuve: he is, I think, trying to construct a critical vocabulary for talking about these fantasy novels he's discussing. So, rather than simply talking about a series or sequence, Mullan turns to roman fleuve. Mostly, though, he uses Lanchester's words to comment on the 'richly imagined world' and the 'prevailing "sense of unsafety and uncertainty"' of that world', presumably because no non-literary critic or novelist would ever have managed to describe it in such terms, or if they did, their judgement has now been validated by an 'accomplished literary novelist'. For example, we are told of *ASOIAF* that any 'connoisseur of narrative drive' who 'crosses that divide' (by which he means the unbridgeable crevasse that Lanchester refers to in his article, although I'm not at all sure Mullan and Lanchester actually are on the same side of that crevasse) will be amazed at the drive and inventiveness of Martin's novels, because obviously neither science fiction nor fantasy as category fiction are ever all about the narrative drive.

By now, it seems clear that if Mullan is going to praise fantasy, that praise will be faint indeed, and mostly backhanded. I eventually realised that what Mullan was attempting was first to construct a lineage for fantasy, and then to construe a kind of reading schedule in which one begins with fantasy-fantasy but gradually, as one becomes more enlightened, moves away from that towards something more literary, like, oh, let's say Kazuo Ishiguro's *The Buried Giant*, which is of course a serious literary novel.

Tolkien, we are delighted to learn, 'has not been entirely cold-shouldered by serious critics'. While I might agree to an extent that *Lord of the Rings* is increasingly more of a cultural artefact than it is a great book, what is a great book? *LOTR* is a much-loved book, it is a book that has moved and influenced millions of people. It has many constructional flaws, undoubtedly; it could be argued that it is guilty of nostalgia, that it lacks female characters, and that the language is stilted. It could equally be praised for its staggering ambition, for the mesmerising beauty and horror of some of its sequences (the journey through the Dead Marshes does it for me every time). And it could be argued that both Tolkien and Ishiguro are in their various ways drawing on the same stuff of British folklore and history to tell their stories, albeit with wildly differing results.

I'm fascinated by an anecdote that Mullan introduces at this point, of the 14-year-old Mullan being taken to meet Tolkien at Merton College, Oxford, because he knew one of Tolkien's grandsons at school, and having his 'battered paperback copy of *Lord of the Rings*, much reread' signed. Fascinated because, if the timeline fits together the way I think it does, while Mullan was getting his book signed, several miles across town a 14-year-old girl was embarking on her umpteenth read of a similar paperback copy, unaware at that point of who precisely Tolkien was, or that she had spent much of her childhood regularly passing his house.

As to why Mullan inserts that anecdote precisely then, I assume it is first to establish his pedigree—he met Tolkien—and second, it is to put *LOTR* in its proper place as a childish thing, which can and must be set aside as one grows older. We can infer this because Mullan then turns to offer us *ASOIAF* as the real deal, because it is 'emphatically fantasy for grown-ups'. It's not just the sex and violence but the Machiavellian principles, apparently, but I daresay the sex and violence helps. (I should say here that, assuming he has actually read *ASOIAF*, Mullan may have the advantage of me, as I have not; on the other hand, I have read the whole of Robert Jordan's *Wheel of Time* sequence, may god forgive my desiccated soul, and I doubt he has, so we are probably even).

Apparently, 'Compared to *Lord of the Rings*, *A Song of Ice and Fire* is morally complex and undecideable', and obviously no other fantasy novel has ever been like that before or since. At least, none that Mullan has read. And here I refer you back to Niall Harrison's observation at the beginning. Mullan is in effect constructing a reading chart based around a few very popular writers, writers who have in terms of that popularity pretty much transcended the category to which Mullan assigns them, and yet it's clear that he has very little idea of what else is going on in modern fantasy writing.

There is a long disquisition on the use of maps in fantasy novels. While Mullan correctly notes that Tolkien almost certainly initiated this habit he seems unaware that more recently the ubiquity of such maps has itself become a source of amusement among certain sections of the readership. Instead, Mullan fastens on the fact that children love to draw maps—you can probably see where this is going.

He notes, citing Lewis's Narnia books, the fact that there is 'invariably a route from our world into a magical one', but while Mullan is correct in noting that Alan Garner's *Elidor* requires the children to cross into another world, the whole point with The Weirdstone of Brisingamen is that the magic comes to them, on Alderley Edge—there is no secondary world, and indeed Mullan for some reason insists on referring to secondary worlds as alternate universes, which is not the same thing at all.

Neil Gaiman is cited as the writer 'of fantasy for adults', whose stories 'admit the deities and demons of different mythologies to this [world]', again as if this has never happened in literature before. I particularly treasure Mullan's announcement that 'Gaiman composes like the TS Eliot of horror-fantasy, patching together stories and personages from incongruous sources, amid a flurry of literary allusions, as if all pagan stories of the supernatural comprised a single compendium of our deepest fears'. And perhaps Neil Gaiman does, but he is not the first to do so nor is he likely to be the last. And you know something? Much as I like both Eliot's writing and Gaiman's writing, Eliot is no more Gaiman than Gaiman is Eliot. I call bullshit.

We'll slide past the embarrassing encounter with the work of Terry Pratchett, and the bit where Mullan suggests that Pratchett stopped writing fantasy and started writing commentary on it instead through his satires, which are apparently not fantastic. 'Many of Pratchett's readers must also be readers of fantasy fiction, able to relish the irreverent parody as well as the real thing'. Perhaps that would be because the irreverent parody as a version of the real thing is actually the real thing. Possibly, just possibly, fantasy readers read Pratchett, and Pratchett fans vice versa. They might also understand what's happening because the tropes that Pratchett is dealing with have already long since infiltrated our culture. That is, long before *ASOIAF* arrived on the scene.

And finally, we return to Kazuo Ishiguro and *The Buried Giant*, confirming my suspicion that the dalliance with *ASOIAF* as the real fantasy deal is but a smokescreen for what is really on Mullan's mind. Is *The Buried Giant* a fantasy? With Mullan's guidance, we've been led from the pastoral nostalgia of Middle-earth through the gritty, sexually and militarily violent, and incestuous reality of Westeros, until here we are, finally, in the rarefied surroundings of imaginary sixth-century England, in a work written by a literary novelist. We have undergone our quest and have won through, and got to the good stuff. Except, how is he going to justify that dragon: 'Dragons are the grandest inhabitants of the genre', which I think means Mullan is wondering how he deals with Querig.

How Mullan deals with Querig is by claiming that *The Buried Giant* is 'no more echt fantasy than *When We Were Orphans* was a detective novel or *Never Let Me Go* a work of science fiction' (a Clarke shortlisted work of non-SF, no less). Mullan, by past account, is keen on representing things that read like category fiction but that he personally likes as having transcended their category. So, like *Wolf Hall* and *Never Let Me Go*, *The Buried Giant* has transcended the perceived limitations of category. 'It declines to provide much of the superstructure that the genre addict would expect'.

What superstructure does Mullan mean, exactly? No map? No gritty military action and incest? He doesn't say, but as Niall Harrison also noted, Mullan is a man who thinks very much in terms of category templates; I suspect that the need to construct a 'three ages of fantasy' for this article is in part born out of his not being able to find one easy template for fantasy (to go along with his past failure to find a single easy template for science fiction). That desire for a category template surfaces too in his endless reiteration of the notion that bookshops have special rooms for, variously, science fiction and fantasy. I assume he means the shelves that are marked 'science fiction and fantasy' as a marketing tool, for half the argument here is really about category in marketing rather than genre qua genre, because that's actually an entirely different theoretical argument, as well he ought to know.

So, what are we to do about that dragon? She is 'disappointingly undernourished and lethargic' ... thank god, she is not a proper dragon after all! Thus, Mullan can confidently state that Ishiguro 'is using some of the conventions of fantasy fiction to produce a fable of violence—always at the heart of the genre—and about the capacity of societies to forget the violence of their pasts. Fantasy has enabled him to do this obliquely, daring us to take seriously a kind of narrative that is often called childish'. Mostly, I would venture to suggest, by mainstream critics. Fable is the weasel word here, a way of saying fantasy without saying fantasy.

And then finally, we're back to GRRM and the announcement that he 'employs a shifting of viewpoints that some critics do not expect from the moral and narrative conventions of fantasy writing'. Because, again, no one ever did that, not even Tolkien—oh, wait.

It is easy, far too easy, to poke fun at Mullan's article, because it is so woefully wrong-headed. He raises some interesting points along the way but rarely in such a manner that is actually germane to whatever he is discussing at any given point. The article is one long betrayal of his lack of familiarity with what is going on in modern fantasy writing and indeed his failure to understand the breadth of modern critical work on the fantastic. The big takeaway for many people from Mullan's article was the fact of no women writers being mentioned, except Amanda Craig as critic, and Trudi Canavan as a quiz answer. But, much as it pains me to say this, Mullan's failure to discuss women writers is not the main issue, but symptomatic of a broader failure to understand fantasy as a category at all.

Making an Emotional Investment – surviving the announcement of the Hugo Awards shortlists

I've spent most of the week stewing on thoughts of award shortlists, or more precisely on thoughts of reactions to award shortlists, the Booker and the Hugos in particular. I first properly paid attention to the Booker Prize in 1984, the year that J.G. Ballard's *Empire of the Sun* was shortlisted, and Anita Brookner's *Hotel du Lac* won. Indeed, I paid attention *because Empire of the Sun* was shortlisted. Insofar as I can now reconstruct what my younger self thought about that shortlisting, it was probably something along the lines of myself as a rather earnest SF fan, a bit fed up with people being rude about science fiction, believing that Ballard's being selected in some way demonstrated the worth of science fiction because he was after all 'one of us'.

Without actually reading *Empire of the Sun*, I was already fairly sure that the Ballard was the best novel on the shortlist (probably basing my opinion on book reviews I'd read and on discussions on TV and radio). I recall being incredibly disappointed that Ballard didn't win, as indeed were many people I knew at the time. There was a sense somehow that we, along with Ballard, had been rejected; that *Empire of the Sun*, although not science fiction, was considered somehow tainted because of Ballard's connection to the genre, and therefore not good enough.

Some years later, by this time having read both the Ballard and the Brookner, I was genuinely baffled that *Hotel du Lac* had triumphed because, to my mind, it was and remains a pallid little book, limp and uninteresting, in terms of technique and subject matter, whereas the Ballard is clearly the better-written book and far more interesting as well.

In fact, only as recently as last year, when letters between Richard J. Cobb, chair of the Booker judges, and friends including the historian Hugh Trevor-Roper were published, was it revealed that Ballard was almost certainly robbed, and so were several other people. Keith Jeffery reviewed *My Dear Hugh: Letters from Richard Cobb to Hugh Trevor-Roper and others* as edited by Tim Heald and, among other things, made this observation about Cobb's handing of the Booker Prize: 'he claimed to have done "a little NEGATIVE good" by keeping Martin Amis and Angela Carter off the shortlist, "and manoeuvred so that Ballard did not get the prize"'.

On the one hand, this confirms that instinctive sense I had then, and again later when I read the Brookner, that something was critically wrong with the award that year. On the other hand, I find myself less surprised now than I might have been in, say, 1990, had I learned that Cobb had been machinating, not because it appears to have been the kind of thing that Cobb did, but because I understand now that judges, juries, chairs of awards often have hidden agendas. The only thing that is unusual here is that Cobb boasted openly about his actions to close friends.

I have not read the letters, so have no idea what his grounds were for keeping Amis and Carter off the shortlist, any more than I know why he manoeuvred to avoid the award going to Ballard, though that he did so clearly indicates that some of the judges that year thought Ballard should have won. Personally, I suspect I would have made less of an emotional investment in the prize had I known then, as I know now, that Ballard did not see himself as a science fiction writer, and had not done so for a long time. I might well have regarded that as a betrayal—because I had a heavy emotional investment in SF, and would have found it difficult then to imagine why anyone might abandon it, not least because, to my mind at least, Ballard was still writing science fiction, even if he did not choose to name it as such.

And in terms of the alienating effects of young Jim's experiences, *Empire of the Sun* did seem science-fictional to me, still does. What upset me most about Ballard's rejection of science fiction was the perceived snub to us, the science fiction community, and to me as a science fiction reader. While I was not then aware of the creative struggle to reposition SF within the literary mainstream, I did realise that many people thought that science fiction and fantasy were inferior forms. At that stage I couldn't adequately articulate why this was not the case, but I could and already did annoy people by pointing out elements of the fantastic where they surfaced in realist writing.

Empire of the Sun winning the Booker would have given me more ammunition for the argument, but *Hotel du Lac*'s victory crushed that hope—and yes, I probably did take it that personally. So even as I discovered the Booker, I was already disillusioned by it. I followed the prize religiously for a number of years, and I'd be lying if I said I didn't still follow it after a fashion, but I lost my sense of personal investment in it almost in the moment of its discovery. Nowadays, I view it cynically, waiting to see which novel possessing clearly fantastical elements is proclaimed as 'literary' or 'mainstream' because it is apparently too well-written to be science fiction or fantasy. Clearly, I still haven't quite got over my original disappointment.

However, the Booker doesn't interest me in the way it once did. I don't have a personal stake in it, not even when there is a novel with clear fantastical leanings in the running. The judges probably do a conscientious job of looking at all the contenders and doubtless give careful consideration to what goes on the shortlist. But I am also acutely aware that the shortlist they eventually choose can only ever be a snapshot of what a particular group of people think about a particular group of books published during a particular year.

It is easy enough to disengage oneself from the Booker because it is so remote. This theoretically should hold true even for awards closer to home, such as the Hugos, the Nebulas, the Tiptree, the Clarke Award, the BSFA Awards and the Kitschies, especially the juried ones, where most of us have no actual input. And yet, as we saw with the 2012 Clarke Award, the furore and passion surrounding the shortlist can still be extraordinary. It seemed like everyone I knew had an opinion—and expressed it forcefully.

It seemed that 'we', the science fiction readers, or stakeholders if you like, felt that the judges, the people we saw as representing us, had somehow let us down by being less expert than we felt they should have been. Although we had no involvement in their becoming judges (this is the prerogative of the committees of those organisations who nominate judges), we nonetheless saw them as embodying our tastes and shaping the award we saw as representative of those tastes, and in this instance failing us by not including the novels we felt they should have shortlisted. This is clearly nonsensical when viewed dispassionately, but the fact is that we tend to view the juried award as a more accurate barometer of what is good, significant, award-worthy, whatever, than an award that is decided by a public vote. Until, of course, it doesn't yield the kind of result we think it should, at which point it becomes treacherously flawed.

And yet, how can it not be flawed? As with any award, judges have their prejudices and biases, ones they may not even be aware of. In fact, these biases are a necessary part of the process. Without disagreement it is difficult to reach agreement. The Clarke Award has the same non-voting jury chair from year to year, with the aim of facilitating discussion among the judges. Even so, it is down to the judges to decide what they are looking for in a Clarke Award winner, and that will inevitably vary each year as the jury lineup changes.

Why is it that we get so exercised over award shortlists when as readers we cannot do anything to influence the result? It is a question that troubles me, because I cannot find a sensible answer to it, and I am not sure there is one. Such an intense level of debate demonstrates that the Clarke Award is an important part of the intellectual landscape of SF, and that is clearly a good thing. On the other hand, are we so emotionally invested that we are unable to step back and reflect more dispassionately on what the shortlist is saying?

The Clarke Award is probably as transparent about its processes as an award can be. The Hugos are a different kettle of fish. My emotional investment in the Hugos probably died in 1995, the year that David Gerrold's 'The Martian Boy' won the Best Novelette category. If you were in the Glasgow YMCA the morning after the ceremony and saw a young woman kneeling on the floor of the foyer, banging her head against the floor, that was me, in despair, and none too particular who knew about it.

Having looked back at the shortlist I cannot for the life of me think now what it was I wanted to win—probably Le Guin's 'The Matter of Seggri'—but I do know I thought Gerrold's story was not only cloyingly sentimental, it was cynically eliciting a particular response from the audience, who no doubt knew that Gerrold himself had adopted a boy and the story was based in part on their relationship. I suspected that this was in turn why the story won the Hugo. We're almost all of us suckers for a happy ever after. However, whereas I accepted that the Booker had some fierce politics going on under the surface, I suppose I still hoped that the Hugo voting was based mostly on literary merit. And clearly it wasn't. After that, while I didn't exactly ignore the Hugos, I found myself less and less certain about what they were for. I had previously tended to regard them as representing a benchmark for good SF writing but after the Gerrold incident I felt I could no longer rely on them to serve that purpose and I wasn't sure where to go next with them. Mostly, I ignored them.

Given that I am now part of a loose online community that regularly discusses science fiction awards, including the Hugos, I've found myself thinking about them again. The arguments go back and forth about the point of the Hugos, especially as regards whether they offer a genuine recognition of a story's intrinsic merit or are simply a vote on an author's popularity. It is probably impossible to provide empirical data to show that, in the novel category at least, it is an author-driven rather than a text-driven award, though I suspect this is the case, not least because the same authors crop up on the shortlists time and again.

Rather than looking at this year's shortlists and thinking 'Jesus Christ', I would like to start thinking about how I can usefully engage with the Hugos as a stakeholder of some sort. Whenever and wherever this matter gets discussed, most people seem to agree that the essential requirement for active involvement is being bothered to nominate. I can't deny the sense of this and I'm as guilty as the next person in this respect. I have not even been eligible to nominate in recent years because, to put it bluntly, however important I might now consider the Hugos to be, as a self-funding postgraduate student with a small debt mountain to my name, a supporting membership of the Worldcon is a luxury I cannot afford.

I have also gained the impression that those who do nominate are drawing on a very limited pool of names, which is why the same candidates seem to resurface so often. There is also the problem that a large percentage of Hugo-related publicity seems to centre upon writers drawing attention to the eligibility of their own work, rather than to the work they have enjoyed.

It occurs to me that one inarguably positive thing I can do is flag up work I come across that seems promising, not just in the period immediately before nominations close, but throughout the year. If there is to be a genuine investment in making the Hugos 'our' awards, the way so many people seem to want them to be, then this kind of general enthusiasm for good writing needs to become an intrinsic part of the process. It may not achieve immediate results, and it's certainly not enough on its own, but it might help to push the argument beyond the usual expressions of horror at this time of year. And frankly, that change would be welcome.

WRITING IN THE MARGINS

Daughters of Earth, edited by Justine Larbalestier

'Feminism is as much a way of reading, as it is of writing,' observes Justine Larbalestier in the introduction to this anthology (p.xvi). To which I might add that there are also as many feminist readings of a story as there are feminists to read it, and to write about it. Larbalestier comprehensively illustrates her point, and mine, in *Daughters of Earth*. Part historical survey of women as writers of SF short stories, and part a critical response to those stories, its format is ingenious, with each of the eleven selected stories accompanied by a critical essay from an SF critic or academic. To read the story, then the commentary, and then the story again, is to have one's eyes opened to their deeper complexities in a most satisfying way. I don't recall seeing this format used before, but I certainly found it incredibly effective.

In the almost twenty years that have elapsed since the publication of Sara Lefanu's *In the Chinks of the World Machine* (1988), the SF community at large has become much more aware of the presence of women as writers, commentators, and as fans. Even so, it can still come as a surprise to realise that women have been reading and writing science fiction since the very inception of the first true SF pulp magazines, and participating in the discussions surrounding the stories. As Larbalestier herself showed, in her previous book *The Battle of the Sexes in Science Fiction* (2002), women's presence as readers and as vocal fans of the genre has frequently been contentious, sometimes distinctly unwelcome, but they have always defended their right to participate, despite the sometimes appalling responses of male fans and editors alike.

One can only wonder what Clare Winger Harris, the first woman to publish a short story in a pulp magazine (in 1927), must have thought when she saw her $500 Cover Contest prize-winning story, 'The Fate of the Poseidonia' damned with the faint praise of Hugo Gernsback's observation that 'as a rule, women do not make good scientifiction writers, because their education and general tendencies on scientific matters are usually limited'. It apparently did not deter Harris from producing further published stories, but Gernsback's comment leaves me wondering exactly how much work he was considering— and apparently rejecting—from female writers, and what, precisely, those worrying 'general tendencies' were. Jane Donawerth's accompanying essay shows how Harris's story touches on issues of feminism, race anxiety, invasion, the effects of new inventions, in a way that the modern SF reader would easily recognise. At this point I cannot help but think of J.G. Ballard's comments about SF holding up a mirror to its own world, but such an approach would clearly be at variance with Gernsback's desire to use SF to promote a positive future, a scientific future.

Gernsback's response was by no means unusual, though we should remember that he, unlike some of his successors, did actually deign to publish science fiction by women. The essay by Brian Attebery that accompanies Leslie F. Stone's 'The Conquest of Gola' (1931), describes a scenario that would become only too familiar to female writers: the editors who rejected the work of women, and here Attebery singles out John W. Campbell as being particularly disapproving of women writing SF; the fans who did not want to see female characters or what they thought of as female concerns in *their* stories; the gradual recognition that the desire for publication would become inextricably mixed up with the need to conceal one's (female) identity behind an androgynous name or initials, or an outright pseudonym. Stone's narrative, as Attebery shows, skilfully up-ends the classic 'planet of women invaded by planet of men' trope, with her women acknowledging but resisting the role that is expected of them. Stone herself eventually left the field, but other women did not, and continued to resist the editors wherever possible.

Things changed after WWII as so many people are so fond of remarking. It's true, they did, but while some writers were intent on documenting the brave new world in which everyone found themselves, for many women the sense of anxiety increased. During wartime, many had found a new sense of freedom; in the UK and in the US women had taken on men's jobs while the men were away fighting. When the men returned, they were expecting to recover their jobs and the apple-pie domesticity they'd dreamed of while they'd been away; women found themselves expected to retreat happily to the domestic arena once again.

The 1940s and 50s saw the rise in SF of the so-called 'housewife-heroine', the mocking term bestowed by male readers on a figure who seems to me to represent a profound expression of women's anxiety at this time—what did this future hold for them? A.E. Jones's 'Created He Them' (1955) addresses the grim possibilities of a future post-war home front, in which the impulse to people the brave new world would be undermined by the effects of that war, meaning that fertile men and women would be forced into loveless coupledom in order to repopulate. Lisa Yaszek's accomplished essay teases out the many subtle implications of Jones's story, with its politically charged critique of the militarisation of daily life, and its examination of sex and gender issues. By contrast, Kate Wilhelm's 'No Light in the Window' (1963) plays with the notion that given the choice between keeping her man and seizing the opportunity of a lifetime, there is of course no choice at all, while Josh Lukin's intriguing commentary explores the ongoing resistance to female autonomy as exemplified in post-war fiction.

As the collection moves closer to familiar territory (that is, to the authors I began reading when I first came to science fiction), I was struck by what I missed at the time, both in terms of the stories I didn't read, and the messages I perhaps internalised but couldn't articulate, at least not until much later. I didn't come to Tiptree's fiction until much, much later than most people, for example, well after James was revealed to be Alice, and I was well into my twenties before I became fully aware of the discussions concerning feminism and science fiction. Whilst I would not necessarily claim that, in good Gernsbackian fashion, science fiction written by women has a specific message that as a reader I was bound to pick up on, I'm sure it had an effect. If your mother is constantly trying to guide you towards a diet of romances in which faux-Gothic heroines of improbable slenderness get their man, the house, and the lovely clothing, because that's what proper women read, while you are tackling Lisa Tuttle's 'Wives' (1976) or some such, it is possible that not only Houston has a problem. I am sure that I am not the only female reader of science fiction who relied on stories such as those included in *Daughters of Earth* to remind her that, yes, there was another way, and while it wasn't all fun, beautiful frocks, and parental approval, it was equally valid and worth pursuing.

Looking at Tiptree's 'And I Awoke and Found Me Here On the Cold Hill's Side' (1972), or Pat Murphy's 'Rachel in Love' (1987), or Octavia Butler's 'The Evening and the Morning and the Night' (1987), or Gwyneth Jones's 'Balinese Dancer' (1997), it's impossible to avoid acknowledging that the science fiction project to examine women's roles in the world just keeps on growing, and that it seems unlikely to run out of themes or subject matter any time soon. By the same token, academic readings of those stories continue to tease out new ideas and insights. In particular, Wendy Pearson's detailed examination of the Tiptree story, '(Re)reading James Tiptree Jr.'s "And I Awoke and Found Me Here on the Cold Hill's Side"' employs many different facets of current literary theory to invest a story that initially seems quite straightforward with immense, resonant depths, and was for me a highlight in a collection in which there are no bad essays at all.

It is invidious to single out favourites, but having already hinted at a favourite among the essays, I must also acknowledge a favourite among the stories, and at the same time make a confession. I have, of course, been aware of Pamela Zoline's 1967 story 'The Heat Death of the Universe' for years, but it was only when I started reading this anthology that I realised, with considerable embarrassment, that I had never actually *read* it. Still, better late than never, and now I know what really incendiary science fiction looks like. If I had to choose one story to express how the twentieth century has seemed for women, I think it would have to be this one, for the way in which it articulates the frustration of a competent woman, struggling to achieve the seemingly impossible.

Justine Larbalestier, along with a stellar cast of critics, has done a marvellous job in assembling this anthology. It's not so much about drawing attention to the women men don't see as showing just what women have seen, understood and written about, and how this has drawn others into an extraordinary discussion between author, reader, and critic that still exists within the SF community.

In compiling an anthology, there is always the problem of who should be included, who left out. In particular, Larbalestier's introduction specifically regrets the absence of Joanna Russ, Ursula K. Le Guin, and Suzy McKee Charnas, while noting that the essayists were free to make their own decisions about which story they wanted to write about. Although the lack of certain authors is going to raise eyebrows, Larbalestier makes it clear that the absence of stories such as 'When It Changed' (1972), 'The Ones Who Walk Away From Omelas' (1973), or 'Boobs' (1989) is not as the result of an editorial oversight. Had *Daughters of Earth* been presented as a definitive historical survey, then these would indeed be glaring omissions. However, according to Larbalestier this anthology has a different purpose. *Daughters of Earth* is 'aimed squarely at newcomers to feminist science fiction' (p.xvi), and as such the contributors have clearly taken this to heart. I think *Daughters of Earth* does a good job of sketching the development of feminist SF during the twentieth century, introducing the reader to a wide range of stories and approaches. Newcomers are inevitably going to hear about Le Guin, McKee Charnas, and Russ as they explore the literature. It makes sense to me that they should hear about some of the other feminist SF writers past and present who also live in the world machine. *Daughters of Earth* ensures that they do just that.

Women's Weird 2: More Strange Stories by Women 1891 - 1937, edited by Melissa Edmundson

When the *Strange Horizons* reviews team discussed the possibility of our reviewing ghost stories for Christmas, it seemed like a no-brainer. Except it turns out that the tradition of telling ghost stories at Christmas is not necessarily a global one. At a recent online seminar organised by the University of Glasgow Fantasy Centre, I was surprised to learn that the telling of midwinter ghost stories, a thing I have taken for granted for many years, is a more specific tradition than I'd imagined. Something of a national tradition, in fact, which in practice means an English tradition, and in reality a London tradition, promoted through print magazines. On top of that, the ghost story tradition we're familiar with is a Victorian reinvention of the idea, the stories more structured, and perhaps a little more respectable, domesticated even, than the older, pagan narratives.

Nonetheless, in the UK, midwinter ghost stories have invariably found an enthusiastic audience. The biggest Christmas excitement for me, as a teenager in Britain in the early 1970s, was the latest BBC adaptation of a ghost story by M.R. James, who, in my entirely uncritical judgement, wrote the best ghost stories ever. Even now, having read my way through the work of the other assorted members of the soi-disant James Gang, I still think James did it best. Or perhaps I should temper my enthusiasm slightly, saying that James wrote a certain kind of ghost story—the antiquarian ghost story—and wrote it very well indeed, while other writers, E.F. Benson especially, wrote equally well but in a more worldly vein. Personally, I still love antiquarian ghost stories best of all.

James's work drew a particularly sympathetic response from Lawrence Gordon Clark, a film director who adapted five of James's best-known stories for television between 1971 and 1975—the most successful, in my view, being 'A Warning to the Curious' (1972) and 'Lost Hearts' (1973)—as well as filming a truly stunning version of Charles Dickens's 'The Signalman' (1976). But after that long run of ghostly hits, the BBC turned to contemporary ghost stories. These, somehow, with the noble exception of Nigel Kneale's 'The Stone Tape', were never quite in the same league as their antiquarian forebears.

As if hoping to relive its glory days by tapping into what was clearly a winning formula, the BBC has returned periodically to James's stories, most notably with a lovely series of performed readings by Robert Powell, reflecting James's habit of reading his stories to his audience by candlelight on Christmas Eve ('The

Mezzotint' is probably the best of these performances, although 'The Ash Tree' is fastidiously nasty), and most recently, there have been a couple of Jamesian adaptations by the tiresomely ubiquitous James fanboy, Mark Gatiss, neither of which was actively bad but neither of which was great (how, for goodness' sake, does one conspire to make 'The Tractate Middoth' dull?). No matter how much he might want to succeed, Gatiss just doesn't have Gordon Clark's filmic eye, and without that the adaptations bump along the ground rather than taking flight. We will also draw a veil over the most recent BBC productions of contemporary ghost stories, again mostly written by Gatiss, because, just no. Meanwhile, the ITV network has never quite managed to top its terrifying 1989 Christmas Eve production of Susan Hill's *The Woman in Black*, the screenplay written by none other than Nigel Kneale.[1]

After the most recent so-so BBC contemporary story, written by Mark Gatiss, featuring Simon Callow and a haunted recording studio, a friend of mine posed this question: which *female* writers of ghost stories deserve to be adapted for TV? The immediate answer was E. Nesbit (and her stories have been adapted for the radio), at which point we all looked at one another and thought, 'Why hasn't this been done already?' I mean, 'Man-Size in Marble' and 'John Charrington's Wedding' are both screaming out for thoughtful, nuanced adaptations. And then I started thinking about the other women writers who were effectively James's contemporaries, none of whom, so far as I can recall, has made it to the screen. In fairness to Lawrence Gordon Clark and his ilk, these writers were all but forgotten back in the 70s, unless you happened to like poking around in old ghost story anthologies, but Nesbit was very much a household name, more so than ever at that point, given the success of the film of *The Railway Children* in 1970. So how come none of her ghost stories had ever received a similar treatment?

In the late 1980s and early 1990s, several publishers drew attention once again to the richness of what Michael Cox and R.A. Gilbert termed the 'literary ghost story'. In *The Oxford Book of English Ghost Stories* (1986), out of forty-two stories selected by Cox and Gilbert, seven were identifiably by women,[2] while in *Victorian Ghost Stories: An Oxford Anthology* (1991), out of thirty-five stories, eleven were identifiably by women, and Cox and Gilbert's introduction specifically acknowledged the existence of many other female writers.

Looking at the tables of contents for both volumes, neither group of names now seems particularly revelatory, but at the time most would have been pretty

---

1. This production is now famous for a particularly long-lasting shot of the face of the ghost filling the screen. It scared me so much when I was taping the broadcast that I accidentally shut down the video recorder and spent what seemed like minutes fumbling with the remote control to get the recording restarted. And still the face was on the screen when I got it going again.

2. Not included in that total is Vernon Lee, who at that point was regarded as writing under a male pseudonym, whereas more recent research has made it clear that Lee thought otherwise.

much lost to a general readership, so both volumes might have been regarded as a useful first step in rehabilitation. *The Virago Book of Ghost Stories* Volume 1 (1987) and Volume 2 (1991), plus *The Virago Book of Victorian Ghost Stories* (1988), all three edited by Richard Dalby, offered up a much broader range of material, although there is a fair amount of crossover in terms of names included, if not duplication of stories (and again, Vernon Lee is included). Around the same time, several small presses (among them Ash Tree Press) began publishing long-out-of-print collections of ghost stories by women writers and creating new collections of stories by writers otherwise overlooked. Much more recently, the British Library's Tales of the Weird series has also included a number of stories by women writers in its various collections, and has volumes specifically devoted to Mary Braddon and Charlotte Riddell.

And yet, the feeling remains that women's supernatural fiction continually requires attention to be drawn to its existence in a way that does not seem necessary for writers such as James or E.F. Benson.

I thought about this subject a lot when the first volume of *Women's Weird* was published, and I find myself thinking about it again now that we have *Women's Weird 2*, edited once again by Melissa Edmundson. That is, what is it about female ghost story writers that causes them to slip so easily from public attention? Based on what is published here, and in the previous volume, I have no obvious answer to that question, because the majority of the stories in both collections can easily hold their own against the likes of James or Benson.[3] The writers featured in the two volumes of *Women's Weird* rarely deal with the scholars so beloved of James (perhaps unsurprisingly, considering the refusal of the universities of the period to admit women as undergraduates), and when they do, it is almost invariably through a male viewpoint character. More often they seem to find their stories in domestic settings.

I wouldn't want to fall into the trap of implying that women writers of ghost stories were producing a distinctively domestic form of weird fiction, because I don't for a moment believe that to be true.[4] While a glance at the table of

---

3. I have wondered if the answer is, simply, that many women writers published their stories in magazines, and didn't have enough clout with publishers to get collections published. From the outset, James's work primarily appeared as hardback volumes, while Benson was a prolific writer, publishing widely, in magazines as well as in hardback. And yet, looking at various bibliographies it's clear a lot of these women writers were publishing collections of short stories all through this period, many of them entirely devoted to supernatural stories.

4. At the same time, James's fictions often touch on matters of domesticity; for a man who lived most of his adult life in college rooms, he understood extremely well how a middle-class household worked. And he had an eye for disturbing domestic images. One of the most horrific is that of a man putting his hand under his pillow for his watch in the middle of the night, and instead encountering a hairy mouth with teeth, while another involves a character reaching over the side of his bed to pet his dog and finding ... something else. Let's just say, there are reasons, even now, why I do not to stick my foot out from under the duvet in the middle of the night if I can help it, and James's stories are several of them.

contents for *Women's Weird* 2 reveals repeated references to both 'house' and 'room', this is to overlook, first of all, the variety of geographical settings, some easily identifiable, ranging from London to India to small-town America, and secondly the use of such places—the English garden, run-down country houses, small, dismal rooms in boarding houses, upstate American cottages—as symbols of a certain kind of life. And while it might be possible to argue that ghost stories by women are often linked to a building before an event, Stella Gibbons's 'The Roaring Tower', Barbara Baynton's 'A Dreamer', Sarah Orne Jewett's 'The Green Bowl', and several others certainly give the lie to this, as indeed does Edith Stewart Drewery's 'A Twin-Identity'.

Drewery's story sets the tone for this anthology, with its first-person account by Marie Lacroix, a female Parisian police agent in London to hunt down a murder suspect, during which process she receives unexpected, and seemingly supernatural, assistance in her quest. Yes, it is hinted that she at times disguises herself as a man in order to carry out her work (and it's not entirely clear to me how much the element of fantasy comes into play here—*were* there female *agents de police* in Paris at this time?), but I find it fascinating that the narrator takes for granted the fact that she should carry out work of this kind. One wonders what her predominantly male audience—the story is apparently told to a group of snowbound railway passengers—makes of it all, but there is no doubt that Marie's position as an *agent de police* is intended to add further veracity to her narration, implying that her story is to be trusted, because she herself is a responsible observer, as much as it is intended to titillate. Her profession is, if I'm honest, far more interesting than the story, which does involve a certain amount of mystical hand-waving, but what it might lack in supernatural interest, it more than makes up for with its depiction of a woman successfully pursuing a profession outside the home.

That easy assumption of personal agency also underpins Sarah Orne Jewett's 'The Green Bowl', a story of clairvoyance and mystical connection between two women of different classes, facilitated by ownership of the titular bowl and its twin, the sister bowls. Again, it's a curious tale, well told, but one of the elements that really stands out for me is the narrator's account of her journeys across New England, either alone or with a female companion. '[D]o you mean to say,' asks a scandalised listener, 'that you really go driving off to strange places, quite, quite alone? Have you no fear of tramps?' Katie Montague, the story's narrator, instead cheerfully regales the company with tales of her resourcefulness, and that of her companion, Frances Kent, when the two find themselves miles from a night's lodging, in the pouring rain, and obliged to put up in a tiny church overnight. Katie Montague casually talks of lighting a stove and having the wherewithal about her to ensure that she and her companion can eat and drink. And they are perfectly capable of tending to their carriage horse.

All this might be incidental to the seeming heart of the story, the meeting with Mrs Patton, the owner of the two green bowls, the eventual gifting of one bowl to Katie Montague, and her eventual coming into her power, but Katie's lavish descriptions of her adventure prior to meeting Mrs Patton are clearly intended to establish the two young women as being entirely self-sufficient. There is also the matter of the queer ... I want to say subtext, but the closeness of the relationship between the two women is so front and centre within the story it would be an act of wilful misreading for a twenty-first-century reader to ignore it. It's not so easy to gauge what the girls' audience is thinking, but the easy acceptance of their friendship suggests that most of the women present are either ignorant of its subtext or else not bothered. Travelling without a male companion seems far more scandalous.

Jewett was best known as a writer of 'local colour', and her account of the young women's experience, driving through the pouring rain and looking for somewhere to stay, is intensely vivid, as is the evocation of Mrs Patton's speech patterns and daily life, which is detailed without seeming patronising. It feels like a lived experience. One feels, too, the connection forged between her and the two young women, and indeed the entire story is suffused more with friendship than it is with any sense of the supernatural. Katie Montague's accession to her powers, towards the story's end, thus becomes a threat to her otherwise delightful life.

Indeed, what is striking about so many of these stories is that the various hauntings are not entirely the point of the story. Take, for example, L.M. Montgomery's 'The House Party at Smoky Island', which does actually feature a ghost, one with something on its mind, and yet the story has little to do with the ghost, and everything to do with the dynamics of a particular group of people at a particular moment, wondering about the deteriorating relationship between two people they all care about. The ghost is not so much a haunting as a vehicle for a revelation that cannot conveniently be made in any other way. Its presence is almost incidental to the bulk of the story, and when it does appear it is almost a relief in that it distracts the reader from feeling rather more out of it, even, than the narrator, who remains at a slight distance from the main social group.

If Montgomery's ghostly revelation is somewhat crude, there are other stories here that are far more intricate. Katherine Mansfield's 'The House' is a case in point. Is it even a ghost story? I think it is, but in so much as it anticipates a future haunting rather than one that has already taken place. It's a story I don't remember reading before (true of all the stories in this collection, in fact, which is itself a novelty), and I'm very glad to make its acquaintance as an excellent example of a certain kind of story where doubt persists throughout as to whether there is a haunting, at least in the physical sense, whilst it is undoubtedly about a sustained act of imagination. Here,

Marion takes shelter on the porch of an empty house during a downpour, only to find that, mysteriously, this is indeed her own house, with her own husband finding her there as he comes home, bearing flowers and gifts. Their life in this miraculously beautiful house is perfect in every degree, until a mystery voice calls from the hall downstairs, drawing Marion away again. It is, if you like, a modern version of Andersen's 'The Little Match Girl', with Marion taking refuge in a dream she and her lover constructed when they previously visited the house, knowing they could never afford to rent or furnish it. But it seems likely that she will always have the house now, as the servants who discover her body fear that she will haunt it. Indeed, perhaps she haunts it already.

Bithia Mary Croker's 'The Red Bungalow' is reminiscent of some of Rudyard Kipling's supernatural stories, but here there is a distinct sense that the narrator is just waiting for Netta Fellowes to get her comeuppance as she refuses to heed the warnings about the Red Bungalow, instead renting it for a pittance, determined to open it up and establish her new life at Kulu. The low-key tensions of life for army wives are laid bare in this account. Netta, with her 'marvellous energy and enviable taste', seems oblivious to the more subtle etiquette of service life, as Liz, the narrator, chides her gently for wanting to advance herself so rapidly: 'Then pray don't look to me for any assistance. If you make such a hasty exit the station will think we have quarrelled'. Netta's response—'no one could quarrel with *you*, you dear old thing'—in turn suggests she regards Liz as rather stuffy. One wonders initially if Liz's throwaway comment that 'our nursery was empty' implies a certain jealousy concerning Netta's two children, but when she refers to herself later as 'a middle-aged Scotchwoman', one wonders instead if she is simply piqued by Netta's refusal to take advantage of her superior knowledge of the area.

What Liz knows intuitively—that the Red Bungalow having remained empty when decent-sized houses are at a premium suggests that something is very wrong indeed—is reinforced by her experience when she visits for the first time.

> As I stood reflecting thus, gazing absently into the outer glare, a dark and mysterious cloud seemed to fall upon the place, the sun was suddenly obscured, and from the portico came a sharp little gust of wind that gradually increased into a long-drawn wailing cry—surely the cry of some lost soul. (p.103)

Her unease increases when an elderly English resident comes to her with other stories, emphatic that the servants will not stay, as indeed proves to be the case. Netta has airily dismissed these stories by noting that 'this is the twentieth century', which brings with it an unsettling second-hand rejection of the local Indian experience. While we can read Netta as merely ignoring the old Raj hands because she is determined to make her mark in local colonial society, she is also ignoring the stories told by the local people, those she hears directly, and those relayed to her by those further up the social hierarchy. As so often happens in these stories, we never quite see the haunting, but the effect of Netta's refusal to take the stories seriously is her undoing, socially and for her family.

Undoubtedly the most oppressively atmospheric of these stories is Bessie Kyffin-Taylor's 'Outside the House', an extraordinary story of a haunting that has driven the family involved to bizarre lengths of denial. Narrated, inevitably, by an outsider, the story focuses on the experiences of John Longworth, a convalescent soldier who goes to stay with the family of his fiancée, Elsie Falconer, in their country house. It soon becomes apparent that there is something very strange about the house and its occupants, not least the family's insistence that no one remain outside beyond 5 p.m. While this may make sense in the winter, it is deeply puzzling during the summer. Even more startling is the elaborate indoor garden created by the family and the shuttering on the windows facing the main lawn of the house. Undeterred by the family's refusal to speak about the issue, Longworth is determined to get to the bottom of the mystery, as anyone would be.

That the story is finished by a friend tells us that Longworth ultimately fails, but his death has far-reaching consequences for the family, now obliged to finally address their refusal to engage with the past. The alleged haunting is unusual—the ghosts of miners who died in a pit disaster besiege the house built on their involuntary grave—and the haunting is tied as much to the failure of the mine owner and his descendants to admit they were in the wrong in their treatment of the miners. Their stiff-necked refusal to admit that anything has happened, even when their lives are weirdly proscribed by this dark family history, sets up the tragedy that inevitably occurs when Longworth will not stop asking questions. Issues of class are clearly in play here. Longworth's failure to take the hint, despite the stern admonitions of his hostess, indicates that he does not understand his position, which does not bode well for any marriage to the daughter of the house. Longworth's strange experiences in the garden resonate too with his wartime experiences, and there is a strong argument for reading this story as a condemnation of the attitudes of those not directly involved in the war, for whom it is an inconvenience to be tolerated.

It is Mary Elizabeth Counselman's 'The Black Stone Statue' that disturbs the hitherto fairly even tenor of this collection of weird stories, because it is so unlike the others (rather as Frances Stevens's 'Unseen—Unfeared' seemed oddly at an angle to the other stories in *Women's Weird*). So far I've dodged the question of 'what is weird fiction?' because the stories themselves have defined the term. They seem, for the most part, to represent a particular, personal kind of engagement with the supernatural, and that includes Helen Simpson's 'Young Magic', which deals with a child gradually coming to an awareness that she might possess strange powers, and then, as an adult, trying to determine whether or not this was the case, and how this might affect her future. Not a ghost story as such but, like 'The Green Bowl', in the same neighbourhood.

'The Black Stone Statue' is something else altogether: an encounter with a mysterious creature that, like some latter-day Medusa, turns everything with which it comes into contact into black stone. The nature of the creature is never discussed, but the narrator exploits its ability to further their career as an artist, until a prestigious commission finally prompts them to confess. Now, it may just be me, but if we are reading 'weird' as 'supernatural', in the traditional sense, how is this story anything but science fiction?

That in turn brings us finally to the question of what is 'weird', and more specifically to what is 'women's weird'? Is it weird fiction that happens to be written by women? Or is there such a thing as a distinct type of weird fiction written by women? And is 'weird' the same as 'supernatural'? I noted in my earlier review of *Women's Weird* (*The BSFA Review* 9, p.22) that 'the proliferation of terms—strange, weird, supernatural, ghost—is indicative that we are in danger of becoming lost in a forest of immense taxonomic complexity'. Limitations of space meant I couldn't explore that issue to the degree I would have liked, but I think it's worth exploring it now.

I have mainly talked in this review about ghost stories, although some of the hauntings are rather less embodied than others. Some are little more than a feeling, or an apprehension, but over the years I've generally considered that it's the sense of uneasy potential that marks out a ghost story for me, even if the spectre never actually manifests itself. So, a story as traditional as Lettice Galbraith's 'The Blue Room', complete with devoted family servant as accessory to the ghost's eventual laying, and a happy-ever-after for the young couple, can sit happily alongside Mary E. Wilkins Freeman's 'The Hall Bedroom', a strange tale of a man who disappears from a small, nondescript bedroom overnight, its narrative framed by the account of the woman who rented him a room, having been forced by economic circumstances to become a landlady.

I could easily reframe all these stories as being 'supernatural', but if we take the definitions employed in *Women's Weird*, I think only the Counselman could be described as truly 'weird'. In her introduction to *WW*, Edmundson invoked H.P. Lovecraft, who observed that '[t]he one test of the really Weird is simply this—whether or not there be excited in the reader a profound sense of dread, and of contact with unknown spheres and powers' (*WW* p.ix).[5] Perhaps I'm doing this wrong, but of all the stories in this collection, I think only the Kyffin-Taylor comes close to meeting those criteria, at least from the point

---

5. Frankly, it pains me to have to refer to Lovecraft at all, but, whatever one feels about his stories, his *Supernatural Horror in Literature* is one of the first modern theoretical texts concerning the fantastic. I am pinching my nose as I write this section.

of view of Longworth, the narrator. Even then, as other parties in the story confirm, the ghosts were embodied, and not the product of an unknowable cosmic horror.

Lovecraft at least writes from the reader's point of view. Other early commentators, such as Mary Butts, author of an influential essay, 'Ghosties and Ghoulies: Uses of the Supernatural in English Fiction', serialised in *The Bookman* in 1933, wrote much more from the point of view of a writer of supernatural fiction (I recommend Butts's 'With and Without Buttons' in *Women's Weird*). Butts wrote that supernatural stories should bring with them 'a stirring, a touching of nerves not usually sensitive, an awakening to more than fear—but to something like awareness and conviction or even memory' (*WW* p.x), and that feels perhaps closer to what we might be seeing with these supernatural stories.

However, in the introduction to *Women's Weird* 2, Edmundson discusses Dorothy Scarborough's *The Supernatural in Modern English Fiction* (1917).[6] In this, Scarborough considers the continuing popularity of the weird in fiction: 'The spirit feeds on mystery. It lives not by fact alone but by the unknowable, and there is no highest mystery without the supernatural' (p.vii). Which feels right, to my mind, but is that weird? Scarborough gets closer to the truth, and perhaps a little further from the weird, when she takes up the matter again in the introduction to *Famous Modern Ghost Stories*: 'Modern ghosts are less simple and primitive than their ancestors, and are developing complexes of various kinds. They are more democratic than of old, and have more of a diversity of interests, so that mortals have scarcely the ghost of a chance with them' (p.viii). And if the ghosts are more democratic, then perhaps so too are the writers. In these stories, the reader is cheek by jowl with expressions of the supernatural. It is an up close and personal kind of experience, and thus maybe not quite so weird as it might at first seem.

I thought about this particularly when reading *British Weird Selected Short Fiction 1893—1937*, edited by James Machin, another collection from Handheld Press. It is a pleasing selection of stories, from names as familiar as John Buchan, E.F. Benson, Algernon Blackwood, and Arthur Machen as well as E. Nesbit, Eleanor Scott, and, once again, Mary Butts. These stories seem much more centred on landscape and the outdoors, and consequently much closer to Lovecraft's sense of 'a malign and particular suspension or defeat of those fixed laws of Nature which are our only safeguard against the assaults of chaos and the daemons of unplumbed space' (*WW* p.ix). Blackwood's 'The Willows' is well-known, and still, I think, one of his best stories. The sense of menace emanating from the landscape itself is matched by Buchan's 'No-Man's Land', a story new to me, one concerning the notion of a preserved race

---

6. Happily, this volume is available on Project Gutenberg, as is Scarborough's anthology, *Famous Modern Ghost Stories*.

of prehistoric people lurking somewhere in the remote Highlands. Eleanor Scott's 'Randalls Round' has a surprisingly contemporary folk-horror vibe, concerned as it is with strange practices in a country village, and so does Nesbit's 'Man-Size in Marble', a story I've previously read as a ghost story: now I'm not so sure. Conversely, both the Machen and Butts's 'Mappa Mundi' deal with the idea of an urban landscape concealing as much as it reveals, and that seems to me to tap into a genuine sense of cosmic horror that is not so far removed from the secret model landscape at the heart of L.A. Lewis's 'Lost Keep', again a story I was unfamiliar with. Perhaps the best thing about this collection, though, is that it reprints Butts's 'Ghosties and Ghoulies', a boon indeed when the original is not so easily come by.

But if the stories in *British Weird* do seem for the most part to live up to that description (I'm reserving judgement on the Nesbit for now), I'm still not sure about the stories in *Women's Weird* 2. I come back to this feeling of a sense of enclosure, even in the Jewett which, despite its upstate adventures, still takes place for the most part in the drawing room and parlour. Weirdness seems to demand wide open spaces, but the supernatural, actual ghostliness, seems to require corners and shadows, its shockingness deriving from the mundanity of its setting. In this respect at least, *Women's Weird* 2 is clearly the natural choice for Christmas Eve reading, while *British Weird Fiction* will suit Boxing Day very well indeed.

Galactic Suburbia: Recovering Women's Science Fiction
by Lisa Yaszek

In 1970, Joanna Russ published an essay, 'The Image of Women in Science Fiction', which discussed the ways in which SF portrayed relations between the sexes: 'In general, the authors who write reasonably sophisticated and literate science fiction (Clarke, Asimov, for choice) see the relations between the sexes as those of present-day, white, middle-class suburbia'. Later in the same essay, Russ notes that science fiction at that point had begun 'to attempt the serious presentation of men and women as equals, usually by showing them at work together', but that this was a 'reflection of present reality, not genuine speculation'. When Russ talks explicitly about science fiction written by women, she categorises it under four headings, including 'ladies' magazine fiction' (which, famously, relies on 'the sweet, gentle, intuitive little heroine' to solve 'an interstellar crisis by mending her slip or doing something equally domestic after her big, heroic husband has failed') and 'galactic suburbia', the latter explicitly linked to the earlier comment on work by the likes of Clarke and Asimov.

Russ's impatience with portrayals of women in science fiction, even when written by women, is evident in her casual dismissal of 'galactic suburbia' stories. These writers, and their characters, were clearly not bold enough for her taste, and yet, as Lisa Yaszek's *Galactic Suburbia: Recovering Women's Science Fiction* suggests, Russ is perhaps hasty in dismissing the work of post-war women SF writers, or rather, in using its deficiencies in order to foreground the emergent feminist SF. To do so, Yaszek argues, is to overlook the significance of women's SF in the development of feminist SF writing; her intention is to recover the work of this post-war generation of female writers and reaffirm its historical significance. Although many of these authors write about conservative sex and gender ideals, Yaszek argues that this doesn't necessarily mean that they support them. Instead, she suggests that many female writers are using the images and tropes of science fiction to provide a powerful and nuanced critique of the new world order.

If America's entry into WWII saw women being recruited to the general workforce, the end of hostilities saw them being told it was their patriotic duty to retreat to the domestic sphere and to relinquish their jobs to returning solders. How best to make this loss of freedom seem more palatable? Developments in technology are reflected in the creation of better household appliances, designed to release women from the drudgery of housework in order to devote more time to raising their children to be good, compliant citizens and satisfying their husbands' needs. Rampant consumerism was represented (as it so often is now) as a patriotic duty. During the Cold War, women were represented by government as warriors on the domestic front, vital in maintaining the security of hearth and home.

Post-war women SF writers addressed all these issues and more, Yaszek suggests. Their work is recognisably SF because of its use of, for example, extrapolated futures, and because it uses classic SF story forms and tropes. However, this style of SF differs from earlier material in that it focuses on the effects of science and technology on women and families, and on the domestic arena in general. Stories are told from the perspective of women who seek to define, or redefine, themselves through familiar roles. These writers are using science fiction to explore their hopes for and their fears about the emerging post-war world and their position in it, which necessarily involves considering sex and gender. One might term it 'feminism by stealth'—clearly it did not satisfy Joanna Russ's need for a more iconoclastic type of feminist writing—and Yaszek's readings of such stories as Judith Merril's 'That Only a Mother' (1948) and Alice Eleanor Jones's 'Created He Them' (1955) are persuasive so far as they go.

And yet, I am left with one huge inescapable problem: when Yaszek talks of 'Recovering Women's Science Fiction', what is it that she's trying to recover, exactly? Early in the book, she observes that in her research she has discovered almost three hundred women writing between the end of the war and the rise of feminist SF. In the discussion, she mentions more a dozen writers by name. The likes of Shirley Jackson, Judith Merril, Marion Zimmer Bradley, and Zenna Henderson are hardly strangers to regular science fiction readers, while Katherine MacLean, Margaret St. Clair, and Mildred Clingerman are by no means unknown either. Some names—Rosel George Brown and Cornelia Jessey—I don't know, but what of the rest? Yaszek notes several times that women SF writers are publishing under 'decidedly feminine names', but given the propensity for genre writers to use gender-neutral names or to hide behind pseudonyms, can we be sure that Yaszek and her researchers caught them all?

And what is it that she *has* caught? Early on, Yaszek comments that 'few if any of the members of the early SF community treated these women writers as a unified group with overlapping thematic concerns or narrative techniques' (p.21). The reason for this is surely not difficult to see. It is easier to identify such themes or techniques in a group of stories if you can actually see that the writers are working as part of an identifiable group or there is evidence that they are actively engaged in some sort of dialogue with one another. While some writers, such as Merril, are associated with groups of male SF writers, there is no sense from Yaszek's account that many of the women writers were in contact with one another at all (if they were, I would dearly like to hear more about it).

Their reasons for turning to writing SF, where known, are likewise so disparate it is difficult to establish any sense of immediate connection between them. For Merril, SF provided the perfect literary vehicle for political dissent, while for Alice Eleanor Jones, the SF market was somewhere to place the 'offbeat' stories she couldn't publish in the glossier ladies' magazines where she generally appeared. Shirley Jackson acknowledged a long-standing interest in magic and the supernatural as 'a convenient shorthand statement about the possibilities of human adjustment to what seems at best to be an inhuman world', and to publish in receptive SF markets would make perfect sense (p.54). The motives of other writers, alas, remain opaque, and there is not always much biographical information available. All this suggests that a number of the women SF writers dropped out of sight as much because they were moving in ones and twos in the chinks of the science fiction writing machine as because they wrote about the increasingly unfashionable galactic suburbs. Without the support of fellow writers, and with markets shrinking, it would have made economic sense to turn to other genre markets.

Perhaps the biggest difficulty facing Lisa Yaszek in presenting 'women's science fiction' is the phenomenon's very evanescence. It lasted perhaps twenty-five years, squeezed in between the end of the Second World War and the feminist revival of the early 1970s. I'm willing to believe that there is a discrete body of work that focuses specifically on the techno-cultural issues Yaszek describes, yet it is difficult to disentangle it from the broader sweep of women writing feminist science fiction throughout the twentieth century (for examples of which see Justine Larbalestier's *Daughters of Earth*) or indeed to raise it above Russ's scornful dismissal. Yaszek's chapter pointing out how the concerns of women's science fiction were taken up by the feminist writers that came later sits as an uncomfortable and somewhat out of place conclusion to her discussion. Is this a discrete phenomenon or not?

I don't think that this is by any means the last word on the matter. Lisa Yaszek has done the science fiction community a great service in recognising and describing this brief literary 'movement', as well as providing a preliminary cultural and technological context for it. And yet, I crave more. I'd like more information about the other writers Yaszek has identified (an appendix listing them would have been wonderful), and some sense of their relationship (or not) to the science fiction community, fans, and writers. I feel too there is a deeper discussion to be had as to what these women were doing when they wrote.

And I hope that in her next book, Lisa Yaszek is more kindly served by her publisher than on this occasion. There is an odd choppiness about some of the chapters, with repetitions of arguments, sometimes of sentences and phrases, as well as a sense that some arguments are more sketchily made than others. These are problems that should have been ironed out in the editing process. There are, in addition, more proofreading errors than I consider seemly in an academic work.

However, despite my reservations about the book's argument and production, I think nonetheless that it is a valuable contribution to the ongoing discussion about the nature of women's SF, in all its forms.

James Tiptree Jr.: The Double Life of Alice B. Sheldon
by Julie Phillips

Even before she was a person, Alice Hastings Bradley was a fictional character. At the age of six, she featured in a children's book, *Alice in Jungleland*, written by her mother, Mary, a well-known author and society hostess. Here, Bradley describes how during a sea voyage to Africa, the young Alice was dressed as a doll and placed in a wooden box, then carried into a fancy-dress party. Much to everyone's surprise, when the box was opened Alice remained perfectly still, 'just like a real doll in a box'.

The sense of relief contained in that anecdote is almost palpable, for Mary Hastings Bradley had a great deal invested in her daughter's good behaviour. The expedition she had helped to fund was headed for the Congo, to film and shoot gorillas. Bradley had been publicly criticised over her decision to take her daughter with her, and she knew she would be permitted to take on the role of explorer only if she could also demonstrate that she was a competent mother. Thus, the young Alice Bradley became the unwilling centre of attention, required to appear immaculately dressed and well-behaved at all times, conforming to society's demands in order to support her mother's claim to a life that society deemed improper. All the while young Alice was, as she later acknowledged, the baggage on the trip, denied the adventures her mother craved because she was too young.

The irony of this was surely not lost on the adult Alice, whose lasting fame rests not on her work as a research psychologist, nor even on her career within the CIA, both carried out in her own name, but for her creation of another fictional character. James Tiptree, Jr. was the by-line that unexpectedly came to life, achieving a strong and vivid existence on the page, and providing Alice (Alli) Sheldon, his progenitor, with a voice for all those things she felt she couldn't say as a woman. As it turned out, Tiptree's existence was to prove as fragile as that of Alice in Jungleland. Just as young Alice proved not to be a beautiful doll, but a troubled little girl who struggled hard to come to terms with life as an adult, when Tip's true identity was accidentally revealed in 1976, Alli Sheldon was effectively robbed not only of her creation but of her voice.

The story of how James Tiptree, Jr. was revealed to be Alice Sheldon, 'nothing but an old lady in Virginia', is now well known, but the territory between Alice in Jungleland and James Tiptree, Jr. has so far been little explored. Julie Phillips's ambitious, multi-layered biography now reveals that the life of Alice Sheldon was every bit as strange and exotic as the life she bestowed on Tip, and more to the point, that much of his life was indeed her own.

For much of her life, Alli was tortured by the sense of not knowing who she really was. A confusing childhood left her with, on the one hand, a very well-developed sense of her own artistic and intellectual abilities (among other things she was an accomplished artist and a gifted mathematician) but on the other, an inability to apply herself to her work in order to improve her skills. She wanted to make her own way, but was reluctant to give up the comforts of her parents' house and money. Yet she was stifled by her adoring mother, and for many years Alli associated love with possession. More than once she described her mother as a 'queen bee', needing to always be the centre of attention, but it is clear that the bond between mother and daughter remained very strong throughout their lives.

Alli's acquaintances—almost everyone interviewed for the biography seems to start by saying 'I didn't know her very well'—clearly regarded her as a strong woman who conducted life on her own terms. However, her journals suggest that she was uncertain about her gender identity and her sexual orientation. She could not come to terms with her wild crushes on women, none of which seem to have been entirely reciprocated, nor reconcile them with the fact that she preferred the company of men. She could ride a horse, fire a gun, fish as well as anyone she knew; she puzzled over how a woman might combine such skills with motherhood and managing a home. In an unfinished essay, 'Femininity and Society: A Discussion from the Standpoint of the Atypical Woman', she wrestled with this dilemma, concluding that male and female were cultural categories, that the sexes are really divided into men and mothers, and that the female reproductive system was a 'vampire', themes she would often return to in her stories. In the light of this, her eventual decision to more fully 'inhabit' her by-line is perhaps not so surprising, in that she was finally able to give voice to a part of herself that had remained suppressed for so many years.

One might still wonder why Sheldon needed Tiptree as much as she seems to have done, considering the remarkable variety of things she tackled during her life as Alice. She had an impressive war-time career in the CIA, working on the interpretation of surveillance photographs. Later, she helped her second husband to run a chicken farm, work that turned out to be far more time-consuming than they initially supposed. Later still, she went back to university, finally becoming Dr Alice Sheldon, research psychologist. However, as Phillips shows, the work always came between Sheldon and her artistic side, rather as motherhood had got in the way of writing and exploration for Mary Bradley. Becoming James Tiptree gave Alli permission to write, providing her with a space as well as a voice. Whereas Woolf advocated that women should have rooms of their own in which to work, Alli Sheldon took this one step further, and created a persona in which to work. All that being said, it is a pity that in presenting Alli as a feminist (and I have never been entirely persuaded of this particular argument), Phillips never really addresses the fact that Alli transforms herself into, effectively, a male version of her own mother—the very man, perhaps, her mother wanted to be.

In Tip, Alice Sheldon seemingly reached her apotheosis, brief as it turned out to be. Critics agree that the stories written after Tip's identity was revealed were never as good as those from before. It seemed that Alli could write only by distancing her creative ability from her physical self; once that distance was removed, her talent began to wither away. With her writing went her reason for being. Alice Sheldon had all her adult life suffered from depression. She was terrified of old age, and terrified of what it would do to her and her husband, Ting. They had made a suicide pact, but at the point when Alli decided the time had come for them to die, Ting's only problem was failing eyesight. It seems likely that her depression convinced her otherwise; consequently, on May 19, 1987, she shot Ting as he lay sleeping and then, after ringing a lawyer and her step-son, she turned the gun on herself.

Tiptree's legacy is well-documented. The discovery that *he* was in fact *she* has prompted much critical discussion on how to read masculinity and femininity in writing, and taught a couple of generations of readers to be more careful about making judgements based on the author's name and supposed gender. The James Tiptree Award is now an institution, promoting work which pushes the boundaries of our understanding of gender portrayals in science fiction; it is supported by one of the most fiercely loyal communities within the SF world.

Alice Sheldon has become very much overshadowed by her own alter-ego, and this biography is therefore a welcome redressing of the balance. It's all too easy for us to be admiring of the carefree Tip, pounding out his stories, or to acclaim Alice Sheldon's audacity in creating this vibrant persona for herself. It is likewise tempting to portray the creation of James Tiptree, Jr. as a conscious feminist statement, a thumbing of the nose to the masculine SF establishment. To do so is, I believe, to overlook what it was that drove Alice Sheldon to transform herself as she did. Julie Phillips's carefully researched account of the life of Alice Sheldon is a stark reminder of what has happened to too many women, and not only writers, who have tried to find a balance between their daily and creative lives. James Tiptree, Jr. triumphed, but it was Alice Sheldon who fought his battles, and Julie Phillips who brings that remarkable story to our attention.

Love Beyond Body, Space & Time
edited by Hope Nicholson

I don't believe that the primary role of science fiction, in any form, is to teach us; about science, or about anything else for that matter. Didactic fiction is usually pretty grim stuff; didactic science fiction especially. If I want to read about rocket ships or space stations or nuclear apocalypse, I turn to non-fiction. On the other hand, I do believe that one of the things that science fiction can do is to speculate about how the future might *feel*. I use 'feel' rather than 'look' quite deliberately. We can take turns to ever-so-ironically point out that *Blade Runner* is set in 2017 and gripe about the fact that we still haven't got our flying cars and jetpacks, but to do so is frankly tedious and facile. The point is, we are forever teetering on the brink of actually living in the future, one second at a time, and we not unnaturally think about what that future is going to be like. I was a young adult in the late 1970s/early 1980s and I genuinely believed that I would not get as far as my thirties, because the threat, real or imagined, of nuclear war loomed so large in my life. Almost all the science fiction I read was extremely pessimistic; I knew my chances of survival were poor, doubly so because of my gender. What I see now but couldn't see then was just how white and straight that science-fictional future also was.

Time passes, and slowly, painfully, agonisingly, science fiction begins to get its act together. By fits and starts we begin to see better representation of women, people of colour, people who are not American or British, marginalised groups, LGBTQIA people. Having said that, this representation is by no means evenly distributed; intersectional representation is clearly one thing that really needs to be worked at right now, and I do not doubt that there are other issues waiting their moment. I find it strange that for so many people who live in a world that is inevitably intersectional, the idea of fiction representing the quotidian world, showing people who contain multitudes, is still a concept too far.

One might argue, I suppose, that science fiction is not realism, but insofar as much of it attempts to represent a realistic future, there is surely something—a lot of somethings—missing. As I once searched for representations of women like me, so other groups search for representations of people like them. A key word here is surely 'people' plural, rather than individual token representatives. And critically, they're looking for life-affirming representations. We can joke about the *Star Trek* 'redshirts' easily enough, but way too often for the person of colour, the gay couple, the non-American … well, it is not going to end well, is it? Tragic renunciation at best; at worst, death.

Recent appeals for 'positive SF' have brought forward yet more lists of novels by mainly white male authors, set in gung-ho mainly white futures. I daresay it's a comfort to them, and at least they have noticed that women now have brains, but if this is positive and life-affirming ... This brings us, then, to *Love Beyond Body, Space and Time: An Indigenous LGBT Sci-Fi Anthology*, edited by Hope Nicholson. All of the stories in this collection are by indigenous writers, LGBT and/or two-spirit and their allies, and they deliberately employ science fiction as a way of imagining a future that is positively indigenous and positively LGBT, but also simply, plainly positive.

The first story in this collection, Richard Van Camp's masterly 'Aliens', sets the tone for the enterprise. There are indeed aliens present: the 'Sky People'. Their ships are huge, shadowy presences; they are apparently cleaning the oceans and the rivers without harming the wildlife. But that is pretty much by the by. This is a story about people, and about community.

'So, some of us—like me—still go to work. The Sky People are here but the bills don't stop. Plus you gotta get out of the house, right? You gotta check the mail and get groceries, hey?' And so, the narrator launches into a story about her niece, Shandra, and Jimmy, the boy who never left town, unlike all the other kids. If you're familiar with some of the structures of Native American storytelling, you'll see them at work in this story. We learn of the narrator's own connection to Jimmy through her grandfather, the healer, who once cured one of Jimmy's relations, meaning 'me and Jimmy are related in the medicine way'. But the story is not about the narrator but about her niece, Shandra, and about Jimmy's slow, gentle courtship of her. We learn what they say to one another, what they do together, but what we never learn is who Jimmy is.

The Aunties may speculate like fury about it, but Shandra isn't saying. But what we do learn is that Jimmy is fascinated by other people's lives, much as the narrator is fascinated by him, by his nature. It's left to the reader to speculate, too. The story's title pushes us one way, because we read science fiction, but what sticks with me about this story is that sense that whatever Jimmy is, he has always been a part of the community. Granted, this story takes a particular angle, but why not this angle?

In her introduction to the collection, Grace L. Dillon notes 'Two-spirit natives swim hard among cultural currents'. For not only are they 'resisting both colonial gender binaries and sexual regimes imposed by the legacy of nineteenth-century white manifest destinies,' but some must also deal with 'scepticism and rejection by some traditional Native communities'. Thus, these stories are, as the subtitle to her introduction has it, 'two-spirit survivance stories', and Van Camp's story is the embodiment of this.

Survivance is significant. Jacques Derrida used it to denote a spectral existence that would be neither life nor death. Used this way, it is a word that evokes how, even now, we are still encouraged to think about indigenous populations in heavily colonised countries. It is implied that they live, so to speak, in the 'cracks of your world machine'; they are lost, vanished, easy to romanticise in their seeming absence. The same is too often true of the LGBTQIA community, even more so if one is already part of an invisible community. But the term has since been co-opted by the Anishinaabe scholar, Gerald Vizenor, who first used it in his book *Manifest Manners: Narratives on Postindian Survivance*, and made it a central tenet of his analyses of Native American literature, culture, and politics. Vizenor defines survivance as 'an active sense of presence, the continuance of native stories, not a mere reaction, or a survivable name. Native survivance stories are renunciations of dominance, tragedy, and victimry' (*Manifest Manners* p.vii). That is, Vizenor takes Derrida's spectral presences, transports them into the contemporary world, embodies them once again, and gives them agency. He is in part as playful as Derrida himself might be (and that –ance ending might well make us think of jouissance, another Derridean usage), but there is nonetheless an urgency in his argument for the renunciation of what he calls victimry.

And there are no victims here. Certainly not Auntie Dave, who takes in the narrator of Cherie Dimaline's 'Legends are Made, Not Born' after his mother is killed in an accident. Only gradually do we realise that where they live is not Earth—i.e. Old Earth—but New Earth. Auntie Dave describes what the evacuation from Old Earth meant to the indigenous peoples: the last to be evacuated, not allowed to bring much with them, and the choices they made as a result, and in particular the choices made by the two-spirit peoples. It's a very short story but we see a future in which the best of the past also continues, not just preserved, but made real.

Daniel Heath Justice's 'The Boys Who Became the Hummingbirds', a story he calls 'a Teaching, and a Remembrance', is perhaps closest to what those unfamiliar with contemporary Native American writing might expect of indigenous storytelling, but we have no idea where in time those 'far ancient days' are located. I read it as a teaching from the future, not the past. Set alongside this traditionally framed tale is Darcie Little Badger's 'Né Łe', clearly set in the future, an uproarious tale of love and Chihuahuas in space offering glimpses of a future in which there is a Diné orbiter, 'sovereign Navajo territory', and a perfectly ordinary part of the off-Earth world, though there are hints that even this habitat is more utilitarian than, say, the Mars colony where Dottie expects to be looking after the pampered colonists' equally pampered dogs.

The two stories couldn't be more different if they tried, yet both clearly emerge from the same traditions of Native storytelling, in which humour has always been an important ingredient.

Gwen Beneway's 'Transitions' focuses on an unnamed narrator, a trans woman in the process of transitioning, her encounter with an Anishinaabe

Elder, and her gradual recognition that, as the Elder puts it, her female ancestors have found her and are acknowledging her. Mari Kurisato similarly explores the process of transition, but a very different, more overtly science-fictional way, as a cyborg moves towards becoming human. What is at issue here is the colour of Aanji's blood, black rather than red, but it is not difficult to see that this story also interrogates the white obsession with Native blood—how much of it do you have to have in order to be indigenous?

And there are love stories here, too: David A Robertson's 'Perfectly You' is a complex story of love and possibility, as Emma tries to decide whether or not to initiate a relationship with Cassie, using a virtual reality program to help her make that choice. Nathan Adler's 'Valediction at the Star View Motel' explores the hesitations of first love between Eadie and Mushkeg, the girl who claims to speak to spiders. In tone, it's much like Van Camp's story, discursive, firmly rooted within the community, hopeful.

There's only one poem included in this anthology, but it is astonishing. Cleo Keahna's 'Parallax' is a short, powerful weighing-up of a person's identity.

In his introduction to this collection, Niigaan Sinclair, comments that 'Two-spirit people [...] have been living, loving, and creating art since time immemorial'. And as Qwo-Li Driskill, Daniel Heath Justice, Deborah Miranda, and Lisa Tatonetti tell us in *Sovereign Erotics: A Collection of Two-Spirit Literature*, 'Queer Native people are far from a monolithic group. We have numerous identities, artistic stances, and political agendas. We come from diverse nations, land bases, and traditions'. *Love beyond Body, Space and Time* can only hint at the breadth of these identities, but it does represent to the world, and most importantly, to two-spirit people themselves, that they are a part of science fiction, precisely as they are a part of the everyday world.

They Are Not Ghosts: on the representation of the indigenous peoples of North America in science fiction and fantasy

Given my interests in Native American literature and genre fiction, it is inevitable that I've become interested specifically in the ways in which the indigenous peoples of North America are represented in science fiction and fantasy. For the purposes of this particular article, I'm thinking primarily of their representation in Anglo-American SF and fantasy, and I'll be focusing on representations by non-Native writers.

I want to begin with Joe Abercrombie's *Red Country* (2012), where we meet Crying Rock, described as 'an old Ghost woman with a broken sideways nose, grey hair all bound up with what looked like the tatters of an old Imperial flag, and a face so deep-lined you could've used it for a plate rack' (p.55). A couple of pages later, one character says of another, 'His Ghosts massacred a whole fellowship o' prospectors out on the dusty not two weeks ago. Thirty men, maybe. Took their ears and their noses and I shouldn't wonder got their cocks besides' (p.57). A few pages later, '[t]he old Ghost woman had the reins, creased face as empty as it had been at the inn, a singed old chagga pipe gripped between her teeth, not smoking it, just chewing it' (p.64). Only on the following page is Crying Rock finally introduced by name, having said a few words '[s]o slow and solemn it might have been the eulogy at a funeral' (p.65). And much later still, we see Crying Rock as tracker: ''Til that moment Shy had been wondering whether she'd frozen to death hours before with her pipe still clamped in her mouth. She'd scarcely blinked all morning, staring through the brush they'd arranged the previous night as cover' (p.301).

Those who've read *Red Country* will know that in this novel, Abercrombie takes on the stereotypes of the Old West, particularly as represented in film: its gunslingers and scouts, bandits and prospectors, its taciturn reluctant heroes and its young women struggling to make a go of pioneer life after the death of a parent. And, as we've come to expect of Abercrombie, he happily sets about demolishing the myths of frontier life much as he has previously devoted his time to undermining the tropes of epic fantasy. It is all very enjoyable, except for one thing, perhaps implicit in the title, but undeniably explicit in the presence of Crying Rock. The Ghosts are clearly the Native American analogues in *Red Country*, but whereas Abercrombie seems willing to stand every other stereotype on its head, that of the Native American remains mostly untouched. There might be some novelty in the fact that this Native American happens to be female rather than male, but it is a very small subversion. Many people are familiar, after all, with the story of Sacagawea, who travelled with Lewis and Clark's Corps of Discovery Expedition in the early 1800s.

All the way through the novel, I kept asking myself why, when Abercrombie had subverted everything else in sight, and often to great effect, he had nonetheless retained the image of the stoical, taciturn Native American, for that is what Crying Rock is, no matter her gender. Perhaps he had decided that writing Native American characters was something he could not undertake, and that to leave these Native American substitutes untouched was the simplest way of dealing with the difficulty. If so, I am sympathetic to the problems that might be experienced by a white European man attempting to create acceptable Native characters, but I nonetheless find it hard to be indifferent to what amounts to a continued silencing of the Native American voice, first in the films themselves, and then through the perpetuation of that stereotype in *Red Country*.

I am also disturbed by the name that Joe Abercrombie uses for these Native American analogues: Ghosts. Within the context of the novel, the name seems to come from the whiteness of the Ghosts' skins, or perhaps from the way they appear and vanish, but I think inevitably of two things. First, there is the simple implication that they are a dead or dying race. Rather as the federal authorities sought to exterminate Native Americans, destroying people they regarded as little more than vermin and taking over their territories, so it seems that the Ghosts have little agency in this novel. We learn that Sweet and Crying Rock—the Lone Ranger and Tonto of this reworked western landscape—have been together for many years, but it is difficult to avoid noticing just how few Ghosts actually appear in *Red Country*. They are mentioned in passing, and almost always in the past tense. In the same way that Hollywood relegates Native Americans to the Old West, so the Ghosts exist mainly in the Empire's past. They have no present, and apparently no future either.

This is by no means a new trope, needless to say. James Fenimore Cooper's *The Last of the Mohicans*, one of the first novels to feature Native Americans, immediately presents the idea that they are dying out, as they inevitably must in order to facilitate the manifest destiny of the white settlers. It is a pity to see this myth being implicitly perpetuated in a novel that otherwise interrogates the myths of the West with considerable vigour.

Tony Daniel's 1993 novel *Warpath*, takes place in the far future on the planet Candle, an alien world that looks suspiciously like the western frontier of the mid-1800s. The twist here is that American colonists land on Candle only to discover that Mississippian Indians were there long before them, having discovered a form of astral projection that has enabled them to take their canoes into space. The inference here seems to be that the mound-building civilisation of Cahokia in the Mississippi river valley vanished because everyone went into space, which is in its way a pretty conceit. However, what seems more dubious to my mind is that after 1400 years, the Mississippians are still using birch-bark canoes, and in many respects living much as they did back on Earth. Yes, there is sophisticated technology at work here—spears that explode—but we are encouraged to see the world of Candle and its inhabitants as though they were a little piece of pioneer America transported across light years. And if we are in any doubt about which stereotypes are being perpetuated, the Indian village is called Doom, and one of the novel's early sequences features an Indian raid, complete with a massacre.

We might also consider Orson Scott Card's *Red Prophet*, one of his Alvin Maker novels, an alternate history in which Alvin meets Ta-Kumsaw, a Native American who wants the white man to leave the western lands to the 'red men'. One might ponder the irony of Alvin's curing Ta-Kumsaw's brother, Lolla-Wossiky, of his alcoholism (how did that alcohol get there in the first place?), but there is something especially pernicious in his being positioned as the one person who can keep Ta-Kumsaw alive, playing into the idea of Native Americans requiring the blessing of the white man in order to survive.

Andre Norton's Beastmaster series features Hosteen Storm, the Navajo in space, a 'noble savage' who speaks to animals, and who also possesses the ability to bond with the Norbies, the indigenous people he meets on the planet Arzor. Storm is interesting in that he begins the series as a former soldier, a reminder of the many Native Americans who have served in the armed forces. Earth has gone, but unlike the other soldiers who can't return home, Storm has not suffered a nervous breakdown, implying that he was from the beginning a loner, detached from the world, though this is a stance at odds with Leslie Marmon Silko's Ceremony and N. Scott Momaday's *House Made of Dawn*, both of which feature former soldiers and lay emphasis on their need to reconnect with the land as part of their healing process.

I've focused deliberately on the ways in which Anglo-American writers, intentionally or otherwise, represent Native Americans using certain stereotypes, and in particular stereotypes that are recognisable from portrayals of Native Americans in film. To redress the balance a little, I'll finish with a brief consideration of R.A. Lafferty's masterly 'Narrow Valley'. It's a clever, knowing tale about a Native American family's efforts to deter a white family's attempts to settle a piece of land under the Homesteading Act. The story begins with Clarence Big-Saddle's determination not to pay tax on the land allotted to him, which he regards as his own. He performs an incantation: "'That my valley be always wide and flourish and green and such stuff as that!' he orated in Pawnee chant style. "But that it be narrow if an intruder come.'" As Clarence himself acknowledges, he's not entirely sure of the incantation's efficacy, as he's used the wrong plants and the wrong words, but in spite of this, the fact remains that no one seems able to find the Narrow Valley, so Clarence doesn't pay taxes, and nor does his son, Clarence Little-Saddle.

And so, things continue until the arrival of the Rampart family, led by Robert, who is determined to settle the land that Clarence occupies. Except, of course, that Robert can't see it. He can see where it should be, and the locals all know about the strange valley that seems to be folded in on itself. Robert's wife and children can walk down into the valley, but somehow Robert himself just can't enter it.

The Rampart children challenge Clarence, refusing to believe that he is Native American: 'If you're an Indian where's your war bonnet?' To which Clarence responds: 'How come you're not wearing the Iron Cross of Lombardy if you're a white girl?' before delivering a brief lecture on which tribes wear war bonnets—the Oglala Sioux, according to Clarence, who is a Pawnee. Throughout 'Narrow Valley', Clarence challenges the Rampart family's stereotypical notions of how a Native American looks and behaves, and this in a story published in 1966. It is largely a comic story, but even the comedy reminds me strongly of the humour found in the work of writers like Sherman Alexie and Thomas King, and the Fus Fixico letters; as many writers have suggested, there is a distinctive 'Indian humour', and Lafferty seems to be au fait with it.

Entertaining as it is, 'Narrow Valley' deals with serious issues around the re-allocation to Native Americans of their own land, the rest to be sold off to white settlers. For all the comic window dressing of spells that aren't spells, it's Clarence's intent that is important; his desire to keep his land and cattle for himself, outside the remit of a federal system he clearly doesn't recognise. In all, he is practising tribal sovereignty in microcosm, and Lafferty's story is clearly arguing in favour of his continuing to do that.

Where to start with Native writers writing SF and fantasy? I'd suggest *Walking the Clouds: An Anthology of Indigenous Science Fiction*, edited by Grace L. Dillon, and *Mothership: Tales from Afrofuturism and Beyond*, edited by Bill Campbell and Edward Austin Hall. It is useful to remember that not all seemingly speculative fiction written by Native writers is intentionally written as fantasy or SF. A text such as Louise Erdrich's *The Antelope Wife*, while being the winner of a World Fantasy Award, deals with beliefs that are important to Native American lifeways; to read it as fantasy is, in a way, to appropriate its content. There is no easy way to square this, other than to be mindful of the ways in which a story might be interpreted and to be cautious in approaching it as an outsider. Neither are Native writers simply here to educate Euro-American readers about their cultures. Reading *The Antelope Wife* will not give you a universal insight into Native culture. How can it begin to?

Similar problems arise for outsiders who choose to work with Native American stories. The history of their gathering is often fraught: anthropologists and ethnologists often collected the stories in secret or through duress, and then published them against the wishes of the indigenous peoples. Sometimes these stories were not meant to be heard outside the tribal band, or were reserved for particular situations. Often they formed part of a ceremony, but have been stripped of context. To use them without understanding, to use them even with only a partial understanding, is to tread on sensitive ground. Whatever the stereotypes of Native peoples in genre fiction might suggest, they are not Ghosts, nor are their cultures simply exhibits in our museums.

Reading Mothership: Tales from Afrofuturism and Beyond edited by Bill Campbell and Edward Austin Hall, and *We See a Different Frontier* edited by Fabio Fernandes and Djibril al-Ayad

As I'm writing this review, the shortlists of two awards have just been announced. One, for the three David Gemmell Legend Awards, featured seventeen white men. The other, for the John W. Campbell Award for Best New Writer, included women and writers of colour on its shortlist of five. Which shortlist then is the more representative of contemporary SF and fantasy publishing? The answer is, of course, the Campbell Award. Yet given the nominating process for the Gemmells is much, much broader in its intake than that of the Campbell, one has to ask why in 2014 so many readers of speculative fiction either do not seem to be aware that SFF is also being written by women and by writers of colour or, worse, simply do not want to acknowledge that fact.

Bill Campbell, co-editor of *Mothership: Tales from Afrofuturism and Beyond*, has frequently asked himself the same question. As he puts it, 'mainstream, American corporate culture whitewashes all culture—past, present, and future—giving people the false impression that America has been, is, and *always will be* the "White Man's Country"'. This is reflected in much of the science fiction emerging from the US in the last half century or so.

I pause here, briefly, so that someone may observe—as someone inevitably will—that the protagonist of Robert Heinlein's *Starship Troopers* is a person of colour. Or that Samuel Delany is a writer of colour. Lieutenant Uhura in *Star Trek*! Octavia Butler! While not denying that all them exist, an argument that relies on such a small number of data points to prove that US science fiction is not a purely white male enclave is a poor one, especially when the same two writers of colour are continually offered as proof of the genre's diversity. We can surely do better than this.

What is all too easy to miss is that fantasy and science fiction *is* being produced by writers of colour, but that it remains, for whatever reason, not as immediately visible as the work produced by Anglo-American writers. In part this might be because such stories are not always published in genre venues (several of the stories in *Mothership* are reprinted from mainstream literary journals) or simply because they are scattered through a variety of harder-to-access small-press publications and anthologies. It takes projects such as these, or small press magazines such as Crossed Genres, which has a specific brief to recognise diversity in what it publishes, to draw the attention of the wider reading public to what is out there.

Mothership, edited by Campbell and Edward Austin Hall, and *We See a Different Frontier*, edited by Fabio Fernandes and Djibril al-Ayad, are part of an informal movement that directly opposes the idea that science fiction is, or should be, exclusively a white male Anglo-American activity. Charles Tan and Lavie Tidhar have been pushing this message strongly for some years through the award-winning World SF blog, now alas in abeyance, and it has also been heavily promoted through social media. These two anthologies, both crowdfunded, take different but complementary approaches to demonstrating the genuine diversity of contemporary SF with *Mothership* offering us a dazzling variety of authors and stories, while *We See a Different Frontier* is more philosophical and structured in its approach.

In *Mothership*, Campbell and Austin have brought together a wide range of authors, a good half of whom are new names to me. If a preponderance of the authors are resident in the US, this only serves to show how ridiculous is the assumption that SF must be by and about Anglo-American men. And if a good percentage of the stories are reprints, this serves only to remind us that the genre has been rather more diverse for longer than most of us realise.

Campbell and Austin also work with a commendably broad definition of genre, what Austin calls an 'open-arms, fantasticated-tales-by-and/or-for-and/or-about-people-of-color approach'. In practice, this means that a story such as N.K. Jemisin's 'Too Many Yesterdays, Not Enough Tomorrows', a neat take on the effects of the tiny universes we build for ourselves online (all the while in dialogue with E. M. Forster's 'The Machine Stops') can sit alongside Charles R. Saunders's 'Amma', about the fate of a woman who can transform herself into a gazelle, told by a griot in the marketplace, while Abenaki writer Joseph Bruchac's 'Dances With Ghosts' is, unsurprisingly, a ghost story, one which wittily reframes themes familiar from Native American novels such as Momaday's *House Made of Dawn*.

These stories challenge the reader's expectations and assumptions in other ways. It is all too easy for white people to look to indigenous writers and writers of colour and either expect to be educated about another culture or to assume that because you read fiction written by someone who identifies with a particular cultural group, this means you have gained knowledge of that group. Throughout *Mothership* there are stories that subvert such assumptions; indeed, the collection's opening story, 'I Left My Heart in Skaftafell' by Victor LaValle, should stop such nonsense in its tracks. LaValle's African-American narrator is on holiday in Iceland and notes the reactions to his skin colour from others on the trip, but his story isn't about that; it's about the narrator's sustained encounter with a troll. Lauren Beukes's 'Unathi Battles the Black Hairballs' is rich with references to animé; it tells us about Beukes herself, not what it means to be a white South African. S.P. Somtow's 'The Pavilion of Frozen Women' is a story about a serial killer, with hints that the killer might have been driven to their actions because of the pressure of being part of an indigenous minority (and the narrator is herself Native American), but it is primarily about the events leading up to the deaths rather than the issues behind them.

There are many different kinds of story in *Mothership*, and stories of such high quality it is difficult to single out particular favourites. Other than the stories already mentioned, I was particularly taken with Tobias Buckell's 'Four Eyes'. This deals mostly with a young Jamaican man, Manny, finally acknowledging that his destiny is to become a 'four eyes' or obeah man. His teacher, Jimiti, easily accepts that La Llorona, the Weeping Woman, is his spirit guide, although 'she ain't even the right mythology for me to see. And she had ask me, "what the right mythology, Jimiti? You a two hundred-year-old blend of cultural mess"'.

Other outstanding stories include Rochita Loenen-Ruiz's 'Waking the God of the Mountain', which deals with issues of territorial sovereignty and deep, powerful ties to the land, as well as Rabih Alameddine's delicate, tender 'The Half Wall'. But there are so many good things in this anthology. If you want to get some idea of just how diverse SF can really be, *Mothership* is a great place to start.

We See a Different Frontier takes a different approach, as its subtitle makes clear: *A Postcolonial Speculative Fiction Anthology*. Aliette de Bodard's preface takes up this theme: 'When we read science fiction stories where colonists leave their home and hearth, and make contact with funny-looking aliens, we are uncomfortably reminded of the days when English or French or Dutch colonists came to foreign shores … and gradually took over everything under the pretence of "civilizing" barbarians'. The voices we hear in *WSADF*, then, are those of 'the invaded; of the colonized; of the erased and the oppressed; of those whom others would make into aliens and blithely ignore or conquer or enlighten'. In other words, these are the voices that supposedly don't exist, the voices of the Gayatri Chakravorty Spivak's famous subalterns. Yet these subalterns are only too eager to speak.

Shweta Narayan's exquisitely allusive 'The Arrangement of Their Parts' leads off the collection. The story's setting appears to be the Mughal Empire in the time of Aurangzeb, its sixth emperor, described in this story as a usurper. One of the sons of Shah Jahan, builder of the Taj Mahal, Aurangzeb engaged in a series of wars to overthrow his brothers and gain the throne. This, though, is simply background to a story in which the Englishman, Sir James, encounters what appears to be some sort of automaton. To judge from his workshop, this is not the first such entity he has encountered; the others he has dismantled. The Artificer Devi, however, has something else in mind.

It is possible to read this story simply as a cyberpunk interpretation of the presence of the British in India, but it seems to me that there is also another more slippery layer of allegory in play, given the significance of the peacock in Indian culture. Sofia Samatar's 'I Stole The D.C.'s Eyeglass' takes us into not dissimilar territory. We see from the point of view of the colonised what it is to be under the rule of an Englishman, but also how supposedly lost indigenous technology is brought into play, not only to escape colonial rule but also, and perhaps more importantly, to escape the mindset inculcated by colonial rule. In Silvia Moreno-Garcia's 'Them Ships', the unnamed narrator, a slum dweller, finds herself enslaved by aliens, along with wealthier members of her own country. Chief among them is Leonardo, who 'acts like we are totally partners … but he would've never even looked at me if we'd bumped into each other on the street'. For the unnamed narrator, life under alien rule is not necessarily that bad—there is better food, better conditions; for Leonardo it is intolerable and he compares her to La Malinche, the indigenous woman who acted as Cortés's translator. The story serves to remind us that under colonial or postcolonial rule, there is no one experience common to all.

As Ekaterina Sedia notes in the collection's afterword, the main theme of all these stories is the 'push-pull of the contradictory demands of assimilation versus appropriation'. We see it manifested in so many different ways through the stories, from the suppression and reclamation of a language in N.A. Ratnayake's 'Remembering Turinam' to Sunny Moraine's 'A Heap of Broken Images', which addresses such issues as guilt tourism and its effect on the culture that has to deal with it. More than one story touches on the presence of anthropologists and their relationships to the cultures they study, including Dinesh Rao's 'A Bridge of Words', which suggests that in the proper circumstances this can be productive rather than appropriative (underlining, of course, that this is rarely so).

Intriguingly, JY[1] Yang's 'Old Domes' considers the fate of old buildings, swallowed up by so-called regeneration. Jing-Li is a cullmaster of buildings, trained to extinguish the spirits of buildings, spirits made out of the history accumulated in their very fabric. Afterwards, the buildings are re-used. In this case, though, the spirit of Singapore's old Supreme Court is reluctant to go. Again, one might read this as an allegorical story, interrogating the assumption that modernisation is good, and that eliminating the old is a necessity in order to achieve that modernisation, but the story is rather more subtle than that, looking at different responses to history and how it affects a relatively new state.

If *Mothership* is a joyful celebration of diversity in science fiction and fantasy, *WSADF* is a more focused, more directly political consideration of the effects of colonisation on writers and how that is expressed in their fiction.

---

1. JY Yang is known as Neon Yang since 2020.

A number of authors have work included in both anthologies, but again in *WSADF* there are several writers whose names are new to me. In reading Mothership and *WSADF* together, I feel rather as I did when I encountered Alberto Manguel's 1983 anthology, *Black Water*, which first opened my eyes to the variety available in fantastic literature if one did but look hard enough. Reading both these books should prompt SF readers to look more closely at the world around them and ask themselves why they are not reading more by such amazing authors. Because the point is that more diverse genre fiction is out there. Even if it is not on the shelves in one's local bookshop, we live in an age where it is easily available online and there is no excuse for not reading it.

AfroSF: Science Fiction by African Writers
edited by Ivor W. Hartmann

AfroSF—that is, science fiction written by African writers, including those living abroad—has already attracted a considerable amount of enthusiastic attention from the Anglo-American SF community. Along with other critics, I welcome its publication. However, I wonder if *AfroSF* as an anthology is quite what it claims to be. In introducing these stories, Hartmann asserts that as a continent Africa has a rich history of science fiction, but then goes on to say that 'SciFi ... is highly underdeveloped in African literature as a whole'. Which of these claims is correct? As Hartmann eschews any form of historical overview, it is difficult to determine who the 'Afro' in 'AfroSF' is actually speaking for. Without a frame of reference, it is hard to contextualise these stories, though one might argue that it is a good thing to come to them without preconceptions. Given that I read them from the point of view of a white British female science fiction reader, my own perception has inevitably been shaped by my cultural expectations.

In his introduction, Hartmann explains that 'the vision I had for *AfroSF* needed to include the forward-thinking spirit embodied so well in SciFi as a genre' and goes on to say that 'if you can't see and relay an understandable vision of the future, your future will be co-opted by someone else's vision, one that will not necessarily have your best interests at heart'. This suggests that for Hartmann as editor, it is the idea behind a story that is important, and he has acknowledged this elsewhere.

In practice this means a number of things. There are stories which, to the Anglo-American eye, might seem to employ familiar tropes, most notably involving insanely automated bureaucracy, the fear of losing one's identity, of no longer being able to participate fully in a capitalist society, or else focusing on the frustrations of maintaining one's position within it, often through corruption. However, given the viewpoint from which they are written, they can't be dismissed as 'tired'. Ashley Jacobs's 'New Mzansi' draws attention to the difficulties of getting medical treatment, while Tendai Huchu's protagonist finds himself ensnared in colonial bureaucracy as he tries to protest against a land sale, while also becoming the victim of the government's intrusive control of the 'natives' health.

Similarly, Sally-Ann Murray's 'Terms and Conditions Apply' examines the problematic relationship between pharmaceutical companies and emerging nations. The narrative tricks of cyberpunk resurface in Efe Okogu's

'Proposition 23', though as a narrative of AIs seeking autonomy in the face of a repressive regime, the story works extremely well.

War is rarely far from the agenda in this anthology. Clifton Gachagua's 'To Gaze at the Sun' prompts us to think about the role of the artificial human in a new way as he describes a society in which couples adopt young men in order to have the pride of sending them away to war. Biram Mboob's 'The Rare Earth' involves Gideon, who leads a militia army and who is apparently directed by God, but seems also to have a remarkable arsenal at his command. Mboob skilfully juxtaposes the viewpoint of those who see Gideon as a magician with those who better understand his resources.

Other stories deal with the relationship between modern society and traditional beliefs, most notably Chiagozie Fred Nwonwu's 'Masquerade Stories', which presents an initiation ceremony that seems also to be based on an alien encounter through the viewpoints of young men of both traditional and modern attitudes. It is, to my mind, one of the most satisfying stories in this volume. Intriguing too is Rafeeat Aliyu's 'Ofe!', her first published story. It is rough round the edges; nonetheless, the combination of ultra-modern detective story and casual recognition of traditional powers is a refreshing counterpoint to modern urban fantasy. Of the more overtly science fictional stories, Tade Thompson's 'Notes from Gethsemane' is a well-wrought piece, successfully combining gang culture in a run-down suburb with the appearance of an alien entity, while Cristy Zinn's 'Five Sets of Hands' explores interracial slavery and cooperation. And sucker as I am for a time-travel story, Liam Kruger's 'Closing Time' comes with a neat twist.

As to whether this is the defining anthology of AfroSF the editor wanted it to be, I remain doubtful. However, it is undoubtedly a useful introduction to science fiction writing from the African continent and diaspora, and contains some excellent stories.

AfroSF Volume 2 edited by Ivor W. Hartmann

The first thing to notice about *AfroSF* v2 is that this time around, editor Ivor W. Hartmann has selected not short stories but novellas. According to Hartmann's introduction, 'I enjoy the length a novella gives to really get into a story, […] and I wanted to challenge both myself and the writers to see if we could claim another first for African SF writers and publish the first Pan-African SF novellas anthology'. There is no doubt that the novella is the story-length of the moment, with a number of publishers (most notably Tor) putting out novella lines, and I know I'm not the only reader or critic who takes the view that the novella (and here I use the Hugo Award definition of a novella as being between 17,500 and 40,000 words) is pretty much the ideal form for writing science fiction. If we think of a short story as being about setting up, in the reader's mind, a situation that continues to unfold beyond the story's ending, then the novella is about expanding the frame of the narrative to take in more than the initial view. While the novella moves beyond the allusiveness of the short story, however, it still demands great precision in storytelling. Just because you have the space for more scenes, more characters, more viewpoints, doesn't mean you can afford to be sloppy.

While I like short fiction because it pushes writers to be concise, too often that concision can lead to a sense of claustrophobia on the page: one becomes crushed within the story. By contrast, a novella's length gives the reader a chance to draw breath, to flex their reading muscles as they proceed. For the writer, it offers the chance to explore a story in more detail. The novella form can also allow writers to take creative risks that might not be so easily sustained within the larger framework of a novel. One thing that is notable about the five stories in this collection is their structural complexity, with all six authors intent on testing conventional linear and chronological narrative constructions.

'The Last Pantheon' by Tade Thompson and Nick Wood, the first story in the collection, gives us two viewpoint characters whose intertwining narratives move back and forth through nearly forty years, with occasional unexpected shifts into the deep past. All the time they circle the same few events, providing a parallax view of these encounters between two former superheroes, Pan-African and Black-Power. Thompson and Wood frame the story as a graphic novelisation (they themselves appear briefly in the story in an amusingly knowing postmodernish cameo), which throws out some intriguing questions as to how, in cultures that increasingly draw more on the 'look' of things, you pin down the visual in words.

Mame Bougouma Diene's 'Hell Freezes Over' follows a different trajectory—not precisely beginning at the end, but not starting in *medias res* either. I did wonder at the halfway point if I had stumbled into a different story altogether. I realised eventually that the story is constructed as a kind of diptych, though there is enough ambiguity in both aspects of the ending to suggest that a bigger historical cycling of events might be at stake, and that backstep in the narrative refocuses the story's issues in a startling way.

Dilman Dila's 'The Flying Man of Stone' and Andrew Dakalira's 'VIII' are more conventionally structured, but Dila's story seems to describe circles around itself even as it moves forward, rather like the flying machine that lies at the heart of the story. 'VIII' takes place in a short, clearly delineated period of time, but in common with Efe Tokunbo Okogu's 'An Indigo Song for Paradise', it has a remarkably filmic quality about it: there are many jump cuts, a constant shifting of viewpoint as the narrative tries to make sense of extraordinary events around the world. 'Indigo Song' is intricately structured, flipping from character to character, leaving the reader breathless with the speed and energy with which the narrative moves.

Something else that is noticeable about all the stories is how urgently they demand of the reader: you will read, you must read. God knows, I'm a jaded reader. Been there, done that; and it often seems as though a lot of Anglo-American SF is retreading familiar paths to little purpose. Part of what these stories do so well is to retread, or rather, repurpose ideas and tropes that are familiar into new ones.

We see this quite explicitly in 'The Flying Man of Stone', where Baba Chuma, a metalworker, is famed for his ability to make new things out of old. When he acquires some alien technology and builds a 'replicating machine', his son Kera recognises that while '[h]is father had built something straight out of a sci-fi movie [...] its system was no more complex than that of a rope pulley. It had to be magic' (p.171). This positions us neatly in Clarkean territory. It is clear to the reader and to Kera, if he but admits it, that he and his father have encountered aliens who have been on Earth for a long time. This, though, is not the story. It's not the wonder of the technology that is of concern, or where it came from, but the uses to which it is put. This is a familiar scenario in which soldiers murder innocent civilians, leaving the survivors to apportion blame, and take revenge as seems appropriate. But who is to blame? Corrupt governments? The colonial settlers who put in place an inappropriate governmental model in the first place?

There is no simple answer, and that is the point: there never is, never can be. Through this, Kera must chart a course, in the flying machine Baba Chuma made. And the story isn't even about that. It's about raw emotions: anger, rage, the urge for retribution, the need for an explanation, and the whole terrible mess of politics.

All these stories are fiercely, viscerally political, directly confronting issues that I think too many Anglo-American stories gloss over, concealing their evasions in 'art for art's sake'. 'The Last Pantheon' represents the struggle for supremacy between the two strands of black political theory made explicit in the names of the superheroes Pan-African and Black-Power, while simultaneously providing a witty commentary on the pervasiveness of American cultural references in African countries. The story dissects many of the familiar tropes of science fiction, in between querying whether science fiction as a written form is even appropriate in these circumstances.

It's clear why Hartmann chose this as the opening story, because it does set an agenda of sorts, presenting the reader with a working model for the concept of Afrofuturism, a conceit that is reiterated in 'An Indigo Song for Paradise', interrogating as it does the nature of Paradise City, a violently assertive alternative culture in which, as various people chase after pieces of a mysterious device, the reader is given a revealing insight into how the city's economy really works. This is not so much a story as a collage of text, verse, and music, employing a similar parallax technique to 'The Last Pantheon', and dealing with many of the same issues in a more informal way. Like 'The Last Pantheon', the story reaches deep into the past, and suggests that aliens have been present on Earth for millennia.

It's a persistent theme, perhaps made most explicit in 'VIII', which posits this world as some sort of game reserve, watched over by sympathetic aliens who fear that at any moment the hunt may recommence. Read in the wake of recent controversies about rich Americans shooting African wildlife for trophy purposes, it's not difficult to figure out, on one level at least, what this story is saying; but it is equally a very compelling portrait of a group of people trying to deal with the incomprehensible when it erupts in their community, as well as slipping in some sharp political commentary.

Mame Bougouma Diene's 'Hell Freezes Over' is set in a future in which the ice age is returning (again, one is reminded of an Arthur C. Clarke story, 'The Forgotten Enemy'). Once again, this is incidental to the intricate politics explored as two specialised groups of survivors vie for supremacy. What is especially interesting about this story, however, is the gender politics at work among the Mole people, in which women play a subordinate role and are valued according to their ability to produce children. Unsurprisingly, much of the story focuses on women who are attempting to change this, in particular Rina Arfazadeh, who becomes the figurehead of a struggle against her own people in a search for equality.

Several of the stories in this collection either put women front and centre in this way, or else represent them as in the ascendant by the time the story finishes, which makes it all the more difficult to raise the next criticism, but it's impossible to avoid.

This is a collection of stories by six men. There are no women writers here. Why are there no women writers here?

There are women writers in Africa. There are women writers within the African diaspora. There were women writers in *AfroSF* v1. I find it impossible to believe that not one single African woman writer ever uses the novella form. There is nothing to suggest that novellas can be written only by men (the Tor novella line gives the lie to this immediately), so one has to ask why Hartmann either couldn't or wouldn't include any women in this collection, especially given that he mentions a number of women writers in his introduction. It is the one glaring flaw in an anthology of fiction that I would otherwise recommend unreservedly. There is so much here to like in terms of wonderful, compelling, thought-provoking contemporary storytelling, and yet still there is no room at the table for women. What kind of message does that send about AfroSF today?

LOST LANDSCAPES AND NEW HORIZONS

Quis Est Iste Qui Venit

Christmas wouldn't be Christmas without ghost stories, and 2010 was no exception. BBC's Radio 7 broadcast a series of ghost stories from Walter de la Mare, interspersed with a set of rather weak parodies of ghost stories by M. R. James (meant, I assume, for the aficionados who know the originals rather than the casual listener, and all the more tiresome for that). Meanwhile, BBC Two, harking back to its own tradition of adapting James's stories for the festive season, offered a new version of 'Oh, Whistle, and I'll Come to You, My Lad', called 'Whistle and I'll Come to You', written by Neil Cross, directed by Andy De Emmony, and featuring John Hurt.

I wondered why we suddenly needed a new version of the story, and how this new version could possibly improve on Jonathan Miller's 1968 adaptation, also called 'Whistle and I'll Come to You', which is still one of the two or three finest adaptations of James's stories ever produced (up there with 'A Warning to the Curious' and 'Lost Hearts', both broadcast by the BBC in the early 70s). Matters were not helped when I noticed Alison Graham's preview in *Radio Times*: 'Silly me. Here was I thinking that the whistle in the title was the essential component in the best ghost story ever written', nor by A. N. Wilson's revealing, in the review on Radio 3's *Night Waves* on 22nd December, that the protagonist dies when confronted by his wife's spectre, something that certainly doesn't happen either in Miller's version or James's original.

In which case, I should begin by revisiting James's story, which follows the fortunes of Parkins, Professor of Ontography at Cambridge, who travels to Burnstow for a golfing holiday. At a colleague's request, he also undertakes to look at the site of a possible Templar preceptory and while doing so, he discovers a whistle concealed in a wall. The first odd event occurs as Parkins returns to the hotel. A backward glance shows him:

> ...a prospect of company on his walk, in the shape of a rather indistinct personage, who seemed to be making great efforts to catch up with him, but made little, if any, progress. I mean that there was an appearance of running about his movements, but that the distance between him and Parkins did not seem materially to lessen. So, at least, Parkins thought, and decided that he almost certainly did not know him, and that it would be absurd to wait until he came up. For all that, company, he began to think, would really be very welcome on that lonely shore, if only you could choose your companion. In his unenlightened days he had read of meetings in such places which even now would hardly bear thinking of.

Parkins cleans the whistle and discovers the inscriptions on it, the longer one of which reads *'Quis est iste qui venit'*. 'It ought to mean, "Who is this who is coming?" Well, the best way to find out is evidently to whistle for him', which Parkins duly does. The result is striking. As James puts it:

> He saw quite clearly for a moment a vision of a wide, dark expanse at night, with a fresh wind blowing, and in the midst a lonely figure—how employed, he could not tell. Perhaps he would have seen more had not the picture been broken by the sudden surge of a gust of wind against his casement, so sudden that it made him look up, just in time to see the white glint of a sea-bird's wing somewhere outside the dark panes. [...]

Subsequently, Parkins dreams of someone being chased along the beach by 'a figure in pale, fluttering draperies, ill-defined', while a local boy sees a similar figure apparently waving to him from Parkins's bedroom window. The story culminates in the figure attacking Parkins in his room, having used the sheets of the spare bed to give itself substance. '[W]hat he chiefly remembers about it is a horrible, an intensely horrible, face *of crumpled linen*'. Parkins is rescued by Colonel Wilson who, having heard Parkins's original story and seen the whistle, has clearly been expecting trouble.

James's ghost stories, for all their inventiveness in terms of individual hauntings, follow familiar patterns. The ignorant or unwary meddle with the supernatural at their peril, and either meet with or narrowly dodge an unpleasant death. Alternatively, an ancient wrong must either be righted or at any rate be recognised for what it is. Often, there is also a mystery to be solved. 'Oh, Whistle', falls into the first category, in that Parkins is engaging with something he simply doesn't understand. This is made apparent in a number of ways, not least Parkins's guileless decision to blow the whistle, presumably in a spirit of enquiry which fits with his position as a Cambridge academic, and indeed as Professor of Ontography, concerned as he is with describing the nature and essence of things. What is not clear is how this process of description might relate to matters of belief. Is it possible to describe something in which you refuse to believe?

Among Parkins's most vehemently expressed convictions is a fervent disavowal of the existence of spirits, an irony not lost on the reader in the light of what is to come. His views stand in sharp contrast to those of the Colonel, who comments on the strength of the wind the previous night: 'In my old home we should have said someone had been whistling for it', and goes on to say that 'there's generally something at the bottom of what these country-folk hold to, and have held to for generations'.

I think it is worth going back to the part of the story describing Parkins's journey back to the hotel after finding the whistle, and that brief reference to his 'unenlightened days'. His loud rejection of the supernatural and his discomfort with the Colonel's stout Protestantism and complex views on the local vicar's 'Papist' practices suggests that Parkins's philosophy is as much of an atheistical bent as it is rationalist. His rejection of superstition, most immediately embodied in his refusal to accept the Colonel's belief in the possibility of whistling up a wind, makes him vulnerable when dealing with the whistle.

I'd also suggest that what has been brought back into play for Parkins is the world of the imagination. When the wind first answers the summons of the whistle:

> Quickly as it had risen, the wind did not fall at once. On it went, moaning and rushing past the house, at times rising to a cry so desolate that, as Parkins disinterestedly said, it might have made fanciful people feel quite uncomfortable; even the unimaginative, he thought after a quarter of an hour, might be happier without it.

There is something so studied about Parkins 'disinterestedly' saying something, when juxtaposed with the 'fanciful' and 'even the unimaginative' as to suggest that Parkins's 'unenlightened' self is being consciously suppressed by his intellectual training, with inevitable consequences. The Colonel recognises this when he observes that the creature's 'one power was that of frightening' and that it could probably have done little else. But what effect might such a fright have on the suppressed imagination? Parkins's nerves are said to have suffered: 'He cannot even now see a surplice hanging on a door quite unmoved, and the spectacle of a scarecrow in a field late on a winter afternoon has cost him more than one sleepless night'. These are surely the responses of a man whose imagination, suppressed for so long, is now in overdrive. As the narrator drily remarks, 'the Professor's views on certain points are less clear cut than they used to be'. The whistle can be thrown into the sea and the bedsheet that transformed itself into a figure can be burned, but this in no way alters the fact of their having existed and been witnessed by Parkins. As a result his perception of the world must inevitably have altered; at what cost to his intellectual practice, we never learn.

James's narrator described Parkins as 'young, neat, and precise in speech' but also as being 'something of an old woman—rather henlike, perhaps, in his little ways; totally destitute, alas! of the sense of humour, but at the same time dauntless and sincere in his convictions, and a man deserving of the greatest respect'. The reader has a sense that for all his foibles, Parkins is a social creature, and his colleagues and acquaintances appear to like the man.

Jonathan Miller's take on Parkins, now Parkin, is rather different. While his production substantially follows James's original story, Miller is not interested in simply replicating the account of an unwary academic's brush with the supernatural. Parkin is no longer an over-earnest but generally collegial figure. Instead, he has become a solitary, anxious man, staying in a hotel filled with long, silent, empty corridors; eating lonely meals in a deserted dining room, spending his days tramping along an equally deserted beach. Michael Hordern invests Parkin with the neurotic tics of a man who does not engage much with others, instead humming and muttering his way through his days, accompanied by a soundtrack of slight noises hugely amplified. He is, classically, a man who lives almost entirely in his own mind, his contacts with other people limited to stilted encounters with the hotel staff. There is one conversation, with the Colonel, about the possibility of an afterlife; yet even this the observer comes to in *medias res*, with no clue how it was originally initiated.

Like his Jamesian predecessor, Parkin does not believe in any spiritual dimension, and rejects the Colonel's arguments that there might be things that he, Parkin, cannot account for through logical explanations. We must assume that the need to explain is fundamental to the Professor's life, and his inability to find an explanation for what happens to him is in its turn essential to Miller's production. Parkin's encounter with the sheeted figure creates a fatal undermining of his philosophy, and our final view of Parkin is of a figure who has retreated to an infantile state, sucking his thumb, repeating 'No', as if this can dispel the evidence of his own eyes.

The BBC's 2010 production seems to owe more to Miller's version than to James's, not least in its visual imagery. We find the same empty hotel, the same long corridors; the broad, empty beach, the same small noises dominating the soundtrack. Here is also the same sense of isolation and of silence. In this production, however, Parkin's experience in the hotel is mirrored by that of his wife in the care home to which he commits her at the story's opening.

In the home, which is as unhomely as you might care to imagine, there are endless doors, endless glass walls, endless rows of chairs, all of them occupied by silent, unresponsive women in identical white shifts. Is this how a distressed Parkin sees it, or is it really as bleakly institutional as represented? The environment appears to be entirely stripped of warmth, and although the nurse (there is only one) appears to be sympathetic, she also seems disturbingly eager to remove Parkin from the scene, urging him to relax and take a holiday. The camera almost always observes Parkin's interactions with his wife from a distance, through a window, through a doorway, placing the viewer in the position of a watcher, as though checking up on him, as though he cannot quite be trusted to be alone with her. (In the *Night Waves* review of this production, Philip Dodd and A. N. Wilson keep returning to the close-ups of John Hurt's face—which, lined and wrinkled as it is, seems to me to stand in for the face of crumpled linen that will never appear in this version of the story—but never posed the question I felt to be most pertinent: at any given moment, through whose eyes are we watching?)

The introduction of a wife already indicates that Neil Cross's script has moved sharply away from the original story. James Parkin is no longer a philosopher but an astronomer, although he holds equally trenchant views on the possibilities of the survival of life beyond death. In this instance though, what most preoccupies him is not the absence of anything beyond death but the horror of absence in life. Parkin's wife, Alice, obviously provides the focus for this concern, although the nature of her condition is not made clear; she is pale, still, always staring straight ahead, and almost entirely unresponsive to events around her. She speaks only once, to utter a few nonsensical half-sentences, and on another occasion, after Parkin has spoken to her, we see her wringing her hands as they lie in her lap. She is physically present, but her body has outlasted her personality. For a man who lives by the intellect, this is clearly a devastating position to be in, but Parkin must, as he notes, reject the idea of the ghost in the machine. Matter rots, after all, but what happens when the issue is not death but disconnection?

We are given to understand that Parkin has been devoted to his wife, but there is no indication of why he has suddenly relinquished her to the care home. He seems to have no family, no friends, no outside interest. Without her, he is utterly lost. What she thought of him, we can have no idea. There is the argument that an outsider can never properly understand the nature of a couple's relationship, but the outsider can always surmise, and the viewer inevitably fills in the gaps. One might suggest that Parkin's apparent uxoriousness has somehow crushed his wife's personality. A dream sequence that occurs after Parkin's first overtly supernatural experience suggests that there is some unspoken tragedy in the couple's lives. We see Parkin's wife holding a posy, like Mary in a painting of the Annunciation, followed by her cradling an invisible something in her arms. The porcelain head of a doll explodes from within. The drama's opening, as it focuses on the photos on the mantelpiece, does not show any family portraits. We are invited to assume that Mrs Parkin has experienced at least one miscarriage and that the couple have been unable to have children. Whether Parkin blames her for this, we are not certain.

There is one curious moment when he finally leaves her at the care home. As he departs, Parkin says, 'Call me if you need me', not as crass as it might sound if one accepts that he continues the pretence that she is alive, but he then leans close to her ear and whispers or, more accurately, quavers 'Oh, Whistle, And I'll Come To You, My Lad'. We might assume this refers to James's story, but we should also remember that James got his title from a poem by Robert Burns, in which a girl exhorts her lover to pretend that he is not interested in her if he sees her on the street, and to visit her covertly, to 'come as ye were na comin' to me'. That Parkin seems to be singing the words suggests that this refers to Burns rather than James. What it means is another matter; is Parkin commenting on his wife's indifference to him, or is he simply saying that he is, as always, at her disposal? Is that a threat or a promise?

I think we are supposed to assume guilt on Parkin's part for committing his wife to the home, and to read his concern as love. Perhaps this explains his attempt to reclaim something of their life together by revisiting some of the places they went as a couple, a refusal to let go. Thus, Parkin finds himself staying in an empty out-of-season hotel, with corridors and stairs that seem to go on forever; walking along a deserted beach, past huge white chalk sea stacks, their weathered organic forms foreshadowing the white figure he encounters on the beach. Whatever I might feel about the storytelling in this drama, it is impossible to deny the power of some of the images.

Then Parkin finds the wedding ring buried in a grass tussock. Strangely, when Parkin cuts the ring free it proves to have something engraved on the inside—*Quis est iste qui venit*—and it is this that provides one of the few solid connections with James's original story. I cannot decide whether it is a weak attempt to acknowledge the original, a showy piece of stage-dressing or a genuine attempt to say something about the nature of relationships. In many respects, this drama's haunting is cruder than anything that appears in either the original story or indeed Miller's production, and not all of it makes sense.

James is always most rigorous in the working out of a haunting; everything happens for a reason and will, in due course, be explained, although on occasion 'explanation' is left open to the reader. Similarly, while Miller takes a more psychological approach to Parkin's experience, he remains faithful to James's storyline, although for reasons that are quite obvious, he edits out one particular manifestation because it would require Parkin to interact too much with other people.

In the 2010 version, we are presented with curious scratching noises, maybe a rat in the wall (although, in fairness, one might allow that the noises are similar to the sound of the rattling windows in Miller's version). There is a bedside lamp which switches itself off when Parkin is asleep (and this preoccupation with the light can be clearly linked to Miller's similar framing of Parkin in bed at night, with the light pull to one side). The viewer's attention is also directed to a particularly unaesthetic white porcelain bust of a woman in the room, which appears to alter its position of its own volition. This is not directly commented on, and indeed seems to be an almost entirely unnecessary piece of business; it is presumably meant to resonate with the whiteness of the figure on the beach and Mrs Parkin's seemingly intrinsic paleness. On his final night in the hotel, Parkin locks the bust away in a cupboard, indicating that we are supposed to invest it with significance, though what kind of significance remains unexamined.

In a genuinely memorable moment of horror that would, I think, have appealed to James himself, someone comes to the door of Parkin's room, turns the door handle and shakes the door violently, attempting to gain admittance. During this disturbance, the unknown visitor's feet are visible in the light streaming under the door. Afterwards, when Parkin sleeps, he experiences the dreams I mentioned earlier. Only on the following day does Parkin discover that he was in fact alone in the hotel that night, and he subsequently seems to decide that his wife is calling him home. For his last night in the hotel, he prepares his room as though for a siege, stuffing a pillow under the door to obscure the light, drawing the curtains tight and, as noted, shutting the hideous bust in a cupboard before getting into bed.

After this, events unfold in short order. The pillow is sucked out from under the door into the corridor, another rather good moment of drama, then the fingers of a small pair of hands appear briefly, trying to work their way through the gap under the door. The next thing we see is Parkin's wife, spectral, still in a white shift, clawing her way up the bed, all the while telling Parkin that 'I am still here'. A small *coup de théâtre* perhaps, reminding me strongly of the extended shot in Nigel Kneale's TV adaptation of Susan Hill's *The Woman in Black*, where the Woman looms over Kidd for many seconds as he lies ill in bed, still the best and most frightening moment in an otherwise rather indifferent production.

However, here, while the image of Gemma Jones crawling up the bed is presumably supposed to provide a visual echo of the scurrying noises that have disturbed Parkin, it seems somehow cheap, a feeling strengthened when those noises are finally revealed as an inept piece of foreshadowing: the movement of the now dead Parkin's arm dragging his fingernails along the floor. The cause of Parkin's death is never stated. One might, I suppose, look to others of James's stories for clues; in 'Lost Hearts', Mr Abney is clawed to death by the ghostly revenants of his earlier victims, their fingernails having continued to grow in death, but I'm not sure this is really the answer, for this is not the end.

The camera returns to Parkin's wife, who seems to have suddenly come to life. A tear slides down her face, she gets up from her chair and is gone. Has she caused Parkin's death? Does this provide her with a release of some sort? We are, I think, supposed to meditate upon the nature of death-in-life, of the fate of the mind trapped in the body, unable to communicate, but I am not clear whether this drama is suggesting that the trapped mind can exact a distant revenge, confounding everything that the victim once believed in, killing him by confronting him with that which he cannot intellectually accept.

In the end, though, I still don't see the point of this adaptation. Its relationship to the original story is so slight as to be inconsequential, and one wonders why the writer and director retained such connections as they did. There is clearly a stronger link between this and Miller's production in visual terms (which, oddly enough, Dodd and Wilson never remarked on), but it still has little to do with it in terms of story content. Wilson can mutter as much as he likes about

Sebald's *Rings of Saturn* and the character's constant perambulations (this is also true of Miller's production) and make comments about the East Anglian setting (there are no chalk cliffs in Norfolk, and indeed the outdoor filming took place in Kingsgate Bay in North Kent), but he comes nearest the truth when he commented that nothing connects.

He also observes that Cross's adaptation is not a ghost story. Not, perhaps, in the classical Jamesian sense, but I'd argue that there is enough of the supernatural as well as the psychological about it to give the viewer pause for thought. At the same time, it seems to be playing into that irritating late-1970s vogue for explaining away hauntings as externalised psychological experiences, something I'm not convinced the BBC has ever quite got over when it comes to dealing with ghost stories.

England's Redemption: an examination of Richard Cowper's Corlay Sequence

W. B. Yeats's poem, 'The Second Coming' (1921), and chapter 8 of Kenneth Grahame's *The Wind in the Willows* (1908) might at first sight appear to be strange bedfellows. The one is a vivid evocation of a civilisation close to collapse, and what this might presage, while the other describes Mole and Ratty's remarkable encounter with the numinous, embodied in the nature spirit Pan, the Friend and Helper to all animals. And yet, both pieces may be cited as clear influences on Richard Cowper's Corlay sequence, perhaps nowhere more clearly than in the novella that begins the series, 'Piper at the Gates of Dawn'.

The lack of a definite article in Cowper's title is itself significant, suggesting not just one piper, but the possibility of many, and as we shall see throughout the sequence, one of Cowper's intentions would seem to be to demonstrate the cyclical nature of the world. To reach a point where redemption is achieved is not to reach a goal, or even a new beginning (though this is again implicit in the choice of title), but rather to begin another cycle in which the balance of power will pass from the individual to the system and back again, like the movement of a pendulum.

But before the revelation must come the collapse, as Yeats's poem indicates, and it seems clear that Cowper uses 'The Second Coming' in part at least, to provide a framework for 'Piper'. The novella is set in AD 2999, a significant date, as with the approach of a new millennium people's minds are already turning towards the possibility of change. As Old Peter the Tale-Spinner puts it: 'The fact is the world's grown to expect something remarkable of AD 3000. And if enough people get to expecting something, then like enough it'll come to pass'[1].

Parts of Britain have been inundated, or Drowned, for nearly a thousand years, the higher ground left as a series of island kingdoms, somewhat reminiscent of Britain in the ninth century. Although Cowper initially portrays it as an idyllic-seeming world of small towns and isolated farmsteads (the infrastructure of the twentieth century having been swept away), there are clear indications that this is no paradise.

---

1. Richard Cowper, 'Piper at the Gates of Dawn', in Cowper, *The Custodians* (London: Pan, 1978), pp.6hl.12 at p.72. All in-text references below, unless defined by the following endnotes, are from this text.

As the story opens, Old Peter of Hereford and his great-nephew Thomas are 'leggin' it' to York. As they travel they hear stories of Irish pirates and border patrols, of poachers and absent lords, of Crows and Falcons. Rumour has replaced accurate information and people away from the large towns live isolated lives, focused on their own needs, dependent on mainly absent lords for protection, and subject to their intermittent demands for men or taxes. The Seven Kingdoms have returned to a feudal state, in which a theocracy holds sway, and the lords temporal and spiritual vie for supremacy.

The impending millennium presents a threat to the Church Militant, which first took power after the inundation a thousand years earlier. In particular, the church is troubled by the talk of a 'forthcoming'. Tom recites a prophecy to Old Peter:

The first coming was the man; the second was fire to burn him; the third was water to drown the fire, and the fourth is the Bird of Dawning.
(p.84)

Marshal Barran, one of the District Marshals of the Church's Secular Arm, puts it thus: 'It is said that at the start of each millennium mankind is given another chance. They would have it that the Drowning in 2000 wiped the slate clean so that a new message could be written on it in the year 3000' (p.97). The snippets of information that filter through to the reader are enough to show that the legend of the White Bird is a story of death, renewal, and redemption. As the mysterious White Bird dies, its blood splashes the breast of the Black Bird, which is transformed into the White Bird, to begin the cycle of life again. For the Church, the Black Brothers, often colloquially referred to as 'crows', the prophecy's meaning is only too clear. The White Bird, whatever it is, represents a threat to their power and the story and its disseminators must therefore be suppressed at all costs.

At the start of the novella, it is not clear how the prophecy will be fulfilled, or indeed whether this will happen at all. The country people talk of the White Bird (though there is no indication of where the story originally came from) as a symbol of hope and expectation, but they appear to see the Bird literally, as an outside agency that will come to help, rather than in a metaphoric sense, representing their own potential struggle with the system, the Church.

The creed of the White Bird seems designed to appeal specifically to society's underclass. 'People want to believe it. They are tired of being afraid,' says Tom (p.81), but this would seem to hold true even for some of those who cause that fear. There is an underlying sense that things should be different, but society is so fragmented, the power resides in so few people, it is difficult to see how a change might be affected.

Constant, the head of the church's Secular Arm, its Chief Falconer, views the matter somewhat differently: 'If the life they already know is all there is for them to believe in, then most of them would be better off dead. [...] It has always been so [...] And what happens ultimately is that they are driven to create their own. Miracles born out of sheer necessity—out of spiritual starvation' (p.97). But: '[...] the Church has no need of Birds of Kinship. The truth enshrined in Holy Writ must suffice us'[2].

Thus, Constant recognises that the Church does not meet the spiritual needs of its followers, even that their lives are thus impoverished, but nevertheless criticises them for attempting to make their own lives better in whatever way they can. At the same time, he refuses to recognise that the Church might participate in any way in improving their lot. Constant's perception of the Church is mechanistic:

> Long ago he had been vouchsafed a vision that would have struck a responsive chord in the imagination of many a nineteenth-century engineer, for he had dreamed of the Church Militant as a vast and complex machine in which every moving part functioned to perfection, and all to the greater glory of God. In such a machine, with fallible men as its components, fear was the essential lubricant... (p.96)

And to that end, people will be made to fit the machine's working, no matter what. In contrast to this Gradgrindian vision, belief in the White Bird offers something very different:

> ...all about his head the air was suddenly awash with the slow, majestic beating of huge, invisible wings. He felt an almost inexpressible urge to send a wild hosanna of joy fountaining upwards in welcome while, at the same time, his heart was melting within him. (p.88)

Here, the emphasis is on joy, celebration, involvement, the antithesis of the cold, intellectual appeal of the Established Church which requires people to serve it unquestioningly without offering anything in return. The apotheosis of this vision of freedom comes when Peter witnesses Tom piping to the assembled crowds in York on New Year's Eve just before he is murdered:

> All around him he seemed to sense a world becoming subtly transformed into something wholly new and strange, yet a part of him still realized that this transformation must lie within his own perception. (pp.103-104)

---

2. Richard Cowper, *The Road to Corlay* (Reader's Union: Newton Abbot, 1978), ch.4, p.41.

The creed of the White Bird offers its devotees the chance to shape their own lives, to break free of the system. As a witness to Tom's New Year performance puts it:

> [...] he took my heart from me and breathed his music into it and gave it back to me [...] He came to show us what we have it in ourselves to be.[3]

And yet, although it is the Church that, to all intents and purposes, murders Tom through the agency of Gyre, one of the Falcons, it is not the Church that orders his death (however much they might have wished to). Gyre appears to have acted according to his own free will, though he cannot himself explain why he did so. In killing Tom, he would seem to have precipitated a new and peculiarly gentle anarchy, in which the people confront the Church Militant, not passively but not violently either, secure in their own beliefs and their ability to express them.

Gyre, the Falcon who becomes the first identifiable convert to the Creed of Kinship, is the literal embodiment of Yeats's poem within the novella. It's explicit in his name and in his later role as the Creed's evangelist; the widening gyre, the widening circle, as the new faith spreads out from him. He is the Falcon who 'cannot hear the falconer' but whereas Yeats speaks of anarchy, Cowper points more towards a careful orchestration of the Creed's emergence. After Gyre is handed over to Old Peter for punishment, the storyteller comes to believe that the incident was orchestrated in some way by Tom, when he entered Gyre's mind during an earlier encounter. Tom has the potential to reach into people's minds (and animal minds also; when we see him first, he charms a salmon from the water with his music, and causes savage dogs to act like puppies). Tom tries to explain this to Peter:

> I join myself to them. I build a bridge and walk to them over it. I take their thoughts and give them back my own. [...] One day I'll do it for everyone, not just one or two. [...] [Morfedd] taught me how to find the right keys. A different one for each person. But I believe there's a master-key, Peter. One to unlock the whole world. I call that key The White Bird. (p.90)

However, Tom's calling his 'master key' The White Bird complicates matters further. Are we witnessing a spontaneous upwelling of faith, or is it something orchestrated by the mysterious Morfedd, Wizard of Bowness, who, according to Tom, 'planned it years ago. Long before he chose me. Before I was even born. It was a secret between us' (p.83), using Tom's unusual skills.

---

3. Cowper, *Corlay*, ch.4, p.48.

Morfedd is a shadowy figure throughout the entire Corlay sequence. We know little of him other than that he had 'stored up a treasurehouse of wisdom from the Old Times' (p.76), and that he was Tom's tutor for seven years, teaching him, among other things, to play the pipe, a strange double-barrelled pipe, and slitting his tongue because 'he wanted me to be able to tongue them both separately' (p.68). Why this should be necessary is never made clear, nor are the properties of Tom's double-flute, with its mysterious 'crystalline facet' (p.67) ever fully explained. We might speculate that it in some way amplifies and directs Tom's abilities—in the later novels, the flute is on occasion used as a sound-weapon in other hands—but Tom himself does not know, and Morfedd remains elusive. Ironically, Peter almost certainly possesses the same skill that Morfedd saw in Tom, though perhaps not to the same degree.

When Peter talks about telling stories, he says: 'I don't hear much above the sound of my own words. I'm hearing it and telling it at the same time. Seeing it too. In a bit of a dream, you might say' (p.82). His skills, however, are honed by years of experience rather than with artificial aids, and the implication seems to be that this was much too hit-and-miss for Morfedd's plans.

Nevertheless, it is fitting that Peter and Gyre will be the two to spread the word about the new Creed. Following Tom's death, he is claimed by the Church as a martyr, in the hope that this will neutralise the power of the prophecy of the Forthcoming. However, Peter and Gyre's proselytising only sends more pilgrims to York, miracles follow, and the Church is obliged to acknowledge the Creed's existence. Even its own Advocate Sceptic is swayed by the power of the White Bird's message, eventually turning apostate and fervently embracing the new belief, although that fervour will distort the Creed beyond recognition. At the beginning, Brother Francis is willing to accept the simple creed of the Kinsmen, which preaches 'only love for their fellows [...] and the doctrine of the Kingdom of the Holy Spirit which lies within our grasp'[4]. However, for Constant, now Archbishop, intellect obscures faith, and because he cannot discern what it is that the people believe in, he rejects it out of hand.

> We can hardly suppose it to be [...] faith in the Holy Mystery we serve. Faith in the Boy Thomas then? Or is it perhaps faith in something which he has let loose in the world and which now, like a pernicious mole burrowing secretly in the darkness of superstition, threatens the very foundations of our Holy Church![5]

Even as Tom has offered redemption through his music and simple vision of a perfect world, awakening people to a realisation of their own power, the Church has rejected the very thing it professes to have offered all along.

---

4. Cowper, *Corlay*, ch.4, p.40.

5. Cowper, *Corlay*, ch.4, p.40.

The Road to Corlay, *A Dream of Kinship* and 'The Singer and The Song' (the first part of *A Tapestry of Time*) between them chart the development of the new belief, effectively the making of its mythology, from its joyous and tragic beginnings, through the grudging toleration then open persecution of its followers, until the Church Militant overreaches itself, interfering in temporal politics in order to eliminate the Kinsfolk, carrying out a massacre within a Kinsfolk sanctuary, an act that cannot be ignored. As a result, the Secular Arm is forcibly disbanded in several of the Kingdoms and the Kinsfolk enjoy a certain amount of security.

Brother Francis, severely injured and on the verge of death, receives a vision which inspires him to renew the fight in support of the Creed of Kinship. Thereafter, he is described as being 'in the grip of some supernatural force'[6]. Constant himself had previously noticed Francis's fanatic fervour, which is now brought to bear on Kinship; Francis sets about transforming it even as Constant once reshaped the Church Militant. The promise of personal freedom and redemption offered by the White Bird is slowly but surely eroded as Francis organises the new religion in the image of the old. As Thomas of Tallon tells him:

> You are taking the Boy's wild Bird and locking it up in your churches and your cathedrals and convincing the Kinsfolk that that is where it belongs. You have clipped its wings so that it can no longer soar up into the skies and carry them with it. You have changed it into a thing of words, into a creed. It is no longer real.[7]

The Kinsmen themselves have become introspective, preoccupied with interpreting Morfedd's Testament, a 'rambling, rhyming prophecy', which not only foretells the death of the Boy Thomas but speaks of the coming of the Child of the Bride of Time. Francis believes he has already identified the Bride of Time: Jane Thomson, whose brief relation with the Kinsman Thomas of Norwich was marked by the discovery that he was carrying within him the spirit of a living man from the twentieth century. Jane, who possesses second sight, is convinced that her child, Thomas of Tallon, is the Child referred to in the prophecy, the Star Born. Francis, when presented with the evidence of this, several times rejects the notion, much as Constant before him rejected the miracles supposedly wrought by the White Bird. Miracles, it is suggested, are the province of the individual but not the system, and that once a religion becomes established, system is always going to be more important.

And yet, even within Francis, the free will symbolised by the White Bird maintains a toehold. When Thomas of Tallon decides he can no longer be a

---

6. Richard Cowper, *A Dream of Kinship* (London: Gollancz, 1981), ch.7, p.71.

7. Richard Cowper, *A Tapestry of Time* (London: Orbit, 1982), p.122.

Kinsman within the structure of the established creed, Francis, on impulse, loans him the pipes that once belonged to the Boy Thomas, later describing it as having been the 'Bird's wish', apparently without irony. For Thomas of Tallon, they are the instrument through which he will retrieve the master-key that the Boy Thomas dreamed about, the Song of Songs, and give it shape and voice. Once he has reconciled his inner and outer lives, as Thomas of Tallon and as the Star Born, he learns to deal with the power and responsibilities he holds within him:

> If pure crystals of sound could ever be imagined then such, most surely were what the Star Born quarried from within himself. Nor did they fade and die. [...] Who shall say whether Tom was truly aware of what he did? The Singer and the Song cannot exist apart. Knowledge of the Self, once gained, is but to know there is no Self to know. I am the thing I make: the thing I make is I. (p.105)

The discovery of the master-key is, or should be, the final redemption of the individual, but at the last, when the fulfilment of Morfedd's prophecy is within Francis's grasp, he rejects Thomas's gift. 'All he had to do was to say the word, to make an act of faith, to believe. And he could not do it. He was too old and altogether too much was at stake. He shook his head' (p.121).

And thus, Francis takes it upon himself, the representative of the system, to turn down, on behalf of humanity, the chance of redemption that it offered. Thomas of Tallon leaves Corlay and travels to Bowness to bury the Boy Thomas's pipes, and the score for the Song of Songs, which are seemingly lost to the world for almost eight hundred years.

The second part of *A Tapestry of Time*, 'The Cartwright Papers', is cast in the form of a scholarly detective story. James Cartwright and Margaret Coley are scholars of the Avian Apocrypha, those tales excluded from the official canon of stories concerning the establishment of Kinship. Indeed, Cartwright has just produced a new scholarly edition of 'Old Peter's Tale', which he has called 'Piper at the Gates of Dawn', believing it, as he says, to have 'a slightly more numinous quality' (p.134). One New Year's Eve, he and Coley witness a child dressed as the White Bird of Kinship suddenly disappear before their eyes. Cartwright regards himself as a rational man, and refuses to accept the evidence of his own eyes.

Although a rigorous scholar herself, Coley's devotion to the Boy and to the White Bird is a matter of genuine faith rather than habitual lip service, and she forces Cartwright to address the 'miracle' he has witnessed and denied, and to consider its ramifications.[8] Coley and Cartwright represent the two sides of the Kinship creed, and indeed the Christian faith before it, she representing the strong, pure faith of the individual accepting miracles, he the comforting

---

8. Cowper, *Tapestry*, p.134.

intellectual structure of the establishment, denying that which he cannot explain.

Their academic discussions on the nature of Kinship lead them to realise that 'our Modern Established Church has been constructed upon the ruins of the Old Faith whose bones are everywhere evident beneath the tissue of living flesh'[9]. Indeed, Coley is moved to wonder:

> Is it not possible that you and I have been chosen [...] to track the stream of Kinship back to its source and there, by clearing away the weeds which have been allowed to choke it, to let the pure truth flow free once more and nourish the hearts of men?[10]

Their scholarly detective work eventually leads them to the discovery of manuscripts that have been suppressed through the centuries because they did not fit in with the accepted view of the Church's history, and to a new, though to them speculative, understanding of the Church's early history, which we as readers could of course confirm, were we to be given the chance. More importantly for humanity, they are led at last to the hillside above Bowness, where Thomas of Tallon, himself now a shadowy figure in the literature, buried the score of the Song of Songs and what is now the only relic of the Boy Thomas himself.

When the Song of Songs is finally played, Margaret Coley describes it as 'the instant when the shutters of my soul were unlocked and thrown back, the window flung open, and through the inflooding brilliance I beheld the transcendental reality of the universe in which I lived and moved and had my corporeal being'[11].

In other words, it is the moment when redemption becomes available to all. Whether all will embrace it remains to be seen.

Beyond the title, the connection with 'The Piper at the Gates of Dawn' in Kenneth Grahame's *The Wind in the Willows* is perhaps not as immediately obvious as the relationship between Cowper's novella and Yeats's 'The Second Coming'. Nevertheless, there are distinct resonances, which suggest that Cowper may have had Grahame's nature philosophy in mind as a model for the Creed of Kinship. Ratty and Mole's night-time journey to find the lost otter cub is described with extraordinary attention to detail, which emphasises the creatures' oneness with the landscape.

Throughout the Corlay sequence, Cowper offers an account of the struggle of the individual to achieve a real and personal redemption through faith, set against the need of organised religion, be it Christianity or the creed of Kinship,

---

9. Cowper, *Tapestry*, p.139.

10. Cowper, *Tapestry*, p.139.

11. Cowper, *Tapestry*, p.186.

to put in place structures that crush the very thing they seek to safeguard. His is always a hopeful view, suggesting that no matter how long the wait, no matter what the cost, there is always another chance of redemption at some point in the future. Even two thousand years hence, this will still be an option. There will never be one moment where everything is finally redeemed, but in the manner of Fortune's wheel, there will be a steady movement between catastrophe and redemption, 'turning and turning in the widening gyre'[12].

---

12. W.B. Yeats, *The Works of W. B. Yeats* (Ware, Herts: Wordsworth, 1994), p.158.

The Owl Service TV series adapted for the screen by Alan Garner, directed by Peter Plummer

By those of us who saw it the first time around, Channel 4's reshowing of this children's classic was greeted with warmest enthusiasm; the videos were set, and the phone taken off the hook every Sunday for eight weeks. Eight weeks! In that respect at least, the series showed its age; who makes eight-part serials for children anymore? Everyone knows the current attention span doesn't last beyond four episodes of fast-moving action. And *The Owl Service* was hardly fast-moving. Each portion of the action unfolded carefully and delicately, leaving the viewer time to savour its ramifications.

In other respects too, it creaked a little. Camera angles were used in a way hailed as highly innovative at the time, but that now seem so ordinary as to be hackneyed, and the shallow brightness of the characters' clothes rather crudely underlined the fact that this was an early colour production. A recapitulation of the plot thus far at the start of each episode is uncommon these days, although I for one welcomed it.

But the story itself? Well, it's as fresh as ever. Ignore the clothing, the attitudes implicit in certain exchanges of dialogue and the story of Blodeuwedd, Lieu, and Gronw Pebyr is still as gripping in 1987 as it was twenty years ago or two-hundred years ago. A touching love story doomed to failure, and riven through with supernatural undertones, *The Owl Service* is undoubtedly one of Garner's finest achievements, both as a novel and a television series. It's frightening, more for what remains unspoken or only half understood, yet there is enough explicit mystery and magic to keep those who are unfamiliar with the legend happy as well. More than that, the central dilemma of two people whose situation means that their relationship can never be sanctified, is still as relevant today as when Garner wrote it.

There are fine performances from all the cast, though inevitably Frances Wallis, Michael Holden, and Gillian Hills must take the lion's share for their portrayal of the three children. Edwin Richfield is excellent as the newly married man struggling to maintain his wife's standards when his own inclination is to live and let live, and Dorothy Edwards's venomous performance as Gwyn's mother still scared me as much as it did when I was eight. Raymond Llewellyn as Huw Half-Bacon, Gwydion the magician, was terrifying in his portrayal of a mad and wise man. The line between the two was indeed fine. I just hope we don't have to wait another twenty years for another reshowing.

'Fusion with a land rescued me': landscape and presence in the writings of Alan Garner

When I first began to think about this paper, a number of people commented on how the presence of landscape in Garner's writing is so strong it is almost like another character in the narrative. What is striking is that Garner writes in great topographical detail about actual places. It is possible to physically trace the routes followed in most of Garner's novels, although, by his own admission, he has occasionally fudged details to achieve a particular artistic effect. In his first two books, Garner practically invites readers to travel with him, by providing maps, while with Thursbitch, his most recent novel, he has been performing an illustrated talk about *Thursbitch* valley at literary festivals up and down the country. His novels are as much about place as about people; this reaches its apotheosis in *The Stone Book Quartet*, where Garner writes in most concentrated and intimate detail about his 'own square mile of Cheshire hillside'. I want to think about why Garner invests so much importance in sense of place, and how this is reflected in the use of landscape in his novels. I want to consider Garner's position within his landscape and his account of it. And I want specifically to use postcolonial theory to examine Garner's relationship to the land, which is, I will suggest, more problematic than it might at first sight appear to be.

Postcolonial theory primarily considers the reading and writing of literatures written in previously or currently colonised countries, or literature written in colonising countries about the act of colonisation. It is built around the concept of 'otherness', focusing on the attempts of the colonised to articulate their identity and reclaim their past in the face of the otherness of that past. What does this have to do with Alan Garner and Cheshire, you might reasonably ask. Although we tend to think about postcolonial theory in geographical terms, about country A invading/colonising country B, and the results of this, the theory can be applied in other ways, depending on how you care to define colonisation. What I want to propose is that Alan Garner's narratives are a response to a sense of estrangement in part brought about by his education and its effects on him and those around him, an intellectual colonisation, if you like. However, I also want to suggest that while his novels are in part an attempt to reclaim his identity in the face of this, they might also be seen in terms of a second act of colonisation in which the colonised, Garner, becomes the coloniser.

I'll begin with a quotation from Emannual Levinas's essay, 'Heidegger, Gagarin and Us': 'One's implementation in a landscape, one's attachment to Place, without which the universe would become insignificant and would scarcely exist, is the very splitting of humanity into natives and strangers. And this light technology is less dangerous than the spirits of Place'.

Garner opens one of his best-known lectures, 'The Edge of the Ceiling', thus: 'I was born, with the cord wrapped twice round my throat, in the front bedroom of 47 Crescent Road, Congleton, Cheshire, at Latitude 53 [degrees] 9' [minutes] and 40" [seconds] North, Longitude 2 degrees, 13 minutes and 7 seconds West, on Wednesday, 17th October, 1934'. There are two striking things about this statement: firstly, that Garner wasn't actually born on Alderley Edge, and secondly, the extraordinary level of detail he employs in marking his birthplace. Most of us could provide a rough location for our places of birth, but why would anyone want or need to give such detail? Why does Garner want to be so precise?

Garner's place of birth in effect marks the first of a series of estrangements from the 'one square mile of Cheshire hillside [where] the Garners are'. These estrangements are spatial, cultural, intellectual, and temporal, and they provide the driving force for his fiction. In his essays, Garner refers again and again to his family's close relationship to this particular area of land—'a hill that Garners have inhabited, and worked, for as long as anyone knows'. The identification is fiercely, microscopically, regional, but 'in this particular place, I find a universality that enables me to write'.

Garner is of course conscious of the dislocations of his own life—education at Manchester Grammar School, and then Oxford University; the shift from the Germanic language of home to the Classical/Romance languages associated with his education—and has discussed them in lectures and essays on numerous occasions. As he sees it, a 'sense of fusion with a land rescued me', in this instance his connection to Alderley Edge, because, as he puts it in 'The Edge of the Ceiling', 'as a family we have always known our place'. This statement seems simple, unequivocal, and yet from it emerges a tremendous uncertainty as to where that place might be, in geographical terms at least, and possibly others too.

To return to the opening of 'The Edge of the Ceiling', to be able to recite the position of one's birth with such precision may indeed be to know one's place, but it also suggests an anxiety about where one's place in the world might be. It's striking that when Garner talks about this sense of place, of home, he is obliged to use words from other cultures—rodina from the Russian, the German heimat. Rev. Neil Hook also draws my attention to the Welsh word for this sense of longing for home, hiraeth (and my thanks to Charles Butler for giving me the correct spelling of this word) This is, one might argue, another form of cultural appropriation; it's interesting that there seems to be no specific English for this conception of home.

Time and again in his fiction, Garner also takes up the theme of geographical displacement. With the exception of *The Stone Book Quartet*, Garner's characters are invariably geographically displaced, usually by events beyond their control, rarely through choice. In *The Weirdstone of Brisingamen* and *The Moon of Gomrath*, Colin and Susan move to Alderley while their parents are abroad; in *Elidor*, the landscapes in both this world and Elidor itself are devoid of people, while the Watson children are displaced in their own world as the family moves house, and doubly displaced by the transition to Elidor. In *Red Shift*, the characters in all three time strands are displaced by war and emotional violence, while in *The Owl Service* every character struggles, often violently, to find their appropriate geographical place. No one is where they ought to be. In *Strandloper*, William Buckley is forcibly removed from his familiar world, through transportation to Australia. And in *Thursbitch*, while the estrangement from the land is as much of a spiritual as of a physical nature, the need to establish and maintain a relationship with that land remains a clear theme.

But through the displacement of his characters, and the subsequent attempts to locate them once again in their appropriate places or to make a space for them, Garner is, I believe, writing performatively, actually writing his home. That is, he is addressing his own heritage and his distance from it, but he is also creating his own place in and through these acts of fiction. The detailed topographical descriptions of Alderley Edge, Barthomley, Mow Cop, and Thursbitch attest to a deep knowledge of the locale, but accompanied by the frequent incantatory recitation of place names, they seem to do more than simply provide context. 'By Seven Firs and Goldenstone they went, to Stormy Point and Saddlebole' in *The Weirdstone of Brisingamen*, or its mirror image in *Strandloper*: 'He walked the Holy Well, by Saddlebole and Stormy Point to Golden Stone and Seven Firs and Thieves' Hole, he walked the Beacon'. Or in *Thursbitch*: 'Jack climbed out of Goyt by Embridge Causey, over Withenlach and passed through Old Gate Nick. The road dropped straight to Saltersford'. These strings of names are no longer route markers but a beating of the bounds, an establishing of boundaries and edges; they are the activity of the boundary-walker, the mearcstapa that Garner describes in his essays.

But to walk the edges is also to secure and enclose the centre, to annex territory and to possess it. Garner assumes the land as his birthright, but I'd like to suggest that, severed from his roots by birth and by education, he claims it also in an act of nostalgia and effectively remakes Cheshire through his writing, evoking a past world as an act of wish-fulfilment, an act of homage and perhaps also as an expression of regret.

Garner's Cheshire landscape is distinctively an historical rather than a modern artefact. He rarely portrays modern dwellings, and if he does, they are transitory places: a caravan, a house which is empty and on the market.

Likewise, modern vehicles rarely appear, except as agents of separation and disaster. Travel is conducted on foot or on horseback. Everything is done in the old way; in a memorable scene in *Elidor*, ancient, otherworldly powers adversely affect modern electrical appliances, burning out their motors. Bess Mossock in *The Weirdstone* would surely have had no truck with such labour-saving devices, any more than Gowther Mossock would dream of owning a tractor. Everything is played out against a background of historical and regional certainty. So long as the land is secure, Garner seems to suggest, the rest will surely follow, and the way of life will endure, and, in his fiction at least, it has.

But in securing his territory, Garner seems not only to have suspended it in time and deprived it of any means to develop—even those novels with a contemporary setting sooner or later reach back to an earlier period for an anchor. It is often difficult to date the modern settings with any degree of certainty, while the earlier settings are almost always precisely identified, their inhabitants in some way transformed into rural caricatures. His use of dialect is striking, but it's hard to avoid a sense that for all his pride in his linguistic roots—Garner presents himself as working in the same linguistic tradition as the North-West Mercian Gawain-poet, and this is particularly evident in *The Stone Book Quartet*—Garner's treatment of the 'Cheshire' characters and their language is paternalistic, professorial even. One feels a little too frequently that one is being invited to view a batch of linguistic specimens rather than a distinctive group of people. It is because of this highly controlled presentation of what he characterises as his own people, his own land, that I suggest Garner has to some extent become the coloniser in turn.

This is most strikingly observed in *The Stone Book Quartet*, four novellas that chart a history of Garner's own family, beginning with his great-great grandfather Robert, before moving to Garner's grandfather, father and, in the last story, a boy who may or may not be a thinly disguised avatar of Alan Garner. The stories are presented as fiction, but in writing them Garner has drawn so heavily upon his own family's biography through the stories he heard as a child and through his own research that it becomes difficult to determine where fact ends and fiction begins. It could be argued that Garner's control over the story extends beyond the text into the life of the family. As the literate, educated descendant of uneducated craftsmen, he has taken over their lives in much the same way as he possesses the landscape, and his version of the story, written rather than oral, becomes the definitive text, unalterable, unchallengeable.

In 'Aback of Beyond', Garner discusses the need among each generation of the Houghites, the occupants of his square mile of Cheshire hillside, to 'do better, or do other than, the one before. It is called "getting aback of"'. In becoming a writer, as Garner himself recognises, 'I get aback of smith and stone-cutter and all of them'. In this, Garner sees the integration of his divided selves, but in getting aback of all of them, Garner has effectively taken possession of his family's history as well as its landscape, exerting a power that earlier his education had deprived him of. If, as I suspect, identification with his territory and its occupants is for Garner much more of a conscious act of making than a simple acceptance of things as they are, this re-accounting of family history seems to be consistent with his detailed recording of the landscape, expressing a continuing anxiety about the certainty of knowing one's physical place in the world, and being aware of one's status.

It is also rare for Garner's protagonists to experience a satisfactory closure of their experiences. The earliest novels might appear to offer a traditional happy ever after, but for Colin and Susan their lives have been disrupted by their magical experiences, to the point where they can never recover the security of their earlier lives; the experience for the Watson children in *Elidor* is similar. *The Stone Book Quartet* aside, the endings of subsequent novels are generally so ambiguous as to defy easy interpretation, but generally suggesting further emotional and physical dislocation. Even *The Stone Book Quartet* concludes with a further dislocation, the death of Joseph, the last connection with Robert, the paterfamilias, with no indication that young William will assume this role.

In *Albion: The Origins of the English Imagination*, Peter Ackroyd notes that 'it is sometimes supposed that landscape shapes human perceptions and that the power of the earth, the ground upon which we stand and move, is greater than that of the heavens in determining human destiny'. This would seem to be so in the case of Alan Garner's work, although it seems to me that for Garner, severed from his roots, through birth and education, those perceptions have been further shaped by a need to return to a landscape so specific that he has been obliged to create it, or recreate it, through his fiction. Salman Rushdie memorably observes that in colonial and postcolonial literature the Empire writes back to the centre, and it seems to me that Alan Garner's novels do precisely that.

Boneland by Alan Garner: preliminary notes

> The Einheriar paled, their forms thinning to air and light, and they rose from her into the sky.
> 'Celemon.'
> But Susan was left as dross upon the hill, and a voice came to her from the gathering outlines of the stars, 'It is not yet! It will be! But not yet!' And the fire died in Susan, and she was alone on the moor, the night wind in her face, joy and anguish in her heart.
> But as they crossed the valley, one of the riders dropped behind, and Colin saw that it was Susan. She lost ground, though her speed was no less, and the light that formed her died, and in its place was a smaller, solid figure that halted, forlorn, in the white wake of the riding.

It had never occurred to me that there was meant to be a *Weirdstone* trilogy, or indeed that there even needed to be. Somehow, the desolation of the final moments of *The Moon of Gomrath*, as Susan is abandoned by the Old Magic, had seemed sufficient. Perhaps the novel ended a little abruptly, perhaps I wondered what happened afterwards, but perhaps the same was true of the novels that came later, few of which could be accused of having easy endings. Alan Garner has said that when he begins a novel, he knows already what the last line will be; writing the novel is a process of hoping he hits the ending squarely rather than veering off to one side. For the reader, the process is just as hazardous, for an author's final sentence does not necessarily offer the neat tying-off that we are taught to look for.

Garner's novels are notable for the uncertainty of their endings. If anything, with the exceptions of the stories forming *The Stone Book Quartet*, which are tied closely to Garner's own history, Garner's endings have become more opaque with each successive work. Which brings me to *Boneland*, Garner's newest novel, possibly his last, or so the interviews are hinting, and the concluding volume in the newly discovered '*Weirdstone* trilogy'. More tyings-off, it would seem.

The Moon of Gomrath was published in 1963, and here we are again, more than fifty years later. Colin has grown up, acquired a surname and a profession, but along the way he has lost his family, biological and adoptive, not to mention everything else he held most dear. Magic has been replaced by science, in his case astronomy, but also, as so often seems to be the case with scientists, by a fascination with the mechanisms of belief. Oddly, Colin cannot now remember anything before he was thirteen, so those of us familiar with the earlier novels already know more about Colin's life than he does. On the other hand, Colin remembers many other things; he can, for example, say exactly what he was doing at any particular moment on any given day since he was thirteen. In his dreams, he is able to reach deep into the prehistoric past and remember things he cannot possibly have directly experienced and may never have heard about.

And there is something else: Colin believes he once had a sister, although everyone else denies this was ever so. He devotes much of his time to looking for her among the stars, in particular among the Pleiades, Messier object M45. It helps that he works at Jodrell Bank; it is less helpful that he pursues this search instead of the project he is supposed to be engaged in. As the novel opens, Colin has reached some sort of physical and mental crisis and has sought help, without being clear what kind of help it is that he really needs other than finding the truth. And that is the short version. The long version? It's going to take more than one reading to sort that out, but I will attempt a first tentative commentary.

The setting returns us to that most familiar of Garner's locations, Alderley Edge, the village and the Edge itself, made famous by Garner's own *Weirdstone of Brisingamen*. Alderley Edge has changed a good deal since that first novel, being now a playground of the newly wealthy, in particular footballers and their wives, but as far back as *Weirdstone*, the first hints were already there. Bess and Gowther Mossock were almost the last remnants of a way of life that was fast dying out: the farmhouse, Highmost Redmanhay, was still lit by candles rather than electricity, while farm work was carried out using horse-drawn vehicles. But there were hints throughout the novel, and its sequel, that they were already at a tangent to the contemporary. One remembers the stir that Prince and the cart caused every time the Mossocks went into Alderley and the sharp contrast with Selina Place's big black car. The Morrigan, source of evil within the novel, naturally embraces the worst of the twentieth century. Similar themes have surfaced in various of Garner's interviews over the years as he notes the changes to Alderley Edge, in particular the gentrification; the issue is addressed here once again, not least in the reference to 'the bimbos of Lower Slobovia' and their tinted-windowed cars.[1]

Throughout his novels, Garner has firmly delineated his territory: Alderley Edge, Macclesfield Forest, the Peak District, the places he knew as a child, using them as his settings, weaving their names into the story almost as incantations. This surfaces again in *Boneland*, but whereas in Weirdstone and Gomrath Garner seemed to be following a ritual—'By Seven Firs and Goldenstone they went, to Stormy Point and Saddlebole' (and a ritual he incidentally reverses

---

1. I still haven't forgotten my shock when I passed through Alderley Edge some years ago, I found myself confronted by a pub that had been turned into 'Brisingamens Brasserie'.

for William Buckley's homecoming in *Strandloper*)—something is different here. Gone are the evocative place names, to be replaced by what at times reads almost like a set of directions from Google Maps. Given that Garner is the most deliberate of writers, this is presumably intentional and significant. Among other things, this internal recitation seems to be one of the ways in which the adult Colin maintains some semblance of structure in his daily life as he cycles round the area. His intimate knowledge of the timings between any two given places, and how to work the gradients to his advantage while cycling, indicates how well he knows his patch. At the same time, once plotted on a map, the directions show how circumscribed Colin's world is. He rarely moves far from the Edge, where he lives in a mountain hut, and then only to go to work at Jodrell Bank; even his new therapist conveniently lives within the small area of country in which he apparently feels safe.

One might also read in this shift from places to roads a different kind of relationship with the land, more tenuous somehow, skimming over the surface, as though afraid to make contact with the ground. Even on the Edge itself, although Colin still walks the familiar routes, some places he now avoids, while when visiting the others he dresses ceremonially in his academic robes. One thinks perhaps of Cadellin Silverbrow, of Colin filling in for his absence, or maybe Colin protecting himself with the trappings, literally, of knowledge.

The ritualistic yet somehow childlike pleasure of articulating place names and roads reaches its apotheosis in the strange twisting and turning of language, the use of nonsense rhymes and cant that marked *Strandloper* in particular but that resurfaced too in the historical portions of *Thursbitch*, although at times they sit oddly with the contemporary elements of the story. While one might expect it of Colin, who has lived in the area since childhood, is Jodrell Bank really staffed entirely by people who speak English salted with Cheshire dialect?

Garner has always used Cheshire dialect in his novels: he cheerfully admitted that Gowther Mossock was based on his friend, Joshua Birtles, whose speech patterns and vocabulary he transcribed. But as time has gone by, the dialect has come more and more to the fore, to the extent that while the volumes of *The Stone Book Quartet*, originally published in a children's imprint, are still easily comprehended, *Strandloper* and parts of *Thursbitch*, while not actually impenetrable, do not make for easy reading. As a rule, Garner does not include vocabulary lists.

Garner has also made great play of the connection he perceives between Cheshire dialect and the language used by the Gawain-poet, writing in North-West Mercian, circa 1400, although so far this has tended to sit in the background.[2] It's invariably been represented by a particular phrase: 'the governor of this

---

2. Garner and his friend, Professor Ralph Elliott, have a party piece in which Garner recites the Lord's Prayer in Cheshire dialect while Elliott simultaneously recites it in Middle English. The divergences are not as many as one might suppose, which is of course Garner's point.

gang'. There is a moment in *Gawain and the Green Knight* when the knight, having entered Arthur's hall, looks around him and: Þe fyrst word þat he warp, 'Wher is', he sayd,'Þe gouernour of þis gyng? That is, who's in charge around here? Arthur, whose kingly bearing should be obvious to all is, at this particular moment in the story, being anything but kingly as he chases round the hall, playing silly Christmas games. The knight, 'oueral enker-grene' as he is, is a far more imposing sight than Arthur. One can read this confrontation in a number of ways, but there is an underlying emphasis on the fact that the Green Knight represents and respects power in a way that Arthur doesn't; the old challenges the new and underlines his own authority. There is a finely judged contempt in asking for the 'governor of this gang'.

The phrase surfaces in *The Stone Book Quartet* a number of times, always spoken by members of the Garner family, members of the so-called subordinate classes, signifying a respect for the older ways, and also the perceived authority of the Garners as craftsmen. It is almost always used mockingly of their supposed superiors. And it reappears here as well, when Colin asks a decorator to let him see round a deserted house where the man is working, and the decorator asserts his own authority: '"I'm the governor of this gang," said the man, "and we're not on piecework."'

At the same time, and pretty much for the first time, Garner goes deeper into the Gawain story. I've wondered at times why we've not seen a version of *Gawain and the Green Knight* from Garner. *Boneland* is perhaps in part an answer, and one in two sections. The simpler, more obvious element lies in an obvious identification of Colin himself with the Green Knight, made explicit in the axe he keeps in his hut for wood-cutting, and in the fact that his academic hood, worn during his ritual walks, is green. The second element lies in the 'prehistory' of this novel, the memories of the Watcher that come to Colin in dreams, centred around a place called Ludscruck, Ludschurch in modern parlance, a place that has been in recent times identified as the Chapel of the Green Knight. The poet Simon Armitage, who has himself recently produced a wonderful new version of *Gawain and the Green Knight*, visited Ludschurch for a TV programme about the poem a couple of years back, which showed the extraordinary cleft in the rock which is, according to some, the 'chapel'.

Boneland, though, seems to hint at the idea of the Green Knight as some sort of shaman, reinvented according to the mores of the time. Or rather, *Boneland* posits the idea of a Watcher, who might be the Green Knight or Cadellin or, indeed, Colin himself. Certainly, this is how Colin sees himself now that Cadellin has vanished; hence, his reluctance to leave the Edge at all, so much so that at the beginning of the novel he discharges himself from hospital after some unspecified procedure rather than stay away from the Edge for even one night. Or possibly Colin feels he has to be there in case Susan reappears.

The novel is rich in language, in the past and the present, yet novel by novel I've had a sense of the language overtaking the story at times, to the point where what seemed natural if initially slightly unexpected in *Weirdstone*, *Gomrath*, and *The Stone Book Quartet* began to seem rather too self-conscious in *Strandloper*. Garner is clearly making the point that it is not so much words themselves as the power and intent behind them that matters, thus enabling William Buckley, Cheshire man, to become the shaman of a group of indigenous Australians without necessarily understanding their language. I gather too that his evocation of criminal cant in the transportation sequence runs close to contemporary accounts of its use; his research is always thorough. However, as I've already hinted, it seems that the words are overwhelming the story, certainly in the present. One might argue, and I think quite reasonably, that Colin has become a kind of conduit for everything that has gone before, that he is in some way sampling the linguistic past of the Edge and its inhabitants. At the same time, I can't help wondering if Garner has strayed too far into the self-conscious use of dialect, old song words and so on, as though the storyteller has been replaced by the folklorist and archaeologist.

I'm not sure, either, what I feel about the way in which Garner is reaching deep into past human experience, far beyond and before history. This is, in terms of Garner's themes, the newest, least familiar material and these are the portions of the novel I really need to think through before I discuss them in more detail. In a sense, allusions to a more personal sense of magic and ritual have always been there, if not so directly articulated—and here I hesitate to use the word 'shamanic', although I think this is probably the word Garner himself would use. To begin with, in *Weirdstone*, it is next to impossible not to read the passage through the Earldelving as anything but some kind of rebirthing of Colin and Susan, fully initiating them into the world of magic, placing them under the aegis of Alderley Edge itself. Here, there are several forms of magic in play. The Morrigan and Cadellin represent a classical approach to magic, for all that the Morrigan is more usually identified with an older Celtic world, but note the use of Latin.

The struggle here is between good and evil, a simple dichotomy, no matter the creatures invoked to carry it out. The Old Magic, personified by the likes of Angharad Goldenhand, is not controllable in the same way; it works for its own purposes, which may sometimes coincide with those of the likes of Cadellin.

It is the Old Magic that drives *Gomrath*, a strangely edgy book, choppily plotted at times and shaped by Susan's seemingly wilful and incomprehensible risk-taking. For a long time I have read this as an attempt to convey the fact that Colin and Susan are now teenagers rather than children, and indeed that Susan is on the threshold of menarche, made explicit in the voice that says, at the end, 'Leave her! She is but green in power! It is not yet!' Indeed my reading is in part confirmed by a comment made by Meg, Colin's therapist, in *Boneland*. *Elidor* edges around similar themes, added to which we have Malebron as Fisher King, wounded, trying to maintain the integrity of his kingdom by moving between worlds.

In *Red Shift*, in the Romano-British portion, Logan, Face, and Macey and the other Roman soldiers are holed up on Mow Cop with the girl who is the tribal corn goddess and who, through the ritual grinding of corn in a place that has significance as part of the grindstone of the world, poisons them. Macey himself is a berserker who has visions that link him with Thomas Rowley and Tom, his historical counterparts. Ritual plays a significant part throughout the novel, as everyone attempts, one way or another, to keep their daily lives intact.

The repetition of ceremonial performance, allied to the recapitulation of certain events through multiple generations, comes to the fore in *The Owl Service*, here with the implication that the pattern needs to be broken in order to achieve closure, rather than maintained and thus prolonging the tragedy. *Strandloper* and *Thursbitch* both look at the consequences of maintaining ritual that has become emptied of meaning and also, perversely, of the perils of failing to maintain ritual.

In *Boneland*, I think Garner is finally addressing the question of where ritual and ceremony come from, what brought them into being, and what is necessary to maintain faith with the original without rendering it meaningless; if you like, how is ritual practice refreshed from one generation to another. At the same time, one can see also that some of Colin's attempts to devise fresh ritual to maintain himself as a whole and complete being in the twenty-first century have clearly failed. Travel directions are not the same as the incantatory weight of 'Seven Firs and Goldenstone and Stormy Point to Saddlebole'. By the end of the story it becomes clear why Colin had eschewed this ritual, but equally, that its necessary restoration comes about through renewal rather than through restitution. This in turn is linked to an exploration of the wellsprings from which story is derived.

There are other things going on in *Boneland*, not least among them the presence of Bert the unusually conscientious taxi-driver, and Meg the not-terribly-professional therapist. Both are marked as being in some way significant by, once again, the strong Cheshire accents. From the beginning, Bert reminded me strongly of Gowther Mossock—the speech patterns are very much the same. But Meg's relationship with Colin, part-mother, part would-be lover, is more complex, though I think she is some kind of analogue of Bess Mossock. As the story unfolds, the reader is obliged to question their corporeality and to wonder whether it is wise to assume that any part of this novel is taking place outside Colin's head or whether it is an entirely internal struggle to make sense of his past experiences, not least because Meg seems so easily able to glean the information that has eluded Colin, and indeed his doctors and therapists, for so long, most crucially to confirm that he had a twin sister.

None of this resolves the question of what happened to Susan. Did she vanish into some other universe, as Colin seems to suspect, or did she drown, her body remaining undiscovered, or run away, or was she kidnapped, murdered? Is Colin attempting to conjure her into existence again in some arcane way, or is he trying to finally reconcile himself to her loss, and indeed to the loss of childhood, the deaths of his parents and the Mossocks, as well as Highmost Redmanhey, his home? Colin has for too long been a man cut adrift, floating in time and space; perhaps this novel attempts to ground him, but figuratively rather than literally.

There is of course more, much more, for Garner's novels are always densely layered, capable of yielding new thoughts and ideas across multiple rereadings. There is a sense that Garner is drawing on his entire output in a way I've not seen him do before. To put it crudely, one might play Garner Bingo: I've already mentioned the various references to the 'governor of this gang', but to take another example, early on, Colin, in some sort of fit, begins to refer to 'blue silver', which immediately brings to mind Tom and his historical counterparts in *Red Shift*, united by their epileptic fits, in which, among other things, they see blue and silver. Indeed, contemporary Tom's explanation of the speed at which he and Jan are moving in relation to the cars on the M6 is reprised in part by Colin when he entertains Meg the therapist to dinner in his hut. One might think also of Sal and Ian in *Thursbitch*, whose dialogue strikingly echoes that of Tom and Jan, as indeed do many of Colin's conversations with Meg. More subtly, I have the distinct impression that Colin, perhaps mistakenly, identifies Meg with Selina Place: his discovery of her long empty house reminds me of the way in which Errwood Hall flutters in and out of existence. And undoubtedly, further readings will produce more resonances. Colin is, for example, much preoccupied with a stone axe he acquires from his project director; one recalls that a stone axe is the linking object in *Red Shift*, but here it will take on a much deeper significance.

This brings me back to an issue I touched on earlier, the sense of this novel being rather more deliberately self-conscious than its predecessors. On the one hand I find myself wondering whether Garner has all along envisaged his oeuvre as a single work; on the other, I wonder if he has quite deliberately attempted to incorporate elements of his earlier books into this, his supposedly final novel, or … well, who knows. One doesn't like to second-guess the intentions of authors, but given what I've read of Garner's biography over the years, it's difficult to avoid recognising descriptions of his own therapeutic processes—and here I think especially of the time surrounding the filming of *The Owl Service* and the fits of vomiting it provoked in Garner, as well as his accounts of his therapist encouraging him to go to the source of the pain.

I think *Boneland* is at its most self-conscious in posing as the final part of a trilogy rather than a stand-alone novel. I can see how, in one sense, it does complete the trilogy, with the return to Alderley Edge, and to Colin bringing with it the sense of closure for reader and story-teller alike. But I wonder too if Garner isn't, in his way, trying also to undermine the narrative linearity of those early novels, to belatedly shatter them into the fragments of story that his later novels are composed of.

It's probably far too soon to pass a judgement on this novel. It will take more than one reading to fully digest what's going on. I haven't even begun, for example, to unpick the Arthurian references beyond *Sir Gawain and the Green Knight*, though they are there from the beginning, in *Weirdstone*. For the time being, however, my sense is that this is Garner's most personal novel and indeed his most complex, a detailed statement of his perception of the world.

> 'That's your modern thought,' said Colin. 'We have to make the imaginative leap into the ancient mind and the likelihood of a different world view. I agree that you could argue that for a thing to have a multitude of possible meanings is tantamount to its having no meaning at all. But perhaps the opposite could once have applied. Perhaps a thing that could be thought to have a multitude of meanings, then, gained strength and importance from the ambiguities. We simply don't know. Nor is there any way of our knowing, whatever "the present" may be; but we must keep our minds open; though, yes, not so open that our brains drop out.'

First Light: A Celebration of Alan Garner
edited by Erica Wagner and *The Beauty Things*
by Mark Edmonds and Alan Garner

In 2016, the author Alan Garner celebrated his eightieth birthday. To mark the occasion, Erica Wagner compiled *First Light: a celebration of Alan Garner*, containing forty-three contributions, including her own, talking about different aspects of Garner's life and work. Garner himself suggested the volume's title, 'first light', an astronomical term referring to the first reading taken with a new telescope. He famously lives a couple of fields away from Jodrell Bank Radio Telescope, which is mentioned more than once during the course of *First Light*, as well as playing a significant role in Garner's most recent novel, *Boneland* (2012). It is an intrinsic part of the Garner mythos.

The contributors to this not-exactly-a-festschrift are a mixed bag: famous readers of Garner's work rub shoulders with writers of his own generation, people who knew him at university. Garner's two youngest children, a writer and a scientific researcher, talk about how being Garner's children has affected their own work. Younger writers discuss his influence on their own writing, while literary critics address particular aspects of his work.

What struck me after reading this anthology was how little, in sharp contrast to the critics and academics, those writers of his own generation actually have to say about Garner's writing: their pieces seem mainly to be based on long-ago acquaintance or meetings in passing. One or two august contributors seem to badly misunderstand the nature of the project. Margaret Atwood and Cornelia Funke especially spring to mind here, the one with a short story that seems to have no connection to Garner, other than it being a modern fairy tale, the other with a remarkably amateurish artwork, allegedly representing Garner as storyteller and shape-shifter. And, in truth, articles on 'how I first came to read Alan Garner and the effect he had on me' are mostly of little interest to anyone but the person who wrote them, and sometimes their most ardent fans. With the best will in the world, I am not that reader nor ever can be, and anyway, I have my own story.

The exception to this rule is John Burnside's stunning 'Reading Together, Reading Apart', in which he charts the effect that reading *The Owl Service* (1967) had on his life, and the way in which it first prompted him to see the fantastic alongside the 'real'. Burnside comes from a family that focused very much on the need for 'advancement', and shunned any expression of the imagination. This is a theme that is hinted at in *Elidor* (1965), but made explicit in *The Owl Service*, and even more so in *Red Shift* (1973), while aspects of it return in subsequent novels, to reach their apotheosis in *Boneland*. It is the raw viscerality of Burnside's response to Garner's work that speaks to me in turn. My own encounters with Garner's writings have left their scars over the years. Met at the right, or wrong, moment, his work can change you in significant ways.

I take a delight too in 'Where the Starlight Sings', Frank Cottrell Boyce's blithe and joyful account of inviting Garner to walk with him through the landscape of *The Weirdstone of Brisingamen*, retracing Cottrell Boyce's teenage explorations of the area. Cottrell Boyce's enthusiasm is unforced and infectious. Having made a few forays of my own into Garner territory, even as far as Geelong, in South Australia, I understand that need to have one's feet on the ground, so to speak—and what better guide?

And that is where things become a little more complicated. Cottrell Boyce quotes a small part of Garner's commentary as they walk over Castle Rock: '*That rock shouldn't be there. That dip is man-made. This was an old path*'. On the one hand, these are the observations of a man who knows an area intimately. Of course he does. He has been here a long time, and so has his family—at least since 1592, according to an observation he makes in *The Beauty Things*, a record of conversations between Garner and Mark Edmonds, emeritus professor of archaeology (who also contributed to *First Light*). Long acquaintance with a place will do that for you. But I wonder if there is something in the phrase '*that rock shouldn't be there*' that doesn't sit quite right. We're given no context for the rock's presence, or how it came to be there, but to say that something *shouldn't* be in a place is to suggest that a landscape should be immutable.

This is plainly nonsense. Left to itself, a landscape will change in small ways day by day, and over time larger transformations will occur, even without human intervention. So, what is going on here? This leads me to consider the other major group of contributors to *First Light*—the historians, the archaeologists, the occasional astronomer—and a motif that occurs over and over, in a very similar pattern. Cottrell Boyce touches on it when he talks of being shown the treasures of Toad Hall, the place where Garner and his wife live. He talks about the axe that Garner hands to him, the one that features in *Boneland*; there are other items he doesn't mention, though I'd not be surprised to learn they include other axes, or the carved Celtic heads, possibly an unbroken Macclesfield Dandy clay pipe. Or a stone book.

I have never visited Alan Garner's house, but the ritual is familiar from other accounts, in *First Light* and elsewhere: beating the bounds of the fiction, then being presented with the tangibility of the objects encountered therein. Perhaps it is a test, or perhaps the objects are the reward for another, previous test, but the description of the walk, followed by the handling of objects, surfaces often enough in these accounts to make one aware that something significant is happening. On the one hand, there is the sense that the tangible fact of the objects validates the fictions; on the other, by walking these historians and archaeologists through *his* landscape, having them handle *his* objects, Garner invites them to validate the existence of his history, the history he has already validated through the fiction. Somehow, while Alan Garner is undoubtedly a historian and an archaeologist in his own right, one who has made important contributions to understanding the story of the Alderley area, and is acknowledged as having done so by his peers in *First Light*, it seems not to be enough. Something is lacking for him.

The attachment to the land is of course a persistent theme in Garner's work, both fiction and non-fiction, and insistent, to the point where one almost begins to feel he protests too much. Indeed, in the past I have proposed that for various reasons, Garner has come to regard himself as being estranged from his own landscape and history, and has sought to write himself back into it. I have previously framed it in terms of a recolonising of his 'one square mile of Cheshire countryside', and the ritualised performances of walking that countryside might be argued as being a part of this, a planting of footprints in lieu of a flag.

But what of the objects that form the other part of the ritual? I've been trying to decide where in Garner's oeuvre the presence of things became overtaken by a preoccupation with things. *The Weirdstone of Brisingamen* (1960) and *The Moon of Gomrath* (1963) follow a conventional fantasy-story trajectory concerning the loss, recovery, and relinquishing of objects of power. This becomes more complicated in *Elidor* because not only are there clearly recognisable objects of power, disguised as ordinary things in this world, but Garner also adds a second layer of significance by displacing familiar objects, such as a porch from a twentieth-century house, a child's glove, a broken jug, and imbuing them with ambiguous fantastical significance.

But it is with *The Owl Service* that the real and the fictional finally converge. It's well known that the story was in part inspired by a real dinner service, belonging to the family of Garner's wife, but it is from reading *The Beauty Things* that we see just how often this near-sacralisation is happening in Garner's work. At the same time, it turns out that not everything is what it initially seems. The original 'Beauty Things' of the title, for example, didn't belong to Alan Garner but to a man named Dafydd Rees. If you've read *The Owl Service*, you'll have met a fictionalised version of him in Huw Halfbacon, the guardian of the valley in which the story of the love triangle involving Lleu Llaw Gyffes, his wife, Blodeuwedd—the woman made of flowers—and Gronw Pebyr is doomed to replay itself over the generations. In a hollow tree, Huw maintains a cache of significant objects connected to earlier iterations of the story: Gronw's spear, a knife, an ancient pendant, objects of power. And among these objects is the set of brake blocks Huw removed from a motorbike belonging to Bertram, the second man involved in a love triangle formed with Nancy, the cook of the house to which Huw is attached as gardener and whose son, Gwyn, is unaware of the identity of his father (spoiler—it's Huw).

In real life, 'the Beauty Things were the artefacts that Dafydd put beyond price. One could say possessions but for some of them at least, Dafydd was as much custodian as owner. Those things carried a certain weight. So it mattered that they passed to someone who would honour them in the telling'. And that someone was Alan Garner. Edmonds goes on to describe how Dafydd Rees came to give those items to Garner: 'One day, Dafydd said to Alan, "I think I shall close my eyes soon. When I am gone, my sons will sell what they can, and throw the rest to the river. You are to take the Beauty Things now, in case we do not meet again."'

There is something almost mythic in this scene, the handing on of significant items to the chosen one. Which is not to mock Garner's account (for it is of course Garner's story; Edmonds is presumably repeating what he has been told), but this is all we have, and it places Garner front and centre as the preserver of other people's beloved trifles. Unlike Gwyn, who has no idea what to do with his inheritance, Garner always knows what to do. To go back to *First Light*, the archaeologist Richard Morris describes Garner the historian and archaeologist at work:

> Yet more excursions were made to rescue things. In the garden stood the shaft of an Anglo-Saxon cross that had been saved from break-up. From Barthomley came the page of a medieval gospel of St Luke that had been re-used as a leaf in a post-Reformation account book and was about to be thrown out when Alan intervened. Two seventeenth-century gravestones had been salvaged from a clearance in Knutsford. An early visit saw us rattling down a lane in Alan's Land Rover to retrieve a boundary marker that had become displaced and was at risk. (*First Light*, p.211)

While I accept the sincerity of the enterprise, a part of me nonetheless feels that there is more of the eighteenth than the twentieth century about this. Archaeologists and historians are taught that context is all, yet here we have a catalogue of objects deprived of context even as Garner swoops in to save them. Morris talks too of Garner asking him, while the novelist was writing *Red Shift*, to find something connected with the Ninth Legion, 'because Alan works through real things'. This much did not surprise me, but I had assumed that the fiction emerged from the objects, rather than the objects bolstering the fiction. At the same time, I found it hard not to see Garner as some sort of historical bric-a-brac collector.

The Stone Book Quartet (2006) possesses the most 'thingness' of Garner's work; it's explicit in the title, of course, but is perhaps best summed up by a description in what is narratively the final book of the series, *Tom Fobble's Day* (1978), of Joseph's junk room, which pretty much contains the remnants of the other stories in the series. In *Tom Fobble's Day*, we see young William collecting shrapnel as the Germans bomb Manchester with no sense of what he might do with it. By contrast, his grandfather, Joseph, about to retire as a blacksmith, brings his skills as a craftsman to bear on one last task: building a sledge for William. The sledge incorporates components of the loom that features in the first volume, *The Stone Book* (1976), and other items that readers will recognise. It has become the embodiment of all the stories, which are passed on to William. I have argued before that William, who is of course Alan, is collecting in a different way, and that the storeroom also represents his brain, filling with fragments of story idea, but since reading *The Beauty Things*, I'm less convinced.

I'd always assumed that the stone book (and it is by no means the only one that exists) was a genuine Garner family heirloom. One might argue that this is testament to the way in which Garner describes its making, but the book's actual provenance turns out to be more disturbing. 'He turned up one day, with this, a stone book that he'd found in a shed'. He was Cedric Wheeler, a man working on the demolition and reassembly of the Medicine House, the storied building that now forms part of Garner's home in Cheshire. Garner had warned the men that they might find things in the fabric of the building as they took it apart (old shoes, old papers, witch bottles, and mummified cats being not uncommon discoveries). Wheeler had been inspired by this and had started to investigate other derelict buildings in his spare time. It was Garner's reported response that startled me: 'He didn't want to give it to me. I had to have it but said that I wouldn't buy it'.

There is something about the transaction described that is uncomfortable. It might be that I'm embarrassed for my younger self's assumption about the object's provenance, but I don't think it is (just) that. I find myself wondering what went through Cedric Wheeler's mind as he displayed his discovery to Mr Garner, who insisted he must possess this thing, but no, he wasn't going to pay for it, at least not with money. Instead, there will be a dedication in the book about the stone book if and when it is eventually written. And this is not the only time such a thing occurs: one of the stone axes was acquired in a similar way, and that not locally either (although, luckily, there is another, local axe that looks just like it, to establish the connection to Garner's own land).

Other things appear to be freely given, but nonetheless there remains a sense that Garner is constructing a museum of Garnerish things, and the means by which he does it are not entirely above reproach. People have things and he has to have those things. There is something presumptuous in the terms he offers, coupled with a patrician sense of his knowing best what needs to be done.

This presumption is nowhere more apparent than in the story of Garner's friend, 'Writer William'. It's not stated, but the death dates agree so I'm fairly confident in saying that this story concerns William Mayne, the children's writer and a long-time friend of Garner's (there is an early story by Mayne, *The Big Egg* (1967), which is clearly about Garner's three eldest children, and set at Toad Hall). Garner tells how William, visiting Australia, comes across a box of stones in an antique shop. He buys them, and on his way home shows them to Garner. 'I recognized immediately that they were artefacts, Aboriginal Australian, with a few intrusions from North America, and William said I could have them, but not yet; he might need the stones for his own stories'.

When William died in 2010, Garner asked those clearing the house to keep an eye out for the box of artefacts—'by then I knew much more about what I was seeing and understood the obligation that it brought. Among the tools were axes that the Kulin people made from the stone of Bomjinna, to chop the trees to prop the sky to stop the sky from falling'. That might be so—Garner has done his research over the years, writing memorably about Aboriginal Australian storytelling in *The Voice That Thunders* (1997)—but if these are, as he appears to suggest, sacred objects, what is he doing holding on to them, allowing them to be photographed and the photographs to be published? How is he so certain that this is permissible? I think in particular of the spear point wrapped in paperbark and tied with a cord made of human hair. There is something very intimate about that assemblage that makes me feel it was not meant for general viewing and I feel uncomfortable even discussing it. Garner writes, 'The wrapping is protection and concealment. It is also pure theatre, a moment when the curtain pulls back to bring the protagonist into the light'. Perhaps we should be asking who is actually entitled to pull back that curtain.

Similarly, there are Aboriginal Australian weapons that Garner saw nailed up on a wall in a neighbour's house. He took them down, he said, because he had to, likening their presence on the wall to Christ crucified. But again, it seems as though he feels no need to make an effort to return them; or if he has, there is nothing here to indicate that fact. Instead, we have what is to all intents and purposes a tourist's cabinet of curiosities. A very knowledgeable tourist, perhaps, one who has done a remarkable amount of homework, but who remains, nonetheless, a tourist.

The whole of *The Beauty Things* is permeated with these twin desires to acquire and to recover, to the point where it seems to me that two very different impulses have become entangled and confused. On the one hand, we have the extraordinary story of how Garner rediscovered the contents of his grandfather Joseph's workshop intact, boarded up in a cellar. This much is undoubtedly Garner's patrimony and we can find genuine pleasure in seeing the things that Garner so lovingly recreated in *The Stone Book Quartet*. But what about that stone book, that axe head, those stones, and the other things we don't know about? What do they represent? *The Beauty Things* invites us to see those also as belonging to Garner, because they have all played a part in the creation of his novels. And that is true in a way, but when you push a certain creation myth, there is something disconcerting in discovering that it is built in part on appropriation.

There is an argument that, stripped of their previous context, Garner has given these objects new context, incorporating them into his own mythos. Of the box of stone tools, Garner says, 'Biography gives way to archetype, the slate wiped clean', which seems to excuse him of the responsibility of doing anything about them. But if my previous argument holds true—that Garner had, in effect, to colonise himself in order to become Alan Garner—then it is hard not to see some of these objects as colonial trophies.

I've been reading Alan Garner's writings for a long time now, and rereading. I have called him one of my favourite authors, and that's still true, but this has never been a simple relationship. When I was young, it was easy enough to buy into the mythos of Garnerland. Somewhere in my study is a talismanic ammonite (*Red Shift*), along with a small, intact clay pipe (*The Stone Book Quartet*), not to mention a bulging file of photocopies about the history and landscape of Cheshire. And maps. So many maps. I've visited Alderley Edge, Mow Cop, Barthomley, Thursbitch, and still vaguely hope I'll one day make it to Ludchurch. For years I wanted to find a stone book of my own. For me, to read Garner was always about looking things up to see if they actually existed. The first thing I did when *Thursbitch* was announced was to type the name into a search engine to see if it was a real place. Of course I did. And of course it did. But I ask myself now if this isn't all some kind of distraction from the real work of reading.

There are passages in Garner's writing I admire intensely—the evocation of deep time, deep history in *Boneland* is a literary tour de force—yet I've become increasingly ambivalent about the man and his work. I'd argue this is a productive state in which to exist. As I've grown older, I've gone from accepting his fiction at face value to arguing with it fiercely. Things that never occurred to me when I was an adolescent or in my twenties leap out at me now, and I find myself wondering how I never noticed them before.

This is not to say that *The Beauty Things* should be regarded simply as a catalogue of disastrous acquisitions for a fictional museum, or that the contributions in *First Light* should be regarded as swerving around the unacceptable. Each is sincere in its way, I don't doubt, but when read together the critical mind must surely ask questions that don't have a straightforward answer. To truly celebrate an author is to keep asking those difficult questions.

The Critic and the Clue:
tracking Alan Garner's *Treacle Walker*

I've been reading Alan Garner's work for more than forty years, and sporadically venturing an opinion in print (even here on *Strange Horizons*). He is one of 'my' writers. Unsurprisingly, then, I read Alan Garner's *Treacle Walker* almost the moment it was published, and my first response was 'how on earth am I going to write about this?'—because I knew I would have to. Here we are, at what might reasonably be considered the twilight of Garner's career; something ought to be said. The man is eighty-seven, after all, and to say I was surprised there was another novel to be had after the, in parts, magisterial *Boneland* (2012) is to wildly understate my reaction when it was first announced. Mind you, I was surprised when *Where Shall We Run To?* appeared in 2018—I had not been expecting an actual memoir of Garner's childhood. Was that story not already familiar to anyone who had paid the slightest attention to his career over the years? As it turned out, there *were* more stories there, about Garner's childhood companions, and a few later stories to boot.

Lots of people seemed to like *Where Shall We Run To?*, but I wasn't sure. What they saw as the considerable achievement of Garner putting himself into a child's mind and telling the story from there, I personally found a little arch. There was a sense, though, that Garner was now tying off the ends. Indeed, I rather thought he had actually tied them off—but then came *Treacle Walker*.

Where, then, to start? Let's begin with the critical response to *Treacle Walker*, which has been curious, to say the least. By 'critical', I mean the reviews in the newspapers and other 'immediate' outlets; in the discussion below I'm sampling just a few that I happened to come across around publication date. This is not an exhaustive survey.

To begin: Melanie McDonagh reviewed *Treacle Walker* as part of a roundup of the best children's novels of 2021 in *The Spectator*. She likes the novel—'it's utterly compelling'—but is flummoxed as to what age group it's written for, which is hardly surprising. Even though it is about a child, it doesn't fit comfortably with our current understanding of what a children's book, or YA novel, should look like. And I doubt very much that Garner intended it for a child audience, but evidently someone in the editorial department thought that a child's viewpoint means a book for children.

Personally, I would have read the shit out of *Treacle Walker* if I'd encountered it as a teenager, because I liked difficult, wordy things, but I'm fairly sure that understanding it would have been a matter for another time and place, with a few more years behind me. Or many more, given that there is no one moment of total comprehension of a novel. Interpretation is a mutable thing and now I do not read *The Owl Service* (1967) or *Red Shift* (1973) in the way I did as a teenager or when in my early twenties.

McDonagh's summary of the novel is briskly efficient: '*Treacle Walker* is a rag-and-bone man who isn't what he seems—a man who emerges occasionally from a marsh—and an unlovely boy called Joe, who's obsessed with comics and sees things he shouldn't'. None of this is untrue but neither does it adequately sum up the novel. It's not even a review as such: Melanie McDonagh had fifty-odd words at her disposal to write a plot synopsis and offer a snap judgement, and she did just that. One cannot expect a considered opinion in those circumstances, and frankly, this novel is not going to be summarised in fifty words (though there were numerous people in private forums who seemed to think McDonagh ought to have done better. In fact, I think she understood her task very well and did her best with an impossible book).

Claire Lowdon's review of *Treacle Walker*, in a roundup of new novels in *The Sunday Times* doesn't do much better. If anything, despite having more words at her disposal (around a hundred), she makes a worse job of it than McDonagh. Even in fifty words, McDonagh's enthusiasm shines through, whereas Lowdon is clearly at a loss. My general impression is that she had no idea who Garner was, so had no idea what to expect from his writing.

> *Treacle Walker* is a peculiar book featuring young Joseph Coppock, a boy with eye trouble who seems to live alone in an old house, and who is befriended by the rag-and-bone man of the title. [...] Walker is an eccentric spiritual guide, and reality soon starts to wobble as comic strips come to life and the letters of an eye test spell out an alchemical formula in Latin. [...] the story itself is none the worse for feeling curiously outdated, like a children's book from yesteryear.

Again, nothing in Lowdon's summary is actually wrong, but neither does she seem to actually engage with the novel. Or, rather, I don't think she particularly wants to engage with the novel. Ironically, however—and possibly unintentionally—she does hit on something significant when she describes the novel as 'feeling curiously outdated', but there is no chance for her to follow up on this.

The Guardian reviewed *Treacle Walker* twice. Alex Preston's review was ... very Alex Preston. Readers are reassured that Preston is familiar with Garner's work, and he identifies Garner's big themes, but once the review is stripped of the reviewer's distinctive stylistic tics, not much is actually said about the novel itself. Preston rightly describes *Treacle Walker* as the summation of Garner's career as a writer, but doesn't give much indication of what that might mean. This, if you like, is the review as performance. We're invited into the world of Alex Preston—a comfortable, gossipy place, brimming with literary references and asides about writers he's met recently, in which the novel under discussion generally plays a fairly small part.

Justine Jordan's review, also in *The Guardian*, is rather different. It's a long review, twice as long as Preston's, and it's clear that Jordan really does understand Garner's recent publishing history: she confidently lays out the links between *Treacle Walker* and other recent publications by and about Garner, including *Where Shall We Run To?* and the 2016 Festschrift, *First Light*, in which the real Treacle Walker is first mentioned. More than that, she recognises how *Treacle Walker* resonates with so many of Garner's other novels, and links it in particular to *Elidor* (1965), that problematic third novel.

Is this review a piece of criticism? No. But it's getting closer than any of the other reviews I've looked at so far, in that it gives readers a sense of the considerable hinterland of Garner's work. It's the sort of review I'd be glad to find if I did not know that much about Alan Garner and was looking for other titles to move on to. We have novels by, and books about, Garner here. And yet. As most reviewers do—and indeed are probably obliged to for reasons of space—Jordan still shies away from discussing the story in much detail, as indeed does Carolyne Larrington in *The Times Literary Supplement*. Larrington's review explores Garner's themes and influences in greater depth than Jordan's, but at the end we still don't know that much about the novel itself.

In some respects, this is probably not surprising. In a mainstream media review there is a perceived requirement to not 'spoil' the novel for those who have not yet read it (though I strongly suspect *Treacle Walker* is immune to being spoiled because it is just so unusual, or 'peculiar', if you like). If a plot summary is designed to address the question 'do I want to read this?', then the average broadsheet or literary journal review might, at its best and most effective, be characterised as 'here are some reasons why you might find this book interesting' or 'here are some reasons why this book may not be quite what you think'. In non-fiction reviewing, of course, there is no need to worry about revealing the end, although non-fiction reviewing just as frequently resorts to summarising the contents of a book in lieu of engaging with its argument or passing any kind of judgement on it. Indeed, strange as it might sound, I felt that, in some ways, Larrington and Jordan were reviewing *Treacle Walker* as a piece of non-fiction, pointing out recurring themes in Garner's work even as they tried not to spoil the novel, which I found rather disconcerting.

There is also another issue for reviewers that is rarely, if ever, addressed, and that is the difficulty of writing about an author who has a long and storied career, and whose work is revered by so many. This is something I have had to come to terms with myself over the years. The post-*Red Shift* novels have never worked quite as well for me as the earlier novels did (I can never quite decide whether *The Owl Service* or *Red Shift* is the better book). For a long time, I thought it was just my not understanding, but as I've grown older—and more experienced as a reader and critic—I am confident in saying that, whereas the more recent novels are perhaps more formally daring, they are as likely to miss their mark as to hit it.

And yet, I can't, offhand, think of a review of any of Garner's work, certainly not his more recent work, that risks anything more than faint puzzlement at the bits the critic doesn't understand, although Penelope Lively did express some irritation over Garner's use of language in *Strandloper* (1996) and was unpersuaded by the connections he sought to make between Cheshire and the cultures of indigenous Australians. Nowadays, I too have my reasons for doubt, although the words I am currently toying with are 'cultural appropriation'. There is probably a case to be made also for reading Garner's work through Bakhtin's theories, if someone hasn't already, but that's a job for another day.

It is a quality of Garner's work, however, that it inspires obsession and adulation in readers, and along with that comes a reluctance to say anything even remotely negative about his work, and a refusal to address anything critical said by others. This happens a lot in private social forums—Garner is a shaman, or whatever, and there is little if any space to say 'maybe, just maybe, he is actually a human being, and this book is not entirely perfect'. To even attempt that in certain company can be unwise.

We began with the critics, but where does the critic begin with *Treacle Walker*, this summation of Garner's career, as people keep describing it? The reviewers we have already encountered have clearly struggled. Over the years, I have come more and more to appreciate John Clute's belief that to write proper criticism one needs to discuss the whole of the fiction, rather than leaving the reader hanging on the edge of a precipice at the vital moment by refusing to discuss the ending. As much as possible, now, I will always try to discuss the ending. In part, it's as simple as the fact that I don't believe, except possibly in some strands of detective fiction, that knowing the ending before you get there is to spoil the novel. It's the journey that I find interesting. I've no especial need to be *surprised* by fiction; I've read enough over the years to recognise how stories are likely to pan out. Rather, I like to be absorbed by the process of reading; a surprise is a bonus.

Reading Garner is, for some people, like a treasure hunt. They eagerly chase the breadcrumb-trail of names and places and historical events. I've done it myself in the past—to be honest, I'm fighting hard to resist doing it now—and it's not surprising that people do. It's very much a mark of Garner's work that it is so deeply embedded in the landscape and history of Cheshire (and Garner has stated more than once that he prefers the company of historians and archaeologists to that of literary people).

But to trace out all those connections is not in itself an act of criticism; it's a process of annotation. It may become valuable later in terms of understanding a novel's context, but it is not a substitute for thinking critically about a work. Indeed, it can become a distraction from the task in hand, and I think that's something that happens a lot in relation to Garner's work. To take one example in relation to *Treacle Walker*, there was huge excitement on one forum when it was discovered that 'Joseph Coppock' was a real person. Yes, and?

More significantly, Treacle Walker was a real person, Walter Helliwell, or Walker Treacle, an eccentric tramp and healer (he claimed he could cure anything except jealousy) who lived in Holywell Green, near Sheffield, in the early twentieth century. But this is not a novel about that man. Garner has appropriated his name for the novel, and I can see good reasons why he might have done that, but they have nothing to do with the man himself.

Criticism is about asking questions and perhaps answering them, too. One question I must obviously ask at this point is 'what is going on in *Treacle Walker*?' It's a very broad question, and not that helpful as it invites a plot synopsis, and we've already had several of those. And yet, another plot synopsis, a longer one, might unearth some clues. The reviews mentioned earlier established that Joseph Coppock, a boy, receives visits from the mysterious Treacle Walker, with his horse and cart. Walker is a rag-and-bone man, and he wants to trade with Joe: '"Rag and bone," said the man. "And you shall have pot and stone."' (p.4).

By trading an old pair of pyjamas and a bone from a lamb, Joseph will receive a pot that he must choose for himself from a chest filled with containers of one sort or another, and Walker will also give him a donkey stone, a type of manufactured scouring stone used for cleaning doorsteps, mainly in northern England, through the early part of the twentieth century. The donkey stone, when Treacle Walker hands it over, is embellished with the sign of a galloping white horse, which many will recognise as the shape of the Uffington White Horse in Oxfordshire.

The mention of the pot and the stone made me think immediately of the artefacts the children rescue from Elidor in the novel of that name—a sword, a stone, a gold cup, and a spear—and how they are transformed into ordinary objects in this world: two pieces of wood nailed together, a brick, a china teacup, and a piece of iron railing, which suggests to me that this is perhaps the novel to keep in mind as I continue writing about *Treacle Walker*, especially as there is also a white horse in *Elidor*, a unicorn, in fact.

Here we should recall that Justine Jordan also recognised the connection, even if she did not elaborate on it. There are other resonances, which I'll come to later. But before I can focus on these, I need to consider the pot that Joseph chooses from Treacle Walker's chest of pots and jars, and the green violet ointment it contains, which is obviously connected to Treacle Walker's green violet eyes. Later, when Joe accidentally smears some of the ointment on his good eye, the one he is supposed to keep covered in order to make the lazy eye work harder, it first causes him pain, and later seems to have affected his vision. It is after this event that Joe first encounters Thin Amren in the willow copse, whom he can see only if he uncovers his 'good' eye.

Who is Thin Amren? He wears a leather hood but is otherwise naked. He has emerged from the marshes and is clearly a bog-body—a remarkably animated bog-body, by his own admission, and as enigmatic as Treacle Walker in the ways in which he plays with language, although he is clearly mistrustful of Walker in the same way that Treacle Walker will turn out to be concerned about him.

It is worth considering the many references to illness and impairment that abound in this novel. As well as having a 'lazy eye', Joe, we are told, has been ill. We know too that Joe does not like to wear his eyepatch as it seems to upset his vision. So, Joe is ill and Treacle Walker has brought him a cureall, as seems appropriate when we consider the possible derivation of Treacle Walker's name. Treacle mines and treacle wells are a little-known feature of the English countryside. Unsurprisingly, they did not dispense a black sugary liquid; 'treacle' is a corruption of an older word, 'triacle', which is associated with healing. The tramp describes himself as a healer, and the treacle wells (such as that at Binsey, just outside Oxford, referred to by Lewis Carroll in *Alice in Wonderland*) reputedly have healing properties.

At one point Joe takes an eye test to check on his progress. Here, in its most literal sense, we see his second sight in action. One eye can see what is on the eye chart, while the other sees instead a Latin phrase: 'This stone is small, of little price: spurned by fools, more honoured by the wise'. We are led to assume that these words refer to the donkey stone and its capacity to repel invaders when it is used to scour a doorstep, but again we might turn back to Elidor, and the four treasures of *Elidor*, and in particular that house brick, of as little price as a piece of donkey stone.

Treacle Walker's surname also reminds us once again of just how many of Garner's novels are centred around walking as a ritual act of 'knowing' or claiming the landscape, even as recently as in *Boneland*, which not only features the adult Colin ritually walking the landscape he has walked for most of his life, but, back in deep time, the original Alderley shaman undertaking a journey on foot from Ludchurch to Alderley. Garner's Strandloper is the novel that most fully expresses the role of walking in his fiction, as William Buckley, transported to South Australia, attempts to walk home, ignorant as he is that Australia is surrounded by ocean, and thus falls in with a group of indigenous Australians, who believe him to be their shaman returned to them.

Treacle Walker, by contrast, is a novel marked by immobility, even stasis. There are no long walks here. Joe Coppock is recovering from an unspecified illness and has lately spent a lot of time in bed (we are subtly prompted to remember that the young Garner was also, as a child, periodically bedridden with life-threatening illnesses, which he credits with the development of his imagination). There is a sense that Joe is in danger if he even sets foot outside the house. He does not do well in the sun, we are told, and his journeys to the copse to look for the cuckoo are constantly fraught with danger. The longest journey he makes is a journey he may not even have made at all. In a vision Joe sees himself following silver hoofprints across the yard and out into the countryside until he reaches a hillock, where the hoofprints stop. Under the ground he can hear the sound of a pipe. But then he wakes to find himself on the hillock in reality. Or possibly not, for when he returns to his house, he finds Treacle Walker inside, talking to Joe's doppelgänger.

Treacle Walker, like Joe, seems curiously static; even though he owns a horse and cart, he seems to materialise in the yard of Joe's house, with no sense that he is on his way from or to anywhere, and never quite leaves. Thin Amren's wandering around is a cause for concern to Treacle Walker, and later it will indeed become imperative that Thin Amren's body is once again secured to the ground, a task that must be performed by Joe. Travel is something that happens for the most part invisibly, away from the house. How did Joe get to the optician's for his eye test? There is a train that passes once a day—Joe calls it Noony, because it passes at midday—but it's never seen, never described, and oddly, it seems to go in only one direction. Only its smoke drifts across the yard.

Indeed, having noted that Thin Amren has become untethered, one might begin to think that much of the novel itself is untethered. Bits of it simply do not fit together. Joe's house is a puzzle. Apart from Joe, no one is there. He does not mention his parents—perhaps they are both out at work—and no one seems to be looking after him. I actually found this less surprising than some people seem to have done; if we remember Lowdon's reference to the book feeling curiously dated, in Garner's day it wouldn't have that uncommon to leave convalescent children unattended while their mother maybe went next door to the neighbour or went to the local shops. But when Joe attends his eye test, he seems to be there on his own, which is more unusual.

We should keep it in mind though that Joe himself does not seem to be unduly worried by this state of affairs. It's perfectly natural to him, so the reader must accept it. Likewise, Treacle Walker's arrival on his doorstep is not particularly surprising. It's not so long ago that the year's cycle was marked by the arrival of rag-and-bone men, knife-sharpeners, onion-sellers from France, women hawking clothes pegs and telling fortunes, and it's clear that Joe understands the ritual exchange of one set of goods for another. When I was a child, rag-and-bone men would often give out artificial flowers or other cheap items as a kind of 'payment' for the unwanted articles that they collected.

Which begs the question: what has Treacle Walker really come to collect? Or, to take up the refrain again, who is Treacle Walker? Thin Amren gives us a clue, when he rails at Treacle Walker, calling him a psychopomp; that is, a guide to dead souls. In Jungian psychology (and Garner has spoken recently of reading Jung), the psychopomp mediates between the conscious and the unconscious realms, and is personified as a wise man (or woman). This opens up some interesting possibilities indeed for the reader.

Let us suppose that Joe Coppock is not an actual child, but someone else's memory. Perhaps he lies in the mind of an older Joseph Coppock, a sick man, drifting in and out of consciousness, remembering his earlier years. Or perhaps it is young Joseph's mind we are permitted to enter, his thoughts mixed up with stories from the comics he so avidly reads. And if Treacle Walker is here to guide Joseph to the afterlife, which afterlife is he headed for?

I've noted already the presence of Noony, the noonday train, seen but never heard. Noony seems also to be associated with the arrival of Treacle Walker. And what else passes once a day? The sun. There is an implication here that Treacle Walker is in some way associated with Helios, the god who drives his chariot across the sky each day. His chariot is pulled by horses, and they are probably white, and, like Noony, Helios travels only the one way before vanishing underground at the end of the day, to re-emerge the following morning. But if Treacle Walker is indeed Helios, he seems to have come down in the world. Helios's glorious chariot is now a rag-and-bone cart, and there is only one horse left, itself diminished, an ageing pony.

If we accept the implication that Treacle Walker is here to collect Joe and guide him on his way, what then of Thin Amren? The description of Thin Amren's body should remind us of Tollund Man (though Cheshire, of course, has its own bog body, Lindow Man, found close to where Garner himself lives). If one accepts the reading of Treacle Walker as an avatar of Helios, from the classical mythological tradition, Thin Amren belongs to a different mythology altogether, something more northern, more instinctive, a joyful and irreverent counter to the more rational linguistic precision of Treacle Walker. Thin Amren is a child to Treacle Walker's austere, world-weary adult. For all they are vying with one another for Joe Coppock's attention, I don't think we should read Thin Amren and Treacle Walker as protagonist and antagonist in the conventional sense. They're competing, yes, but not fighting. It's tempting instead to read them as two worldviews, each struggling for supremacy, inviting Joe to choose.

Supposing that Joe Coppock is standing in for Garner himself, then one might choose to see Treacle Walker as an avatar of the rational, educated Garner (who of course began reading Classics at Oxford, though he did not complete his degree), while Thin Amren represents the intuitive child-Garner who roamed Alderley Edge, learning the stories of his forebears. And both are deteriorating. Thin Amren is drying out because he has left his bog, while Treacle Walker is rag and bones himself. Joe notes several times that Treacle Walker smells terrible, but this is not the stench of an unwashed tramp. Treacle Walker is literally rotting. The healer cannot heal himself.

In the end, perhaps it is incumbent on Joe to reinvigorate Thin Amren's purpose by once again pinning him in the bog, where he belongs. It's not clear what has dislodged him other than sheer antiquity, and possibly a failure of belief in his presence and efficacy at healing the land. Having discharged this task, Joe is then free to leave with Treacle Walker, which we might choose to read as symbolising his death in this world. Except that Joseph Coppock doesn't leave with Treacle Walker; instead he takes over from him. How one might interpret this is anyone's guess.

All of which is a perfectly workable reading of this novel, except for one thing: there is the vagueness engendered by a mind scattered by the transition from life to death, and there is also just plain untidy writing. As I have noted several times, a number of commentators have justified the narrative bric-a-brac of *Treacle Walker* as representing the summation of a long and storied career. Why wouldn't the author revisit old themes? Why not, indeed? Some have suggested that Garner is having fun with what has gone before. And that is also a possibility.

And yet, I cannot get rid of the feeling that it would be just as easy to read this novel as an untidy gathering-together of Garner's greatest hits, so to speak. As you've probably realised, one can play 'spot the reference' for hours with this novel, but to what purpose? In some situations, I would stick my neck out and call this 'fan service', a pandering to the writer's admirers. In this instance I might be inclined to call it 'self-indulgence', though the two are closely related. I've tried to steer a course between playing 'spot the reference' and making the very necessary connections with the constant themes in Garner's work, but it's not easy.

You could argue of *Treacle Walker* that it is a novel of two parts. On the one hand, a person apparently on the point of death debates the nature of time and the possible existence of an afterlife with two embodied mythic figures; on the other hand, there is a framework of folktales, local history, and dialect that teeters on the brink of being incomprehensible. In the past I might have suggested that Garner was commendably preserving his own history within his work, but as time has gone by, I've felt more and more that, as his use of dialect grows more evident, and the dialect itself has become stronger, Garner is using language as a means of keeping readers out rather than inviting them in.

When Joe Coppock first meets Treacle Walker, he invites him into the house—bear in mind that thresholds are always a contested place in Garner's work. They sit at the fireplace, until a hammering sounds on the door. When

Joe investigates, he sees through the window that no one is there: outside it is high summer, the yard is quiet, empty but for Treacle Walker's pony and cart. Yet when he opens the door, as the novel so memorably puts it, 'night spilled in […] night was in the room, a sheet of darkness, flapping from wall to wall' (p.2). It's a powerful moment. But in the aftermath of that, as Joe goes back to the fireplace, Walker says, 'It was a hurlothrumbo of winter […] a lomperhomock of night. Nothing more' (p.15). More Cheshire dialect? A new way to say 'fimbulwinter'? Curious, I searched online for the word, and vanished down an intriguing little rabbit hole involving Samuel Johnson of Cheshire, or Maggoty Johnson as he was later known, who created a spectacle called *Hurlothrumbo*, which was performed in London, and created a certain amount of scandal.

From what little I've managed to find out, the play sounds fascinating, and may indeed have some relation to *Treacle Walker*, but why mention it at that particular point of the story? To defuse a tense moment? Or because Treacle Walker likes to play with words? Because he saw the play when it was first performed (which, if he is as old as I think he is, is very probable)? Or because this is a sign that Treacle Walker's mind is deteriorating, along with his body? Whatever the reason, what was Garner expecting to happen when he put those words there? If this is wordplay, it seems to be very unequal wordplay. This may be Garner having fun, but if so, he is having fun at the expense of his reader, surely? Or is he teasing readers, knowing full well they will be hitting Google immediately? Whatever the reason, most of these breadcrumbs feel a little … tiresome?

We have reached the point where critical appraisal struggles to find a way through, because there are too many routes to the end. Every potential flaw can be countered with a proposal that in fact the author might be doing something else. The novel's epigraph is a quotation taken from Carlo Rovelli's *L'ordine del tempo* [*The Order of Time*] (2017): 'Il tempo è ignoranza/Time is ignorance'. Rovelli works on quantum mechanics and *The Order of Time* is a piece of popular science writing that investigates what we understand by 'time'. It seems clear from this where Garner wants to lead us, but can invoking quantum mechanics excuse a wobbly plot? Is a chase in and out of comic-book panels a plausible way to explore time? Possibly, and I suppose we could argue that we are seeing it through the eyes of a boy, Joe Coppock, so it is unsurprising if it seems simplistically presented. Yet I don't believe that myself, and I don't think it's an argument that can stick.

For a critic, going against the prevailing opinion on a text is fraught with danger. To disagree is to worry that perhaps your critical faculties are at fault. It is uncomfortable to be out of step with everyone else, and yet you have to say what you see. We have already seen that almost all of Garner's reviewers now back away from anything but the usual bromides. But I have spent enough of my life thinking about Garner's work, and writing about it, that I am reasonably confident in my opinion, and able to support it with arguments, even if it does go against the prevailing opinion. No work, in my view, is immune to criticism. *Treacle Walker* is not a bad novel, but neither is it a work of towering genius.

You may disagree. Awesome! Now we can talk about it some more. That, for me, is what criticism is about. My job as a critic is to talk about the text, and explore it. Not to promote it by providing quotable nuggets for the back cover of the paperback edition, or to provide feedback to the author. I've never written for authors. If I am talking about the text I am writing for readers, and to some extent for myself, so I can find out what it is I think about a particular book.

What I think about this particular book is that it is trying very hard, possibly too hard, to do several things, not the least of which is to be an Alan Garner novel. However, its considerable ambition is not always matched by its execution, to the point where, at times, it is opaque, while at other times, in attempting to be a summation of the writer's career, it runs perilously close to becoming a scorecard of the writer's ongoing preoccupations. To fully achieve its effect, the text requires the reader to be more than an average reader, though even knowledgeable readers are struggling with it. This is not reading as a collaborative effort so much as reading as a full-time research project, and that is not how people generally read. Which feels like another kind of gatekeeping to me.

Garner has said many times that when he begins a novel, he always knows what the last line is, and the entire novel is spent working towards that and hoping he doesn't miss. In this instance, I can't help feeling that Garner knew from the beginning what the last chapter would contain, but struggled to find his way there. Because, even considering how short the novel is, the journey has been arduous, and I have wondered at points whether it was worthwhile. And yet, in this final chapter there is a sense that Garner has stopped messing around, or being playful, or whatever you choose to call it, and is getting down to the business of just writing.

It's not entirely perfect, but the best of it is extraordinary. Paragraph by paragraph, less has become more. Suddenly, Treacle Walker is all terseness, as he summons Thin Amren from the bog, and instructs Joe in the matter of preparing the five alder withies he will need to pin him down. Thin Amren's job, we learn, is to sleep in the bog in order to remember Joe and allow him to continue to exist. One assumes this ritual was also at some point performed by Treacle Walker himself. It was Joe who woke Thin Amren, and so it is Joe who must sacrifice Thin Amren to the bog again before he leaves, literally taking up the reins of Treacle Walker's pony and cart, and disappearing towards evening.

Still, one can't help wondering how long it will be before Joe's youthful vigour is ground down by the demands of Treacle Walker's job, and he is reduced to plodding stoically along as Treacle Walker has done for so long. I can't help feeling that here, at the end, rationality still trumps instinct, and the old wild magic of intuition is rejected in favour of the more reliable but less interesting magic of Newtonian science. Even quantum mechanics cannot save Joe from the quotidian routine of the day. This seems an oddly downbeat ending, yet it is entirely characteristic of Garner's work, because this is what happens every time. Garner may valorise the old magic but inevitably he, or his characters, rejects it, as though there is no permanent place for it in the world, because it is too unpredictable. Not even death, or a flirtation with quantum mechanics, offers respite.

There are many forms of critical writing, as I've already noted. I could have opted for the 'rationality' of academic writing, and dragged up the big guns of theory to make a point or two. On this occasion, I opted for something a little more 'instinctive', teasing out themes and ideas, finding and testing links, sketching in arguments to follow up later. And, to some extent, I have tried to write about the reception of *Treacle Walker*, and examine the dialogue among other reviewers. As it turns out, there seems not to have been dialogue so much as a nervous toeing of a party line, which is interesting in itself, although I profoundly disagree with that party line. For me, disagreement is very much part of the critical process. And reviews are part of the critical process too, even if, in this instance, they do not offer that much critical insight into the novel.

And it is the insight I'm in search of, both when I read criticism and when I write it. I'm not interested in whether X likes a novel, any more than you should be interested in whether I dislike a novel. The questions should always be: 'What is this piece of fiction doing, does it work, and if not, why not?' Everything else unfolds from that.

A Field Guide to Reality — Joanna Kavenna

Joanna Kavenna's novel attracts me partly because it's set in a version of Oxford, my home city, and I'm a sucker for anything about my home city; partly because it seems to be illustrated and I'm also curious about attempts to bring together text and art, especially as they are often unsuccessful and I want to see if this wins rather than loses; and mainly, because I like the sound of a novel that partakes of quantum theory and metaphysics, and I want to find out if a novel that might be about science might be science fiction too. And it has to be said that if one is going to read a novel about alternative or imbricated realities, it is interesting to begin from a place one knows well.

So, because I am not sure I know how else to shape a review of this novel, I shall take those reasons as sub-headings.

The dream of everyday life

Oxford is the city of my birth, and though it is no longer my home, it is still *home*, the place where everything started, the place I will spend the rest of my life moving away from. There is no going back in reality but Oxford persists as 'the consolatory elsewhere', the place I can return to in my imagination, and especially through fiction.

Though, having said that, it is difficult to find fiction that offers up an Oxford I truly recognise; unsurprising, given my Oxford is not your Oxford, and never can be, any more than yours will be mine. Sometimes it's a matter of evoking places and names in the right way at the right moment: old favourites include Penelope Lively's *The House in Norham Gardens* and Philip Pullman's *Lyra's Oxford* (more so even than the His Dark Materials trilogy). Sometimes, it's more a matter of creating a particular atmosphere, something *A Field Guide to Reality* turns out to be remarkably good at, all the more so given that Kavenna's Oxford is itself an alternative city, where some of the names have stayed the same but some, especially those of things pertaining to the university, have changed. Is this important? Maybe.

What I know as the Ashmolean Museum is, in Kavenna's Oxford, the Tradescantian Ark, reflecting the fact that the collection Elias Ashmole gave to Oxford University was in part composed of John Tradescant the Younger's collection of artefacts, known as the Ark, which he gave to Ashmole (or, depending on who you listen to, which Ashmole swindled him out of). So, perhaps we are in an Oxford that is less a 'home of lost causes, and forsaken beliefs, and unpopular names, and impossible loyalties', as Matthew Arnold memorably described it, and instead a place where potential wrongs have been righted even before they were committed, and Jeremiah Tradescant's ownership of his family's remarkable collection is justly celebrated. Perhaps, but rather as light is both particle and wave, so wrongs can be righted even as the lost causes and forsaken beliefs persist.

Fluidity, of belief and materiality, is the essence of this Oxford. It's signalled in the way this winter city is so often wreathed in mist, or rimed with frost, seeming constantly to be about to be erased as the fog swirls or the ice melts. It is a world without light, yet made of the purest light, according to Robert Grosseteste, philosopher, who believes that white is 'created by such fiery furious light in pure diaphaneity'. What is more diaphanous than misty veils? Except, perhaps, that concept of Oxford that I can never quite convey to you but that is as seductive to me as it is to Eliade Jencks, who came to Oxford because her mother believed she was destined to work at the Tradescantian Ark, and found she could stay only by becoming a waitress in the café in its basement.

Light is replaced by opacity; Eliade believes herself to have 'lost the diaphanous realm, or transparency. Now she is immersed in the turgid reality of the Oxford beyond the city walls, living somewhere up the Cowley Road, in an 'atmosphere [that] was desolate'.

The art in the text, the text in the art

'*And what is the use of a book,' thought Alice, 'without pictures or conversation?*'

I read *Alice in Wonderland* often as a child, even before I fully understood its connection to Oxford. The edition I read had pictures, of course, but I was more puzzled that Alice, so terribly grown-up as she seemed to be, didn't understand the cachet of reading books without pictures, the sure-fire marker of adulthood.

Even now, I wonder a little about illustrated novels for adults; not graphic novels, but novels like this, with artwork dotting the pages, inserted between chapters. Some pictures are like doodles on a manuscript, left by a bored or inattentive monk. Their strength lies in their seeming artlessness: a gargoyle here, a sketch of a man in a deckchair there. They make me smile. They're probably meant to. They're heirs to a long tradition of entertaining marginalia. Other illustrations are more obviously intended to evoke a particular atmosphere: a rainbow on Port Meadow, the mist swirling around streetlights somewhere on the Cowley Road; Solete's house on Mesopotamia, that narrow strip of land in the Parks, between two strands of the River Cherwell; and a sketch of the café at the Tradescantian Museum, which suggests to me it is a very different building to the Ashmolean I recall. These illustrations seem to transform the novel into literally a guide, a guide to the Oxford that exists within the novel.

Strangely, though, it is when the art engages most closely with the text that it seems to be at its weakest, especially when figures are involved. It is as though Oly Ralfe works best as an evoker of feelings rather than as an illustrator of events and people. Certainly, I find his figures somewhat unconvincing at times. Eliade herself is a vague presence, sometimes lurking at the front of the picture: we always see her back, and seem to look over her shoulder, as though viewing her dreams and visions almost but not quite through her eyes.

But, I have come to realise, the presence of the art is important, because this novel is all about light and visibility, and how better to emphasise that than through illustration? Fiction is both word and picture.

Perception is a prevailing mystery of thought

Finally, we come to the novel itself. I was struck, looking at newspaper reviews, how critics have struggled with it. It defies a quick *précis*, as a result of which reviewers have focused on what seems to be the meat of the matter, the hunt for Solete's life's work, the Field Guide itself, while almost entirely ignoring the rest of the novel's content. This is perhaps unsurprising, given it wrestles with a lot of complicated material about philosophies of light and visibility, but to ignore it is to present only a very limited view of the novel.

The novel opens with a scene on Port Meadow, ancient grazing land north and west of Oxford, and the appearance of a huge double rainbow in the year 1216. A sign from God, some people believe; others would argue that 'rainbows derive from the reflection, by clouds, of the sun. The colours are caused by the dimming effect of clouds'. We know now that rainbows are caused by the reflection, refraction, and dispersion of light through water droplets, generally rain, but this opening sequence tells us an important thing: people are theorising about the nature and causes of the phenomena they see around them. Nowhere is this more intensely thought about than in Oxford, site of the first English university. As if to emphasise this, Kavenna then takes us on a whirlwind tour of early Oxford and the thoughts of its first chancellor, Robert Grosseteste. The mutability of his name's spelling reminds us of myriad explanations of the natural world that already exist, even then.

We travel with Grosseteste as he reviews the various theories of perception in what seems to be the most literal fashion imaginable. Such is his imagination he's there, as philosophers propound their theories; if we're wise, we take this as a pointer for what is to come later.

Fast forward to 2016, and to our narrator, Eliade Jencks, living in Oxford, living an in-between life, neither student nor don (as though these are the only options available in Oxford, even now), working in the Tradescantian

Museum café, and carrying out unspecified research in the Great Library in the evenings. A phone call announces the death of Professor Solete, with whom Eliade was friends, and summons her to Nightingale Hall, where a box lies, waiting to be opened, her name written on it.

So far, we seem to be caught up in an academic turf war, as Solete's colleagues, who have been frantically searching for Solete's *magnum opus*, which they now believe to be in Eliade's box, come up with reasons why the box's contents should belong to the college rather than to Eliade. It is deliciously naked and oh-so-Oxford in its way, and there is a great satisfaction in discovering, once the box is opened, that it is empty.

As most of Solete's colleagues lose interest, it's left to Eliade and Anthony Yorke, a don, to figure out what Solete was actually working on and where he has hidden it. Which makes the novel sound like a detective story. In fact, it's more accurately characterised as a journey through theories of perception and epistemology, how we come to understand our world, set against the history and geography of Oxford and varying perceptions of the city (though the one thing that is perhaps lacking is a fully-formed Town perspective. The Gown are inevitably contemptuous of the Town but Eliade herself is again neither one thing nor the other).

The novel can also, I think, be read as a kind of journey through the underworld of forsaken theory, each clue leading Eliade on to the next set of ideas. This would also account in part for the sense of the hallucinatory and the elusiveness of Eliade's experiences, coupled with her as yet not fully articulated grief for her own father's death as well as that of Solete as perhaps a substitute father. I'm prompted to say that in part because of Eliade's unusual forename, which immediately makes me think of Mircea Eliade, the historian who posited the idea of the myth of the eternal return, and the shift between sacred and profane time and space. Early in their acquaintance, Yorke tells Eliade a story of how as a child he convinced his brother that if they tossed a dead mouse into the river, the dead creature would return to them. Oxford, surrounded by rivers and by marshes, seems to be a place where the dead might come back to life, or at any rate lie uneasily, as witnessed in Robert Grosseteste's visions and Eliade's own dreams.

The novel's denouement (and avert your eyes now if such things bother you, but I cannot discuss this novel without discussing its ending, not least because in this instance the ending is the novel) centres on Solete's long journey through different theories of perception, to reach the understanding that 'the fundamental mystery and central property of reality is light'. Solete could not express this in writing and instead built a construct to express his revelation: a theatre of dust, in the cellar of his house. 'Seven rays of light seeped through the holes, and clouds of dust floated along these beams of light'. It echoes the work of Alhazen, mentioned at the novel's beginning, and famed for his work on demonstrating that light travels in straight lines. This of course is not what Solete's colleagues want: they want papers they can edit and publish in a neat volume with their names on the front as editors. They will have their volume, but for Eliade and Yorke their quest has also come to an end. As Yorke notes of Solete's work, 'in a perverse way, it is a theory of everything. Just not the one they want'. Are Eliade and Yorke happier for the knowing? It's hard to say, but ultimately that is not what the novel is about. It is the journey rather than its ending that is important, the accruing of knowledge, the constant demand that we see the world anew.

The question has to be asked: is this science fiction? It is undoubtedly fiction about science, but fiction about science isn't necessarily good science fiction. I think there is a case for *The Field Guide to Reality* being described as science fiction, but in the same way that Arthur C. Clarke noted that 'any sufficiently advanced technology is indistinguishable from magic'. I'm going to suggest that in this instance it's remarkably difficult to disentangle the philosophical and the fantastical from the scientific. And that is the point. I could argue that *A Field Guide to Reality* is an alternative history, but that is a thin argument, and makes for thin fiction too. Equally weak and flimsy is to suggest that it might be a time-travel novel. My own feeling is that the time-travel is entirely in the imagination, ours and Eliade's. I'm going to suggest instead that this novel is about the wonders of science and philosophy and the ways in which they have seemed magical and fantastical to those who have struggled to grasp the intricacies of theory. It may be that Eliade has dreamed the whole thing, but I don't think that undermines the nature of her quest for knowledge.

The first time I read this novel I enjoyed it, but there was so much to take in, it was difficult to gain any mental purchase on it. The second time, having stowed away my preoccupations with its portrayal of Oxford, it was easier to start trying to get to grips with the theories underpinning the novel. Easier, but not easy. There is an image employed in one section of this novel of a giant chrysanthemum unfolding its petals. It's a disconcerting image when it arises, but looking back it's tempting to see it as a metaphor for the novel itself, in the way that it unfolds in complex patterns, different each time. And the more I read, the more I find to read.

Walking with Tolkien and Macfarlane

As an aside to all the hoo-ha about the new screen adaptation of *The Hobbit*, I wanted to say a little something about *Smith of Wootton Major*, my favourite story by Tolkien. It was originally published as a tiny hardback, almost a board book, which turned up in my classroom library when I was ten or eleven, and which fascinated me, for its size and for the Pauline Diana Baynes illustrations, I think, rather than for the story, which I did not especially remember. It was only some years later, when my interest in Tolkien was already well alight, that I rediscovered the story, made the connection, and finally got my own copy of the little hardback. I reread it over Christmas, in the midst of the current Tolkienfest, and though it has perhaps lost some of the charm it had when I was younger, I still rather like it.

The setting is quasi-medieval, with a dash of Norse saga. The village of Wootton Major (which is, of course, bigger than Wootton Minor) is famous for its craft workers, in particular its cooking. There is a Kitchen that belongs to the Village Council, and the Master Cook is an important personage within the village. His House and the Kitchen are adjacent to the Great Hall, used by the village for its meetings and celebrations, for which the Master Cook caters.

William Morris would have doubtless approved of Wootton Major. Quite apart from its annual round of festivals, it is in every way the perfect medieval fantasy. With a Village Council to keep it running smoothly and apparently no feudal lord, Wootton Major's workers are able to get on with being good at what they do. There is commerce, clearly; Smith, who is at the heart of this story, travels regularly to buy raw materials, and the finished goods go somewhere other than the village, but the ugly details of capitalism are not foregrounded. Everyone is happy and well-fed, warm and decently clothed, not least because this is an allegory rather than an attempt at fantasy realism. The emphasis on artisanship and creativity are clear indicators that we are in familiar Tolkien territory, theorising about the nature, significance and formation of fairy stories. As ever, art and good workmanship go hand in hand.

We first meet the Smith of the title when he is a child, an attendee at the Twenty-Four Feast, a festival which comes about only once every twenty-four years, to which twenty-four children are invited, and that is marked by the creation of a Great Cake, the production of which is considered to be the Master Cook's finest moment. At the story's opening, the village is in turmoil, first because the Master Cook has been away on holiday, something that has never happened before, and then because he has brought home an apprentice from outside the village. Not of course that there is anything wrong with the Cook having an apprentice, or with his coming from away, but one immediately scents disapproval from among the villagers. When, a few years later, the Master Cook suddenly retires and leaves, it does not occur to the village to appoint Alf, the apprentice, to the post of Master Cook. Instead, they appoint Nokes, a mediocre local man, whom Alf assists, and indeed does most of the work for.

Nokes's lack of imagination is specifically reflected in his Great Cake: 'Fairies and sweets were two of the very few notions he had about the tastes of children. Fairies he thought one grew out of; but of sweets he remained very fond'. And so, Alf makes a cake iced with mountain peaks, with a delicate fairy queen on a pinnacle, and Nokes takes the credit. In the cake are twenty-four little trinkets, but also a mysterious silver star that Nokes found in an old box. Alf identifies it as a 'fay-star' and disapproves strongly of Nokes's dismissal of fairy things, but approves putting the star into the cake.

The star is swallowed by a small boy, the blacksmith's son. He is unaware of what he has done, but on his tenth birthday something strange happens:

> He looked out of the window, and the world seemed quiet and expectant. A little breeze, cool and fragrant, stirred the waking trees. Then the dawn came, and far away he heard the dawn-song of the birds beginning, growing as it came towards him, until it rushed over him, filling all the land round the house, and passed on like a wave of music into the West, as the sun rose above the rim of the world.

It will come as no surprise to anyone familiar with how this sort of thing works that Smithson, later Smith, becomes a famous worker of metal. The goods he makes, although primarily 'plain and useful', are 'strong and lasting, but they also had a grace about them, being shapely in their kinds, good to handle and to look at'. Pure William Morris, though unlike Morris, Smith doesn't have a factory behind him.

But Smith is not simply a skilled and inspired worker of metal. 'For Smith became acquainted with Faery, and some regions of it he knew as well as any mortal can: though since too many had become like Nokes, he spoke of this to few people, except his wife and his children'.

And here we reach the section of the story that interests me most, not for what now seems like rather heavy-handed allegorising of the creative process (although Tolkien suggested that this was not intended to be an allegory), but for the journeys themselves, the explorations of this mysterious country of Faery to which Smith has access.

Smith, we are told, travels under the aegis of the fay-star, and 'was as safe as a mortal can be in that perilous country'. He is favoured, if you like, but after several strange encounters, 'he understood that the marvels of Faery cannot be approached without danger'. Nonetheless, 'his desire was still stronger to go deep into the land'. On the surface, this seems quite reasonable and yet I confess to a sense of unease when confronted with this deliberate attempt to penetrate the mysteries of Faery. Of course, one might argue that it is the work of the artist to keep going despite obstacles and obstructions, but I can't help thinking there is an art, too, in knowing when not to go on, and this is something that Smith, for all his gentle and unassuming ways, does not grasp. He is rebuked by the young maiden with whom he dances. We already know her to be the Faery Queen, but Smith will recognise her only years later when summoned to the Queen's presence.

> She wore no crown and had no throne. She stood there in her majesty and her glory, and all about her was a great host shimmering and glittering like the stars above; but she was taller than the points of their great spears, and upon her head there burned a white flame.

She is as far as can possibly be from the doll on Nokes's Great Cake, but forgives this as being better than 'no memory of Faery at all'. After this final meeting, having achieved his heart's desire, Smith 'knew that his way now led back to bereavement'. In fact, although Smith will travel no more to Faery, we are led to understand that his desire to create will continue to be satisfied with hammer and tongs, the understanding being that he has seen his fill and can now distil the life of experience.

This seems slightly at odds with the philosophy at work in *The Hobbit* and *The Lord of the Rings*. In *LOTR*, Frodo recalls how Bilbo used to say 'that there was only one Road; that it was like a great river: its springs were at every doorstep, and every path was its tributary. "It's a dangerous business, Frodo, going out of your door," he used to say. "You step into the Road, and if you don't keep your feet, there is no knowing where you might be swept off to."'

These are journeys fashioned by chance and happenstance, but Smith, for all that he is a learner and explorer, is driven by a goal—to penetrate as far into the land of Faery as he can, and he assumes this as his right.

For Christmas, I received a copy of Robert Macfarlane's much-acclaimed *The Old Ways: A Journey on Foot*. Macfarlane's intention is to explore the ancient tracks that cross the British landscape and the surrounding seas, and establish a connection with the world beyond Britain. It's a fascinating enterprise and Macfarlane writes well. One might, I suppose, invoke the word 'psychogeography', but if one does, one needs to reach for a meaning other than Iain Sinclair inscribing increasingly frivolous lines across London and South-East England.

Like Tolkien's Smith, Macfarlane also has a goal of sorts, as expressed in his Author's Note, 'of walking a thousand miles or more along old ways in search of a route into the past, only to find myself delivered again and again to the contemporary'. '[d]elivered', passive, rather like a parcel, subject to the whims of others. Macfarlane goes on to describe his book as being 'about walking as a reconnoitre inwards, and the subtle ways in which we are shaped by the landscapes through which we move'.

There is a subtle distinction, I think, between 'reconnoitre' and 'explore', a hesitancy that Smith's perambulations through Faery seem to lack. There is an assumption on Smith's part, or Tolkien's, that walking is a mapping, a marking out of territory, whereas for Macfarlane the act of walking is a rediscovery of the mappings of others. Macfarlane's landscapes are real rather than allegorical, but it occurred to me as I read that his landscapes are as inaccessible to me as are the landscapes of Smith's Faery. I can trace his perambulations much as Macfarlane himself is inspired by the journeys made by the poet, Edward Thomas, but does this bring me any closer to what Macfarlane himself is doing?

And the answer is 'no', but it is a complicated no. I can follow Macfarlane's walks in the belief that this somehow enriches and transforms me by proxy, but it would be a mistaken belief and a foolish enterprise. Alternatively, I can be inspired to walk in my own way, shaped by what I encounter, but to do that I must put down Macfarlane's book and walk away from it, finding my own path. I can follow in his footsteps to an extent, maybe sampling the texts he's read over the years (some of which are familiar to me already), but my discoveries must be mine, and mine alone.

Review: *Mothlight* by Adam Scovell

At the heart of Adam Scovell's *Mothlight* (2019) lies a mystery. Why did Phyllis Ewans hate Billie, her sister, so very much? Even to the extent that when the elderly Billie scalds herself with a hot drink, Phyllis ignores her injury until Thomas's grandmother discovers what has happened and has Billie admitted to hospital. In spite of sharing a house with her, Phyllis has effectively turned over all responsibility for her sister's care to Thomas's grandparents. When Billie dies, it is they who arrange her funeral and deal with the legalities. Meanwhile, Phyllis has gone about her business as usual, even as far as going on holiday, apparently determined to forget as soon as possible that her sister ever existed. Photographs of Billie still exist only because Thomas's grandmother, realising what Phyllis Ewans would do, rescued them to ensure she was not forgotten.

As mysteries go, the solution proves to be relatively banal, although underlying it is a matter of profound importance to Phyllis, and to one other person. Yet Thomas, the narrator of the story, will apparently be unable to comprehend the nature of the mystery or its solution, refusing to see what is staring him in the face. Perhaps this is because Thomas himself is out of kilter with the world around him, though why that might be is unclear. We could start with his having been 'a shy and inward-looking boy' (p.11), at least according to his grandmother. Why he spent so much time with his grandparents is not explained, but there is already a sense of something lurking unacknowledged in his early childhood.

His parents seem to be entirely absent, and his grandparents have taken over the parental role. They are also the facilitators of his first meetings with the Ewans sisters, even as they later forbid him to keep in touch with Phyllis Ewans. Their own connection with the Ewans sisters seems to be through business—Thomas's grandfather runs a grocery shop and the Ewanses are customers, albeit customers who rarely pay their bills. With hindsight we may wonder why it was that Thomas's grandparents tolerated this running debt, but it is not a question that Thomas ever asks himself.

As he grows older, Thomas will describe himself thus:

> I became a lonely teenager, interested only in things that could excuse such loneliness. These were namely an insistence on long walks in Wales at the weekend and an increasing interest in moths. (p.28)

Whether the loneliness begat the walking and the pursuit of moths, or whether the walking and the pursuit of moths begat the loneliness is uncertain, not least because Thomas himself seems not to know, but as the novel unfolds it becomes more and more difficult to imagine that Thomas ever had an existence that was separate from either Billie or Phyllis Ewans, so closely is his life entwined with theirs. Indeed, it is almost as though the sisters somehow brought him into existence. When, after Phyllis's death, he painstakingly begins his examination of her possessions, one has the sense that Thomas is as much hunting for himself as for the explanation of Phyllis's animus towards Billie, and the deeper secret that Phyllis herself hides. For all that he has long been obsessed with Miss Ewans, he has come to stand in relationship to Phyllis much as she once stood in relation to Billie, and she is as much a necessary part of his life as she is an annoyance.

By his own admission, Thomas begins to haunt Phyllis's life, infected as he is by 'the parasite of her interests' (p.37), and yet he seeks to suggest too that his early interest is superficial, something he has picked up 'in the way that many do when young and impressionable, and so I took to the most obvious ways to express this interest by fumbling around in an amateurish manner, and with little success' (p.39). But the opening words of the novel undermine all of this:

> To my knowledge, Phyllis Ewans had only two great preoccupations in her long life: walking and moths. An interest in these same two subjects also grew within me after a number of years of knowing her; such was the power of her influence. (p.10)

So which is it to be? Has Phyllis exercised a magnetic influence over Thomas since the moment they met (although, by his own admission, Phyllis first takes an interest in him because Billie has already taken an interest in him), or has Thomas, for whatever perverse reason, modelled himself on Phyllis Ewans, and taken on her interests and perhaps also her life? There is undeniably something strange about the interest that both women take in him, and indeed about their relationship with one another. Billie is described as being 'much older than her sister' (p.11), and Thomas will later say 'they were only sisters in name, and I still harbour daydreams surrounding the likelihood of their differing parentage' (p.11).

One has to ask if in fact Billie is Phyllis's mother rather than her sister. And, eventually, one can't help wondering if Thomas has come to imagine he is Phyllis's son.

Thomas's narrative proceeds in fits and starts, as though he struggles even to find the right place to begin his story. He constantly backtracks, pulled between the past, present, and future, unable to locate himself in his own narrative. Or to put it more accurately, he circles the story like a moth drawn to a flame, only to find himself caught in a death spiral, unable to resist his attraction to the light but unable to explain it either.

At one point, just after Billie's funeral, Thomas talks of 'following blindly towards the light if only to uncover the reason for [Phyllis's] character. This was the curiosity she had imbued in me with parasitic precision' (p.28), implying yet again that Phyllis Ewans is herself responsible for Thomas stalking her, when it is his own fascination that drives him, a fascination that his grandparents do their best to counter:

> I was not allowed to write or converse with her due to the great divide between her and my family [...] and could not have done so at any rate as there was no forwarding address for her new London home. (p.41)

In fact, Thomas is reunited with Phyllis Ewans by accident, when he starts work in a university entomology department and hears her name mentioned. They begin to meet regularly and talk, which is when Thomas begins to sense a deeper mystery. He insinuates himself into her life, becoming her *de facto* carer. Whether she actually requires this is unclear, though as Thomas puts it: 'She needed to be healthy for as long as conceivably possible in order to pass on her secrets to me' (p.68).

What does Phyllis Ewans get from this arrangement, apart from a devoted slave? According to Thomas, it's stories. 'This was an explicit requirement, as Miss Ewans seemed to draw energy from them, almost as nourishment' (p.68), and Thomas devotes much of his time to telling her stories of his experiences while out moth-hunting, altering and embellishing them in the process.

It is at this point that the novel takes an even stranger turn. Or rather, that something that has been happening already becomes more explicit. Thomas calls them 'visions'; the first occurs at the graveside when Billie's coffin is lowered into the grave. Thomas describes himself as being somehow attacked by 'a skein of moths' (p.27), an image drawn from a photograph of Billie with, behind her, an ornament of some sort that looks precisely like 'hordes of moths' (p.27). The fluttering of paper wings will dog Thomas as his mental health begins to deteriorate.

Another time, walking alone in Snowdonia long before meeting Phyllis Ewans again, Thomas experiences a vision of a lake, and a woman staring at him from a jetty. 'I had become aware of my own detachment from reality. I could feel the spray of water from the breeze and sometimes felt a hand holding mine' (p.42). Later, he finds a photograph taken by Phyllis Ewans that appears to document this exact same scene, and asks himself, 'whose hand had held mine' (p.43).

By his own admission these teenage experiences have an 'accumulative, traumatic effect on my own psyche' (p.43). Later, as an adult, the hand returns. In one particularly disturbing scene, Thomas tells Phyllis about a visit to a nature reserve, one they had both visited, though not at the same time.

> I felt a hand grasp my own. It was, I just knew, the same hand that had held mine in the forest in North Wales: a woman's hand, slender and friendly. […] More unnerving than the feeling of the hand in mine was the uncanny change it seemed to make to my own. I looked down to my side in my memory of walking around the reserve and found my hand to be slender and feminine with longer, ill-kept fingernails. (pp.70-71)

The visions increase after Phyllis's death, particularly when Thomas is sorting her photographs, many of which appear to document other places he has visited, though Phyllis herself has repeatedly denied ever having been there. Thomas chooses to interpret these synchronicities as Phyllis Ewans attempting to communicate with him from beyond the grave.

All first-person narrators are unreliable to some extent, but Thomas regularly undermines his own recollections by repeating them with variations, particularly when it comes to his own creation story, rather in the same way that he has repeated stories to Phyllis. Yet, while his interpretation of the strange encounters might be suspect, there is a sincerity in the way he describes them that suggests that he at least believes that they are genuine. It is only after Phyllis's death and on the point of breakdown that Thomas is finally able to solve the central mystery of her life, following a breadcrumb trail of hidden photographs, entries in an address book, and a name: Elsa.

And perhaps Thomas has understood the nature of the 'hauntings', if such they are, all along. Even as a teenager he realised that place is often emphasised in his visions, and later recalls Phyllis Ewans talking of 'place being essentially the ghost of all our lives' (p.44).

> I imagined her amused look, peering over my shoulder when the synchronous moments occurred, and found much likeness between her past and my past, albeit my past already had hers intertwined within it. Such dizzying thoughts would plague my mind as if we were, in fact, the same person: a reflection of simulacra displaced by some impossible mistake. All of this could simply have been down to our shared geographies and our shared passion for moths, but it went deeper than that. (p.44)

The inside of Thomas's head is a rather exhausting, self-pitying, and self-justifying place to be for long periods of time, not to mention having to spend much of the novel watching him fail to grasp what has become obvious to anyone reading it. But this is not where the novel ends, and perhaps is not even where the novel begins. For this is a novel with photographs. In the acknowledgements at the end of this book, Adam Scovell tells us that *Mothlight* is constructed around a series of photos he inherited from his grandmother and the 'real Phyllis', although the circumstances remain vague. The novel acts therefore as a piece of found art, with the photographs acting as prompts and the novel constructed around them.

For all we know, the story being told by Scovell might be the same as the story told by the original photographs, or some version of it, but there is something disconcerting about the idea that these photographs might as easily have come from somewhere else, and that perhaps one day the subjects of the photographs, or their descendants, might accidentally find themselves pressed between the pages of a piece of fiction that has nothing to do with them.

This is perhaps the risk a creator of 'found' pieces runs, and maybe it adds a frisson to the act of creation, but I can never escape the feeling that there is something misguided about such ventures. As readers we become reluctant voyeurs, colluding in someone else's act of appropriation. One might argue that *Mothlight* is in itself one massive act of appropriation, with the author supposedly producing this extra evidence as 'proof' when it is nothing of the sort.

I think, though, that these photographs are not so much about co-opting unsuspecting people as attempting to establish a relationship with another text, W.G. Sebald's *The Rings of Saturn*, a novel that is intensely present throughout this text, especially if one considers the section in which Sebald recalls Thomas Browne's *Musæum Clausum*, and his inclusion of the bamboo walking canes in which two Persian friars smuggled silkworm eggs out of China, a section illustrated with a black and white photograph of a plate from a book of moths. The only visual representation of a moth to be found in *Mothlight* is in Vince Haig's collage cover design, where the moth's wings are a patchwork assemblage of the photographs which lurk at the heart of this novel.

The Rings of Saturn is ostensibly a record of a walk Sebald makes around the coast of East Anglia, in part as a celebration of recovering from illness. Each chapter spirals out from Sebald's direct experience to a consideration of previous inhabitants of East Anglia and beyond, intertwined with the history of Sebald's own family in Germany. Although it is at heart a narrative in search of a rootedness, it is an outward-looking book, even when the narrative returns us to home at the end of each chapter. It is illustrated with a mixture of Sebald's own photographs of his journey and appropriate material from photographic archives. Scovell's approach is, we might say, Sebaldian, but it is also antithetically Sebaldian. While Sebald looks outward, recording his discoveries, Scovell's narrator turns ever inward, somehow finding less and less to record.

Sebald's photographs can be seen in terms of a mundane act, documenting an account of a journey—sophisticated holiday snaps, but holiday snaps nonetheless, their interest lying in the fact of Sebald having taken or curated them—but can the same be said of the photos taken or collected by Phyllis Ewans? What is it that Phyllis is actually documenting?

We can choose to read her photographs as documenting an innocent series of journeys through North Wales, or the covert documenting of a love affair. But, in discussing a particular series of photos Phyllis Ewans takes of Billie's bedroom after Billie's death, Thomas seems to be suggesting that Phyllis uses the photograph to physically imprison her subjects and memories in the same way as she captures and mounts a moth:

> Phyllis Ewans forced the ghost into the space, capturing it within an image of itself to control the existence of its memory. (p.31)

When I searched online, I was surprised to discover that the title *Mothlight* is not original to Scovell, but is also the title of a short collage film made in 1963 by Stan Brakhage. Brakhage's *Mothlight* was created without the aid of a camera; it involved pressing found objects between strips of splicing tape and then running them through a projector. Brakhage was inspired by seeing moths drawn to a candle flame. He identified powerfully with 'these crazy moths [...] flying into the candlelight, and burning themselves to death' and wanted to incorporate them into his artistic practice. He struggled to film live moths and eventually turned to dead ones instead:

> Over the lightbulbs there's all these dead moth wings, and I ... hate that. Such a sadness; there must surely be something to do with that. I tenderly picked them out and start pasting them onto a strip of film, to try to ... give them life again, to animate them again, to try to put them into some sort of life through the motion picture machine.

Watching *Mothlight* is an odd experience. An intense storm of detritus appears on the screen, some of it identifiable as insect body parts, the rest unrecognisable. There is some debate about how the film would originally have been experienced, some suggesting that the whirr and clatter of the projector would evoke the idea of wings beating, while the light from the projector would illuminate the dust motes floating in the air.

It is difficult to know how to respond to these images of carnage; the natural impulse is to construct a narrative around them, but the story, such as it is, lies in the film's provenance rather than the film itself. The insect parts are momentarily animated but they die all over again once the film is run.

Such images in their turn suggest an alternative way to read *Mothlight*;

not as a text constructed around a series of found prompts or clues, but as a collection of artefacts pressed between the pages of another book, tumbling out into the reader's vision, to be made into a story according to how they fall.

By this point the novel is becoming as much a treasure hunt as it is a novel. On the one hand, I'm up for a treasure hunt; on the other, it quickly becomes annoying. Is this what I'm supposed to be doing? Or is the fact that I have to keep going away to do the research a mark against me? But still I continue, uncomfortably aware that as a reader I am now, like Thomas, painstakingly if reluctantly rummaging through the material made available.

The novel's epigraph quotes words spoken by Jacques Derrida in Ken McMullen's 1983 film, *Ghost Dance*. The film itself claims to explore the beliefs and myths surrounding the existence of ghosts and the nature of cinema, which might in turn prompt us to consider *Mothlight* as an act of cinema on the page. I am, I admit, suspicious of this as an idea. I don't think the two are analogous, and inserting pictures into a novel really isn't going to change that.

Ghost Dance is a mesmerising film, reminding me of Chris Marker's *La Jetée*, another 'found' story. Derrida appears near the beginning of the film, as himself, theorising to one of the characters in a highly entertaining cameo. He's obviously enjoying himself, and in turn we enjoy his pleasure at being in the film. But it is what he has to say about ghosts that should be the focus of our attention. 'To be haunted by a ghost is to remember something you've never lived through. For memory is the past that has never taken the form of the present'. And this seems to me to be at the heart of Thomas's experience. He might be reliving Phyllis's memories through his handling of her photographs, or maybe he is trying to relive something that never happened at all.

What really caught my attention though was a section of narrative later in the film. An unseen man says: 'The more things break up, the more myths flourish, attempting to make historical sense out of historical chaos', and this seems to me to be how we are initially invited to read *Mothlight*. Yet, one of the characters poses a question that undermines this: 'Do you think these myths are an attempt to avoid something?'

The question remains, hanging, as the novel ends. As does another question: does this novel need to parade its props and influences so blatantly when the story itself is sufficient?

READING FOR THE FUTURE

Reading for the Future

I read Rebecca Mead's *New Yorker* article about children's reading habits, 'The Percy Jackson Problem' (22/10/2014), with mounting irritation. And then wondered *why* I was so irritated by it. Children's reading habits are of no particular interest to me, except, of course, they are, as they must be to us all, so long as we continue to live in a word-based culture. And despite the doom-laden claims people like to make about the shape of the future, my feeling is that our lives will be dominated by words for a long time to come.

How would I express the content of this paragraph in images? The intermittent claim that the written word is dying generally seems to boil down to the fear of the electronic page superseding the printed, which is not the same thing at all. In my world the two happily co-exist. I prefer print to pixels for study (though at some point I must train myself to annotate electronic texts the way I annotate printed texts), but I will happily read an ebook for pleasure—one tablet device can contain a mighty travelling library, and I need never be stuck without a book again (though it will probably be only a matter of time before I start carrying an extra e-reader just in case).

Whatever else I feel about them, for me books are a delivery system; I am more interested in the content of the text rather than the mode of its presentation. I'm a critic and reader, not a bibliographer or collector. And while I may be sentimental about books at times, as are most of us, I think, I hope this won't ever slide over into a misplaced nostalgia about the superiority of print on paper. (And although there is an argument for print on paper being more permanent, that argument disintegrates, as do the pages, when you look at twentieth-century texts printed on cheap, badly made paper. Ink on parchment is far more durable).

That misplaced, or perhaps over-nourished, nostalgia often resurges in discussions of how we expect children to engage with texts, and in particular, the way in which a story should be told. This, I think, is at the heart of Rebecca Mead's complaint. Her concern is with Rick Riordan's Percy Jackson books, or rather with *Percy Jackson's Greek Gods*, in which our eponymous hero has been asked by his publisher to retell the Greek myths in his own inimitable way. In case, like me, you've missed the Percy Jackson phenomenon, Percy has discovered that he is not an inept adolescent but a demigod, a son of Poseidon and a mortal woman. As a result, he is sent to Camp Half-Blood where he meets various other demigods and starts to learn the skills that befit his position. Hogwarts for classical bastards, you might say.

I've not read any of the Percy Jackson novels, and I suspect a steady diet of them might pall about as rapidly as the Harry Potter series did. But that's not a problem because on the whole they are not meant for middle-aged women, unless perhaps they're studying classical reception in the twenty-first century, and I'm not. The Percy Jackson stories are written with a very specific audience in mind by a man who taught that audience in school and knows what they like. Which is, as Mead put it, 'a slangy, casual style [...] which often reads like a faithful transcription of teen uptalk'.

Mead is at pains to suggest that the books are deliberately written to keep adults away (unlike the Harry Potter novels, which are, of course, for everyone; Mead is keen on a number of occasions to represent the Harry Potter novels as being so much better). From Mead's brief descriptions, it seems that Riordan has very cleverly adapted the gods of classical mythology for contemporary America in a way that appeals to teenagers while being faintly reminiscent of Neil Gaiman's *American Gods*.

So what, you might ask, is Mead's problem? Apart from the sense that there's something going on here that her children have access to while she doesn't? She seems prepared to concede the popularity of the main series, but has baulked at *Greek Gods* because of its being 'inscribed with obsolescence' (Craigslist, iPhones, and the Powerball lottery are invoked) and 'delivered in the kind of jaded teen argot that proves irresistibly cool to kids from grade school up'. Apparently, actual retellings of myths and legends require something else. But what might that be?

If I think of retellings of myths and legends from my childhood, I immediately turn to Roger Lancelyn Green and Ruth Manning-Sanders, both lovely storytellers—indeed, I still own several retellings by Lancelyn Green and reread them with pleasure. But we have to face the fact that the language is rather heightened for modern tastes and while they're texts I would read to a child, they're not texts I'd ask a child to read on their own, though if a child were to find them in the library and read them of their own volition, I'd naturally be delighted.

This, I think, is Mead's difficulty. *Percy Jackson's Greek Gods* is a book a child will happily read by choice, but it is not a text a parent can so easily engage with. Mead as good as admits it herself when she draws on her own reading memories and on school syllabuses and comes up with *Ingri and Edgar Parin d'Aulaires' Book of Greek Myths*, which I suspect is better known in the US than over here. It was originally published in 1962; in other words, it's over fifty years old.

I took a look at the opening sentences:

In olden times, when men still worshiped ugly idols, there lived in the land of Greece a folk of shepherds and herdsmen who cherished light and beauty. They did not worship dark idols like their neighbours, but instead created their own beautiful, radiant gods.

Compare this to:

In the beginning, I wasn't there. I don't think the Ancient Greeks were, either. Nobody had a pen or paper to take notes, so I can't vouch for what follows, but I can tell you it's what the Greeks thought happened.

At first there was pretty much nothing. A lot of nothing.
The first god, if you can call it that, was Chaos—a gloomy, soupy mist with all the matter of the cosmos just drifting around. Here's a fact for you: Chaos literally means the Gap, and we're not talking about the clothing store.

Interesting differences, I think. The d'Aulaires start from the point of view of the people who created these gods, and their gods are beautiful and radiant. No mention of Uranus being castrated, for instance. The Percy Jackson retelling, by comparison, is more upfront and features a chapter called 'The Golden Age of Cannibalism'. The Jackson retelling is colloquial and vivid, like an older sibling telling a story, while the d'Aulaires' version is very serviceable but not really that exciting. Indeed, it seems rather to talk down to its audience. It's clear which version a modern child is going to choose, and a parent who is surprised that it's the Percy Jackson version is clearly not paying attention.

Which brings us to a further problem, again one highlighted by Mead. Should we leave children to find books for themselves or should we be prescriptive? In her article, the *laissez-faire* approach—'just so long as they're reading'—is expressed through reference to Neil Gaiman's lecture given on behalf of the Reading Agency, which argues that it's all too easy to kill a child's enthusiasm for reading by forcing texts on them. It's a view I have some sympathy with.

Like Gaiman, I'm a product of the *laissez-faire* approach to the extent that I was pretty much left to my own reading devices as a child, though I suspect his libraries were rather better stocked than mine, and if the story I heard is true, I did not have sufficient chutzpah as a teenager to blag a reading ticket to the Bodleian in the same way Gaiman managed to obtain one to the British Library. Then again, we both liked books, we both liked reading, we were always going to find ways to discover what we wanted to read. My siblings grew up in exactly the same circumstances as me, with the same outlets available to them. One read nothing but Mills and Boon, while the other eschewed fiction for extremely dense books about the architecture of the Great Western Railway, which he could discuss with great enthusiasm from an early age. My siblings might not read the *Guardian* Reviews or have an opinion about the Booker Prize, but the fact remains that they function perfectly well in the world, perhaps more so than I do.

The contrasting argument comes from Tim Lott, who suggests that if you don't give children and teenagers 'good' stuff to read, they won't find it on their own. In effect, they must be made to find it, or have it forced upon them. His argument, that E.L. James does not lead to Shakespeare, is valid so far as it goes, but then again, did anyone ever claim that it would? Lott's problem seems to be that young adults don't have the grounding in literature they once did, which might point to a problem with the way the educational system delivers its literature teaching these days but does not, I think, suggest that children themselves have changed. Rather as I disliked reading Jane Austen as a teenager, most of the students in my first-year lit class did not enjoy *Northanger Abbey*. On the other hand, they spoke knowledgeably about a wide range of so-named classic writers and at times gave extremely nuanced readings of the texts they enjoyed, not all of which they had read in order to pass exams.

Which is what one would hope for, given that they were students of English Literature. But that is surely the point. They studied in order to be there, they (mostly) wanted to be there. They could read E.L. James for fun, and discuss Shakespeare and Plath as well. Somewhere behind them are all the people who were obliged to read *Romeo and Juliet* to pass an exam, who will never read one of Shakespeare's plays ever again. Are they intellectually impoverished? Maybe, if they decide to go to university later and find they have a lot of catching up to do, but on the whole, probably not.

It seems to me that there are as many experiences of reading as there are people reading, but Mead does not want to admit that the world is not going to end if her children learn about Greek myths from the Percy Jackson stories (she admits herself that they know a good deal as a result of this encounter) rather than from the d'Aulaires' version or older translations. If they're interested, they're going to read more. If they aren't, why make them? We might even end up with a generation of children that know more about the myths than their parents did, because the Percy Jackson books have encouraged them to read further.

The same holds true for other cultural artefacts. I've always thought that if you want to interest teenagers in Shakespeare, take them to see the plays or act in them, rather than reading around the class, as happened in my day. My first trip to the theatre to see Shakespeare performed was a revelation. Or why not try a film adaptation, if it sparks interest? The original text hasn't gone away just because there's a new version in town.

I think we should reject Rebecca Mead's fastidious veiled snobbishness and accept that just because a book does not appeal to us, does not mean it has no value, and that just because we loved Aesop's Fables or The Famous Five, it doesn't follow that our children will too. The world has moved on.

The Children of Green Knowe and *A Traveller in Time* – a tale of two novels

Among other Christmas presents I received the DVDs of the TV adaptations of *The Children of Green Knowe* (1986, from the 1954 novel by Lucy M. Boston) and *A Traveller in Time* (1978, from the 1939 novel by Alison Uttley). The two novels have been favourites of mine since I was young, and I remember enjoying both screen adaptations immensely when they were first broadcast. I've seen *Children* a number of times over the years, thanks to a video transfer available on YouTube, but *Traveller* only came out on DVD in late 2015. The BBC never repeated it after its initial airing and I had been longing to see it again.

The short version of this is going to be that the TV adaptation of *Children* has lasted far better than the adaptation of *Traveller*, in part for technical reasons, in part because the adaptation of *Traveller* manages to highlight all of the novel's weaknesses and none of its virtues. There is less than ten years between the two adaptations, but that decade saw a number of technical advances. *The Children of Green Knowe* looks as fresh as ever; it's difficult to believe that it is thirty years old. *A Traveller in Time*, only eight years older, is visually awful; in parts it looks terribly bleached, and there is occasional interference visible on the screen. This was clearly a quick and dirty transfer to DVD, with little in the way of titivation. The shifts between studio scenes and outdoor scenes are often awkward, and the painted backdrops of 'outside' glimpsed through doorways are quite obviously fake. The soundtrack is also very fuzzy at times (though the choice of an over-ripe orchestral version of *Greensleeves* as the theme tune is a problem in itself). It's made even more awkward by a decision to update the story, moving it into 'the present', a decision which provided some unexpected visual distractions that I'll return to.

Before looking in more detail at the adaptations, I'd like to step back slightly and revisit the novels. *The Children of Green Knowe*, I've written about before, but not *A Traveller in Time*, and what had not occurred to me before my Christmas viewing was how similar in some ways the two novels are. Each concerns a child moving effortlessly, inexplicably, through time, becoming caught up in the stories of the people they meet, in the history of a house, and then having to face up to the deaths, long since, of the people they have encountered.

I tend to refer to these novels as 'ghost stories', simply because that's what I've always called them, but the very title of *A Traveller in Time* indicates it is a story of time-slippage, though the situation in *The Children of Green Knowe* is made more complicated by the seventeenth-century Oldknow children's knowledge that they are dead. Here, it is not Tolly who moves through time, so much as the Oldknow children who fade in and out of Tolly's own time.

And in both novels, the houses—Green Knowe and Thackers—stand as characters in their own right. Both fictional houses have real-life counterparts: Hemingford Grey manor house, owned by Boston herself, and Dethick Manor farmhouse, originally owned by the Babington family, and known to Alison Uttley in her childhood. Each house is dominated by a woman, Mrs Oldknow, and Tissie/Dame Cicely Taberner, respectively, who functions as the *genius loci* of the place, and possibly bears some resemblance to the author in each instance. Beyond that, it would not be unreasonable to say that Boston and Uttley themselves had a certain amount in common, given that they both seem to have had rather challenging personalities.

Both novels begin with a decision to send the child protagonists away to the country. In *Green Knowe*, Toseland, or Tolly, is to spend Christmas with a great-grandmother he didn't know he had, rather than languish at the rather dull boarding school where he normally lives; in *A Traveller in Time*, the three Cameron children, and Penelope in particular, have been unwell, and their mother decides to send them to an aunt in Derbyshire to recuperate.

The first major event in each novel involves a train journey, with the protagonists moving away from all that is familiar, heading deep into the uncertainty of the countryside. These journeys present us with a picture of close-knit community; in both cases, the children are identified by other passengers as not being from around here, and in neither case is there a clear sense that they *belong*, even though they have a family connection to the area. Tolly's first name, Toseland, is recognised as a local place-name but oddly, despite the family being known locally, there seems to be no awareness that Toseland is also a family forename. For all that he has lived in the interim setting of a boarding school, we are to understand Tolly Oldknow as returning to *his* house. Boston specifically frames his arrival as a return, and has Tolly anxiously ask if the house is partly his.

Penelope's attachment to Derbyshire is indicated first by her middle name, Taberner; it is her mother's maiden name, and the family name of the aunt and uncle, brother and sister, with whom they will be staying. Penelope, we will also discover, is also a Taberner family name, so Penelope's local connection is doubly emphasised. Her family name, though, is Cameron—her mother married a Scot, and I think from this we are supposed to see Penelope as both belonging but being somewhat 'other' too, in that a part of her comes from even further north.

You could say that both novels are about strengthening that connection to a family place by involving the protagonists in the history of houses that are, in a sense, also 'family'. The treatment of the two houses marks the first major point of divergence between the two stories, a divergence that I think makes *The Children of Green Knowe* the more successful of the two novels as a story. Boston provides Hemingford Grey/Green Knowe with a mostly fictional history, but begins from a point of close familiarity with the house itself. Uttley never actually lived at Dethick/Thackers, although as a child she played with the child who did live there, and this only partial familiarity does show. Her descriptions of the house are doubtless accurate, but there is always the sense that they come from an outsider.

I can't help feeling that Uttley rather badly wanted to live at Dethick—so much so that when she bought a house in Beaconsfield from her royalties, she called it Thackers, although it was about as unlike Thackers or Dethick as one might possibly imagine—and that *A Traveller in Time* is her attempt to write herself, as Penelope, into that history. There is an obsession with the house as artefact that isn't present in *Children* in the same way. And while Tolly doesn't have to claim his family history because it comes to him, in *Traveller* Penelope's real fascination is with the Babingtons rather than her own Taberner family. The question that is never posed is how, if this is the Babingtons' house, does it come to belong to the Taberners now? The implication is that they reside there as stewards of the Babington history, but a few uncomfortable questions are elided.

The TV adaptation of *Children* was mostly filmed at Hemingford Grey; even if one didn't know that, one would feel a 'rightness' about the adaptation's setting, inside and out, in a way that just isn't there with the adaptation of *Traveller*. My sense that the interior shots are mostly studio-based arises simply because of the enormous amount of room available for the actors and crew to move around in, not forgetting those unconvincing outdoor backdrops glimpsed through open doors. The shots of the modern-day farm interior, the kitchen at least, do seem to have been filmed on location, which makes the juxtaposition all the more uncomfortable.

The second major difference between the two novels lies in the protagonists themselves. In *Green Knowe*, Tolly is seven years old. Alec Christie was twelve when he played Tolly in the TV series, and I'd place the character he plays as being about nine or ten. Either way, in both novel and series, he is a very active child, exploring, investigating, asking questions, eager for encounters with the other children living in the house and for stories about them. As Mrs Oldknow comments, he's ready for anything. He is, if you like, coming into his birthright, finding out who and what he is. He might start as an outsider, but he is very quickly subsumed into the house and its history.

The central theme of the novel is celebratory restoration. Tolly's arrival at Green Knowe sets in train a process of rejuvenation. While his great-grandmother is aware of the existence of the children, it is Tolly's open desire to engage with them that initiates a series of discoveries—the key to the children's toy chest, Linnet's bracelet previously lost in the shrubbery—as well as a series of magical experiences. We might suppose that the encounters with the children are simply the imaginings of a lonely little boy stuck with an elderly relation, except that Mrs Oldknow matter-of-factly confirms Tolly's account of things. She might be humouring him of course, except that Boggis the gardener, as much a *genius loci* as Mrs Oldknow, also knows the stories, and can add one or two of his own. By doing so, either Boggis is engaged in some sort of unholy conspiracy with Mrs Oldknow, or he acts as a confirming second party.

This is all very real if you are part of the family, and Boggises have been associated with the house for as long as Oldknows. For the most part, the novel is remarkably unthreatening. Tolly is being inducted into the history of his family, and the house where they live, the house that by implication will one day be his. *The Children of Green Knowe* is an introduction to his inheritance, tangible and intangible.

By contrast, *A Traveller in Time* is an account of that which has been lost and can never be regained. It begins as nostalgia and ends as mourning the loss of old ways. Penelope is clearly writing as an adult, describing childhood experiences. She notes how, when offered a treat, she chose to rummage through the old things in a family chest. We are, I think, supposed to see Penelope as being a little old-fashioned, even in her own time. And if Tolly is part of the presiding family in his house, Penelope Taberner Cameron is very different. She is much more passive, an observer but not a participant, and I think this is in part because she is a Boggis rather than an Oldknow, so to speak.

Aunt Tissie is aware of the continuing presence of the Babingtons at Thackers, but 'the secret of Thackers' is something that is not discussed. The job of Taberners is to keep secrets, and as a Taberner, Penelope can never be a participant, only a guardian. The novel may try to account for this by representing her as a sickly, solitary child, as 'fey', but the fact is that the linear inevitability of history precludes her from doing anything other than witnessing the beginning of the downfall of the Babington family. She can tell Francis (and in the novel, Anthony) what is going to happen, but insofar as either of them believes her, neither of them can do anything to prevent it.

One of the enduring difficulties of the novel is how to account for Penelope's presence at Thackers, how to explain her comings and goings, her strange clothes, the fact that unlike most girls of that time, she can read and write, but unlike her aunt, she has not the remotest idea of how to do anything practical, such as identifying herbs. Her position at Thackers is constructed in such a way that she is constantly privileged and her odd behaviour excused; she rides out with Francis Babington, waits on his mother and step-grandmother, but works in the kitchen too. And to round this off, Francis falls in love with her, and she with him. It is the perfect teenage relationship.

This is not to say that *A Traveller in Time* does not have a story, but that story always circles back to what cannot be done. Anthony has lost his heart to Mary, Queen of Scots, and is plotting to rescue her while she is at Wingfield. An old tunnel between Wingfield and Thackers is to be reopened and the Queen is to be brought along it to Thackers and thence onward to freedom. The plot will inevitably be discovered, though for the purposes of Uttley's story, Babington will not be implicated, and a handy fall of snow will conceal the digging.

But while this may be the story, it is not the plot, not least because Penelope already knows what will happen. There is a sub-plot in the novel in which Arabella, the Babingtons' jealous cousin, imprisons Penelope underground in an abandoned tunnel. She is rescued by Jude, a mute farm boy, who seems to be more fully aware of Penelope's nature than everyone else. But even though this sub-plot is given more prominence in the TV adaptation (complete with Arabella roasting the wax figure of Penelope that she's made), it's not really what the novel is about.

According to Denis Judd's biography of Alison Uttley, *Alison Uttley: Spinner of Tales*, the novel was originally rejected by her publisher and had to be reworked, though he provides no detail as to what this involved. He does though refer to Uttley describing *A Traveller in Time* as the 'darling of my heart', and sees Uttley as having written herself into the novel as Penelope. He seems to regard the novel as being more successful in its construction than I do.

If Alison Uttley does have one great theme as a writer, it is her childhood in rural Derbyshire, at Castle Top Farm. Her love of the countryside, and of rural ways, is reflected in much of her output, from *The Country Child* (1931), through the myriad Little Grey Rabbit books, to *A Traveller in Time*. By far the most successful parts of the novel are the descriptions of country life—if we assume that the novel is originally set in the late 1920s and early 1930s, we might also assume that Uttley is drawing on memories of her own childhood. Indeed, many of the scenes, customs, and events described in *The Country Child* resurface in *A Traveller in Time*, where they are used to establish a continuity between the Elizabethan period and the novel's present day.

The narrative disparity between the two novels is also reflected in their TV adaptations. Although both stay close to their original stories, the adaptation of *A Traveller in Time* inevitably elides many of the long, lingering descriptions of farm life, meaning that there is less material for the screenwriter to work with. The adaptation of *The Children of Green Knowe* is visually gorgeous. The opening sequence, as Tolly travels deeper into a flooded landscape, swapping train for taxi, taxi for the taxi-driver's back (a metaphorical nod to St. Christopher, who plays an important role later in the story) is especially magical.

The adaptation of *A Traveller in Time* has more of the atmosphere of a ghost story. While the weather in the novel is often warm and sunny, in the TV version it is bleak, misty, grey, and altogether lacking in joy. I'm not sure where they filmed the outdoor shots, but the crew seem to have deliberately gone looking for the most unprepossessing fields they could find. Even the railway station is not exactly a gateway to adventure. The shots purportedly in the farmhouse garden appear less magical than they should, and the shots of Wingfield are grim in the extreme. I suppose it could be argued that this vaguely threatening atmosphere is a more appropriate tie-in with the clandestine nature of Penelope's experiences, but it seems to me to be a strange artistic decision.

I noted earlier that the story has been updated for a modern audience, although the visual clues were maddeningly vague at times. Mostly, one had to rely on what Penelope was wearing as a guide, given the farm, the farm vehicles, and the Taberners themselves were behind the times. In the original story, Penelope would have been dressed in clothes which, if outlandish by Elizabethan standards, could at least be excused as 'London fashion'. 1970s Penelope by comparison would one moment be in jeans, boots, and a smock top like any normal teenager of that time, and the next wearing something oddly formal or out of time. A quilted dressing-gown is frequently brought into play, because it can pass muster as some sort of over-dress that isn't too un-Elizabethan. Also, a cloak that no self-respecting teenager of that period would have been seen dead in.

In conclusion, I have to admit that in spite of my fond recollections of it, I am disappointed in the TV version of *A Traveller in Time*. I'm glad to have seen it again, and to have it to hand for reference, but the novel, for all its faults, wins hands down. The series is awkwardly put together, emphasising the novel's flaws, and just can't seem to find a story for itself. By contrast, the screen adaptation of *The Children of Green Knowe*, despite its own occasional moments of clunkiness (we'll draw a veil over the business of the walking tree) is joyful and magical, capturing the spirit of the novel very effectively. It's a lovely thing to look at. Watching it will, I think, become a Christmas tradition, rather like rewatching *The Box of Delights*. There is the same sense of craftsmanship about it.

'We were all monsters and bastards and we were beautiful' – Rachel Hartman's *Seraphina*

I had an odd moment of *déjà-vu* when I began reading Rachel Hartman's *Seraphina*. Its narrative tone reminded me intensely of something else, and I eventually realised that it was Alison Uttley's *A Traveller in Time* (1939). At first glance, it would be difficult to find two novels with less in common, but I do think they have certain similarities, which raises some interesting questions about the way in which children's (or teen or young adult) fiction has or hasn't changed over the last seventy years. They also have one very obvious difference, which will be addressed in due course.

Uttley's novel is either a ghost story or time-slip, depending on how you choose to frame it. The story's main character, Penelope Taberner Cameron, is sent to recuperate after an illness with relations who live in the ancient Derbyshire farmhouse of Thackers (Dethick Manor, in reality, and owned at the time of writing by former *Blue Peter* presenter Simon Groom).

The house was once owned by the Babington family, and during the reign of Queen Elizabeth I became the focus of a plot, organised by Anthony Babington, to rescue Mary, Queen of Scots from imprisonment at nearby Wingfield Manor. It is to this historical moment that Penelope finds herself travelling, a process managed simply by her walking into a room or turning a corner in the passage and finding she has gone back in time. Through her, the reader learns the story of Anthony Babington, though, perhaps wishing to spare her young readers some anguish, the story closes before Babington is imprisoned in the Tower of London and then executed in a fashion so horrible Elizabeth ordered his co-conspirators to be hanged instead. In the novel, we are left to breathe easy because snow has concealed the tunnel's entrance, while Francis, Anthony's younger brother, is making plans to flee to Paris, as the young men of Catholic families so often did.[1]

Seraphina, on the other hand, could be described as a full-blown immersive fantasy. It deals with the life of Seraphina Dombegh, the only child of a father who is both emotionally absent and over-protective, and a mother who died giving birth to Seraphina. Through her own determination, Seraphina has pursued an education—she is a talented musician—and has found herself a job as assistant to Viridius, the court composer. What drives the novel, however,

---

[1] I have found it difficult to establish what happened to the historical Francis Babington, though he was later described as being 'unthrifty', which is presumably in part why the house and lands passed out of the family during that time.

is the quest to discover the murderer of the Prince of Goredd, a mystery in which Seraphina becomes involved. Rufus's death threatens the peace that has been established between humans and dragons, some of whom live among the humans, taking on human form.

Both novels are told in the first person, though from what point in the narrators' lives is hard to tell. The tone in each case is detached, cool, leaning towards the analytical, as though they are observing the experiences of their younger selves with a certain wry amusement at the follies of youth.

Both protagonists are solitary, bookish, imaginative, the difference being perhaps that for Penelope, solitude is a choice. She does not seem to mind either being alone or being thought odd. Indeed, she seems to be proud of her strangeness; in a family of three children, and the youngest to boot, it marks her out, makes her distinctive. Seraphina, on the other hand, is by her own admission incredibly lonely. Her solitary life has been forced on her by her father, for reasons that have only recently become clear to her. Throughout her life, he has seemed to obstruct her every wish, and she has, according to her own account, been forced to find ways round his prohibitions, often forcing him into acquiescence by directly challenging him.

In older children's books, serious illness often prompts the transformation which places the child in a position to begin their adventures. In the case of *A Traveller in Time*, both of Penelope's visits to Thackers are precipitated by illness, while for Seraphina, witnessing the Treaty procession in which the dragons shed their human form brings about the first of her mysterious visions, and causes a physical transformation, namely the appearance of scales, and hence the revelation that her mother was a dragon and she is part-dragon herself.

For Penelope, her convalescence is a time of excitement and discovery—her Aunt Tissie knows about the ghosts, is aware that Penelope can see the Babingtons, and is thus a kind of guarantor for her safety in that other world. For Seraphina, the dangers only multiply as she must now conceal her scales as well as learn to cope with the side-effects of her visions, which are severely debilitating. Her guide in this new world in which she finds herself is her uncle, Orma, a dragon constantly under scrutiny for his undragonlike behaviour, and thus less helpful as a guarantor of her safety, though he is not entirely without resources.

Another feature that marks both narratives is what one might call privileged access. Penelope is able to be in contact with all levels of society at Thackers, and though it is initially noted that she should not be in this place or that, it is remarkable how quickly everyone accepts her intermittent presence, even though her tie to the place is through Cicely Taberner, the housekeeper and a servant, albeit a powerful one. One might argue that Penelope's friendship with Francis Babington grants her a kind of social passepartout but even that friendship is effectively a narrative contingency. The narrative does to some extent acknowledge Penelope's extraordinary privilege, and at least one character is deeply suspicious of it, although cast as the villain of the piece for making the point that this is all wrong.

Seraphina, on the other hand, although she has more right to a measure of privilege, given her father's role, given her talent, given her job (and through that access of a sort to the members of the royal family) never stops pointing out that she is a nobody. Of course, she has taught herself to be as self-effacing as possible as a survival mechanism, but this constant underlining of the fact becomes wearing.

In both narratives, Penelope and Seraphina need this level of access in order to tell their stories. It's a matter of narrative contingency, but in the case of Penelope in particular we're being asked to take a rather large step in terms of willing suspension of disbelief. One could argue that Penelope's situation is at least partly rationalised by the fact that she is dealing with ghosts or, just possibly, figments of her own imagination. For Seraphina, the danger is real, and in deadly earnest.

And, finally, there is the upstairs-downstairs romance. In Penelope's case, her relationship with Francis is spread across time and therefore doomed to failure, the implicit moral being that one should know one's place, both socially and in time. For Seraphina, however, things are different: Lucian Kiggs, the bastard prince, can show an interest in her, an interest which she can in theory reciprocate, though of course her mixed parentage may well get in the way of this. On the other hand, Kiggs's illegitimate status may offset that. Nobility of birth is in this instance trumped by outsider status.

It is here that the stories begin to diverge. The Babington family and their loyal servants, including the Taberners, are already out of step with the times by keeping to the old Catholic ways, and as the reader already knows, the weight of history is against them. The plot to rescue Mary, Queen of Scots will be discovered, the fate of Anthony Babington, and indeed of Mary herself, is set in stone. Without transforming *A Traveller in Time* into an alternative history, which is clearly not Uttley's intention, there is no other way the story can play out. Whatever Uttley's political and religious views might be, I am sure her attachment to the story has more to do with its Derbyshire setting and childhood memory than with any need to make redress for the treatment of Catholics during the sixteenth and seventeenth centuries. Uttley knows how her story will end, and is content to interpolate it into the broader sweep of history, without questioning its outcome.

In *Seraphina*, things are much more complex and troubling, politically and theologically. The setting might be most aptly described as 'cathedral city gothic'. In its general tone it reminded me of Elizabeth Goudge's *Towers in the Mist* and *The Dean's Watch*, and on occasion Lucy M. Boston's *The Children of Green*

Knowe. There is also a dash of steampunk in the quigs' love of mechanisms. The story has many of the visible trappings of medievalism: characters wear 'houppelandes', there are knights, albeit banished ones, and the presence of a Christian church much preoccupied with saints. Goredd (and note the Celtic inflection of that double d) is a mature medieval world that has persisted for many centuries. Technology seems to have remained mostly in stasis among the humans, and there is something that smacks of children's fairy tales; take, for example, the ethereal loveliness of Princess Glisselda.

And here indeed be dragons. Dragons that can transform themselves into human shape if need be. Dragons that have signed a peace treaty with the humans. Dragons that have sophisticated technologies. Dragons that live among humans, though rather as we might equip a cat with a bell to alert its potential prey, or a leper with a bell to warn people away, so dragons must also wear bells to alert us to the fact that they are not what they seem when they are moving among humans (except, of course, for the few given permission to conceal their origins). I wonder how many people raised an eyebrow when they read 'Orma didn't need facial hair to pass' (p.12), or at the point where Orma speculates as to whether the saints whose writings inveigh against human-dragon miscegenation (and this word is used specifically) 'had experience with half-breeds' (p.36). We are no longer in a place where a girl can dally artlessly with an historical character, but in a world where something altogether darker is taking place.

But how are we supposed to read the dragons in this novel? Hartman's choice of terms like 'passing' prompts us to think of the Jim Crow laws, and light-skinned African-Americans 'passing' for white. Similarly, when I see 'half-breed' I immediately think of how this word is used with reference to Native Americans, and in particular how those of mixed race have been mistreated as outsiders in Anglo-American society. Should I read the quigs, the dragons who cannot transform, as representing undocumented immigrants and border-crossers? For that matter, given that faint hint of Celticism in Goredd, do we read the dragons as Welsh, oppressed yet again by the English? And that's before we get on to the form of Christianity practised in the novel, a mix of the Celtic and the Catholic, filled with many obscure saints, not a few of whom appear to be dragon-slayers, useful when one needs to invoke religion in order to attack the Other.

Dragons are of course the traditional fairy tale enemy of humanity. We have dragons that must be appeased with human sacrifice, and dragons that dispense wisdom, dragons that represent order, dragons that symbolise chaos. In *Seraphina*, we have two extremes. On the one hand, the quigs lurk on the edges of society, like beggars, barely able to communicate with anyone, shunned by pretty much everyone they encounter. They are, if you like, the descendants of Tolkien's Smaug—only the nature of the hoard has changed.

On the other, we have the dragons who can disguise themselves as humans, though they are not thought of, so far as I can see, as lower-class humans. They have a diplomatic or academic role, mediating between dragons and humans, or studying humans. They are represented as unfailingly logical, baffled by the morass of human emotions. They are portrayed as thinking machines, and essentially Other.

The reader's contact with dragons is mediated through Seraphina, the half-breed, positioned as the bridge between the two groups, but it is a very particular view. For all that Seraphina protests she is a court nobody, for all that we are told that Orma is not a conventional dragon, we are nonetheless dealing with people who possess privilege, who are variously protected, people who are atypical within their communities, and we are then expected to use them as the point from which to extrapolate ideas about all dragons. Even in fictional terms this is too easy, too reductive.

One might argue that Hartman is making the point that this is what we already do, but that argument can be countered by saying yes, so why do it all over again? One cannot overlook the fact that this novel is told exclusively from a human point of view; even Seraphina is identified from the beginning as a human with dragon scales rather than as a dragon with human skin. We never see the dragons on their home ground. To parley with humans, they must mimic humans. The frame of the argument is always human, never dragon. To sympathise with the dragons is not only to fraternise with the enemy but also, perhaps, to become like them.

On top of that, the view we receive is broadly that of the governing classes, the insiders. The 'lower orders' are anxious about the presence of dragons, even though many of them are far too young to remember the war with the dragons, thus it is not clear what their anxiety arises from. The Sons of St. Ogdo roam the streets, pretty much looking for dragons to beat up. One is invited to substitute other identities in that sentence, and to an extent the analogy exists, but it is a crude, one-size-fits-all approach, and I for one wish that Hartman had been bolder in dealing with this.

As if this external struggle weren't enough, we must also deal with Seraphina's struggle with the voices in her head. They are not, as we might suppose, hallucinations or visions but actual voices, the thoughts of other human-dragon hybrids. As it turns out, there's a fairly large group of half dragons, passing for human, some even in the court itself, but also apparently representing human diversity in that they are male, female, not all from Goredd (at one point Seraphina notes how one of them, Lars, speaks Goreddi as though his mouth is full of pebbles). As Seraphina's hallucinations are transformed into people, it is perhaps worth noting that some of them at least exercise autonomy, so they aren't precisely Seraphina's 'gang', though the sense of her authority persists.

There's also a murder mystery to solve, almost the least interesting thing about the novel, though it is a competently executed mystery thriller. On the other hand, there is no denying that the novel's ending is as convenient as that of *A Traveller in Time*. Seraphina and Kiggs may be in love with one another but he is also Princess Glisselda's fiancé and she is now a terribly young ruler of Goredd and needing all the help she can get. For now, Kiggs and Seraphina must bide their time; this is another relationship that must remain invisible.

So, what to make of *Seraphina*, a finalist in the Kitschies Golden Tentacle Award for first novel? Entertaining? Yes, very. For all it seems to reach right back to Uttley's novel, I like the narrative tone, and Seraphina is, in her way, a narrator appealing in her determination to succeed and in her honesty about her struggle. Intelligent? That's more problematic in that Hartman is dealing with difficult issues, which I applaud, but in ways that frequently make me deeply uneasy. It's a well-written novel, one overflowing with thoughts and ideas, but one that always seems to pull back just when things are getting satisfyingly complicated.

Which leads me finally to 'progressive'. Is this novel actually progressive? Superficially, it might seem to be, given the issues it appears to be tackling, but as I hope I've shown, superficiality is something of a problem. We skate across the surface of the issues rather than diving into them, and we tackle them from a very particular point of view: bluntly, a white Euro-American point of view. The subaltern dragon is mediated through the mimic human. The assumption, no matter how little it is actually articulated, is that human form trumps dragon form. Dragons need to learn from humans, particularly about such complex things as emotions, but humans seem not to need to take anything from dragons. Even the dragons regard humans as superior.

And then there is the narrative structure: however sophisticated it might appear, we still have a narrative shaped by privilege, and a romance that can never come to fruition because of the unequal status of the two participants.

In all, this is a novel that could have gone far but doesn't go far enough.

Reading *Diana Wynne Jones: Children's Literature and the Fantastic Tradition* by Farah Mendlesohn

Like many people, I first came to Diana Wynne Jones's novels as an adult rather than as a child. More than twenty-five years later, I still read her fiction with the greatest pleasure, as do many other adults I know. I mention this specifically to support Farah Mendlesohn's introductory contention: while Diana Wynne Jones may be a writer of children's books, her audience is much broader, and it is therefore entirely legitimate 'to discuss her not as a children's writer but as a fantasy writer' (p.xiii). I cannot speak for anyone else, but I always found Jones's fiction to be 'different' in a way that wasn't easy to explain but that felt good to read. Her books are well-wrought, which always brings satisfaction for an attentive reader, and I was pleased with the way that Jones often employed mundane, contemporary settings and characters. But there was also a sense that Jones was doing something else with the fantastic, something unusual, and doing it in plain view of the reader if she could but understand what was going on. This sense of 'doing something else' is what Mendlesohn sets out to examine.

I have more than once described Jones's work as subverting fantastic tropes, which is why I find Mendlesohn's overall thesis so intriguing. She argues that 'Jones is both a fiction writer and a critic', and contends that 'her fiction can be viewed as a sustained metafictional critical response to the fantastic' (p.xiii). This suggests then that Jones is not so much subverting the genre as holding it up to scrutiny in a subtle but distinctive way. As Mendlesohn puts it, '[f]iction as written by Diana Wynne Jones is a critical process' (p.191). We know from *The Tough Guide to Fantasyland* that Jones is both critically aware and critical of the construction of fantasy as a genre; some of the entries in the *Tough Guide* were memorably scathing about the assumptions made by those writers who used the trappings of the fantastic without understanding what made them work. Jones's approach, Mendlesohn argues, is very different.

Jones's fiction constantly tests the reader's expectations and assumptions about fantasy, and also about reality. The magical and mimetic worlds both operate according to certain conventions, but nothing is quite as it seems. We might wish to assume a comforting binary opposition of real and not-real, magical and mundane, good and bad, but Jones points out time and again that nothing is ever that straightforward. Mendlesohn suggests that in *Wilkins' Tooth*, Jones is developing 'an alternative cartography of fantasy' (p.7), picking up on the concept of the rough *Tough Guide*. In other words, Jones is teaching her readers how to read fantasy, and more importantly, how to interpret and question what they're reading. More than that even, she is also engaging with what might be considered the standard fare of 'children's fiction' and querying how it is presented to a child reader.

Agency and the passage to adulthood are topics that figure in literature for children, and in fantasy literature as well. The acquisition of power is often used to signal a move into adulthood; too often, however, the assumption of an author is that power automatically confers maturity. By contrast, Mendlesohn argues, Jones 'reverses the route map to adulthood'. It is therefore the acquisition of agency that brings power, and Jones is concerned in all her novels to address the notion of what it means to acquire agency and to gain access to power. If agency is about making conscious choices, with choice comes consequence and also responsibility.

As Mendlesohn points out, Jones's characters are constantly having to address the meaning of power, and indeed are learning to operate within moral constraints in order to exercise their powers most effectively. Throughout Jones's work, characters are brought to the understanding that intent is as important as external behaviour when they attempt to use magic. It's far too easy to assume that magic confers agency, when in fact to use magic effectively one must be aware of how power can and should be used. 'It is the intelligent negotiation with magic, rather than magical power, that leads to agency' (p.44).

The most complex chapter of Mendlesohn's study focuses on the way in which Diana Wynne Jones uses time in her novels. Jones's use of time travel is itself complicated; Mendlesohn notes that her approach is 'distinctively that of the writer of science fiction' (p.53) rather than merely using time-travel as a fantastical convenience. Here she draws on John Ellis McTaggart's theory of A-Series and B-Series (relative and absolute) time to examine the ways in which Jones uses past events to establish the story in the present, and also destabilises the use of a linear narrative in order to move back and forth through the story, presenting it from different viewpoints. For anyone used to a straightforward linear presentation of a series of events, the time shifts in Jones's writing can be a challenge, but for those who relish complexity, Jones's fiendish plotting is a joy. Here, Mendlesohn's theoretical exposition opens up the beauty of the narratives' construction in a whole new way and effectively demonstrates the skill behind the plotting.

For me and for many other readers, the most striking feature of Jones's narratives is the way in which she renders the mundane fantastic. This is sometimes achieved through the setting—Jones was one of the first writers I ever encountered, along with Ann Halam (Gwyneth Jones) and Alan Garner, who seemed to be comfortable about placing characters in worlds recognisably analogous to our own, with characters for whom the encounter with the magical, the inexplicable, was bruising rather than comfortable and easily resolved—but just as often through the kinds of domestic dilemmas her characters encounter. The key seems to be that 'the dividing line between magic and reality is deliberately blurred, unassailable by logic' (p.136). Jones's novels 'manipulate irony and equipose to challenge the presumptions behind the concept of realist fiction, and to reverse some of the conventional patterns of fantasy' (p.137). This I think is at the heart of Jones's work, that desire to challenge and test conventions.

Mendlesohn further contends that: 'Each novel Diana Wynne Jones has written takes children through the art of logic, the nature of story, a writing and editing course, and a discussion of ethics. She demands of them that they continually question the assumptions on which any happy ending rests' (p.193). This is true, I think, for all readers of Jones's work, whatever their age, if one accepts that reading is a serious engagement between reader and author. I began this review by saying that for me there was a sense that Jones was doing something else with the fantastic. As a result of reading Mendlesohn's book, I genuinely feel I have a better understanding of what Jones is trying to do with her oeuvre. If Mendlesohn's argument is correct—and it is certainly extremely convincing—the implications of Jones's undeclared project are breathtaking, and Mendlesohn has done a great service in laying them out for further discussion.

More Than This by Patrick Ness

In the moments before one dies, one's entire life supposedly flashes before one's eyes. It is also claimed that drowning is a peaceful death. The opening to *More Than This*, Patrick Ness's latest novel, suggests that this is far from the truth.

In fact, it is a moot point as to whether the protagonist of *More Than This* actually drowns. In two and a half exquisitely drawn-out pages, he is rolled by the waves, strength diminished by the cold water, then battered against the rocks, the bones of his body broken one by one, his lungs gradually filling with water, until finally his skull is fractured as the current throws him against the rocks and he dies.

The prologue suggests that even if a drowning teenager doesn't review his life in an instant, time is nonetheless subjectively altered. A brief moment becomes an eternity as a life is snuffed out. And after the terrible exactitude of that death, the 'afterlife' seems, perhaps appropriately, to be a little fuzzy. The boy drifts now in time, confused as to whether he is alive or dead. On the one hand, this might be some sort of religious experience—limbo, purgatory, oblivion. Or it might be, and Ness hints gently at such a possibility, a hospital, with the boy on life support.

Such is Ness's skill as a writer that in a couple of brief chapters he has laid out a wealth of possibilities for the rest of the novel. It might be an extended flashback: how did the boy come to be in the sea? Or this might be an adventure in a life beyond the corporeal. Or even, given the way in which Ness stretches time, a dream, though this would seem too conventional. In the space of a few pages, Ness has teasingly guided the reader through a series of fatal possibilities, yet it is impossible to accept the boy's awakening, when it finally arrives, as anything but the real thing. Perhaps it is the presence of the weeds.

> Every yard is as overgrown as this one. Some that had lawns are now sprouting fields of grass, shoulder-high. The pavement of the road is cracked, too, with more weeds almost obscenely tall growing out of the middle, a few approaching the status of trees. (p.21)

It is hard to believe that an afterlife or a dream will have weeds, or dust, or dirt. That these are all present hints at a new possibility: that the boy is the only survivor of an unspecified apocalyptic event. Yet, as he explores, his experience continues to be strangely dreamlike, slow-moving, intensely detailed. The reader begins to wonder just how long Ness can keep this up before fascination turns to boredom, and as if sensing that, Ness shifts gear. The boy suddenly recognises the house as his former home in England, where he lived before his mother moved to the US to escape. For him at least, all is suddenly clear: 'He's died, and woken up in his own, personal hell' (p.29). Overcome by exhaustion, he collapses.

For the reader, though, there is suddenly a new strand of story, one that is obviously not part of the boy's current experience. Four friends decide to steal a figure from a neighbour's Christmas nativity display. From this ... dream the boy finally retrieves his name, Seth. For the reader, the story's pattern is temporarily settled as Seth moves between a present in which he must figure out how to survive in a now where there is no power, the water supply is dodgy, and he must scavenge for food, and a then in which he had a family and friends, though the family seems to have been blighted by an unspoken tragedy involving his younger brother. His friendships are uneasy, not least because Seth has fallen in love.

The present-day story has, as various commentators have noted, a distinct flavour of *Robinson Crusoe* about it. Seth adapts to his new surroundings and learns to make his way in them, before discovering that he is not alone in this place. What sets this apart from other similar stories is the quality of Ness's prose, the precision with which he evokes each moment of discovery and understanding as Seth tries to work out what has happened to him. This becomes even more striking once Seth meets Tomasz and Regine. 'Survivors' like himself, it is clear that they also remember their own death, but each is reluctant to talk about it. The delicacy with which Ness sketches the tentative development of the friendship between the three is breathtaking. This delicacy is similarly in evidence as Seth recalls his own previous life as a teenager in a US town, and his adventures with H, Gudmund, and Monica, Gudmund's girlfriend, culminating in the theft of a baby Jesus figure. Running through this is Seth's gradual realization that he is gay, that he is in love with Gudmund, and that Gudmund has similar feelings for him.

All this would be a novel in itself, but Seth is determined to find out what is going on, and it is here that the story finally starts to creak. It has moved from possible afterlife to dream to post-apocalyptic survival, but now moves towards a possible explanation that seems surprisingly formulaic after what has gone before. Or rather, it is not the idea that falters so much as the actual mechanics of the storytelling. Much hinges on the presence of the Driver, a humanoid robot apparently programmed to hunt down living humans, for reasons that are not immediately clear; it is the only thing this creature does, and after a while the inevitability of its behaviour begins to grate. However, its presence leads Seth to a revelation about his own situation, though by 'revelation', I actually mean 'recourse to disappointingly banal trope'. To elaborate further would be to reveal the story's ending, so here I must stop.

I was disappointed by that ending, I can't deny. Having so carefully opened up multiple explanations for the situation in which Seth finds himself, to then narrow it down to the one that seems on the one hand the most hackneyed, on the other the least plausible, seems baffling. Even in this, there is a most teasing philosophical problem, but one that, irritatingly, Ness seems to edge around. Maybe there are more volumes to come (and if there are, I doubt I'd complain), but even if that is so, one might wish this novel hadn't so much ended as fizzled out.

Nonetheless, despite its flaws, there is so much about *More Than This* that deserves praise. It is a genuine pleasure simply to immerse oneself in the prose. Ness writes smoothly but never glibly. The craft is evident throughout but is not ostentatious. Even when the plot falters, the prose continues to shine. There were moments when it reminded me of such things as Jan Mark's *Divide and Rule* (1979), which from me is high praise indeed. Although I still mourn for the lost possibilities of the early chapters, right to the novel's end Ness still made me care very much about three troubled characters trying to make sense of their world and their situation.

SEEING STARS

'Recordings alone aren't sufficient' – speaking *Arrival*

Before we begin, I want to say that I enjoyed *Arrival* immensely. Indeed, it acted so powerfully on my imagination that I dreamt a whole sub-plot for it the night I saw it, something to do with people discovering things about past situations they'd found themselves in, information that would have been helpful at the time, and now vouchsafed to them because they'd at last slipped free of the constraints of time and language.

Having read Ted Chiang's original story just before I saw the film, my first thought was how do you adapt a text like this, so heavily reliant on shifts in time and narrative tense, into a film? After the movie, Paul Kincaid and I initially thought that *Arrival* could be seen as an improvisation on 'Story of Your Life', but thinking about it some more, I wonder now if it isn't perhaps a commentary on the difference between telling a story with words and telling a story with images. To which you would pityingly say, 'well, obviously, because it's a film, right?' And it is, and you are right, but what I'm thinking about is the different ways in which words and images (sounds, too) evoke thoughts in the mind.

I have said before that I am generally not that keen on film or TV; in part this is because I don't like the way film-makers attempt, sometimes very crudely, to manipulate my emotions. Obviously, writers do this too, but I've always felt that words are something I have control over—I can stop reading if it all gets too stressful—whereas images I don't—I cannot pause the cinema film. Images are just there, projected into my mind, something I find much more difficult to filter out unless I close my eyes and stuff my fingers in my ears.

'Story of Your Life' and *Arrival* tell the same story, more or less. Odd details change—Gary Donnelly becomes Ian Donnelly, Hannah's cause of death will be different, but essentially, the stories remain the same. It's the emphases that are different.

One of the several reasons why I like Ted Chiang's stories is that while they contain much in the way of ideas, on the page they are very pared down. He gives me as much as I need and no more. He is not a writer who indulges in lush description unless for a very specific reason, and if he does, I would take notice. Mostly, he leaves it to me, the reader, to fill in the gaps between the words and the sentences. I don't want or need it on the page. It doesn't seem like promising material for a film.

One could imagine a film-maker looking at 'Story of Your Life' as nothing more than a synopsis, an opportunity for the special effects department to run riot, and I don't doubt we could think of directors who would have done just that, allowing spectacle to overwhelm all else. But, for the most part, that didn't happen here. At the heart of 'Story of Your Life' is an achronological, universal language, in which everything is said simultaneously. I've come to the conclusion that one of the things *Arrival* is trying to do is to explore how the film image tries to be everything simultaneously, but how the experience can differ, according to what visual memory you bring to it. OK, so this is hardly original, but too often it seems to me that locating the intertextual references in film turns into an easter-egg hunt. How smug we all feel for spotting the shop called Micklewhite's in *The Muppet Christmas Carol*, knowing that Michael Caine was originally called Maurice Micklewhite. That's an in-joke, not an intertextual reference; it's also an artefact, and I'm thinking much more about mood.

Let's take a few examples from *Arrival*, some more overt than others. If *Arrival* is in direct dialogue with any film, it is surely *Close Encounters of the Third Kind*, though I must admit I also read it in part as a riposte to or subtle reproof of some aspects of *CETK*, particularly the Special Edition. To begin with, while the huge spaceships have shown up all over the world, the film chooses to focus on one that has taken up station in Montana, which I do not doubt is meant to prompt us to think of the Devils Tower in Wyoming, the dominant image in *CETK*. There is also the moment when the helicopter sweeps over Louise Banks's house at night before landing in the meadow. The slanting light through the slats of the blinds, the confusion of dark and light, the distortion, the figure at the door, all echo the events as they occur when Barry is taken from his mother's house. And are meant to—the audience is anticipating what Banks is likely to find when she opens the door, and there is the sense of relief that it's Colonel Weber (though anyone who recalls *E.T.* might perhaps wonder whether authority figures should be trusted).

The shots of the house by the waterside, the child playing at the water's edge, and the way the water moved all made me think immediately of Tarkovsky's *Solaris* (and, as Andrew M. Butler pointed out after the film, there is also the shot of the wheat field moving in the breeze). The reference to 'the zone' can't help but invoke *Stalker*, but what about the quality of the stillness of the vast ship, hanging in the air? I thought then of *District 9*. And surely everyone who has seen *Arrival* had at least one moment when they thought of *2001* and the monolith. I doubt any of this is a coincidence, any more than it is a coincidence that every film I've mentioned here is very specifically about attempting, or failing, to communicate with an alien group in ways that don't simply involve trying to shoot them out of the sky.

So, what I'm suggesting here is that Villeneuve is offering a bank of specific references for the viewer to draw on if they so desire, his version of leaving spaces between the words. Because, one of the things that does strike me about this film is how comparatively sparse everything is on the screen. Not the spaceship, perhaps, but we'll come back to that shortly. It is as if Villeneuve has striven to put the minimum necessary on screen to actually tell the story. We see unremarkable public spaces that are in no way distinctive (the campus, the garage); they could be anywhere. Contingent spaces, like the cafeteria, could again be anywhere, and the people in them could be anywhere as well. Banks's own house is more distinctive, but what we note mostly is how isolated it is, how impersonal, how see-through. The army camp is inevitably marked as temporary—we see it put up, and taken down. We see a hundred little reminders—in the furniture, fittings, cramped accommodation, banks of phones for the soldiers to call home—that this is not a place where people will settle. The room where Banks sleeps is small, functional, a place to lie down but not to be comfortable. The only space we ever see that actually seems to belong to someone is Banks's study, with its book-lined walls; this is where she spends most of her time, and it's the place she goes back to while everyone else is wondering how to deal with potential alien invasion. (It's noticeable too that the lecture theatre is the only other place that seems in any way 'warm'. It's bigger than her study but it's still a cocoon; she is prepared to keep on lecturing in the face of the arrival of aliens, no matter how few people attend).

In all of this it seems to me that Villeneuve is giving us what we need, but no more; anything else we will need to bring with us. It's the visual equivalent of saying 'Banks's office' or 'the army camp'. The camera rarely lingers; it's always scurrying along behind Banks, on her way to somewhere else, taking no notice of her surroundings, because they do not interest her. We only really notice the surroundings when, in Montana, Ian is also present, or when Banks is with Hannah. Perhaps we might see these as a visual equivalent of the passages of the original story that are directly addressed to her daughter. These richer settings are important because they reflect engagement, affection.

I deliberately excluded the spaceship from my discussion of the minimalism of the settings. In Chiang's story, the ships are simply referred to as 'the ships'. Indeed, they're really not important except as vehicles to bring the heptapods to Earth. More important are the alien devices, deposited on the ground. They're called 'looking glasses' and described as being 'semicircular […] over ten feet high and twenty feet across'. Later, it will turn out they're made of fused silica, nothing exotic. Chiang's description renders them as being nothing fancy, and I think that's the point. You could imagine one, on a smaller scale, as a mirror over a mantelpiece in an ordinary house. It's just that these are bigger.

The story doesn't need a spaceship; it's taken as read, but the film? Well, maybe it panders to a section of the audience by including an actual spaceship, but I wonder too if a twenty-foot mirror isn't harder to explain than a spaceship. And here the spaceship can be used to tell us something about its inhabitants as well. What I particularly love about the spaceship is its texture, which will echo, to some extent, the texture of the heptapod when we finally see it in detail. (Paul Kincaid thinks this is part of a dream sequence; I am not so sure of that, but even if it is, the texture has clearly imprinted itself on Banks's dream consciousness as well). I like too how the curvilinear form resonates slightly with that curved-mirror artefact that Chiang describes. And also, and maybe this is my imagination, when it finally turns in the sky, I couldn't help thinking of a contact lens, a huge, grey contact lens, something else that says 'seeing' rather than hearing, and again picks up on something that is present in both story and film, the dichotomy between speaking and writing, and the need to utilise both in order to make contact. I could get all Derridean about this and start invoking 'Plato's Pharmacy'—maybe at some point, when I've refreshed my memory, I will—but for now I will simply draw your attention to Colonel Weber's impossible demand that Banks translate the alien speech from a tape recording, with no other clues at all.

Here I should back up slightly—the reference to the mirror in Chiang's text suggests faces; something that is very noticeable in the film is the emphasis on faces. We often see them in close up, Banks's face in particular, and it occurred to me that in these moments we are being urged, literally directed, to take note of their expressions. Why? It could be frantic telegraphing of points, yes, but I don't think so; this film is too good for that kind of cheap manipulation. Instead, it seems to me that Villeneuve is quietly suggesting that not only should we not be relying on words alone when it comes to communicating, but that we can't.

The facial thing struck me in particular because I experience tinnitus and deafness in one ear, and it turns out that I've been compensating for this for years by lip-reading; I really don't like it when I can't see the lower portion of people's faces when they're speaking, and that includes in films. What brought this home to me in *Arrival* is the scene when they first enter the spaceship in hazmat gear and attempt to communicate with the aliens. It is obvious from the beginning that at least some of the team will have to divest themselves of their gear in order to communicate properly, but while one might think of this in terms of showing oneself as a 'human', and what a human actually looks like, it is also about revealing the face, the place where communication starts with humans. Similarly, when Banks lays her hand on the screen, it's tempting to imagine the heptapods thinking, 'OK, now we can talk' because she has, perhaps inadvertently, acknowledged their means of communication.

But, of course, this also links back to Colonel Weber's inability to 'see' that communication isn't simply about words, or recordings, but about bodies, faces, presences, positioning. And as it turns out, vocalisation is not actually the heptapods' primary means of communication. In Chiang's story, which is made of words, the emphasis is on humans figuring out *what* the heptapods are saying and what this means; by contrast, I'd say that the film is more about *how* they figure it out, inevitably, because it is a very visual thing. In the story, the heptapods' writing is described first as 'a doodle of script, vaguely cursive'; later, as they learn more, it becomes like 'fanciful praying mantids drawn in a cursive style, all clinging to each other to form an Escheresque lattice, each slightly different in its stance'. Later, as Banks begins to appreciate the full significance of the heptapods' written language, she talks in terms of calligraphic designs, while noting that 'No one could lay out such an intricate design at the speed needed for holding a conversation. At least, no one human could'. And this, to my mind, is one place where the film does something the story never can—it can attempt to represent the semagrams, shown as ink coalescing in liquid, in black and white. The designers have opted for circular forms, with complexes of strands branching off all over the place, as if emphasising the conceptual all-at-onceness of heptapod communication. Chiang's story has scientific diagrams, but it doesn't, and I think can't, ever have anything quite like this, because words don't work like that (as I am inevitably showing here).

And there is one thing I haven't yet raised—how much of this film is about a lack of communication. It would be impossible to resist such a theme in a film about first contact, but Villeneuve is subtle in his approach to it. Yes, later, we get the inevitable diplomatic tantrums, and threats of war, and it would be wrong perhaps to exclude them, in the same way that we know the military is going to insist on a need-to-know basis, and close down discussion when it most needs to happen. There is something perverse about the way in which the US military always seems to try to control the flow of information, while being staggeringly inept at achieving any kind of meaningful exchange. I'm sure that is a point not lost on Villeneuve.

But think back to the beginning, after we've seen the death of Hannah, at the point where we might still be thinking that Banks is grieving. By the end of the film, those who don't know the story should have made the connection, and realised that first contact comes prior to the birth of Hannah, in which case, what is striking when the alien ships arrive? Yes, we note that a linguist is ignoring all the screens as she walks through the campus building, and has failed to notice everyone gravitating towards them. Yes, we note that she presses on with her lecture even though the auditorium is almost empty (you do—I've given that lecture, too). But what happens in that lecture theatre? People's cell phones start ringing, with others passing on the news that the aliens arrived. Now, we could say that for the sake of professionalism, Banks has switched her phone to silent while she lectures, but for the sake of the film, let's assume she doesn't, and that it is on vibrate. It doesn't ring before she goes into the lecture theatre, it doesn't ring while she's in the lecture theatre. The students have to ask her to switch on the screen so they can see what's happening. In other words, the communications specialist has no one communicating with her socially, has no one to communicate with socially. We can only speculate about what her life at the university is like; apparently, it does not involve collegiality, yet she equally obviously has nothing to do outside except gravitate back towards her university office.

By contrast, everyone around her seems to be communicating furiously but with little effect. Screen after screen of news reports, the bank of screens communicating with specialists at the other contact sites, and yet no one can figure out what's happening. The screens provide a handy visual reference for the compartmentalisation of information. Everyone has a question they want to ask, variations of the question Colonel Weber asks: 'what is your purpose here?', but it is as if everyone has suddenly forgotten the etiquette of communication. And both story and film suggest that people are surprised, outraged even, that the aliens abide by the same rules of deliberately withholding information. Except, of course, that they are not withholding it, if only people choose to collaborate, or finally recognise that they must collaborate.

It's here, I think, that the film seems a little weaker, presenting us with the idea of Banks seeing into the future, and saving the world from global war. The story is rather more low-key—as I said before, it's about 'what', so the problem-solving is, in and of itself, sufficiently satisfying. A film needs more overt drama, I assume, so we have the sub-plot of the group of soldiers deciding to blow up the spaceship, for example. I did like how this was done. It's never discussed but is communicated to the viewer through expressions, significant glances, a mention of something on the radio. I particularly liked the way it was assumed by the plotters that the aliens wouldn't, perhaps couldn't, understand what was going on, so it was fine to bring in the explosives in plain view. Or, because they were aliens, maybe they were invisible. There's a lot going on in just that small sequence.

The larger sub-plot, how Banks saves the world, reaching forward in time to memorise a phone number, stretched my willingness to believe just slightly, but if you look back at the original text, while there is no Chinese general, the text does begin to break down in such a way as to suggest that as Banks works with the heptapod language it is changing her experience of the world, moving back and forth in time. It's subtle; I missed it the first time, but it is there. In the film, though, it seems to need to be made more explicit.

And yet, it is reinforced in less immediately tangible ways. Paul Kincaid and I have disagreed slightly over the film's opening. I thought initially it was a little deceitful in synopsising what comes later, perhaps tricking the audience into assuming that Banks is grieving rather than being crashingly lonely, only to reveal later that ... The story, I realised after a second reading, is actually a circular thing. The end is the beginning—the question 'Do you want to make a baby?' is asked twice, once at the beginning, once at the end. There is an overlap. The film doesn't do that, I thought, until Paul Kincaid pointed out that at the beginning of the film, in the first shot of the house's interior, there are two wine glasses, as there are at the end of the film, when the question is asked. The overlap is, as it must be, visual.

Is *Arrival* an adaptation of 'Story of Your Life'? I think I would prefer to call it a translation. Or, if we 'spoke' Heptapod, there would be a frighteningly elegant semagram that would bring together words like 'adaptation' and 'translation' and 'reworking' as facets of a larger concept. But we are stuck with words and images, and must do with them the best we can.

The view from G21: watching
Star Wars: The Force Awakens

Princess Leia was at the cinema yesterday.

She was a very small princess, but she had a lightsaber, and her hair was perfect.

I couldn't see what her brother was wearing, but her parents seemed to be dressed appropriately for the twenty-first century.

I would have loved to ask her what she thought of General Leia, and of Rey, and Finn, and Kylo. And grizzled Han Solo. And bearded Luke.

For that matter, I wonder what her parents thought, given they looked about the age to have grown up with all this.

The experience of growing up with a film or franchise seems to be important right now. I was struck a while ago by people complaining about how the new *Ghostbusters* would ruin their childhood because they'd watched the original endlessly when they were younger. I saw it for the first time when I was 25; it's one of my favourite films even now, but I don't have that kind of investment in it. I noticed people talking about the significance of *Labyrinth* in their childhood after David Bowie died. (I've never actually seen *Labyrinth*; perhaps I should). And I suspect there are people who feel similarly about *Robin Hood: Prince of Thieves* or *Galaxy Quest* now that Alan Rickman is gone.

But head and shoulders above all these stands *Star Wars*. I didn't see the original film when it came out in 1977, for various reasons involving a boyfriend who didn't like science fiction. I first saw it around 1980/81, in a double bill with *The Empire Strikes Back*. I was the last one into the cinema, because there was one seat left and I was the first person they found in the queue who was on her own (I'd married a man who didn't like science fiction).

The seat was high up at the back of the cinema, higher than I normally preferred. I don't really remember much about either film from that viewing, except that sequence when Luke Skywalker acts as gunner while Han Solo and Chewbacca fly the shit out of the *Millennium Falcon*. Had I been prone to saying 'holy shit' in those days, I'd have probably said it then. It was … awesome. (I didn't say that in those days, either). Never mind the carnage, I was all wow! explosions! can they do that?!?

I saw *Return of the Jedi* six times when it came out. At least six times. Lots of widescreen shooty-shooty but mostly I loved it for that moment when Luke Skywalker suddenly emerges from the shadows, and hey, we're back in business again. What can I say? I was 24, went to a lot of films on my own, and was coming to the conclusion that maybe I didn't want any longer to be married to a man who didn't like science fiction.

I didn't watch SF films critically in those days. I consumed them like sweeties—empty calories to fill the void. I found it hard to disentangle myself from the best of them (*Blade Runner*. Always *Blade Runner*) and laughed at myself for going in when I emerged from seeing the crap ones (and if you think I'm going to admit to some of the films I saw …)

Return of the Jedi? Good, definitely. Great? Possibly. But it wasn't *Blade Runner*. Nonetheless, it offered a fairy-tale narrative of redemption and renewal, and restoration. We could all get through this and find something better. It would be fine. And I'd go and see it again the following week on my afternoon off, just to convince myself again.

I skipped the prequels. Well, wouldn't you?

And now, here I am, in a cinema, in Folkestone, married to a man who likes science fiction (the man who took me to see *Ghostbusters* on our very first 'official' date—I pretty much had to marry him eventually), and we're about to watch *Star Wars: The Force Awakens*. It's been thirty-three years since I saw a *Star Wars* film in the cinema. Holy shit, it's been *thirty-three years*!!!

I had a rough idea of what to expect, from trailer snippets, from things people had written (I don't lose sleep about spoilers, as you may know, though it turns out there was one thing I didn't actually know; we'll come to that later).

First impressions. It's a *Star Wars* film. There's the summary scrolling up the screen. And the music. Oh gosh, the music. This is like coming home, isn't it? So exciting …

And then there's this feeling that it is all a bit … familiar? Haven't we been here before? I mean, actually. Been. Here. Before?

Well, OK, things have changed, a little. Rather than bumping off a few innocent civilians while looking for a droid with information, let's annihilate entire settlements, and show the annihilation in progress. 'Plosions, spaceships, stormtroopers, fires, people running and screaming, shooting, ker-pow!!! Isn't this great???

Er, I don't know? Is it? My younger self remains silent on this issue, though I suspect she might have liked it. Especially in 3D, had it existed in the cinema then (I mean, really existed), as her eyes were still about as good as they were likely to be and she didn't yet wear glasses (although as she had no depth-perception she needed them).

Me? I'm thinking 'holy shit!', and not in a positive way.

And oh dear god, did they really just do that thing with the bloody handprint so you know which stormtrooper to follow? Oh god, yes they did.

face:palm as we also didn't say in the old days.

I just don't know … Actually, I do know, and am busy composing a brisk paragraph in my head about the director not trusting the audience, making it too easy, and so on.

A ghastly sense of inevitability begins to impinge.

I'm old, I've watched a lot of films in my time, including *Star Wars*, and it's actually not that difficult (mostly) to see what's coming. Stormtrooper becomes human, decides to rescue captured pilot as ticket out. Escape from the Death Star Mk. II, in one of those cute little ships that looks like a diablo, and … whee, shooty-shooty. Apparently, my inner twenty-something is still big on the space gunnery. Which is handy, as there is going to be more of it. Yee-ha!

Wait! Why are we on Arrakis? Or Tatooine? No, they're calling it Jakku this time. Was that a sandworm? Whatever, we are back in a marginal desert settlement-thing, allowing everyone to dress up in flowing robes, absolutely not being orientalist, no sir, look, we've got goggles and respirators, too, see?

Twenty-something me approves desperately of Rey. Current-me wonders why she doesn't cover up her lower legs, as though they are magically immune to sunburn, sand burns, bugs, etc. I guess it's for the climbing scenes.

Finn loses Poe Dameron, his new pilot, who has already lost his cat, sorry, droid (see *Inside Llewyn Davis* if you don't get that one; and as Paul Kincaid points out, actually, this time the cat's lost Poe). Finn finds Rey—are two people incapable of meeting around here without another fucking firefight breaking out? Apparently, they are. Boom. More innocent bystanders shot up.

Let's fly away. No, that ship's just been blown up. Let's fly away and use this ship instead. Holy shit (for real, this time), it's the *Millennium Falcon*, hotly pursued by someone who looks remarkably like a remade Bombur from *The Hobbit*. I'm no longer entirely sure which film I am in.

But this, it turns out, *this* is what I am here for: this sequence as Rey flies the *Millennium Falcon* in, out, and upside down, across the face of Jakku, trying to escape Nazis-from-the-Antarctic, with Finn as her gunner. Because I cannot do this in my beloved Peugeot 208, not even on an empty motorway, for reasons involving gravity and traffic regulations. Young-me and current-me have bonded over the joy of watching the *Millennium Falcon* do handbrake turns all over hyperspace. Sigh.

The reappearance of Han Solo and Chewbacca is almost a grace note but there they are, and it's all so … sorry, seem to have got something in my eye. Is that a speck of sentiment or is it just something that's shaken its way out of the air duct? Despite what I might have already said about Luke Skywalker in *Return of the Jedi*, it was always about Han Solo for me. And apparently, still is. Older … much, much older … and superbly grey and grizzled.

And being weirdly meta about the whole thing, as though he is also thinking what I'm thinking. Harrison Ford is certainly not phoning in his performance, but I'm not entirely sure he's always in the same film as the others. It's funny but also disconcerting, as though he is not taking it entirely seriously. And he reminds me of someone, and I still don't know who.

Later, once they've got back to the resistance planet, and he and Leia are quasi-amicably bickering, I find myself thinking of Fonda and Hepburn in *On Golden Pond*. And I'm torn. Because on the one hand, I am thinking that it's fabulous to have an action movie with older people in it, even if one of them is staying at home rather too much (please give her a gun, later). On the other hand, Hollywood still apparently can only account for older couples on screen by having them estranged/squabbling/testy, and I'm kind of hurt by that. I'm looking to Han and Leia to represent me on screen, and … no, it's not entirely working, is it? Perhaps I am too old for this. I smile as Chewbacca fusses about Han putting his coat on when they're wandering around in Antarctica, sorry, on the ice planet, looking for the First Order base, but at the same time, I am thinking that this is like being a thirteen-year-old, reading *Lord of the Rings*, and identifying with Strider because there is a chronic lack of women who aren't elves in *LOTR*, and not realising that this was a problem.

I see it now. Because I'm a 56-year-old woman who is identifying with a character played by a 73-year-old man, and it's 2016. Maybe I should identify with Rey, and to some extent I do, but not enough. There seem to be a number of younger visible women—pilots, bystanders, vamps, and so on—but this film gives me, me specifically, Leia, the doctor played by Harriet Walter, possibly Phasma but who knows under that armour, and Maz Kanata, the Guinan *de nos jours* (also played by a woman of colour, a young woman of colour, and a lot less visible under that than Whoopi Goldberg ever was. And I haven't got time to stop and think about the mystical person of colour shtick). It's not a lot to go on, is it? Maybe I can pretend there's a middle-aged mechanic on the Resistance base.

And, wait, I'm lost now … what were we shooting up in this section? As Maz's trading post is being destroyed, I suddenly realise I'm done with seeing things explode, masonry crumble and fall, and stormtroopers fly through the air every few seconds. The attrition rate is appalling; no wonder they are constantly recruiting. I'm slightly surprised they've not yet taken the orc route and started breeding them, but I can see that might be a franchise too far, and anyway, it's always a good idea not to cross the streams.

Sadly, there is a lot more exploding to go; indeed, the entire film seems to be predicated on blowing things up, including planet-sized weapons. I'm going slightly deaf by this point, and my eyes are suffering from the flashes of light as another person or object goes up in flames. And that includes what is now a mere shell of a plot.

I'm getting impatient with the film, which seems to be getting impatient with itself. There's none of this nonsense about training to be a Jedi. In this generation, Rey can lay hands on a lightsaber and immediately start hacking away at Kylo Ren with considerable aplomb. Of course, she's used to fighting, as is Finn, and though neither was trained to skewer things, they do quite well. Kylo may be trained to fight, but to add to his general woes, he's not that good at it, which is unfortunate, and to compound things, Rey is naturally ace at doing things with the Force as well. Damn. At least he'll be in demand for his Snape impersonation.

I'm being facetious now, because, really, there is little else left to do. Other than to debate the one thing I didn't know about. The death of Han Solo. He has to come back, right? Though given the way things have been so far ... Paul did express disappointment that Han Solo didn't cry 'Fly, you fools', as the Balrog got him, sorry, as he fell into the void, but I have already warned you about the dangers of crossing the streams. But seriously, does he come back? Logic demands that he must, because the logic of film franchises like this is that no one named ever really dies, unless they die, and he hasn't died yet. Not properly. I mean: like the White Witch, you can always get them back if you really want to, and probably with more success than resurrecting her. Rather as we're fairly sure that we've not see the last of Kylo Ren, might we hold out some sort of hope for the return of Han Solo? At least so he can get his revenge on Emo Kylo for stabbing him through the heart with a lightsaber (a move that is incidentally used at least once too often, taking an element of surprise out of it)? Or was that it?

I admit, after that I lost a certain amount of interest, even when Rey goes off to find Slavoj Žižek, sorry, Luke Skywalker, who appears to have gone to ground on Skellig Michael, presumably because he can. Take that, New Zealand!

I did enjoy *The Force Awakens* up to a point. But only up to a point. I like that there is another *Star Wars* movie in the world that includes things I enjoyed about the originals (OK, the *Millennium Falcon* doing handbrake turns—so sue me, I'm shallow), but I look at it now and all I can think of is how thin, how stretched, how like butter scraped across bread this plot is. How this film is really one long series of nods to its predecessors, with very little in the way of newness. Some adjustment of gender roles, to be sure, and some foregrounding of actors of colour, at long last. And I will just say here that Daisy Ridley and John Boyega are both outstanding actors. Along with Harrison Ford and Chewie, they are the most watchable things on the screen. I love the moment when, having evaded the First Order, they're excitedly dancing around, talking over each other. I love that Rey is so good a pilot she can match Han Solo. I love the giddiness of Rey and Finn falling in love. It reminds me of ...

And that's my problem, right there. It reminds me of ... well, it reminds me of things I don't feel inclined to talk about right now, but if you knew us then, knew us well, back in the day, it reminds me of that. And that takes me back to the hurt I feel about Han and Leia. We can be reminded of, but we can't actually be …

But back in the cinema, the film was over. Princess Leia was on her way home. She'd obviously had a good time. In the foyer there was a man with learning difficulties, bouncing up and down excitedly, asking us all if we'd enjoyed seeing the film. I enjoyed his enjoyment.

As for me, it was time to go home. I felt hammered by sound. My ears were tired, my eyes were tired, my brain was curled in a foetal ball, screaming 'enough with the self-referentiality, already. You have ticked every single fucking box, and pleased everyone by recalling their special memory of the first *Star Wars*. Please stop it now'.

On the plus side, there were, thank god, no Ewoks.

'he had a remarkable gentleness and courtesy in his dealings with women' – the *Sherlock* Christmas special

[Mrs Hudson] stood in the deepest awe of him and never dared to interfere with him, however outrageous his proceedings might seem. She was fond of him, too, for he had a remarkable gentleness and courtesy in his dealings with women. He disliked and distrusted the sex, but he was always a chivalrous opponent.
(Arthur Conan Doyle—'The Adventure of the Dying Detective')
'What exactly is the point of you?' Sherlock Holmes to Mrs Hudson
(Steven Moffat—His Last Vow, *Sherlock*, Series 3)

I mostly abandoned *Sherlock* at the beginning of series 2, because I found it so irritating, and at the time I had too little patience with things that irritated me to set about finding out why they irritated me. I suspected back then it might have something to do with the show's being insufficiently canonical, which probably meant that I was actually being a bit too stuffy about the whole thing, and that was the kind of self-examination I wasn't really prepared to deal with just then.

So, new year, better attitude: I decided to watch 'The Abominable Bride', the *Sherlock* Christmas special. The premise looked intriguing and, I admit it, I was curious about the fact the show would be set in Victorian London. Foolishly, I had assumed it was a genuine one-off show, an honest-to-god Christmas special, a return to the textual taproot, so to speak. You would think I would know better than that by now, but I apparently still have much to learn about the Way of Moffat.

The first thing to recognise, perhaps, is that anything I might know, he will know better: he will know anything better than me. I'm not a dyed-in-the-wool Sherlockian by any means—I don't possess that obsessive character quirk that appears to mark the genuine fan of anything—but I've read, watched, and listened to the stories in various adaptations enough times to have a decent working knowledge of the canon, even if I don't have a minutely detailed recall of every actor who has so much as sneezed in one frame of film.

However, two things in particular I have learned over the years. One is that while Sherlock Holmes may not particularly like women, as a rule he behaves well towards them and listens sympathetically to their problems. Conan Doyle states this most clearly through his mouthpiece, John H. Watson, in 'The Adventure of the Dying Detective', but one sees ample evidence of this trait elsewhere. One might cite, for example, 'The Adventure of the Copper Beeches', in which Holmes several times praises the resourceful Miss Violet Hunter, who takes a post, aware that something is amiss, and takes the precaution of contacting Sherlock Holmes before leaving London. One might note his behaviour towards Mary Morstan in *The Sign of the Four*, or any number of other examples throughout the texts, up to and including the landlady in 'The Adventure of the Red Circle' or 'The Adventure of the Veiled Lodger'. Holmes is canonically far more sympathetic than people realise.

The other thing I know is that Conan Doyle himself created the metafictional aspect of the Sherlock Holmes stories, with Holmes regularly making disparaging observations about Watson's prowess as a writer. 'The Adventure of the Blanched Soldier' is recounted by Holmes himself in response to Watson's urging.

> For a long time he has worried me to write an experience of my own. Perhaps I have rather invited this persecution, since I have often had occasion to point out to him how superficial are his own accounts and to accuse him of pandering to popular taste instead of confining himself rigidily to facts and figures.

'The Adventure of the Lion's Mane' seems to emerge from Holmes's need to record a peculiar case at a point when Watson is not there to be his amanuensis. 'Thus I must act as my own chronicler'.

Radio 4 took up the metafictional aspect of adapting Sherlock Holmes well before Steven Moffat came on the scene, and with much more subtlety. Those familiar with the Clive Merrison/Michael Williams Holmes and Watson productions will be aware that the fact of Watson writing about Holmes was a frequent topic of discussion in the narrative frame, and not just Holmes disparaging Watson's flair for melodrama. Think of it more as an ongoing low-key examination of the nature of fictionality, to the point where the narrative raises some very interesting philosophical points about identity.

Cut then to 'The Abominable Bride', and to Una Stubbs as Mrs Hudson, complaining to Watson about the paucity of lines for her in his stories. This is actually entirely true—in the canon, Mrs Hudson is mentioned a bare thirteen times, yet somehow she seems to be more present than that, a fact that has seeped into TV and radio productions, where she often has more lines than she ever did in the originals.

But then, as we have been reminded constantly, what is the point of Mrs Hudson, of Mary Morstan, Molly Hooper, and the various other women who have drifted through three series of *Sherlock*, other than having to put up with Sherlock's petulance and rudeness? Unlike their counterparts in Conan Doyle's stories, these women are rarely accorded respect by Sherlock Holmes, whom we must, I fear, regard as Moffat's mouthpiece.

Moffat has been called out on this constantly over three series, yet has pretty much stuck his fingers in his ears and gone la-la-la to indicate how he doesn't mind, in between throwing tantrums whenever he feels a little too beleaguered by the fans' failure to appreciate his ongoing wonderfulness in delivering up this amazing show. Like his creation, Moffat lacks respect; he lacks respect for a good percentage of his audience while being complicit with the other portion, who of course appreciate his laddish witticisms. But this has all been said before, so I am hardly bringing anything new to the table.

I think, though, that 'respect', or the lack of it, is perhaps key to understanding what Moffat does, or doesn't do, and the main reason why he gets up my nose so much. He may love Arthur Conan Doyle's creation with an unreasoning nerdy joy, and that's fine. There is a place for someone to hold all those little fragments of information in their head and trot them out for our edification as the circumstances allow. But Moffat does not respect the idea of 'Sherlock Holmes', and that's a whole different thing.

And by 'respect', or lack of it, I don't mean the playing fast and loose with the canon, but the manner of that playing fast and loose. It's one thing to insert knowing references to 'The Adventure of the Blue Carbuncle' or 'The Five Orange Pips', and a slyer reference to 'The Adventure of the Greek Interpreter' (which I spotted immediately, so go me). It's another thing to take the canonical figure, move it to contemporary times, and then effectively trash it simply because you can. Because it seems to me that this is what Moffat does every time he puts a woman into *Sherlock* and silences her or demeans her in some way.

While contemporary Sherlock Holmes has a range of skills available to him that are different from those of his nineteenth-century counterpart, he is nonetheless still Sherlock Holmes, Conan Doyle's character. Except that Moffat has entirely stripped him of his humanity because he apparently doesn't have the skill to read the deeper character. Or rather, he may think he does—because it's all about Irene Adler, isn't it?—but *I* don't think he does. He might even argue—maybe he has, and I missed it—that *his* Sherlock Holmes is intentionally the complete antithesis of the original. Except that I don't believe this either. Moffat's Sherlock doesn't seem to me to be a radical departure from the canonical figure so much as an excuse for a badly behaved Millennial to rampage around London with impunity. Or to put it another way, you don't get to label yourself as a sociopath; that's a job for others. And if you are going to be openly misogynistic, you'd better have a damn good reason—'Irene made me do it' doesn't count.

To judge from the Christmas episode, however, it would seem that word has finally reached Moffat's brain that women are not pleased with him. That, in fact, they are really displeased, and given they form a significant chunk of the fanbase, it has become clear to him that he must do something. 'The

Abominable Bride' could be read, therefore, as some sort of attempt to address past deficiencies, an attempt to ask oneself as writer how one could have let things get so bad. Mrs Hudson could indeed ask John H. Watson why she had so few lines in his stories. Mary Morstan could find her way, heavily veiled, to 221b Baker Street to ask John Watson why the hell he hasn't been home lately. His parlour maid could ask John Watson why he never mentions her in his stories. Poor John—everyone wants to know why he's being so nasty to them, and of course he has no answer, because he can't really say 'the scriptwriter made me do it'.

Sherlock Holmes remains silent, because this is not his department. He's got a dead body to worry about. The body of Emelia Ricoletti, who the previous afternoon blew out her brains before a large audience of bystanders, only to re-appear later the same day, armed with a shotgun, to blow two large holes through her husband. It was the Ricolettis' wedding anniversary, Emelia was dressed in her wedding gown, and killed her husband outside a Limehouse opium den, again before witnesses, before vanishing into the fog. By the time Holmes and Watson reach the morgue, her body is lying chained down on a mortuary table, because, apparently, her fingers are smeared with blood, and someone has used that blood to write 'You' on the wall in rather shaky letters (see 'rache', in *A Study in Scarlet*), all of which suggests that the corpse of Emelia Ricoletti committed the murder of her husband.

Naturally, the highly rational Holmes will not have any of this. Nor will he accept any of Watson's faintly ludicrous explanations, such as that Emelia Ricoletti has a secret twin. It is never twins, he says firmly, and indeed it never is. But as he surely knows himself, it doesn't have to be a twin, just someone who looks similar. As in 'The Adventure of the Copper Beeches', say, though canonically that hasn't happened yet, as it's five stories after 'The Adventure of the Blue Carbuncle', which provides the anchor for this story. Or as in a story of a man who fakes his own suicide at the end of series 2 of a TV show at some point in the future.

And here I have to say that whatever else I feel about 'The Abominable Bride', the little nugget of actual story was gorgeously done, one of those moments when you think to yourself, 'thank god, they do actually know what they're doing', even though you know you'll inevitably be disabused of that notion a few scenes later. I assumed the sensationalism and melodrama of it all, complete with an outing for one of my favorite stage effects, Pepper's Ghost, was a nod to the original Holmes's regular complaint that Watson dressed up his stories with flagrant disregard for the actual facts. If so, this was, I think, far further over the top than anything Conan Doyle's Watson could have dreamed of. I was really quite excited about it.

A string of murders follows—Holmes not unreasonably dismisses them as copycat murders. Then Mycroft directs Holmes and Watson to take on a case from one Lady Carmichael, concerned for her husband, Lord Eustace, who has received five orange pips in an envelope in the post, which apparently signifies his death. Later, he sees the Bride in the grounds of his house. Lady Carmichael has come to Holmes, asking him to protect Lord Eustace.

In directing the case to Holmes, Mycroft comments ominously that they will be battling an enemy who lurks constantly at their elbow: Watson rattles off a shopping list of nineteenth-century concerns (read Conrad's *The Secret Agent* if you want a sense of London at this time), all of which Mycroft dismisses. Watching a second time, you get a very clear sense of what Mycroft is hinting at, something that both Holmes and Watson have so far failed to grasp. Holmes has apparently not noticed that Hooper, the surgeon at the mortuary, is in fact a woman. Watson has spotted this, and kindly lets Hooper know that he is aware, making a snide comment about the things people do to get on in the world. Our first view of the doomed Lord Eustace includes him making similarly snide remarks about his wife's plans for the day, assuming she will either do embroidery or visit her milliner, when clearly she has two children, a husband, and a house to take care of, and that's just for starters.

To protect Sir Eustace, Holmes and Watson stake out the house, waiting in a convenient conservatory until something happens. This is the stuff of so many of Conan Doyle's stories—waiting under cover of dark for something to happen—but here Moffat decides to fill in the gaps by having Watson try to persuade Holmes to open up about his past. Thus follows the painful stuff of bromance, and this viewer at least shared Holmes's relief when the 'ghost' showed up and they could do some running around.

Perhaps the most spectacular moment comes as Watson stands guard by the window they have smashed to gain entrance to the house, and the 'ghost' appears behind him. We know, of course, that the ghost must be corporeal, but we might feel a certain sympathy for Watson when he legs it in search of Holmes. There was a genuine frisson of fear at that moment. I savoured it, little realising that things were about to go seriously off the rails.

But maybe I should have guessed. Because, at this point in the proceedings, I couldn't help noticing that, with half the show still to run, we didn't exactly seem to be going anywhere. And what about Mycroft? Conan Doyle's Mycroft is described thus by Watson, when he meets him for the first time in 'The Greek Interpreter':

> Mycroft Holmes was a much larger and stouter man than Sherlock. His body was absolutely corpulent, but his face, though massive, had preserved something of the sharpness of expression which was so remarkable in that of his brother. His eyes, which were of a peculiarly light, watery gray, seemed to always retain that far-away, introspective look which I had only observed in Sherlock's when he was exerting his full powers.

'I am glad to meet you, sir,' said he, putting out a broad, fat hand like the flipper of a seal.'

Fat, yes, but not a glutton, so far as we can tell. Conan Doyle's Holmes notes that Mycroft leads a very sedentary life, moving between his home, his work and the Diogenes Club, whereas MoffatMycroft seems to owe more to the Pythons' Mr Creosote, revelling in his gourmandising. And Mycroft draws attention to his increasing girth when Holmes visits him again the next day, and to something else when he describes Holmes as the virus in the data, words that simply don't belong in Victorian London. Something is not right here.

Indeed, a lot of things are not right. And I don't just mean in terms of Moffat's Sherlock Holmes being his usual obnoxious self, rather than being on his best Victorian behaviour. Back at the beginning, Mary Morstan receives a note that is signed 'M.' There are two possibilities—Moriarty, who is dead, or Mycroft, who most certainly is not (nor likely to be as he is played by Mark Gatiss, and it seems unlikely that Moffat and Gatiss will be writing out Gatiss's character any time soon). At this stage, I can't tell if this is Moffat attempting to misdirect us—oh my god, Mary's conniving with Moriarty, who is not dead after all—or whether he's assuming we'll assume the obvious, because, well, it's obvious. Is he playing mind games with his audience, or is he just being an incredibly clumsy storyteller?

Given Moffat can never resist throwing the entire rack of seasonings into almost any story he writes, it's reasonable to surmise that both Moriarty and Mycroft are involved (and for Sebastian Moran to be there too, for all I know). And that is the last we see of Mary Morstan for over half the show. Her absence is marked *chez* Watson, where Watson is having trouble keeping the maid in order (it is, after all, Mary's job to supervise the household staff, not Watson's), but Watson himself is irritated rather than puzzled by this. It is an inconvenience rather than a cause for concern. Does this happen all the time? What a remarkably modern marriage, we might think.

So it's hardly surprising when Moriarty, still dead at this point, appears in Holmes's rooms as he tries to puzzle out the business of the Abominable Bride. Hold on, let's run that past me again. Moriarty is dead and yet here he is, large as life, not quite twice as natural as he seems to have a large hole in the back of his head …

At which point we come to realise that we are not in Victorian London in a one-off Christmas special, but are in fact in MoffatSherlock's memory palace, which is of course set up to look like Conan Doyle's Holmes's world. And we have just been summoned back to the twenty-first century to appreciate the cleverness of it all. The sense of disappointment I felt at this moment is difficult to convey. Primarily, I felt cheated of the entertainment I had been promised, because yet again Steven Moffat felt the inexorable desire to disappear up his own metafictional fundament, a tendency that will always, always, always trump any attempt on his part at decent storytelling.

The clues pointing to the fact that Moffat and his creation are locked in some sort of battle to the death within an infinite regress are all there if you remember that Moffat has, essentially, only one subject, and that's Sherlock. Or rather, insofar as *Sherlock* is a show about making a show, it is really all about Moffat's efforts to turn Sherlock into Doctor Who. So, actually, it's really all about Steven. Again.

We'll come back to why Sherlock is in his dolls house, sorry, memory palace, in a moment. First, we need to go back to Victorian London and those murders, and luckily Sherlock is able to take us there. By this time, we have probably accepted that we are not going to get a straightforward solution to the murders, except … wait, Sherlock surmises how it was done—with the use of a substitute dead body (never a twin), enabling Emelia to murder her husband later that night. Then Emelia herself must die, but that's OK, because she is making a sacrifice for the cause, and has consumption so is going to die soon anyway.

This is me giving Moffat the side-eye for that one.

It's at this point that Holmes and Watson receive word from Mary Morstan—remember her? She has been absent for almost the entire drama so far—who has apparently tracked down the people responsible for the murders and asks for their help. She is, according to Holmes, now in mortal danger. Which is how we find ourselves in the crypt of a (very badly CGI'd) half-ruined church, witnessing a peculiar ceremony with a lot of flaming torches, Latin chanting, and people parading in hooded costumes. Either they're penitents or a hitherto unknown English branch of the Ku Klux Klan—I assume Moffat drew this from 'The Five Orange Pips', where the Klan was involved. Or maybe Moffat has been reading up on the English folk-horror movement lately.

At which point Holmes reveals he knows exactly what is going on (and doubtless has done all along) and breaks into an impassioned explanation of how these mysterious costumed people are women who have been wronged in various ways by their menfolk and who have decided to act for themselves, murdering the men who have treated them badly. So, Emelia Ricoletti, the Abominable Bride, is a symbol they can utilise. Anyone can be Emelia (I'm Emelia; no, I am) as and when needed.

So there you have it. This is the culmination of all the odd comments about silent women, powerless women, Watson worrying about suffragists and overly perky housemaids, Mrs Hudson feeling overlooked, Lady Carmichael being slighted by her husband, Emelia Ricoletti murdering her no-good man, Molly Hooper having to conceal her gender in order to get the job she wants. I mean, look, it was Mary who practically solved the case by finding out where the ceremony was happening. But not to worry. Sherlock is here now, to mansplain how badly women are being treated. There, everything's better, isn't it?

Isn't it?

Well, what do you think?

What I *did* think was that this might be Moffat's attempt to try to make amends for his past cock-ups in the feminism department. He's acknowledged how women are so often demeaned and silenced in his stories by having everyone comment on how they are demeaned and silenced. And then, like a deus ex machina, Sherlock makes a speech—during which he demeans and silences women all over again by reminding them of how they are demeaned and silenced. That is, he speaks for them rather than letting them speak for themselves. And yes, I did notice that Mary's investigation is conducted entirely off-screen, and we see it only at the end, when Sherlock arrives to take over. I have no idea whether or not that was intentional, but if it wasn't, and even if it was—you begin to understand why the women are assuming the identity of the Bride and offing their annoying spousal units. (And were I Sherlock Holmes I'd lock my bedroom door at night, just in case Mrs Hudson got an idea or two).

Nor has it escaped my attention that this is supposedly all Sherlock's rancid drug-addled imagining anyway, so it would be easy to dismiss the entire thing out of hand. Except that I think Moffat really believes he is giving the ladies a decent crack of the whip in this show. Which is to miss the point entirely, as Moffat usually does.

Ladies and gentlemen, I give you feminism the Moffat Way. Because everything must always be about Sherlock Holmes; that is, everything must always be about Steven Moffat. This is not an apology for ignoring women, mistreating them, exploiting them. Perhaps Moffat thinks he is acknowledging those concerns with his oh-so-amusing metafictional criticism, having Mrs Hudson go on strike in the name of satire, or having Mary Morstan vanish to solve the case. Perhaps he thinks he's done a good thing by having Sherlock speak up on behalf of downtrodden women. He may think that, but let's not forget the pay-off. Mary, it turns out, was indeed summoned by Mycroft, and asked to keep an eye on Sherlock, because Mycroft worries about him. Yes, thoroughly modern Mary Morstan is effectively working as a superior sort of nursemaid. Either that or someone got hold of a box set of *Elementary* and knew a good idea when they saw it.

I've said before that it seems to me that Gatiss and Moffat, despite being almost my age, continue to behave like a couple of rather clever sixth-formers, showing off their cleverness. I don't deny for a moment that they love Sherlock Holmes, but I contend again that they don't really 'get' Conan Doyle's Sherlock Holmes. They seem incapable of taking that character and making something of him in the way that Brett, Merrison, Rathbone, and the writers of *Elementary* have done. The thing is, you can only do so much standing around being amazed that you get to work on the characters you've loved ever since you were old enough to be aware they existed. Sooner or later, if the stories you are telling are shit—and they are—you will be found out. Be you doctor, consulting detective, or script-emperor, sooner or later enough people will notice you have got no clothes on. And, in fact, more than a few of us have been noticing this for quite a while.

Don't you think Steven Moffat looks cold?

The Hobbit, or Madly in All Directions

The trouble with the internet is that it's all too easy to feel you've been to see a film before you even set foot inside the cinema. Having spent the last week or so bombarded with information and opinions about *The Hobbit* Part 1, it was almost an anticlimax to be settled in a seat at our local picturehouse, waiting for the movie to begin.

And before you ask, there will be no discussions of cinematic technicalities. I saw the film in 2D on the poky second screen. The cinema was less than half-full and the proprietors presumably thought that *Life of Pi* would be more popular (tigers, oh my!). I am not as upset about this as you might suppose. I wear glasses because, among other things, I suffer from a lack of depth perception, and I find that they don't play nicely together with 3D specs. Perhaps Erebor or the goblins' stronghold would have been more exciting in 3D, but I was happy to sacrifice that experience if it meant I didn't feel queasy and vertiginous throughout the film. (The Mines of Moria in 2D were quite bad enough, thank you). On the other hand, I would have liked to have seen it on a bigger screen.

However, because it is, as we know, a long film, the cinema thoughtfully provided a short intermission part way through. It felt like going back fifty years in time, though mercifully they no longer expect everyone to stand for the National Anthem at the end of the film. (You think I'm joking, don't you? I'm not). So, full water bottle—check; iron rations—check. Are we sitting comfortably? We should be, for we will be undeniably sitting here for some time. Cue music, roll credits, and it's time for ~~Back to Middle-earth I~~ *The Hobbit: An Unexpected Journey. The Film of the Book.*

The question, I suppose, is what should I expect from a film that is an adaptation of the first third of an average-sized book for children, and that clocks in at ten minutes shy of three hours? I was less bored in the first hour than a lot of people seem to have been, but the film undeniably picked up once Bilbo finally raced out of his front door, waving the dwarves' contract in his hand. Not quite how it happened in the novel, as I recall, when Bilbo had to be chivvied away from the breakfast table by Gandalf, but then this is certainly not the film of the book. In fact, having rewatched *The Lord of the Rings: The Fellowship of the Ring* last night, I was struck by how similar in many ways the two films are in their construction.

In each case, a settled and affluent hobbit is suddenly propelled out of a comfortable existence by external forces, in both cases orchestrated by Gandalf the Grey. In *Lord of the Rings*, of course, the Ring itself is another external factor, but in *The Hobbit*—in the film, at any rate—Gandalf's twin motives in involving Bilbo appear to be a conviction that Bilbo is too settled (great emphasis is laid on Gandalf's distaste for Bilbo's fondness for doilies and crockery), and the need to find a *species* with which Smaug is unfamiliar. Such motivation is not, I think, present in the book, but Jackson, as many commentators have noted, is busy doing infill for *Lord of the Rings*.

In each case, too, there is a sense of the hero of the piece being ineffectual when it comes to surviving beyond the borders of the Shire. In the novel of *Lord of the Rings*, Frodo seems incapable of commanding his group of hobbits on the journey to Buckland and then on to the Prancing Pony at Bree, although he is at least able to keep moving; in the film he seems remarkably passive, inclined to put on the Ring at every available opportunity and place himself in harm's way. Bilbo, by comparison, is cheerfully open about his incompetence throughout *Hobbit* 1, redeeming himself in the eyes of Thorin through an act of physical bravery, whereas in the novel, although he is aware of his physical shortcomings, he is able to counter this through his cunning and a facility with words. That ability is only intermittently on show in *Hobbit* 1, most notably in 'Riddles in the Dark', the famous encounter with Gollum. We see it also in the encounter with the trolls, although it is left to Gandalf to split the rock and send in light, inferring that Bilbo can't quite be trusted to deal with the trolls alone.

And of course, he can't be. The film's arc demands that he gradually redeem himself in the eyes of the dwarves; to do too much too soon would be to topple the story's tower of tropes before its time. Instead, Bilbo has to go to Thorin's aid and kill a goblin before he is worthy of notice. There is a not-fully-articulated argument going on here about the value of brains over brawn.

Rereading *The Hobbit*

As a teenager I read and reread *Lord of the Rings* to the point where I can no longer read it at all because I still remember most of it too clearly. I probably haven't read it in its entirety for something like thirty years. I was never particularly enamoured of the geneaologies when I was young and now, even if I were to reread *The Silmarillion*, I could never recapture the intense concentration of the teenage reader, who could have absorbed and retained all this material if she'd so desired. And yet, although I was delighted to discover that *Lord of the Rings* was about hobbits, I rarely reread *The Hobbit*. It remained vague in my mind—a dark place, filled with woods, trolls, heavily bearded men, dwarves and, best of all, a dragon.

Rereading it in the run-up to seeing the film, I enjoyed it a lot more than I'd expected to, even though this reading is fuelled by academic interest rather than simple pleasure. In particular, many of Tolkien's sources are clear to me in a way they were not to my younger self. Beorn, the bear-man, the shape-shifter, is familiar to me now as a figure in Norse sagas. The dwarves are more problematic, part Nibelung, part Disney, but I can better understand why I find them so difficult. Other sources are more elusive. I knew George MacDonald's *The Princess and the Goblin* when I was a child, thanks to readings on TV, though I doubt I made a connection between it and *The Hobbit* at the time. In MacDonald's story, the goblins live under the mountain. They hate humans, from whom they are descended, and are planning a war on them. Curdie, a miner's son, rescues Princess Irene when she is captured by goblins, and the two of them set out to thwart the goblins' plan. The thematic connection with *The Hobbit* seems quite clear.

There is in addition a strong sense of *The Wind in the Willows* about this story. Bilbo's snugly appointed hobbit-hole is reminiscent of Rat's riverside abode, while the dwarves' perception of their home underground reminds me of the way in which Badger's house reaches back into the hillside, down through history. The general obsession with food and feasting can, I think, be traced back to this book as well.

Familiar too, and I'd genuinely not noticed this before, is the likeness of Lake-town to *Lud-in-the-Mist* by Hope Mirrlees, published in 1926. I'm thinking here not of the strange interweavings of human and faery life, but of the venality of the men who run Lake-town.[1]

Indeed, *The Hobbit* is suffused with commercial calculation. If Smaug is dead, who does his hoard belong to? There are many groups interested in it, and this much is made plain in the film. Peter Jackson makes plain the irony in the fact that the dwarves, the group most interested in the gold, are also seeking a home, and from this we are prompted to believe their motives are pure. Whether this will change in *Hobbit* 2 and 3 remains to be seen.

The novel is, I think, more ambiguous, not only about the motivations in play but also in its portrayal of the dynamics between the various groups. The relationship between elves and men is built on commerce, the purchase of alcohol, and, we guess, other things as well. The elves of Mirkwood are more hard-headed than many of those we will later encounter in *Lord of the Rings*. Yes, they love singing and song-making, and Bilbo responds to this, but they seem more robust, more tangible, than the ethereal beauties of Lothlórien and Rivendell.

---

1. Mirrlees and Tolkien lived for a number of years within a brisk fifteen-minute walk of one another's houses in Oxford; I have never been able to find out if they knew one another, though I've always suspected they didn't. On the other hand, I would be astonished if Tolkien did not know *Lud-in-the-Mist*. I frequently passed by Tolkien's house when I was a child without realising it. And I only found out that Hope Mirrlees lived in Oxford when I read her death notice in the local paper. It was years later that I found she too lived fairly close to my family's house.

Trouble with Dwarves

One of the mildly amusing running jokes throughout *Hobbit* 1 was Gandalf counting up the number of dwarves every time they got themselves out of trouble, making him not so much a wizard as a slightly harassed schoolteacher trying to keep track of his pupils on a school trip. Add to that the 'hobbit dwarves flowchart' that recently surfaced on the internet and it's clear there are *too many dwarves*.

The film is easier to parse than the novel in this respect, given that most of the dwarves have distinctive physical characteristics, generally in the department of facial hair. In the novel few of the dwarves, other than Thorin, Balin, and, because of his size and the eating jokes, Bombur, emerge as distinctive personalities. As a child I never did sort them out. To judge from the rhyming pairs of names (many of them pulled from Norse saga), and the odd number of dwarves, with Bombur almost invariably the last name, my guess is that Tolkien supposed that children would enjoy chanting the lists: ' … and *Bombur*!'. Possibly I was not the child for whom this activity was intended.

Whether the dwarves are to be taken seriously, or are intended simply to be comical, is an issue neither Tolkien nor Jackson fully address. Their back story is entirely serious. The dwarves are a displaced people who want their ancestral home back. Their love of gold and their greed for more gold have proved their downfall, as it was the oversized hoard of treasure that attracted Smaug in the first place. In both the novel and *Hobbit* 1, the dwarves are separated from their kind. The Men of Dale move down to Lake-town, the elves always retreat to the forest, and hobbits live quietly, unobserved, in the idyll of the Shire. But always they are in groups. It is the dwarves who seem to lose contact with one another all too easily.

And yet, Tolkien frequently portrays the dwarves simply as a troupe of Disney characters, concerned with eating, drinking, and generally messing about; this is a group that apparently doesn't know how to conduct itself in the wilderness whereas Bilbo, used to being unobtrusive, knows how to avoid attracting too much attention to himself.

Jackson takes his cue from Tolkien, and so we have extended sequences of bad table manners, jokes involving flatulence and belching, and, dare one say it, a reluctance to engage with threats if they can send in the Burglar first. It is a far cry from *Lord of the Rings* where, although Jackson had (lack of) height jokes, dwarf-tossing jokes, and so on, Gimli was also the embodiment of courage, bravery, ferocity, and, finally, loyalty to his friends. Perhaps the trajectory Jackson plans to follow is that of a people finding self-respect again, though it must be noted that Gimli's table manners remain a little messy; it must be all that facial hair.

For Children or Adults?

Tolkien's uncertainty as to how to deal with the dwarves seems to me to suggest a deeper unease as to what *The Hobbit* is supposed to be: children's story or something deeper. The tone veers all over the place, from patronising Victorian fable to medieval romance to Norse saga and back again. Given that Tolkien was already an inveterate scribbler of stories for his children, one has the sense that *The Hobbit* was similarly intended, at least to begin with. But clearly, Tolkien got sidetracked somewhere along the way. We move from an opening assuring us that the hobbit-hole was not a nasty hole (foreshadowing the abode of Gollum, perhaps) to a point where Bilbo stands at the deathbed of Thorin Oakenshield, a sequence that seems to come from a completely different story.

This uncertainty seems to persist in Jackson's film. Plate-juggling and snot jokes are interspersed with wargs, fight scenes with goblins, wargs, attack bunnies and more wargs, oh, and elves. It's all very decorative but too often it feels like fan service for those who loved the original franchise. The battle scenes in the goblin stronghold are preposterous and at times horribly jokey considering they're mostly about slaughter. They may be bad guys, but this film frequently holds life very cheap, especially if you're a goblin. One detects a distinct whiff of that nineteenth-century fear of the teeming masses, faceless, endlessly replaceable, running out of control at the drop of a hat, needing to be cut down to size.

Whereas Tolkien intermittently finds a sense of grandeur, mostly at the points when the story reaches back to the Norse sagas, whenever Jackson finds the action flagging, he gleefully reaches for the CGI, and we have another battle.

Riddles in the Dark

In narrative terms, the encounter between Bilbo and Gollum is a digression from the main action, namely finding the dwarves. Bilbo has managed to conceal himself in the tunnels of the underground fortress, and is sneaking around, trying to figure out how to rescue the dwarves, when he finds the Ring and meets Gollum. When he discovers the Ring's ability to render him invisible, he will use it to rescue the dwarves, but at this point no one knows of the Ring's deeper significance. Anyone watching the film cannot escape the significance of Bilbo's finding the Ring; Jackson's challenge then is to make the encounter seem as fresh and new as it would have been for a first reader of *The Hobbit*. Rather as I felt the first sight of the Black Riders in *LOTR* 1 and the encounter at the ford were test pieces for Jackson's ability to get *LOTR* onto the screen in a form I recognised, Riddles in the Dark would inevitably provide a measure of the quality of *Hobbit* 1.

Riddles are an intrinsic part of Anglo-Saxon literature. The asking and solving of riddles is akin to sacred ritual, and the riddle-telling process is taken very seriously by both Bilbo and Gollum. You note how familiar they both are with the process, the ease with which they solve the first riddles, and how even when Bilbo wonders aloud, 'what have I got in my pocket', which is not a riddle at all, Gollum is nonetheless bound by the rules of riddle-telling to honour the question.

In the novel, it's a beautifully constructed sequence—the dank setting, the two riddlers manoeuvring in the darkness, physically and verbally, Bilbo not sure where Gollum is, the play with words as intensely anxious as his need to know the identity of the creature he is dealing with. Thankfully, Jackson stays close to the original, and close to the actors. No huge vistas here, just two incredibly skilful players doing a fantastic job. While the rest of the film is undoubtedly entertaining, this sequence is where the adaptation stays most faithful to the original novel, bringing out the drama of the moment without feeling the need to change a thing.

You Want Backstory with That?

Hobbit 1 (and I must stop thinking of it as *Lord of the Rings: The Phantom Menace*) covers the first 121 pages of a 317-page novel, and draws to a close with Thorin acknowledging that Bilbo the Burglar might be a decent sort of chap after all, something he will not do for another 200 pages in the novel. As noted, it's a three-hour film, more or less, and there are three of them. While smearing the story of *The Hobbit* across three films, like butter spread too thinly on bread, Jackson is also attempting to develop the *Lord of the Rings* backstory and show how the situation that pertains at the beginning of that novel came into being.

It's an interesting idea but oh, I don't know … It seems to me more as though Jackson couldn't quite bear to let go of Middle-earth, and came up with this merry wheeze to keep things going. There is an element of fan service about the whole thing, including fan service to Jackson himself. Whereas in the three *Lord of the Rings* films, the cutting between storylines revealed the simultaneity of the different stories in a way that is often difficult to decipher in the novels, in *Hobbit* 1, the drawing together of such disparate threads seems to generate more confusion than it dispels. Perhaps it will make more sense in subsequent films, but too often I felt *Hobbit* 1 was struggling to keep its various elements properly in play.

I enjoyed seeing the film, and I'm looking forward to the next one when it eventually shows up. Whether it is *The Hobbit* is another question altogether, though I'm not sure this is a question that matters all that much.

Watching *Hamlet*

We have all been waiting for Benedict Cumberbatch's *Hamlet*, haven't we? Haven't we? Well, I don't know. It's the kind of role he should be thinking about, given where he is in his career, and there is no denying that a Cumberbatch Hamlet would be highly bankable. And there's the rub. This production was always going to be a Cumberbatch event rather than a staging of *Hamlet*.

The tickets sold out in seconds. There were endless press shows, amidst much carping from the production team that the critics had based their reviews on the preview nights. Worst of all, apparently, the director had moved the 'To be' speech to the beginning of the play, until a general outcry forced them to move it back to its customary place.

I saw the production as a National Theatre Live broadcast at the Gulbenkian cinema in Canterbury. According to the person fronting the live transmission from the Barbican, not only was the play being simultaneously broadcast at cinemas nationwide, it was being shown worldwide as well. We were definitely part of an EVENT.

And after all this, was it worth the fuss?

Yes. And, alas, no.

The short version is that Benedict Cumberbatch, much as I expected he would be, is a very good Hamlet. Unfortunately, he is stuck in an appalling production of *Hamlet*.

The long version? Well, where to begin?

My theatre posts wrestle endlessly with the conundrum of how one produces a cinematic experience that 'faithfully' recreates the sense of a theatrical performance, because I do realise that not everyone watching on screen wants what I want. I'm aware that some of my criticisms undoubtedly emerge from the fact that I really miss live theatre. Watching a performance on screen, while it can be good, just isn't the same for me. Or rather, in some respects it's so much better it's not like being at the theatre at all. I want to be in the theatre.

I've been watching Royal Shakespeare Company broadcasts, live and recorded, for a number of years, and they do a decent job of conveying a genuine sense of theatricality. Critically, they never lose sight of the fact that there is an audience present. I always feel that I'm watching a staged production, with occasional nods to the fact that I am seeing it from a different perspective.

The Royal National Theatre follows a different philosophy, in that their broadcasts mostly seem to want to eliminate the audience altogether. We might see them briefly at the beginning, but once the play begins, they exist only as laughter or applause. The RNT's productions seem to be staged with more of an eye as to how they will look like on camera. This isn't a crime per se, but it seems to me to lose sight of the fact that even at the cinema I'm expecting to see a play, on a stage. I think the RNT does best with more contemporary works—my favourite of the things I've seen from them is Alan Bennett's *The Habit of Art*, which had a very plain staging and was simply filmed. There was no theatrical or cinematic fussiness and I could concentrate on the words and acting.

I'm not clear what the relationship is between the RNT and Sonia Friedman Productions, the company that staged this new *Hamlet*, but the screened version was produced under the aegis of NT Live. Consequently, I don't know who made choices about camera angles and so forth, but for the purposes of this discussion I am going to assume that Lyndsey Turner, director of the play, was involved to some extent in decisions around camera positioning, and that the play was originally designed with the understanding that it would be filmed and broadcast.

Because the first thing I need to say about the Cumberbatch *Hamlet* is that throughout the performance it's impossible to ignore the play's staging, even for a moment. That might sound odd, because surely the whole point of a play is that it is a work intended to be performed on a stage? But there is staging and there is stagey, and this production falls definitively into the latter category. I remember someone once telling me that actors hate it when the curtain goes up and the audience applauds the set, because it means their focus has already shifted away from the actors. Whilst there is no actual applause in this production, I nonetheless had a strong sense throughout the broadcast that I was being invited to mentally applaud the set. The staging (and for the purposes of this discussion I include set, business, lighting, and music) was the dominant presence throughout, and it frequently got in the way of the actors.

Remember the decision to situate 'To be, or not to be' at the beginning of the play? It is highly likely that Shakespeare and his contemporaries were constantly shuffling around chunks of play, trying to get the right effect, so it shouldn't be a problem if a contemporary director wishes to do the same. In more contemporary settings, like the Royal Court, such an approach might be effective; on a West End stage, which is, like it or not, a fairly conservative arena, people are paying for a certain thing, and expect to get it.

The play begins not on the battlements of Elsinore as is traditional, but in a room somewhere in the castle. The room is empty but for a few packing cases, and Hamlet is listening to an old record on a portable record player. This is, we are led to believe, all that is left to him of his father, who has of course recently died. Inserting the 'To be' speech here was presumably intended by Turner to provide a clearer insight into Hamlet's state of mind. Without it, the opening is weak, but neither can I see what placing it here achieves, other than to emphasise something that will become clear anyway: that Hamlet is moody and introspective. Perhaps Turner wanted to head off the 'mad or not?' dispute, but I'm not convinced it works.

Hamlet is summoned to attend his mother's marriage to his uncle, at which point, in a grand theatrical gesture, the backdrop is whisked away and we are transported to the cavernous hall of a grand country house, with a staircase to one side, a balcony along the back of the stage, a doorway opening into a corridor, and another doorway that seems to lead out to a porch. All the world's a stage, but in this instance, it seems that Elsinore itself is intended to be the stage and contain the outside world within it. On those occasions when the action moved theoretically 'outdoors', it seemed more as if the outside world had irrupted into the world of Elsinore. This is most evident at the point when the players come to the castle and perform *The Murder of Gonzago* for the court. They perform first within a tiny toy theatre, brought into the entrance hall, and then the Player King, in his role as Gonzago, steps down into the court audience, which itself sits among off-stage scenery, to sleep in an orchard composed of leafy twigs and dried flowers set in musical instruments (no, I don't know why either. Improvisation?). Hamlet himself steps out of the audience to take on the role of the murderer. All of this is clearly intended to blur boundaries, but I found it rather awkward.

What struck me particularly about this production was how focused it was on the threat of war. In the other productions I've seen, the presence of Young Fortinbras on the borders has seemed vague, rumbling away in the background as the Danish try and work out what to do with their problem child. Here, the implication seems to be that Hamlet's behaviour is really very, very vexing, as he's getting in the way of this war they're trying to deal with. This might be an interesting way to examine Hamlet's story, but unfortunately I couldn't help feeling it had emerged from the staging decisions rather than the other way round.

So, while the stage is filled with the various accoutrements of a war office—desks, telephones, maps, flocks of secretaries dressed in tailored serge or khaki, everyone clutching files or making notes, Claudius and Polonius in sashes to show their status, Gertrude in a vaguely Eva Peron hairdo—Hamlet appears in the middle of this in a toy soldier uniform, with a drum, marching up and down on the table. Later, he sits in a toy fort, surrounded by almost life-size toy soldiers, pretending to fire off his rifle at all and sundry. It's a credit to Benedict Cumberbatch that he actually makes this seem reasonable—he's a good physical actor, and has excellent comic timing—but OK, we get the point: toy fort, toy theatre, Hamlet is reverting to childhood and acting up because his mum has remarried barely two months after his dad died, and he's not getting enough attention.

For the life of me, I still can't work out why all the doors and windows had to be blown in at the end of the first part, when Claudius has decided that something has to be done about Hamlet once and for all. The stage is left covered in paper soot and fake rubble, which is all still there in the second half. I presume this is to indicate that any chance of family unity, and by implication Denmark's own sovereignty, has now failed, but it's all a bit *Fall of the House of Usher*. Not so much something being rotten in the state of Denmark as a complete architectural failure in search of a restoration project, with Young Fortinbras finally arriving to preside over everything like Kevin McCloud.

I have come across reviews of the screening that praise the way in which the characters seem so tiny on the stage, as if to suggest 'As flies to wanton boys are we to th' gods. They kill us for their sport' (wrong play, but you take my point). I grant you it's been maybe fifteen years since I saw a play onstage at the Barbican, but my recollection is that the stage, while sufficiently capacious to accommodate Henry V's surprisingly substantial army and a rainstorm in the production I saw (Branagh's *Henry V* in 1985), is nowhere near as cavernous as the screening seems to indicate, while the auditorium, although large, was fairly intimate in atmosphere. Even in the cheap seats I never felt I was as far from the stage as the filming seemed to suggest the audience was, and so again, I find myself wondering exactly what the theatre audience saw.

To me, it seemed less that the screened version was making a point (and presumably a point that the theatre audience would not be experiencing) as that the cast appeared to be rattling around in an unfeasibly large space, which is odd when *Hamlet* is, to my mind, a fairly intimate sort of play, very interior. And if that is the case, why was I given this entirely different experience of the play from the audience in the theatre that night (this strikes me as a very Cameronian interpretation of 'all in this together'. I suppose I could argue I was being compensated for having to see the play as a cinemagoer, but it sits badly with my idea of what I thought I would be seeing).

In fact, I entirely lost track of where the audience was in relation to the stage. To me, the balcony and staircase that dominated the stage was at the back of it, with the long corridor, up which Ophelia climbs once she has resolved to drown herself, at the side. Yet this makes no sense if the seated audience is to see Ophelia vanish from the stage, which means that I must have been 'watching' a good portion of the play from an angle not available to the audience, effectively from the wings. The implication seems to be that the balcony was set at a slight angle across the stage, but even so, it still suggests that what I saw is nothing like what the audience in the theatre saw. Plus, if the stage was as enormous as the broadcast suggests, I got the benefit of many, many close-ups of Cumberbatch in a way that the theatre audience never could. So, lucky me, I guess, and poor theatre audience.

The inescapable conclusion of all this is that it was never intended to be a theatrical production in the truest sense, but was imagined from the outset as a film. Which is very different, I'd argue, from filming a theatrical production (see Julie Traymor's *A Midsummer Night's Dream*, which is unequivocally a film based on a theatrical production, and never pretending to be anything other than that). This might explain some of the other things that made me unhappy, not least the sound design, which emphasised every significant moment with huge crashing chords, and the lighting design, which performed a visual equivalent. Very little was left to the imagination. Much was elaborately signalled. And yet, every now and then there would be a delicious little moment, purely theatrical, such as when Hamlet's father's ghost descends into the grave; I'd spotted someone flipping up the trap door under cover of dark, but it looked for all the world as though he was simply vanishing through the floor. The groundlings would have loved it. I certainly did, and it was probably the simplest special effect on display all night.

At other times, I found myself wondering about such things as how Hamlet would stab Polonius behind the arras when both arras and sharp pointy weapons were distinctly lacking. As it turned out, the curtains of the toy theatre were pressed into unconvincing service as the arras, and even as I'd wondered about the dagger, my eye drifted to the display of weaponry on the wall, and it became obvious—the reverse Chekhov principle, so to speak. However, given that the play appeared to be set in Upper Romanovia, it did make a nonsense of the last act: Claudius's sudden desire, in the midst of ruin and gunfire, to see Hamlet and Laertes fight a demonstration duel with foils seems bizarre. One could almost see an unvoiced 'WTF?' forming on Cumberbatch's face as he considered the proposal.

The one thing I can't speak to as it's been so long since I read it, is how much Turner has moved the script around. 'To be, or not to be' was restored to something approaching its customary place, but as I noted earlier the play no longer begins with the sighting of Hamlet Senior's ghost, and this decision really does feel wrong. We also thought some of the other speeches had been moved around or edited. I know this happens all the time and we don't really notice, but there was in this instance something oddly breathless about the play. Events frequently arrived suddenly and unexpectedly; neither of us was convinced that the grave-digging scene was quite as we'd seen it before, and the whole of the second half seemed generally very perfunctory, especially the final collective death scene, with bodies dropping like ninepins. Perhaps Turner wanted to avoid the long, drawn-out savouring of Hamlet's death, but something was indeed rotten in the state of Denmark by this point.

Having somehow devoted two thousand words to the play's staging before considering the actors, let's turn to them. Front and centre, Benedict Cumberbatch. The one thing that is so very, very good about Cumberbatch is his sense of timing. We can talk about the energy and physicality of his performance as Hamlet, but it's really all about the timing. He brightens the action every time he is on the stage.

I'm trying to avoid falling into the trap of designating his Hamlet as mad or feigning madness, as has been the custom. Neither is, I believe, appropriate in this case. Cumberbatch's is a very confused Hamlet, and that's not entirely down to having to fight his way out of a very confused staging. I found myself thinking that here is a man who has not been allowed to mourn properly. It's been barely two months since his father died, he's been dragged back from university to find himself attending a wedding with added funeral, he's surrounded by people telling him to brace up because there is war imminent. There is no room here for him to process his own feelings. He throws tantrums, yes; he lashes out, undoubtedly. He's surrounded by people exhorting him to get on with life, and life is defined as war.

The problem, of course, is that Hamlet seems not to be interested in war, or in politics. You wonder why Claudius doesn't just let him go back to his studies. Hamlet seems to be less concerned about the usurpation of his kingdom, more about the usurpation of his mother's bed, but even that I didn't find convincing. Mostly, he seems to want to be on his own, to grieve. And this perhaps is the problem at the heart of this production. Turner can't seem to reconcile the exteriority of war—the excitement of uniforms and noise filling the stage—with Hamlet's necessary interiority. The latter is frequently lost to the big gesture.

Both Gertrude and Claudius seem to enjoy the imminence of war, as though it gave them purpose even though they're revealed to be politically inept—because obviously, the thing you do when you have secured an assurance that Young Fortinbras isn't going to war with you is to then let him march through your lands on his way to an irrelevant skirmish somewhere else. What the elder Hamlet would have done about it, had he lived, I'm not sure—he makes his appearances in a rotting military costume, which might be a clue, and perhaps also an explanation for why the younger Hamlet dresses himself up as a red-coated soldier. But given that Claudius and Gertrude favour a more modern style of battle dress, one wonders if the production is pointing at a theoretical clash—old school honour versus modern military pragmatism. If so, it doesn't really come to anything. The fact that Claudius has effectively usurped Hamlet's position as king is addressed only obliquely, when Hamlet, in *The Murder of Gonzago*, assumes a coat on the back of which is painted 'King'.

One might argue that Young Fortinbras's refusal to obey his uncle, Old Fortinbras, stands also as a reproach to Young Hamlet, as is the readiness of the populace to proclaim Laertes king, but this is never really explored. Perhaps the strongest moment comes when Hamlet, on his way to the ship to England, passes through Young Fortinbras's camp, and it suddenly dawns on him what's happening. At this point, he seems to decide that he has been focusing on the wrong issues, and it's time to go back and save his country from his family. It is, of course, already too late for that, but in the fencing match we get a glimpse of that Hamlet, the dashing young man who might have been king. At the same time, would that Hamlet have ever given in to Claudius's command that he fight Laertes?

I can't say I warmed to either Ciarán Hinds's Claudius or Anastasia Hille's Gertrude, at least not in the first part of the play. Hinds seemed somewhat out of place, as though he had stumbled in from a film about gangsters, while Hille was performing generic hard-faced practical bitch. Things began to improve at the point where Hamlet observes his uncle's soliloquy and debates whether to kill him there and then. The scene was genuinely powerful, perhaps because it was stripped of flummery and focused instead on two people acting their socks off. In the second part, confronted with Ophelia's madness, both Hinds and Hille seemed genuinely moved but unable to adequately respond. Again, I think, because it's impossible to do anything other than to take this sequence straight, without gimmicks (well, until the crashing chords at the end, to tell us this is a dramatic moment—no shit).

It did strike me, though, when Gertrude talks about having imagined that Hamlet and Ophelia would marry, that you really never would have guessed that from the first part of the play. OK, partly it is that everyone is telling Ophelia that this relationship won't work, can't be allowed to work—in this production Laertes is more unsympathetic as a character than I recall seeing before—but neither has there been the remotest hint of an indication from anyone who isn't Hamlet that this might have been on the cards.

And Ophelia, let us talk of Ophelia, and Sian Brooke's storming performance, the best thing in the play after Cumberbatch himself. Actually, better than Cumberbatch. The presentation of Ophelia is the one genuinely interesting thing about this production. This is no dalliance that turns sour because Hamlet is either feigning madness or genuinely ill. From the first moment we see Ophelia she is nervous, twitchy, her speech stumbling; she finds it hard to meet anyone's gaze. In fact, Ophelia constantly carries a camera and photographs everything, as if only through the camera's lens can she actually see the world. That camera stands as a shield between her and reality. She has no job as war looms (unlike Gertrude and the other court women). The fact that she has no autonomy, no purpose other than to make a marriage of some sort is heavily underlined. She would, in another world, be a war photographer or reporter, but here no one is going to allow her to do anything other than stay home and play the piano. In her 'mad' scene, she will drag a huge trunk down the stairs; after she's gone, Gertrude will open it and see huge piles of photographs. It's hard not to read that trunk as a coffin in which Ophelia has buried her creativity and her hopes for the future.

She is constantly lectured to by men—Laertes, Polonius, Claudius, and Hamlet himself. I'd never really noticed this before, but it is painfully evident here. If we assume that Hamlet is her only hope of escaping her overbearing family, his 'get thee to a nunnery' is a bitter rejection. In which case, I suppose we are to read Ophelia's suicide as a means of taking control of her life. And it is about taking control. Brooke's mad scene is heartbreaking—not a word I use lightly—and the most powerful piece of acting in the entire production. You see the moment when she makes a decision, when she knows what she has to do, and the determination with which she marches up the hill of rubble towards the light, towards the outdoors, away from Elsinore, is just extraordinary. It's at that moment you might just begin to reassess the production.

But so much else is unsatisfactory. Jim Norton's Polonius never really rises above caricature. I know one might argue that Polonius is nothing but a caricature, but Oliver Ford Davies showed that it is entirely possible to produce a Polonius who is a little fussy, a little annoying, a little too fond of dispensing good advice, but who is trying to do his best for his daughter and for his king, no matter how misplaced his ideas. Kobna Holdbrook-Smith's Laertes was dull, and Leo Bill's Horatio seemed to have little to do except turn up at intervals looking worried. I'd always seen Horatio as the one person holding Hamlet together, however imperfectly, but here, Horatio's role seemed negligible. I forget who said to me that Rosencrantz and Guildenstern (Matthew Steer and Rudi Dharmalingam) were portrayed as Hamlet's hobbit sidekicks, but sadly, they were spot on. Karl Johnson, on the other hand, showed how to make sufficient of comparatively little, in a lovely cameo as the Grave Digger, marrying the spiritual and the prosaic as he digs a grave, listens to the radio, throws skulls casually across the stage, pretends a leg bone is a microphone.

So, while it may have been an event, I'm not convinced that this production of *Hamlet* was great theatre. Indeed, had I paid to see it at the Barbican, I would have considered myself robbed. Cumberbatch is a pleasingly complex Hamlet, but I think the production itself is a bit of a mess. It's not structured in such a way as to give the actors a reasonable chance. Cumberbatch and Brooke shine, but the others struggle to make the impact they should have done.

THE STORIES THAT SHAPE US

Reading van Vogt's *Slan*

I'm just about to start teaching the second term of a first-year course in science fiction. Coming up is a seminar on fandom (I am also giving the lecture on fandom as subculture), and listed as secondary reading is A.E. van Vogt's *Slan* (1940). I am of course familiar with the slogan, 'fans are slans', but it suddenly dawned on me that I'd never actually read *Slan*. So, being a conscientious academic, I fixed that last night.

First reaction: hmm, hasn't aged well, has it?

Second thought: I wonder how it was regarded at the time? That is, other than as some sort of rallying cry for young bookish adults of the early 1960s who saw themselves as outsiders, smarter than the people around them but with their mighty intellects having so far gone unrecognised.

Exceptionality of some sort or another is a theme that figures over and over in certain strands of SF, appealing directly to the disaffected reader. In particular, I found myself thinking about how many stories I'd read that feature telepathic abilities: it is easy to see how telepathy seems particularly attractive if you can't figure out how the world works and are not adept at picking up clues. To gain the inside track by plundering someone else's mind—well, who wouldn't want to?

I recall being very taken with James Schmitz's Telzey Amberdon stories when I was young—Telzey Amberdon was everything I felt I wasn't: attractive, cool, wealthy, omnicompetent, and above all, clever. As a gawky, confused post-adolescent, I very much wanted to *be* Telzey Amberdon. What I did not notice at the time is just how insufferably smug Telzey actually is. Anne McCaffrey's Menolly, protagonist in one set of her dragon stories, sweet and innocent, and constantly amazed that everyone admires her skills, is nothing more than Telzey without the ego; one might indeed see the Menolly stories as being about developing an ego. All very life-affirming for the teenage reader

I was similarly devoted to *The Tomorrow People* on British TV, 1973-79, which focused on a group of young people who are supposedly the vanguard for the next stage of *Homo sapiens*, known inevitably as *Homo superior*. In adolescence, they develop special 'psionic' powers, such as telepathy and teleportation, and an equally smug attitude. *Homo superior* pretty much says it all. Ordinary humans, that is, you and me, are known colloquially as 'Saps', with that nicely judged mixture of affection and disparagement. Looked at from the distance of adulthood, one notes again the smugness of the 'superior' adolescent, now coupled with disdain for our failure to be like them.

I read Zenna Henderson's 'The People' stories as an adult, but while I found them very attractive in their way (a distinct flavour of Ray Bradbury lingers around them), the glamour of wish-fulfilment no longer exerts itself over me in the way I suspect it might have done when I was younger.

Lurking behind all of these is Colin Wilson's *The Outsider*, the now-classic text on alienation published in the United Kingdom and the United States in the mid-1950s, and before that, L. Ron Hubbard's *Dianetics*, a pseudoscientific belief system that first came to the attention of science fiction readers in 1950 when Hubbard published an article about it in *Astounding*. What I had forgotten was that van Vogt himself was involved in *Dianetics*, and was briefly Hubbard's head of operations in California in 1950.

I'm not sure what I expected of *Slan*, but now that I've read it, I mostly feel a sense of ... disappointment? Actually, no, not even disappointment so much as mild surprise at just how banal plans for world domination through nuclear weapons and telepathic hypnosis can turn out to be. And that's not something I ever thought I'd find myself saying.

The story opens with a young Jommy Cross and his mother entering Centropolis. The city's name immediately suggests that we are in some sort of tightly structured future setting; how far into the future is never made clear. We also learn that Centropolis is the capital of the world, so clearly political structures have changed considerably, yet one can't help feeling that this sounds like a US-centric future and that this mysterious world capital is probably somewhere in North America, below the 49th parallel.

We quickly learn that Jommy and his mother are telepaths. Jommy being only nine, his skills are still limited, though as a slan he is already twice as intelligent as any human child his age. The expositional lump already sits heavy in the gut; almost immediately the reader comes to realise it will be with her from now until the end of the novel.

Yet, in its own strange, broken way, there is something oddly compelling about this novel's beginning. Thrown into the deep end, weighed down with information, on one level the reader still has no idea what is going on. Slans are not a good thing, that's for sure, even if we don't yet know what they are. Van Vogt's opening has a flavour of Dos Passos's *Manhattan Transfer* about it as Jommy samples the thoughts of those about him, particularly after his mother is murdered and he is forced to go on the run.

Jommy's flight across the city is very well-handled; it's tense and exciting, particularly as Jommy learns to make sense of the mind-traffic around him, and use it to his advantage. Jommy eventually manages to conceal himself within the walls of a building; van Vogt does well in conveying his mounting panic as he comes to realise that someone knows about his hiding-place and is on his trail.

That's the problem, though—after this brief tour de force there is nowhere else for the story to go but down. Jommy finds himself in the hands of Granny, mad and devious but also canny enough to figure out how she can exploit a young slan; at the same time, Jommy himself, despite his comparative youth, realises quickly that he needs Granny as camouflage for the next few years. They become locked in an unhealthy relationship, like Fagin and Oliver, as Jommy uses his skills to thieve for Granny and she ... well, she gives him the space to transform himself into a miniature Count of Monte Cristo, educating himself, reconstructing her home, building himself an escape tunnel.

Jommy's relationship with Granny is one of the oddest aspects of the novel. He hates her, he uses her for his own ends, abuses the relationship, and yet, in the end, she seems to represent family for him, no matter how warped the relationship might be. He can never quite bring himself to discard her, and her presence, malign and resentful, persists throughout the novel.

Jommy himself seems to be implanted with all sorts of strange mental imperatives. Almost immediately after being cast adrift, he discovers that there are other slans in the city; he hears their thoughts but realises that although they can communicate with one another, they cannot detect his presence. Unlike 'true' slans, by which Jommy presumably means people like himself, these slans do not possess the mysterious tendrils in their hair which are the marker of the slan. When he reveals himself to them, he is puzzled by their response, which is to attempt to capture him, the understanding being that few if any true slans still exist and they represent a danger to whatever it is the tendrilless slans are up to.

The political dimensions of the relationship between true slans and the other sort is not made entirely clear, at least not until the end of the novel, and even then it is facilitated with a lot of hand-waving. For now, Jommy's task is to find other true slans who, according to his parents, must be in hiding, preparing for the time when they can finally assume the task of running the world. One of the key questions revolves around who is in charge of the tendrilless slans. Another turns on why Kier Gray, ruler of the world, hates slans so much, and why John Petty, his chief of police, hates Gray and slans in about equal measure. The biggest question of all is where are the other true slans?

The novel returns to Jommy at intervals as his search continues, as he retrieves his father's scientific secrets and makes use of them, as he battles with the 'tendrilless' slans, who appear to have infiltrated the world monarchy to a very high level. In the end, it comes as no surprise to discover that Kier Gray is himself a slan, a fact that has been heavily signalled throughout the novel, if only by his peculiar behaviour every time slans are mentioned.

Along the way we gather some sense of why it is the slans are so feared; propaganda has it that they are a machine-made mutation, created by Samuel

Lann at some point in the past. Their super-intelligence is apparently causing all human enterprises to wither away, because no one can be bothered to do anything knowing that slans have either already done it or will do it better when they get around to it. The revelation that slans are the result of natural mutation makes everything fine (though the fact that their continuing survival is down to incest, as Lann begins his 'breeding progam' with a boy and his two sisters, seems not to be considered a problem). Likewise, the 'tendrilless' slans are an intermediate developmental stage, created in order to allow the mutation to persist undetected until such time as acceptance of their presence allows the full tendrilled version to reappear. So that's all right then.

The novel works from the presumption that the slans have the right to assume control of the world, and contains little in the way of reasoned discussion about the continuing engagement between slans and humans. The human response to the slans in their midst has historically been hostile, resulting in hunting and killing. Van Vogt is very vague about this, and in fact the only example we ever see of a slan being hunted is the relentless pursuit of Jommy Cross himself. The only other slan with any significant presence in the novel is Kathleen Layton, ward of Kier Gray, who from the novel's opening pages is in a constant state of jeopardy from Gray's lieutenants, who want to use her to find out whether slans and humans can interbreed (the received wisdom is that they cannot). She is clearly intended to eventually become Jommy's love interest, though she does retain a certain level of agency when the plot demands it.

The novel becomes increasingly absurd as the story unfolds. The science is nonsensical, Jommy's motives become ever more confused, his disregard for humans ever more pronounced. Yet the situation is resolved in his favour and could even be regarded as a happy-ever-after of sorts, no matter how repugnant the novel seems to a human reader.

I'm not sure whether one is supposed to come away from the novel with the message that it's OK to be a complete shit so long as one is part of the brave new world of superhumanity, but this seems to be, in essence, what van Vogt is suggesting. Jommy Cross's behaviour is excused because he is a slan and thus, by definition, better than everyone else.

The question I am left with is this: why on earth would fans want to be slans? Yes, of course, I see the appeal of being *Homo superior*: slan, outsider, disaffected, smarter than the rest of humanity, whatever. But van Vogt's vision of the future makes it clear that slans, at least as personified by Jommy Cross, behave in a staggeringly high-handed way, with no regard for others. While one might tolerate the superior smugness of Telzey Amberdon and the Tomorrow People, given their comparative youth and lack of experience, *Slan* goes way beyond their earnest endeavours in its misguided quest to make the world a better place. The idea that humans and slans might co-exist peacefully is given very short shrift; this is apparently only ever going to be achievable if humans are hypnotised, with all that implies. On the other hand, I suppose, if you feel the world is against you, this is an entirely admirable approach.

I'm now wondering if any of my students will have read *Slan* by Thursday, and what they will have made of it.

The Weird – *The Dunwich Horror* – by H.P. Lovecraft

I was not, as a younger reader, a huge fan of Lovecraft. It wasn't the language that put me off, as I loved the flood of words, but I think I recognised instinctively that while he can describe things, he cannot make you see them, and he is not a great storyteller. Historically, he is interesting, a significant milestone in the history of the weird. But his fiction is too much of its time, irreparably marred by its author's snobbish and anti-semitic attitudes, obsessed with racial purity and terrified of anything he considers even vaguely monstrous. I cannot think of another writer who has used the word 'degenerate' as often. As a critic, one should always endeavour to separate fiction from biography, but the frequent recurrence of certain themes in Lovecraft's work makes it almost impossible to do so.

I wonder what it says about this story that the first moment that genuinely shocked me is when Wilbur Whateley gallops into the village to use the *telephone* to call for a doctor. There is no reason why this should be such a surprise. Lovecraft hasn't been coy with dates, and Whateley's telephone call occurs at a point in the story's timeline that is after 1923. One of the salient features of *The Dunwich Horror* is its scrupulous historical accounting. WWI is referred to, as are visits from government officials, reporters, and cameramen; this is a story that takes place recognisably within an organised, mechanised society. As we will see later in the narrative, the telephone is at the heart of one of its more frightening episodes. The story is unequivocally 'modern', and yet that telephone … why does it bother me so much? Perhaps it is the suddenness with which Wilbur Whateley emerges into the contemporary world. Which says a good deal about what Lovecraft has been doing in the previous five pages of his narrative.

The first sentence of *The Dunwich Horror* is quite arresting: 'When a traveller in north central Massachusetts takes the wrong fork at the junction of Aylesbury pike just beyond Dean's Corners he comes upon a lonely and curious country'. There is the geographical precision of 'north central Massachusetts' and 'Aylesbury pike just beyond Dean's Corners'; even the 'wrong fork' seems to be a recognised feature, given that the country beyond it is 'lonely' and curious'. There is the sense that to take this route is to voluntarily leave behind the mapped and familiar, where taking the wrong turn becomes a rite of passage.

Whatever else one may feel about Lovecraft, he demonstrates an undeniable skill in building a sense of unease from topographical description. I love the way the walls 'press closer and closer', while the trees are 'too large', and the vegetation has an unnerving 'luxuriance'. Are these the fears of the townie lost in the country, afraid of everything, or the concerns of the native countryman who suddenly knows that things are not as they should be? No one seems to feel easy in this landscape, with mountain summits that are 'too rounded and symmetrical to give a sense of comfort and naturalness', dotted with 'gnarled solitary figures [...] so silent and furtive that one feels somehow confronted by forbidden things, with which it would be better to have nothing to do'. There is a sense that this landscape is unnatural, that it has been shaped by some supernatural force, and that's before we get to 'the queer circles of tall stone pillars' that crown those oddly symmetrical mountain tops.

However, if there is one thing Lovecraft is incapable of doing in his descriptive writing, it is knowing when to stop. Two well-observed paragraphs of topographical dread become four distinctly over-egged paragraphs. Suddenly, nothing at all is right about this place. Ravines are 'problematical' in their depth, while bridges are 'crude' and 'dubious', and the sides of the mountains 'loom up [...] darkly and precipitously'. It goes on and on. One might say it represents the burgeoning fears of the nervous traveller in a dangerous place, his imagination beginning to run riot, but there is a dry precision about these descriptions, more evident if you hear them read out loud, that suggests otherwise. This is Lovecraft hammering home his point, just in case you missed it. And not just hammering home his point. Reading *The Dunwich Horror*, I am struck by how manipulative a writer Lovecraft is. He is absolutely determined that the reader will hear his story the way he wants it to be heard. He is like an imp sitting on the reader's shoulder, whispering into his ear. Reading these early paragraphs of *The Dunwich Horror*, it becomes easy to understand why Lovecraft is parodied so much; so prescriptive an approach is simple to imitate.

Having finally arrived in Dunwich, with its 'faint, malign odour about the village street, as of the massed mould and decay of centuries', one should be clear by now that this particular provincial outpost is not a good place to be. In case there is any doubt, the story's narrator reaches back into history to establish that travellers have been avoiding it for centuries, thanks to claims of 'witch-blood, Satan-worship, and strange forest presences', making the point that as we reach the modern day, they still shun the place but no longer have an explanation for why. Modern science has perhaps stripped away the older superstitious frames of reference, so the narrator offers another, more scientific explanation for the outcast nature of the people of Dunwich:

They have come to form a race by themselves, with the well-defined mental and physical stigmata of degeneracy and inbreeding. The average of their intelligence is woefully low, whilst their annals reek of overt viciousness and of half-hidden murders, incests, and deeds of almost unnameable violence and perversity.

Even the gentry, and Lovecraft seems to have a certain preoccupation with 'gentry', are not immune. Some 'have kept somewhat above the general level of decay; though many branches are sunk into the sordid populace so deeply that only their names remain as a key to the origin they disgrace'.

At the same time, Lovecraft as narrator seems able to absolve these gentlefolk to a degree for their own degeneracy, pushing the blame back in time to the Native American population and their arcane ceremonies. It being New England, there are of course no longer any Native Americans around to defend themselves. The key takeaway, though, is that the community in this 'lonely and curious country' is, and always has been, different. This sense of difference and distance is centred upon the Whateley farmhouse, which lies a little distance outside the village of Dunwich itself. Beyond the farmhouse is the hill, the ultimate symbol of otherness and wrongness, a point emphasised by the farmhouse being 'set against' the hillside. Lovecraft couldn't be more specific if he tried.

Candlemas, 2nd February 1913, is the birthday of Wilbur Whateley, son of Lavinia Whateley and an unknown father. In Christian terms, Candlemas is the feast of the purification of the Blessed Virgin Mary, and the presentation of Jesus in the Temple. But Candlemas, one of the cross-quarter days, halfway between the Winter Solstice and the Spring Equinox, is also associated with older festivals marking the beginning of spring and celebrating fertility. Lovecraft's story hints that the inhabitants of Dunwich celebrate it under a different name. Whatever the festival, it is made plain that Wilbur Whateley's birth is 'special', to his family at least. Old Whateley has a reputation as a wizard, and Wilbur's birth is attended by strange noises and other mysterious signs. Wilbur himself is a 'dark, goatish-looking infant', forming a stark contrast to his mother's 'sickly and pink-eyed albinism'. His family show an immense amount of pride in him, and are inclined to make puzzling statements about his future.

It will come as no surprise to anyone that Wilbur develops at a prodigious rate: 'within three months of his birth he had attained a size and muscular power not usually found in infants under a full year of age'. Everything about him signals that something is wrong, and Lovecraft goes to immense lengths to establish this in his descriptions of the boy. On the one hand, 'his firm and precociously shaped nose united with the expression of his large, dark, almost Latin eyes to give him an air of quasi-adulthood and well-nigh preternatural intelligence', while on the other he is described as being:

...exceedingly ugly despite his appearance of brilliancy; there being something almost goatish or animalistic about his thick lips, large-pored, yellowish skin, coarse crinkly hair, and oddly elongated ears.

Given Lovecraft's own well-documented views on race, it's difficult not to feel he is pouring all his feelings about non-Caucasians into that one short passage.

And so, we see the young but apparently gifted Wilbur hard at work, studying his grandfather's eclectic library and stuffing his head full of arcane knowledge. Meanwhile, his grandfather is renovating the farm, the barns in particular, and buying astonishing quantities of local cattle—'anaemic, bloodless-looking specimens'— paying for them with gold coins. Twice a year, mysterious ceremonies occur behind the house on Sentinel Hill. In 1917, the family is the subject of outside attention from newspaper reporters, but then are apparently left to their own devices again. It is obvious that the inhabitants of Dunwich know perfectly well what is going on but choose, for whatever reason, to overlook the matter, either out of fear or misplaced pride.

And I can't help feeling that Lovecraft himself is playing games. I can't decide whether he is toying with the reader, signalling the outcome of the story with outrageously visible clues, or whether he is subtly mocking the yokels for their failure to take action and thereby suggesting their complicity in what is to come.

Either way, it leaves a nasty taste in the mouth, and one that persists as Lovecraft recounts Wilbur's adventures in scholarship and his bruising encounters with academe. There is an element of tragedy here, as this shabby-looking and peculiar young man keeps turning up at university libraries, struggling to cross-reference the material they hold with the information he has gleaned from the piles of decaying books that belonged to his grandfather. Seen through the superior eyes of Dr Armitage, fully aware of the stories from Dunwich, Wilbur Whateley is presented now as being like 'the spawn of another planet or dimension; like something only partly of mankind, and linked to black gulfs of essence and entity that stretch like titan phantasms beyond all spheres of force and matter, space and time'. There is a new sense of sniffy superiority in this assessment and the nature of the story shifts too, from scared tolerance to outright concern as Armitage makes more enquiries about Wilbur.

Matters are brought to a head when Wilbur raids the library in his desperation to get his hands on the *Necronomicon*. Lovecraft is lavish in his revelatory description of the true physical nature of Wilbur. One honestly wonders how, in sheer physical terms, this creature could actually have existed from one day to the next, but Lovecraft is clearly enjoying himself so it would be perhaps churlish to quibble. Wilbur's death is the turning point of the story.

As Lovecraft himself notes, this is but a prologue to the actual horror, which is, of course, the rampaging Horror itself, tramping invisibly around Dunwich, leaving huge footprints, crushing and devouring all living things in its path.

This might all be dismissed as risible—and indeed, the story as written up for the newspaper wire takes precisely that tone—but there are moments when Lovecraft catches the sheer raw horror of a community being faced with something they cannot identify or contend with. The most disturbing moments come when the villagers are trying to reach each other by telephone and either there is no answer or the line goes dead. So much is achieved with so few words, far more than in the over-lavish descriptions of the footprints. The sense of desperation and uncertainty experienced by the villagers is never plainer than here. And finally, indirectly, the telephone is the instrument of their salvation when Armitage sees the newspaper report and realises that his half-formed plans to do something about Wilbur's papers need to be accelerated.

We are now back among the scholar-heroes, with Armitage working long nights to decode Wilbur's diary, work out what he has done, and come up with a solution. It's a familiar world of competent men undoing the mistakes of ill-informed dabblers, and one cannot escape the feeling that this is where Lovecraft himself feels most secure. The yokels can stand by and watch while the university men sort things out, make reparation, explain, tell the locals what to do to make things safe, and admonish them not to do it again.

There is an underlying implication that knowledge should not be left in the hands of the ignorant, because they cannot make proper use of it. On the one hand, having Yog-Sothoth roaming the countryside is not the best thing ever, but so many questions remain unanswered. Were the Whateley family guided by some outside force, or were Wilbur and his brother an ungodly accident? We will never find out. 'We have no business calling in such things from outside', says Armitage, exhibiting his own kind of parochialism, and that is that.

Yet Lovecraft does seem to imply that there is something deeper even than the understanding of Armitage can fully grasp, a strangeness that can appear unexpectedly, like a flower emerging from a crack in the pavement. And that, perhaps, is the weirdest thing about this story. It's not the odd happenings themselves, which are expected, it being Dunwich, but those elements of the story that remain inexplicable, such as how the Whateleys came by their knowledge, the mundane intrusions like the rush for the telephone, that make this story really weird. It's not about fulsome language or overwhelming scenery, it is about the still moments of wondering.

Embassytown – China Miéville

I am by no means up to date in my reading of China Miéville's oeuvre, and that is something I regret because I so liked *Perdido Street Station* and *The Scar* when I read them. (I have also in the past read *King Rat* and *Un Lun Dun* but they didn't capture my attention in quite the same way). So, approaching *Embassytown* is a little like starting all over again.

First, there is the prose itself; there is something about the way Miéville chooses words, employing them with a sense of precision, every word placed just so, as though the writer aspires to be a mosaicist. Everything has weight and meaning, or at any rate everything seems intended to have weight and meaning, which is not always quite the same thing.

Embassytown is a novel about language, or rather, a novel about Language. Or perhaps it is intended to be a novel about language, or Language, except that partway through it wanders away and transforms itself into a novel about the consequences of language and the failure of Language before returning to where it began.

The story is set far into the future on a distant planet that has been colonised by humans. The main city is known to the humans as Embassytown, which expresses its purpose unequivocally. It is home to the Ariekei, a mysterious race most notable for the strangeness of their language, which requires each speaker to have two mouths in order for it to be vocalised. Many humans understand Language but only a few surgically altered and highly trained Ambassador couples can speak directly to the Ariekei; even then it is not always clear that communication is successful.

Added to that is the fact that the Ariekei are physically unable to speak of that which they do not directly experience. They only understand words with sentience and intent behind them. They do not, for example, understand Language generated by speech synthesisers. They have no symbolic language, no polysemy (i.e., the capacity for signs, that is, words, to have multiple meanings). Metaphor is unknown to them, although they can construct and therefore concretise similes, that is, make things for other things to be like, though how they know what it is they want things to be like remains rather fuzzy. Critically, they cannot lie or dissemble. They speak truth; one might even argue that they manifest Truth.

The central question raised by the novel is whether this is a mangling of the Sapir-Whorf hypothesis, that is, the idea that the structure of a language affects the ways in which its speakers are able to conceptualise their world, or whether

Miéville is going after something else.[1] On the basis of only one reading, this jury of one is out on the Sapir-Whorf idea, not least because I don't think the novel engages fully with the idea of how language might come about in the first place.

While keeping in mind the unique properties of Language, as they are important to what happens later, there are other aspects of this novel that I'd like to consider, not least Embassytown itself, and its position so far from anywhere else. It is a colony—somewhere out in the immer, there is a place called Bremen, which seems to have responsibility for Embassytown and the planet. Miabs—unmanned cargo ships—arrive from time to time, and so do manned vessels, but contact with the world beyond is fragile. The human colonists are heavily reliant on the Ariekei and the extraordinary flora and fauna of the planet, which contribute to their technological needs. The animate and inanimate blend unexpectedly; it's a persistent theme in Miéville's work, and here it produces some extraordinary low-key world-building. Embassytown and its environs are not flashy and hi-tech, but they are consistently unfamiliar to the reader, although we of course see them through the matter-of-fact eyes of someone who grew up on the planet, which makes the whole scenario all the stranger.

I like too Miéville's concept of space, the immer. Again, it might have been glossy, as we're used to seeing on screen, but there is a flavour about immer that is more reminiscent of old-style navigation on sailing ships, a perception of space being filled with reefs and shoals, swirls and eddies, unchartable vastnesses, together with a sense that others have been here before, because there are lighthouses, warning the voyagers of unseen dangers. Avice Benner Cho's struggle to explain immer is instructive; she too is stripped of language when it comes to describing her experiences beyond the planet.

Yet, quick as she was to leave, Avice comes home, bringing with her Scile, her husband, a linguist fascinated by the thought of the Ariekei, or the Hosts as they are known. For him, the unique nature of the Ariekei is the lure; Avice is less certain as to why she has returned, other than to please Scile. It is an unspoken rule that those who leave Embassytown do not return, indeed do not want to return once they've seen the breadth of the world beyond. There is almost a sense of embarrassment about Avice having come back, as though she has in some way failed.

But outside eyes are necessary for considering what is to come. For me, one of the most interesting aspects of the novel is Miéville's portrayal of the colony of Embassytown and its relationship with the Ariekei, the Hosts, as well as its relationship with the outside. One might linger on the use of that word, 'Host', with its implication of invitation and welcome. There seems to be no foundational myth about the settling of Embassytown, though we hear a

---

1. I am indebted to Ian Sales and Paul C Smith for a fascinating discussion about this on Twitter.

little of how humans struggled to understand the Ariekei and to communicate with them. The Ariekei move through the novel, strange presences (how to visualise them? I end up thinking of praying mantises, especially when the Ariekei unfurl their fan- and giftwings) exotic to the humans, unknowable.

At this point it is perhaps helpful to turn back to Scile, attempting to study the Ariekei. Scile is excited in a way that perhaps only a researcher can be, determined to understand every nuance of what is happening. But significantly, he is a researcher who discovers that his subject is changing, an anthropologist disturbed to find that the culture of the people he is studying is becoming 'contaminated' by encounters with the outside world. And Scile's impulse to preserve the Ariekei and Language in their 'pure' state, in spite of what the Hosts themselves might want, is conventional enough.

And certainly some Ariekei do want change; they want, for example, to be able to lie. They are trying to train themselves to lie, even though they find this almost physically impossible to do. Their purpose in wanting to lie remains unclear, but there is no reason why it should be obvious. Perhaps they will feel more able to communicate with the humans if they can do so within a mutually familiar framework. Whatever their motivations, I find it more interesting to focus upon Scile's arrogance in seeking to deny the Ariekei the choice to do what they will with Language. In fact, as becomes clear later, the relationship between the humans, Ariekei, and Language is more complex than anyone could have imagined. Used in a certain way, spoken Language is addictive, and many of the Ariekei are in fact hooked on the slightly stilted renditions of Language delivered by the Ambassadors, who are not the facilitators they might have imagined.

And it is here that the novel is no longer about Language but about the consequences of language, as the arrival of a new unmatched Ambassador, Ez/Ra, precipitates a crisis among the Ariekei because of the way he speaks. It is perhaps the most unlikely cause of a revolution, and this is the most unlikely of revolutions. Indeed, for much of this portion of the novel, it is difficult to understand that a revolution is taking place. Instead, Miéville presents an extraordinary and sustained picture of a microcosmic society on the verge of collapse, brought to a standstill by addiction and by the power of words. Sad, elegaic, terrible, and most of all melancholic, this portrayal of the end times of Embassytown is extraordinarily vivid. One is so swiftly caught up in events that it is easy to lose sight of how they reached this point.

Only latterly does the story suddenly, almost wrenchingly, return to the issue of Language. Losing Language, losing culture if you like, is the key to surviving the addiction for the Ariekei, something many of them have figured out already. There are some tempting postcolonial interpretations waiting in the wings, especially when one considers the fact that the authorities in Bremen, suspecting that the humans of Embassytown were about to make a bid for independence, were plotting to secure their grip on the colony because of its strategic position on the edge of known space.

It's not difficult, for example, to think of the Embassytown humans, people like Avice who have initiated the destruction of Language, as complicit in transforming the Ariekei into citizens of this little empire, prioritising the need for the Ariekei to learn Anglo-Ubiq (the name itself says it all). I could go on, but my Truth is that this novel needs more than one reading to fully appreciate what is happening in theoretical and philosphical terms.

At the end of it all, however, I am not certain how successful a novel this is. It raises fascinating issues, it is amazingly atmospheric, the world is vividly painted, and yet, and yet, something is lacking. I don't quite know what it is but in some mysterious way this novel has failed to communicate its Truth to me, perhaps because it is not entirely certain itself what its Truth actually is. I like it a good deal but there is something unfinished about it, rather like some of the stranger creatures that fill its pages. It lies in shadow, not fully realised on the page, perhaps because it cannot ever be.

Osama – Lavie Tidhar

A feature of those of Tidhar's novels that I've read so far is the way in which they draw on his own prodigious knowledge of genre fiction, and not just science fiction. Intertextual references abound in his work; at times it can be like taking part in a literary treasure hunt, though at other times one can walk away feeling like an ignorant fool. In *The Bookman* and its sequels, the references are blatant, not surprisingly, given the nature of the eponymous character, and there is a sense that the reader is engaged in a pleasant battle of wits with the author to collect the set.

But in *Osama*, Tidhar's engagement with fiction in general and genre in particular is an altogether more serious business, though this doesn't prevent him from once again playing intertextual games. And here I should note that while it is possible to manage without spotting most of the references, it would have helped me first time around had I been just a little more familiar with Philip K. Dick's *The Man in the High Castle*.

Joe, the novel's central character, is a private detective in Vientiane, Laos. We learn very little about him other than that he is fond of the Osama novels by one Mike Longshott. They're clearly a generic series, Longshott is probably a pseudonym, possibly even a team of writers. Anyone familiar with the history of genre writing knows how this works. Excerpts from the novels are interspersed between chapters; terse, laconic descriptions of actions and events, recognisable as bomb outrages that have occurred in the reader's world, suggesting some odd connections already.

Then a woman arrives in Joe's office, asking him to search for Mike Longshott. Joe begins a curious odyssey across the world, hunting for a man who has covered his trail well, so well one might wonder whether he exists at all. I use the word 'odyssey' advisedly, because it seems that there are certain similarities between these two wanderers, undergoing strange adventures but somehow never quite coming closer to the truth, or finding a way home. There is a touch too of Orpheus about Joe, descending into a private underworld, hoping to bring back … who? The strange fading girl he encounters first in Paris, as he searches for Longshott's publisher, Papadopoulous? Or someone else?

And what of Joe himself, this fictional everyman, plagued with memories of having been to places before, though believing himself never to have previously visited them? Gradually we come to realise that Joe's world is not ours, but an alternative world. But how many worlds are there? He seems to be slipping from one universe to another, most of them similar, distinguishable from one another and from the home world of the reader by small details and discrepancies, easily missed or discarded.

When Joe himself employs a private eye to help him in London, he describes Mo as having a 'grubby, well-used look, like a paperback'. We begin to wonder then if this whole adventure is an act of imagination by a Vientiane detective with time on his hands and a penchant for reading genre fiction. Is any of this happening, or does Joe still have his feet up on his desk at home as he places himself in one of the novels he loves so much? Given that I have mentioned *The Man in the High Castle*, readers familiar with that novel may have worked out what is going on, and guessed that there is a reason why Joe seems to have little 'reality' beyond what is happening to him at any given moment. One could of course lay out a case for Joe's having come to self-awareness within the fiction he inhabits, and now literally trying to find himself.

There are, though, other things going on in this story. The novel's title is a powerful indicator of this. One feels an immediate sense of shock at seeing a novel named after the great bogeyman of the early twenty-first century. What light does it shed to see him cast as the 'hero' of a series of novels? It perhaps reminds us that however abhorrent his acts might seem, there is more than one side to this story, and in this instance Joe literally stands on the other side of that story, although the veil between the worlds seems to be thinning all the time.

And that, for me, is what is most interesting about this novel, the way in which it engages with theories of genre and reading, through the form of the novel itself. At least, I think that is what Tidhar is doing. The novel constantly collapses in on itself, like a wave on the shore, only to return again and again, building gradually to a revelation that is as inevitable as it is shocking. What delighted me so much about *Osama* when I first read it was its shape-shifting quality, the way in which it constantly reinvents itself. I liked too the way the novel explores how readers engage with the fiction they love. There is even a convention for fans of the Osama books, where people gather to speculate about the identity of Mike Longshott and deliver learned papers on the topic.

That is one form of fantasy, of course, and we have already speculated that the novel may indeed be Joe's own fantasy, but similarly, the possibility remains that we are ourselves trapped in a book, looking out of the pages into a very different world. In the end, how can we ever know? The refusal to permit certainty lies at the heart of this novel as Tidhar posits a series of interleaved worlds that from time to time bleed into one another, complicating the reader's perspective. It's an ingenious and subtle use of that old science fiction trope of the alternate world, invigorated by the energy of Tidhar's storytelling.

Azanian Bridges – Nick Wood

I want to focus in this review not on the alternative historical setting of *Azanian Bridges*, but on the relationship between Martin van Deventer, the white psychologist, and Sibusiso Mchuna, the young black man he is attempting to treat. Sibusiso, a trainee teacher, has withdrawn into himself after witnessing the murder of his friend, Mandla, at an anti-government rally. At a loss to know what to do for him, his father has agreed to his being admitted to the local mental asylum for treatment. We can only speculate as to why his father did this rather than taking Sibusiso home, but for now consider it as only one among many markers of the fact that Sibusiso is metaphorically as well as literally a long way from home, living in a white world, among people who have no idea how to relate to him.

In an early conversation, Martin asks Sibusiso what he enjoys most about the music of Aretha Franklin, Stevie Wonder, and Gil Scott-Heron, which he has apparently been listening to (Martin is uncertain as to who Scott-Heron is, and wonders if he might be black). Sibusiso replies: 'The fact that black people make such wonderful music'.

> What to do? How to respond? I am a liberal Afrikaaner, non-racialist in my attitude. For me, colour is not an issue, not here, not now. (p.30)

But colour and race are all Martin can think about at this moment. However unintentionally, he simply cannot stop 'othering' the people around him. That Sibusiso smells of sweat sends him into a consideration of whether this is just bad personal hygiene, poverty, or a 'cultural factor' rather than 'does he have access to a deodorant?' Why is Sibusiso unresponsive to his questions? Martin notes that Sibusiso initially wouldn't talk to the Zulu nursing staff either (for all his 'non-racialist' attitude, Martin can't kick the habit of using tribal designations), and wonders if he is afraid they might be government informers.

> Here, our task is to make him better, not to vet his political views or activity. [...] Psychology is politically impartial in South Africa—even if we have no trained black psychologists to see Sibusiso either. (p.30)

Martin knows that he is ignorant in some way, but nonetheless, he just can't fathom it out. The answers are right there in front of him but he cannot see them, because he is himself beset by 'cultural factors', the ones that mean he cannot put himself in the place of his patient and think about how it feels for a black man to be questioned by a white man in an institutional setting.

He doesn't even get it when he introduces the Empathy Enhancer box into their consultation, and Sibusiso says: 'It looks a box the Security Police would use'.

> I look at him with surprised shock: forthright views indeed for an endogenously depressed patient, especially a black one. (p.33)

Sibusiso's own narrative of the same incident is much more revealing. 'You're not going to connect that to my genitalia are you, Doctor van Deventer?' he asks, noting how Martin's hands freeze on the switches. So, we can see that Martin lies even to himself, is squeamish, a little prudish even. Sibusiso notes wryly that Martin finds it hard to believe that he can speak English—'What's wrong with my English, black man that I am?' (p.34)—and wonders if Martin will in turn wonder how he knows the word 'genitalia'. Whether Frantz Fanon's *Black Skin, White Masks* exists in this alternate world can only be guessed at, but it is clear that Martin is uneasy at Sibusiso's able use of English, and that Sibusiso himself is deeply insecure, not for the reasons Martin supposes, but because he is struggling to exist at all.

Sibusiso continues to annotate Martin's lack of comprehension at his reluctance to use the EE box—'There are things in my mind that are precious to me'—and shows how he is himself conditioned to not ask questions of a white man, making it difficult to ask the most important question: 'Why should I trust you, Doctor?' (p.50). Only when Martin reveals he is a draft-dodger can even a tenuous link begin to form between them. Sibusiso poses another question to himself at this point: 'Why does he *need* his box? It looks like he is not such a bad reader of my expressions, after all. [...] Ah, it is a toy that smells both of his sweat *and* his ambition' (p.51).

Here, perhaps, Sibusiso slightly misreads Martin, but it's not surprising. If, as SF critic Mark Bould suggests, the novel itself is an Empathy Enhancer, the one thing we do learn about Martin is that he is terrible at understanding people. Not just Sibusiso (and by extension, his other patients at the asylum), but Dan Botha, the co-inventor of the EE box, and Martin's childhood friend (except, as we see, Dan was also his childhood tormentor, and it seems that Martin has never truly been able to break free of his influence). Martin is divorced, estranged from his parents, and barely capable of spotting that he is the victim of a honeytrap until it's too late. The one thing we never see is Martin treating a white patient—one wonders if he actually has any. And yet, without a trace of irony, Martin can say of himself that 'I build bridges' (p.48). After being visited by the Security Police, who want his box, Martin does experience an epiphany of sorts in facing down a number of his own fears. But even so, his belief in himself as a bridge-builder, however genuine, is romantic and almost delusional. He still has a long and uncertain road before him.

The early part of the novel is shaped by the metaphor of the Umgeni Bridge, a rope bridge that Martin visited with his wife on their honeymoon, tried to cross but failed because he was too afraid. Martin's moment of epiphany comes when he revisits the bridge, which seems oddly different, and this time crosses it. Martin obviously sees the EE box as his bridge to working with his black patients, a technological means to short-circuit his ignorance about them. Martin's struggle to use words properly arises in part because he has never had cause to know how dangerous words can be. Nor can he truly see how his box might be exploited by others, not until the Security Police arrive.

For Sibusiso, of course, there are never enough words. Or the right words. Or words addressed to him. As the activist Nombuso argues with Sibusiso's friend Bongani about where Sibusiso is going for the weekend, Sibusiso notes, 'I tire of people talking about me as if I were not there'. And indeed, for much of the novel, Sibusiso has been rendered invisible, one way or another. Lost in the city, lost in the asylum; once the activists learn of the existence of the box he becomes, as much as anything, a means to an end, a small cog in a larger machine.

Yet in these encounters, and especially in his conversations with Jabu the nurse, Sibusiso finds strength and purpose. Martin comments several times on Sibusiso's transformation, noting how he takes up more space, and takes control of that space. Sibusiso himself, when he meets Mamma Makosi, notices that she 'speaks as if we own the borders and spaces within' (p.83), and it is through her intervention that he begins to come to terms with his own private landscape in a way that Martin, even with his EE box, cannot. Put simply, their terms of reference are too different for them to make easy connections. The white man's terms of reference cannot help him; in a way Martin is not wrong in understanding that there are 'cultural factors' at play. Martin's problem is that he can never fully understand their true nature; what is really needed is his acknowledgement that he cannot understand them; that language can and must fail him, EE box or no.

Which takes us back to that bridge. In North America, the white colonial settlers believed that the children of indigenous people and colonisers (variously called half-breeds, mixed breeds or mixed bloods, or métis, depending on where and when they were speaking from) were somehow better placed to act as translators and facilitators between the two groups because of their mixed parentage. In truth, the métis often found themselves caught between two cultures, not entirely comfortable with or welcome in either, but nonetheless burdened by the expectations of both groups. There is a sense, then, of various responsibilities having been placed on Sibusiso by others—his family, his college, Martin, the various activists he becomes involved with—to act in part as their bridge to one another.

Sibusiso learns quickly how to take up actual space and cross physical borders, but something else is also happening. Martin talks at one point of Sibusiso's psyche becoming 'colonized with identity politics', but having raised Fanon's theorising about the oppressed black person who is obliged to navigate a white world according to how they perform whiteness, there comes a point for Sibusiso when he rejects the bridge. Or, rather, one might argue that he has himself crossed a bridge but, unlike Martin, he has not returned. Instead, he is pushing on into new territory, the territory of his own psyche.

At various points during the novel, Sibusiso has sought to express his inner state through invoking figures such as the Beast and the Bird, symbols that resonate powerfully for him, but that Martin cannot hope to interpret. When Sibusiso is finally, almost inevitably arrested, he is tortured physically but also mentally, with the EE box. He has already discovered a way of subverting the machine's use, to some extent at least, but if I understand the novel's final section correctly, Sibusiso is exploiting the box in order to construct and explore his own psychological landscape, to 'own the borders and spaces within'.

What precisely happens in Room 619 is difficult to determine. Somehow Sibusiso manages to get out of the window, or is pushed out, and, depending on how you read it, jumps or falls to his death. In our world, Police Room 619 is the room where, in 1977, the anti-apartheid activist Steve Biko was interrogated so brutally that the walls were left splashed with blood from the appalling injuries he would later die of. The authorities claimed he died on hunger strike; the photographs taken by the campaigner, Donald Woods, clearly indicate otherwise. Biko's death became a rallying point for anti-apartheid protesters worldwide and initiated an intense period of campaigning against the South African regime. 'Biko', recorded by Peter Gabriel and released in 1980, generated further awareness among people, myself included, who would perhaps at that point have described themselves as non-political.

Sibusiso will have a similar posthumous existence, with recordings of his thoughts, taken from the EE box, sent out onto the internet by the activists, enabling everyone to walk in his shoes and gain some sense of what is happening in South Africa. Finally, perhaps, Martin's box has found a use, but only because of its theft by Sibusiso, and the involvement of others in transforming its theory into a practical form. One of the few genuinely delightful moments of a dark novel is when the box is converted into a computer game and small hand-held units distributed for free via drug-courier networks.

There's more, so much more, to this novel, and it would probably take a few more thousand words to unpick it to my complete satisfaction, but even that wouldn't be the end of it. And that's partly the point. This is not a story with neat and tidy endings. It's a moment among many moments; a pause as one sequence of action reaches its climax and before the next begins. We know that apartheid was finally abandoned in South Africa, but we know also that all over the world similar situations are developing all the time, requiring constant action. Martin will continue learning what he can and can't do, and how to exploit his privilege for the benefit of the cause of freedom. There is no end to that struggle, and therefore there is no end to *Azanian Bridges*. We can only ever draw breath, ready for the next assault.

The Book of Phoenix by Nnedi Okorafor

The Book of Phoenix is a prequel to Nnedi Okorafor's World Fantasy Award-winning *Who Fears Death*. As the title suggests, it is the story of Phoenix, 'mixed, grown and finally birthed' in Tower 7 on the island of Manhattan, two years old but an accelerated organism with the body of a forty-year-old woman. She is able to read a substantial book in a couple of minutes, plants grow unusually fast when in her presence, and her body's temperature has begun to soar. Later, she will discover other unusual abilities. Phoenix, as she finally comes to realise, is an experiment in a building filled with other genetic experiments, many of which have gone horribly wrong. Her ultimate purpose will be to become a weapon. And yet, to begin with, Phoenix is happy enough with her life. Things change after the death of her only friend, Saeed, when she realises that her home is in fact a prison, and becomes determined to escape from Tower 7.

These experiences are recounted by Phoenix herself, but in a roundabout way. Indeed, for all that the novel is ostensibly about Phoenix, the reader is well advised to also pay attention to that Book in the story's title, for this is also a novel about storytelling. Phoenix's own story is embedded within another narrative, set further in the future, in which an old man, Sunuteel, caught in a storm in the desert, discovers a cache of old computers. The computers were hidden by the Okeke, of whom Sunuteel is a descendant, at a time when things began to go wrong on Earth: 'just before Ani [the Earth goddess] turned her attention back to the Earth'. The Book of Phoenix downloads itself onto Sunuteel's 'portable', and he listens to it while he sits out the storm, a storm which seems itself to be something to do with the spirit of Phoenix.

It's not too much of a stretch, I think, to see this cave as some sort of repository for latter-day Dead Sea Scrolls, the computers hidden in haste and then left, their stories untold; the very title, *The Book of Phoenix*, suggests a flavour of the biblical, while much of *Who Fears Death* hinges on interpretations of the mysterious Great Book. As for Sunuteel, he is a recorder and a reciter, a man who speaks many dialects of Okeke, as well as a number of other languages. This in turn suggests that it is no accident that he has been brought to this cave at this time. We are also dealing with a character who proudly carries a copy of Roland Barthes's 'The Death of the Author' on his portable, although Barthes's perception that 'the author enters into his own death, writing begins' will be vigorously challenged during the novel. The point being made is that once written, a story lives. It can be rewritten, yes, but the story itself also persists. And persistence and endurance are very much at the heart of this novel.

Alongside Phoenix's own persistence in understanding how she came into being, disentangling her true story from the lies told to her by the managers of Tower 7 and its sister towers in other US cities, we are also led to understand that Phoenix's own story has shaped the world that Sunuteel now lives in. However changed they might be, stories about her have lasted. Sunuteel is better qualified than anyone else to see the truth of this, however terrifying this may be to him, in a future shaped by Phoenix's actions.

The intricate storytelling forms that frame *The Book of Phoenix*, as well as the recognition of the need that everyone's stories should be heard, may seem strange to those who prefer their genre neat, but frankly, that is their problem, not the author's. Quite apart from drawing on traditional storytelling forms, and peopling her world with characters who are emphatically not white, Okorafor delivers a searing (almost literally so in places) commentary on big pharma, experimentation on human beings, the theft and misuse of genetic material, globalisation, companies that function way beyond the law, and all of this from the point of view of the people who are routinely on the receiving end, the people who struggle to maintain their humanity in the face of the appalling violence regularly inflicted on them. This makes for hard reading at times, but it's rewarding work.

The Testament of Jessie Lamb – Jane Rogers

Jane Rogers's *The Testament of Jessie Lamb* is a near-future science fiction novel based on a rather vague premise about a virus that produces an effect similar to CJD, but only in women, and only if they become pregnant. The child may survive, but the mother will die. The virus seems to have been released at airports, thus ensuring maximum distribution across the world, and women die in massive numbers. There is no escape. Who caused it, or why, no one seems to know.

Most of this set-up happens off the page; the only real description of its full impact comes with the mention at the beginning of the novel of a mass funeral at York Minster and the huge traffic jams this causes. There are other hints: a scene in a charity shop when Jessie disposes of some of her possessions is especially telling—the shop is already full of containers of women's clothes that no one wants to buy or keep. What Rogers does not do, except in the broadest, vaguest way, is to give any indication of how these events might affect daily life at the most practical level. For example, what happens to the economy when a large part of the workforce isn't there anymore, and another significant chunk of the workforce has to suddenly consider childcare? Somehow the world seems to continue much as normal, yet the last pre-2012 fuel crisis showed how close to the edge this country habitually teeters, even without a mass die-off of women.

As one or two other commentators have noted, this novel seems to fit into an older model of science fiction—John Wyndham would be an excellent example—that relies less on hyper-accurate, heavily researched detail about what would happen *if*, and more on creating a certain kind of mood. Close to the beginning of the novel, for example, Jessie and her friend Sal are talking about the impact of Maternal Death Syndrome and coming to a realisation that the world they are familiar with is probably going to end soon.

> We thought about our houses slowly falling to bits, the doors blowing open, the roofs caving in, birds and animals nesting there.
> 'Some other species will dominate,' said Sal, and we began to argue about what it might be. All the animals in zoos etc would have to be let out before the last people died. Which would probably kill off a few more of us even sooner. And those animals that could adapt to life in their new territory might take over. There might be wolves again in England, and bears. Tigers might live off untended herds of cows. Tree branches would spread out over roads,

and hedges would grow huge and wild, and weeds burst through the tarmac. After a hundred years the world would be one great nature reserve, with all the threatened species breeding again, and great shoals of cod in the sea, eagles nesting in old church spires. It made me think of the garden of Eden, how it was supposed to be beautiful before Adam and Eve messed things up. (p.9)

Wyndham, to the best of my recollection, never actively considered the zoos, but this scene reminds me of the latter parts of *The Day of the Triffids*, when Masen returns to London for provisions, which in turn seems to draw heavily on Richard Jefferies' *After London*. This similarity to *Triffids* and its ilk is not coincidental. Wyndham and Rogers are less concerned with the 'how did this happen?' and far more preoccupied with 'how do we manage now it has happened?' And by 'manage' I mean on an emotional level rather than the nuts and bolts of day-to-day survival.

Rogers's refusal to engage with 'how did this happen' is helped by her choice of protagonist, Jessie Lamb, sixteen years old, and as self-absorbed as any sixteen-year-old trying to figure out how the world works. To begin with, MDS doesn't really figure in Jessie's life except as a traffic jam. Only later does it begin to acquire a name and a face: a girl at school, a friend's aunt, and then personal significance when Jessie, along with all the other girls, receives a compulsory contraceptive implant at school. Events elsewhere are filtered through Jessie's consciousness—what she sees on TV, hears from other people; the picture is fragmentary because it doesn't impinge on Jessie herself.

But as the crisis continues, Jessie becomes more and more aware of how MDS will change her life. What is the point of continuing with things like GCSE exams? She and her friends experience a growing sense of impatience. Why isn't anyone doing anything? They blame the adults and decide they must take action themselves, but in what way? At the behest of her friend Baz, Jessie attends a meeting where young people are trying to decide what it is they want to do, and incidentally, who to blame. There are any number of scapegoats available, from climate change deniers to research scientists, and any number of strategies. One girl wants to set up centres for motherless children, run by the children themselves, without interference from adults. Others want to promote a greener lifestyle, by force if necessary. Still others want to take the campaign to the scientists, Animal Liberation Front-style. For her own part, Jessie is convinced of the need to punish 'old people' for what they've done, but her perception of who is to blame is no clearer than that.

Jessie's journey through this confused post-MDS landscape might be an allegory for the teenage experience generally, of being half-child, half-adult, expected to make decisions then criticised for doing so. And once again, it is reminiscent of the journey that Bill Masen makes across England, moving from community to community, searching for Josella, but also testing and discarding any number of models for living in a world shaped by Triffids.

Jessie's understanding of what she needs to do comes gradually, influenced by a number of things. First, there is the experience of her mercurial aunt, Mandy. Recently dumped by her partner and desperate for a child of her own, she is about to undergo fertility treatment when it is cancelled by the MDS crisis. Later, Mandy becomes involved with the Noahs, a new religious group who, as their name implies, are trying to preserve something of the present to take into the future, but they reject her as a potential mother because she is too old. Then Jessie's friend, Sal, is raped by a group of her boyfriend's friends, and Jessie herself is spat at, threatened, and robbed by a group of boys. Young women are suddenly expendable in the eyes of young men, and treated accordingly.

At the same time, young women are intensely valuable as a commodity, it having been discovered that so long as they are kept sedated and on life-support, babies can be brought to term. These are the Sleeping Beauties. People are very excited by this possibility of continuing the human race, not least as it buys time to do the research to counter MDS, but already there is conflict between those who are pro-research, those who are against it, pro-Sleeping Beauties, against them. A woman's body is once again a battleground, and for Jessie this is to become all too personal when she decides to volunteer to become a Sleeping Beauty herself.

Her choice is prompted partly by her aunt Mandy's experiences, but also, it seems, by her growing unease at what is likely to happen to her as the world changes. To become a Sleeping Beauty—a point made more explicit if one thinks back to the fairy tale[1]—is to be protected, not by a hedge of thorns but by the laboratory. From Jessie's point of view, the decision is not as bizarre as it might at first appear. More disturbing is the response of Jessie's parents, who imprison their daughter in her room in the hope they can persuade her to change her mind. Some of Jessie's testament is written while she is imprisoned; some of it while she is awaiting the implantation of the fertilised egg.

We are meant to understand Jessie's decision as being one that is taken freely, an adult decision made with the full understanding of what it involves, that it would be wrong to try to undermine Jessie's own perception of what she is doing. Nonetheless, Rogers does an excellent job of showing the vested interests that mass around her. There is Iain, from the youth movement Jessie is involved with, who uses her to promote the cause, a course of action that is in part a front for his own predatory activities. Her parents' refusal to accept Jessie's decision represents a denial of their daughter's having reached adulthood. Rosa, another girl about to become a Sleeping Beauty, is obsessed

---

1. And there is at least one version of the story in which Sleeping Beauty awakes to discover that the Prince has been and gone, and she has become pregnant in the meantime.

with the notion that in this way she will find love and celebrity at last, although she will not be there to experience it.

The assumption is that the human race must persist, come what may, and that any means is acceptable in order to ensure its survival. Inevitably, this will be the burden that women bear.

I remain in two minds about this novel. It is, as I've noted, representative of a certain kind of science fiction, and done rather well, though I don't think it is especially innovative. But still, there is something slightly off-kilter about it. I've recently been watching Dominic Sandbrook's TV series *The 70s*, matching my fragmentary perceptions of that decade against Sandbrook's admittedly sketchy account, and I can't help feeling that Rogers is reaching back to this time—the beginnings of the Greenham Common Women's Peace Camp and a new iteration of the women's movement, the dawning awareness of AIDS—in order to underpin her creation of a near-future society, rather than drawing on the contemporary world as it now exists. There is something oddly dated about the world of MDS, no matter how many references to climate change denial and CJD Rogers includes. Which leaves me with an odd sense of dissatisfaction that at present I can't quite dispel, in spite of Rogers's skill in capturing the sense of uncertainty, the internal and the external anxieties of being a teenager. It may be that a second reading is required, as *The Testament of Jessie Lamb* is undoubtedly more subtly layered it initially appears.

Gods Without Men by Hari Kunzru

Some places in the world possess a palpable, if inexplicable, atmosphere. People are drawn to them, often without being clear why they feel such an attraction. In time, these places may become the focus of ritual, the goal of pilgrimages. Belief in their significance may persist for thousands of years as large, thriving communities develop around them. This attracts yet more believers, to the point where the presence of the people has more importance than what drew them there in the first place, and power is now derived from their continuing presence. Anything intrinsic to the place itself has long since been smothered, yet this is now unimportant.

However, other places retain that mystery. They are significant to a small group of people, but for the rest it is a matter of accidental discovery rather than a conscious seeking out. There is an instinctive recognition that such places are special, but no story to account for why. In Hari Kunrzu's *Gods Without Men*, the Pinnacles or Three-Finger Rocks, a group of rocky spires in California's Mojave Desert, fall into this second category. For the local Native Americans, the Pinnacles have since time immemorial represented 'the threshold, the opening between this world and the Land of the Dead' (p.240), and are the home of Yucca Woman, who guards the entrance to that other world, weaving the two together as she makes her baskets. The former aircraft engineer, Schmidt, who arrives at the Pinnacles in 1947, immediately senses their special nature, although he must confirm this through instrument readings. For him, the rock columns are like 'a natural antenna' (p.5), channelling the power he believes is running along a fault line 'and up through the rocks' (p.5).

For Schmidt, for the People, and for others such as Fray Garcés, an eighteenth-century missionary priest, and Nephi Parr, a nineteenth-century Mormon miner driven half-mad by the murder of his family, the Pinnacles act as a transmitter; they establish some sort of connection with the place and receive messages. Garcés converses with an angel, Parr sees a ghostly airship that will eventually take him away, while Schmidt meets alien visitors who he believes have come in response to his own transmissions, seeking galactic intervention for the world's problems. What the People have seen is not recorded, as such stories are not for outsiders, but surfaces occasionally in hearsay about glowing figures and men capable of prodigious feats of running. It might be that all these people have experienced hallucinations, except that a certain consistency about their stories suggests the Pinnacles are a focus for something beyond familiar experience. What it might be remains part of the mystery, except to note that their experiences are all intensely personal.

Difficulties arise when outsiders become involved. For those following in the wake of the 'visionaries', their relationship with the Pinnacles is inevitably more fraught. In 1920, Deighton, an Anglo-American anthropologist, visits Kairo, the name given by Garcés to the place where the People camp, determined to gather as much information as possible about Native American cultures, which he believes to be on the brink of extinction. His intentions may be good, but driven by a belief in the universality of knowledge, Deighton fails to understand that he cannot simply strip the People of what they know for his own purposes. Schmidt's simple belief in a world beyond Earth has been hijacked by others and transformed into an elaborate belief system in which he is now the Guide, communing with the Space Brothers of the Ashtar Galactic Command, until he dies in a fire caused by his own elaborate communications system. The idealism of a 1970s counter-cultural community, also set up at Kairo, is quickly undermined by the arrival of drug dealers and other criminals before being finally shut down by the locals. In all these encounters not only is there a failure to make proper connections, but also a brutal severing of previous connections. These followers, having escaped from their previous lives, are distinguished by their desperate need to belong.

Whatever it is that manifests itself through the Pinnacles is able to make the distinction between the two groups, to sift out those for whom it has no use from those who, in some way, further its purpose, suggesting that a keen intelligence is at work, sorting and discarding to a pattern that isn't available to those who are a part of it. The careful layering in the structure of Kunzru's novel reveals this to the reader without ever entirely indicating what that pattern might be, or who or what is making the choices.

It seems, though, that in the twentieth and twenty-first centuries, the pace of change accelerates, as more outsiders arrive, more connections are made or ignored, and more data becomes available. It is perhaps ironic that Nicky, the washed-up rock star, the least connected and yet bizarrely the most grounded of the contemporary visitors, the one who doesn't even make it as far as the rocks, perhaps offers the most telling observation as he blunders around in the desert night, trying to find himself spiritually and geographically: 'The stars were like pinholes in a cloth. You could believe you were seeing through to some incredibly bright world on the other side of the darkness' (p.31). If the Pinnacles reject him, it is because he should simply go home to London and plug himself back into the web of connections he has there.

Kunzru's compiling of story fragments, although criticised by a number of reviewers, mirrors not only the actions of the Pinnacles' 'intelligence' but also of Jaz, a mathematical genius, who works for Bachman, a financial engineer and the creator of Walter, a computer whose function is itself mysterious: 'It was more like an organism than a computer. It felt *alive*' (p.134). Bachman's attempts to explain precisely what Walter does are as inarticulate as any attempt to speculate on the nature of the power flowing at the Pinnacles. Jaz is told that Walter identifies minute but predictable behaviours, however fleeting and unstable, and trades on the stock markets accordingly. Jaz, however, is puzzled by the wide variety of data he is required to examine, looking for patterns, or 'rhymes' as Bachman calls them. 'It was as if Bachman were trying to fit the whole world into his model' (p.135).

Later, Bachman tells him that they are hunting for '[c]osmic slips of the tongue' (p.138). His mission, he assures Jaz, is to discover the face of God, and he appears to be serious. Yet if Walter is in some sense alive, it also appears to lack any moral understanding, and Jaz is increasingly disturbed by the apparent extent of Walter's power, believing the computer's trading activities to be responsible, among other things, for bringing down the economy of a Central American country.

If Jaz is rather too intimately acquainted with the interconnectedness of the world through his work, his private life is by contrast a mass of brutally severed connections. The talented child of Punjabi Sikh immigrants, he has remade himself as the all-American boy, rejecting his beliefs and his culture, and then compounding the sin, in his family's eyes, by marrying a white American woman. Lisa, the indulged daughter of secular Jews, has already admitted defeat in attempting to bridge the cultural divide between her and Jaz's family and instead, with Jaz, builds her own set of cultural connections in New York, itself that most connected of cities.

However, the birth of their son, Raj, reflects the illusory nature of this construction, first as the families argue about the cultural rituals surrounding birth and naming, and then more significantly when Raj is diagnosed as being severely autistic, a developmental condition characterised by the child's failure to communicate or to engage in social interaction. Raj is, literally, as disconnected as it is possible to be, but so, by virtue of her role as his primary carer, is Lisa. Both Jaz and Lisa are now attempting to deal with the utterly unknowable, as a result of which their own relationship comes under severe strain. While Jaz tries to fend off his family, which views Raj's condition as a punishment for Jaz's marrying an outsider, Lisa rejects their village remedies as superstition, instead pursuing the high-tech version of quackery, subjecting Raj to untested therapies of dubious merit, desperate for a breakthrough that never comes. Her need to believe in modernity rather than superstition is such that even while she scrutinises Raj's every waking moment for signs of improvement, she cannot accept that playing with his aunt's amulet might soothe him, even for a short while.

By the time the family arrives at the Pinnacles, as part of an ill-conceived road trip intended to bring them closer together, both Jaz and Lisa know what they really want, without daring to say it out loud, and the Pinnacles mysteriously oblige when Raj apparently unfastens himself from his pushchair and disappears. Most reviewers have focused on this moment in the novel, perhaps in the light of recent child disappearances such as that of Madeleine McCann, and the subsequent criticism of the McCanns for not behaving as the public feel bereft parents ought to. Indeed, some reviewers have gone so far as to dismiss the other story elements as so much clutter, I think unwisely. The novel's main focus may indeed be on the contemporary, but only insofar as it is the most visible and accessible iteration of a much deeper pattern.

For all that Kunzru delivers a tour de force account of Lisa and Jaz's trial by media, this is not a novel about a missing child (and indeed Raj is not the only child who disappears during the novel). Instead, it is in part a novel about the stories we tell ourselves in order to survive, and this is its most extreme expression: people so desperate to find meaning in their own lives they will happily extract it from the lives of others without a moment's thought for the pain they're inflicting.

The mystery then is not that Raj disappears, not even that he eventually reappears many miles away, and somehow changed for the better, but that his parents, after everything they've been through, still persist in questioning the experience rather than simply accepting its miraculous resolution. The stories they choose to tell themselves can lead only to self-destruction or to a terrifying revelation they are neither of them equipped to deal with. Even with the wealth of information the reader already has, it is difficult to avoid the conclusion that Lisa and Jaz will join those who wait, and will participate in another iteration of cultish behaviour. Or will Raj become a variable in the pattern, throwing it off course?

The presence of the reader throws yet another uncertainty into the mix. The structure of this novel is so intricate it is difficult not to wonder whether the reader isn't another layer of world that the characters can only vaguely apprehend. Do we lurk behind the Pinnacles, or are we part of Walter? For me, that is part of the pleasure of reading *Gods Without Men*; for others it clearly makes reading the novel a chore rather than a delight. Nevertheless, I would rather have a novel that continues to unfold its meanings rather than one that has a clear, unambiguous narrative thread, and *Gods Without Men*, a wonderfully constructed and fascinating novel, undoubtedly satisfies that need.

By Light Alone – Adam Roberts

If, as we are rather fond of telling ourselves, science fiction is a literary form that is very much in dialogue with itself in the way that writers run with one another's ideas, testing them, developing them, extending the creative conversation, then where in this extended discussion should we position Adam Roberts? He is undoubtedly writing science fiction, but his engagement with it might seem, to an observer, to be rather casual, perhaps a little offhand, as though he weren't really taking it seriously. I admit I've struggled with his work over the years, and indeed have not read any of his novels since *The Snow*. Paul Kincaid wrote about his own critical blind spot concerning Roberts's work just over a year ago, and proposed that one needed to read it as 'Menippean satire'. The critic Northrop Frye preferred the term 'anatomy' (as in Burton's *Anatomy of Melancholy*), and that is the term I shall use in this discussion of *By Light Alone*. Because it seems to me now that Roberts's contribution to the conversation is not so much an attempt to extend ideas as it is a merciless interrogation of the tropes we already have.

In his most recent novel, *By Light Alone*, by undergoing the appropriate gene modification and then growing their hair long, it has become possible for people to photosynthesise and thus avoid starvation in a depleted world. But while many science fiction writers would present the modification as something positive, and write from the point of view of those who have undergone it (a relevant comparison would be Nancy Kress's 'Beggars in Spain'), Roberts does something rather different. First—and this is in itself overtly science-fictional—he suggests the practical downsides to the ability to photosynthesise, such as how long it might take to feed, how easy it is to kill someone by cutting off their hair, and, most significantly for this novel, how photosynthesis can only support life to a particular degree. It is impossible, for example, for a woman to carry a pregnancy to full term without supplementing photosynthesis with so-called 'hard' food. This means that women need to work in order to earn money for food, while men need to do very little.

Shiny science is overwhelmed by economic necessity, and in Roberts's world there is no reason to invest in resolving this problem because, well, why would men do that when it is not to their advantage, and the women are working too hard to have time to dissent?

The reader explores this post-catastrophic world through the eyes of George and Marie, a wealthy couple with two children, Leah and Ezra. Or, rather, they don't, because the family are so self-absorbed it is almost impossible to gain any sense of what is going on beyond the boundaries of their immediate existence. To take notice of the news is considered vulgar. To eat 'hard' food is a marker of wealth, and to chew and spit out one's food is currently the height of fashion. Short hair is a sign of high status; Marie recoils from the 'longhairs' who serve them at their fashionable ski resort. The 'leafheads' are disparaged for their habits, but true scorn is reserved for the 'job suckers', those who work to earn money for hard food but who keep their hair short; in other words, those who aspire to be wealthy too. Class, it turns out, is very much the issue at the heart of this novel.

All this the reader learns obliquely, through snatches of conversation and troubling glimpses of other ways of life, like a child observing but barely comprehending the adult world. Except that here it is the adults who are like pampered children, able to deny or get rid of anything they don't like the look of. Roberts is presenting us here with a classic science fiction scenario: the untrammelled community that is about to be brought to a decisive moment of self-awareness by an intrusion from the unnoticed outside world. Except that when Leah is kidnapped by persons unknown, George and Marie are astonished to discover that no one seems to be particularly interested in the child's disappearance or prepared to do much about finding her. Marie takes her sensitive nerves back to New York, leaving George to ineffectually struggle with local bureaucracy before himself returning home.

Marie's response to the situation is a mix of indignation about the injury done to her (Marie is more usually indifferent to her children) and rage at the failure of everyone around her to jump to it when she demands a resolution. Marie is simply not used to being thwarted. George is a little more emotionally engaged but also completely baffled by the situation. Even their friends seem mostly indifferent. One might compare this with Hari Kunzru's *Gods Without Men*, which also features the mysterious loss of a child, but which in sharp contrast details the contemporary response to such a loss, with total strangers all trying to find a place in the drama. In other words, we learn as much about Roberts's world from what people don't do as from what they are doing. One of the most startling moments of *By Light Alone* comes when Marie resituates herself as an active agent in her own drama, when we already know that she refused to participate in any way until her daughter was returned.

The return itself presents another point of interest. One of George's acquaintances hires a woman who is skilled in tracking down lost people and she, almost miraculously, perhaps too miraculously, recovers Leah after a year. It is clear from the outset that something is not quite right, and as the story unfolds the reader can happily speculate, yet none of the characters in the novel ever challenges the situation, perhaps because of their customary indolence, or perhaps because, deep inside, they don't dare. The fact of Leah's apparent return is sufficient to bring about a collapse in George's and Marie's relationship. George becomes a little more curious about the world around him. He tries, somewhat ineffectually, to experience it by becoming a longhair and getting involved in 'politics'. Marie begins to participate in a project to return parts of New York City to 'the wild', which basically means driving people out of their homes and bulldozing them.

One could draw parallels between Marie's project and attitudes towards the presence of Native Americans in pre-catastrophe and pre-Columbian America. Roberts counters this view of the situation in an oblique way that only really makes sense through subsequent reflection, but that is in its own way telling. Again, there is the refusal to engage at a personal, emotional level; instead, Roberts recounts the story of Issa, a girl who seems to come out of nowhere into the world of the longhairs, in terms that hint at allegory. Who or what Issa actually is we never really learn; her own understanding of where she comes from doesn't seem to fit the other portions of the story, but with a mass of viewpoints that are partial at best, it is difficult to reach a definitive truth.

And that in part is what I like so much about *By Light Alone*, that refusal to follow the standard narrative trail. There is a distinct flavour of Ballard about this novel, with its semi-drowned world and images of longhairs lying in the sun, their hair fanned out behind them, but at the same time, Roberts undermines the chilly melancholy of Ballard's writing by using such shockingly solipsistic characters, thereby demonstrating the unreliability of the grand science-fictional idea.

Zone One – Colson Whitehead

I have never found zombies especially interesting. In terms of genre tropes, I've never been quite clear what they are actually for. Narratively speaking, it seems there is not a lot to be done with them except to get rid of them by any means necessary, the more violent the better. This in turn becomes mind-numbing, which may or may not be the point.

It is hard to feel any emotional connection with a zombie, unless it's someone you knew well in their life before, and that bond is quickly destroyed by the way the zombie must by the laws of genre inevitably behave. A story's response to the presence of zombies in its midst is either to make them a slow-moving and endlessly disposable background against which to play out a drama that may be utterly irrelevant to their presence, or else to lumber them with some sort of metaphorical burden for the rest of the novel.

And so we come to Colson Whitehead's *Zone One*, unequivocally a zombie novel, but one with a curious tagline on the cover: 'A zombie novel with brains'. This of course references the one thing we all know about zombies, their alleged appetite for brains. Yet there is also the implication that Whitehead's novel is different, special even, because Whitehead is not known as a genre writer but as an inhabitant of the 'literary' end of the island, just as his publisher, Harvill Secker, is not a genre imprint.

Goodness knows whose idea it was to include this tagline. I dislike the air of sniffiness it generates, its suggestion that Whitehead's novel is somehow better than other—genre—zombie novels, especially given that Whitehead has previously written of his longtime enjoyment and appreciation of horror cinema. The trouble is, based on the small sample of zombie novels I've read in the last two or three years—the first two volumes of Mira Grant's lamentable Newsflesh Trilogy and Alden Bell's curious but frequently irritating *The Reapers are the Angels*—*Zone One* really is head and shoulders above both.

In this novel, as in others, zombification comes about because of infection by a virus and is spread by the dead biting the living. We are given no idea of how the plague began, and we learn only incidentally of the havoc it has wrought. What is noticeable from the start is that Whitehead avoids the trope of having his protagonists make long journeys in search of other survivors as a convenient means of presenting the broader post-apocalyptic situation. Whitehead's protagonists stay more local, hunkered down in a military-run refugee camp in Manhattan, part of a force whose job is to clear the island of zombies and make it safe for human residents again. Government, such as it is, has retreated to Buffalo, NY, but with the goal of regaining control of New York, Manhattan especially, because it would be good both for morale and for public relations.

Zone One is the lower part of Manhattan, now cordoned off behind a hastily thrown-up barricade, and already cleared of ambulant zombies. It is the job of the civilian volunteers to go from building to building, clearing out the so-called 'stragglers'. Being tied to a particular place, at the mercy of poor communications, emphasises people's vulnerability, but on top of this Whitehead's narrator, 'Mark Spitz' (we never learn his real name—much of this novel is engaged with what it means to be forced into a new life, and a new identity), is introspective and always has been, even before the apocalypse. It is as though he has viewed his life at a distance, waiting for the moment when he will finally engage with the world. For Mark Spitz, that moment happened during his period 'in the wild', fighting zombies, surviving, finding his way to the refugee camp. Since then, he has merely existed, biding his time, waiting from day to day for … well, for what?

One might argue that for much of his life, Mark Spitz has lain dormant, waiting like an insect pupa for the particular circumstances that will allow him to realise his full potential. Occasionally, a different person shows himself. Mark Spitz is a *nom de guerre* bestowed after Mark refuses to jump off a bridge to save himself, because he can't swim, and instead shoots his way out of a trap, singlehandedly killing seventy-something zombies in the process. Mostly, though, Mark Spitz gets by; the only real indicators that he is in any way distressed are his comparative silence and his belief that he sees white ash falling around him all the time.

While Mark Spitz may be geographically confined, there are no such restrictions on his thoughts. In the three days that we travel with Omega patrol (Mark Spitz, Gary from Connecticut, and Kaitlyn)—their last three days together, as it turns out—we travel back and forth through Mark's memory, gradually learning his story and something of his companions' stories as well.

Being confined to Manhattan and its environs is, for Mark, something of a dream come true. The novel opens with a lengthy passage concerning his memories of childhood visits to his Uncle Lloyd, who lived in Manhattan: 'in the long stretches in between visits he daydreamed about living in his apartment' (p.3). In part it is because Uncle Lloyd's flat contains everything missing from Mark's life. While Uncle Lloyd has all the latest devices, Mark's parents have 'a coffee machine that didn't tell time, dictionaries made out of paper, a camera that only took pictures' (p.3).

One might speculate whether Mark isn't really in love with Uncle Lloyd's heavily consumerist lifestyle. One might equally ask why it is that Mark's parents are so resistant to these markers of progress. It's not a question of money, so far as we can tell, nor even a conscious resistance to rampant consumerism, so much as a sense that they just don't need these things. As a result, Mark exists in a state of consumerist feast and famine, seeing these wondrous objects only when he visits his uncle.

And yet it isn't just about the gizmos and gadgets. Mark describes watching the skyline from the windows of his uncle's apartment, 'feeling weird about the pull the skyline had on him':

> He was a mote cycling in the wheels of a giant clock. Millions of people tended to this magnificent contraption, they lived and sweated and toiled in it, serving the mechanism of metropolis and making it bigger, better, story by glorious story and idea by unlikely idea. How small he was, tumbling between the teeth. (p.4)

As Mark walks through the streets of the deserted city, he has an acute awareness of what it was once like.

> Up and down the island the buildings collided, they humiliated runts through verticality and ambition, sulked in one another's shadows. Inevitability was mayor, term after term. Yesterday's old masters, stately named and midwifed by once-famous architects, were insulted by the soot of combustion engines and by technological advances in construction. Time chiseled at elegant stonework, which swirled or plummeted to the sidewalk in dust and chips and chunks. Behind the façades their insides were butchered, reconfigured, rewired, according to the next era's new theories of utility. Classic six into studio honeycomb, sweatshop killing floor into cordoned cubicle mill. In every neighbourhood the imperfect in their fashion awaited the wrecking ball and their bones were melted down to help their replacements surpass them, steel into steel. The new buildings in wave upon wave drew themselves out of rubble, shaking off the past like immigrants. The addresses remained the same and so did the flawed philosophies. It wasn't any place else. It was New York City. (p.6)

This seems to me to encapsulate much of what is going on in this novel, reflected in Mark Spitz's thoughts as he and Omega patrol go about their work. They clear stragglers. Stragglers are zombies who might best be described as having become stuck in time and space. For whatever reason they have returned to a place, a memory, that holds significance for them and have become frozen in a pose that is a part of that memory. They seem to be harmless but, if Manhattan is to be reclaimed, they must be removed, so Omega patrol, like all the other patrols, sweeps each office block, each apartment block, up to twenty stories high, putting a bullet through each head so they cannot come back to life, before bagging and disposing of the corpses.

Mark is constantly aware of the ways in which buildings have been altered, retrofitted, converted. He's sensitive to the reiterated layouts of flats and offices, as well as to the consumer choices people have made. He is also acutely aware of the fact that however familiar each situation seems to him, for the people he finds this was their unique experience. It is, though, also a powerful reminder to Mark of what he might have become; although he finally worked in Manhattan he never quite made the move to live there too, instead returning to his parents on Long Island, saving for the transformation that never came about. The reader suspects that it never would have, even without the apocalypse.

Mark Spitz 'believed that he had successfully banished thoughts of the future' (p.26), but it is obvious that for all his silence, he hasn't banished thoughts of the past, and late in the novel, revisiting a restaurant he went to many times with his parents as a child, Mark Spitz addresses the fact that he is himself a straggler of sorts, fluttering around Manhattan, unable to bring himself to leave. He wonders what sort of straggler he might have been, already knowing the answer: 'What did he love, what place had been important to him? Job or home, bull's-eye of cathected energy. Yes, he loved his home. Perhaps he'd end up there, installing himself in his worn perch on the right-hand side of the sofa' (p.155). We are beginning perhaps to understand why Mark prefers to live in a constant state of 'now', suspended in time.

However bizarre it might seem, Mark Spitz is a survivor. He has always seen himself as a student, doing just enough to get by, yet one could as easily interpret this as a knack for knowing instinctively what a situation demands in order to survive as comfortably as possible without too much effort: 'There was a code for every interaction and he tuned in. ... He staked out the B or the B chose him: it was his native land, and in high school and college he did not stray over the county line. At any rate his lot was irrevocable' (p.9). In perilous situations this is translated into 'a knack for last-minute escapes and improbable getaways' (p.26)—remember his famous shoot-out with a huge crowd of zombies. It is a skill uniquely suited to his present situation, but does this mean that between these short bursts of drama Mark Spitz functions like a zombie? That most other people do too? It is perhaps not surprising that Mark Spitz takes some time to realise, after Last Night, that anything is wrong, because to all intents and purposes his neighbourhood seems much as it always is.

One wonders also how Mark Spitz will function in a future that already has its own theme tune, in which low-grade looting by volunteers is allowed, but only from the goods of the reconstruction's official sponsors, and to a certain price level. This is a reboot of civilisation being organised by creatives and business types. When Ms Macy, all stilettos and highly buffed nail polish, visits from Buffalo to note progress, she is disappointed to find broken windows and shot-out locks, but is more concerned with changing the décor of the apartments to be commandeered for the new inhabitants of Manhattan. It is difficult to imagine that someone could be so out of touch as Ms Macy and indeed, to judge from the reports we see, the government seat at Buffalo is a fools' paradise, about to be rapidly disabused of its belief in its own rhetoric.

As Whitehead shows, rebooting civilisation is not about anthems and changingdécordecor but about tiny achievements, like growing a field of corn and harvesting it, working from the bottom up rather than top down, which suggests already that this government's attempt at regeneration is, if not doomed to failure, then bound to follow a different path than that laid down by the authorities. Those who remain in the countryside or holed up in an apartment are referred to as 'homesteaders', the implication being that those pioneer skills are what's needed in order to survive, not corporate sponsorship. It is also clear that one cannot survive in isolation, yet big gatherings bring bigger dangers, attracting the zombies.

Disintegration, when it comes, is as swift and as dreadful as one might imagine. Alongside the zombie invasion comes the revelation that the patrols were only ever a PR stunt to provide a little of that vital morale-boosting copy, no matter the lives wasted in the process. We've been with Omega patrol for three days, an intimacy that has made us come to care about these people, however artificial the circumstances. Yet, when the system fails, we run with Mark Spitz because what else can we do? It's been three short days in the middle of something incomprehensible. We're no closer to knowing why there are zombies, what the zombies want now that there are more of them. Maybe they wanted what New York City represented for them in their former lives, and have been migrating across the country, struggling to reach this beacon of prosperity, success, and consumer durables. Perhaps plague has stripped them of everything except their deepest capitalist impulses, and here they are, unstoppable.

And that is why *Zone One* is in fact a zombie novel with brains. Whitehead undoes those flights of survivalist fantasy in which the survivors win the day, examining the standard tropes in which humans can and finally will outnumber the zombies, set up a new civilisation and go on as before. He seems to be suggesting that our survival as a species can only be accomplished through a mode of living so new and so radical it remains difficult to articulate, though it is perhaps embodied in the unlikely shape of Mark Spitz and people like him.

There is an argument that Whitehead's approach is not new, that zombies as symbols of rampant consumerism are a device that has been in use since the 1980s. This is true, so far as it goes, though Whitehead departs significantly from the genre route map through Mark Spitz's commentary. Spitz is fully aware that he is as much a zombie as the stragglers he encounters, and he recognises also that the zombies were once living people, like him and his parents, with hopes, fears, aspirations which, however absurd to others, meant something to them, and it is his understated tenderness in accounting for that which offers something new. Spitz may be a straggler, but he is also a living witness, providing a poignant testimony of that which has been lost.

This is the first of Colson Whitehead's novels that I've read, but I doubt it will be the last. My response to his writing is similar to how I felt about Hari Kunzru's *Gods Without Men*; in each case I was drawn to the work because of its genre connection but the quality of the writing prompts me to seek out their other novels, irrespective of subject matter. I've not been disappointed with Kunzru so far; I'm hoping Whitehead won't disappoint me either.

Reading *Elysium* by Jennifer Marie Brissett

The text as puzzle

There is a temptation to treat a text as though it were a puzzle box. Execute the correct series of moves and the object springs open neatly, revealing all its secrets. We are taught to do this at school (or at any rate, I was), and although when we reach university age we may be encouraged to think there is no right or wrong way to approach a text, and that each interpretation is equally valid, some interpretations still seem more valid than others. That is, some interpretations receive more support and discussion than others, thus privileging one reading of a text above all. When disagreement does arise, it's more usually a matter of engaging with the reading rather than the text itself.

Recently, I've been reading Jennifer Marie Brissett's *Elysium* (2014), and I was struck by how it both invites and rejects the puzzle-solving approach to literary analysis. Invites, because the structure of this novel comprises many thin layers of narrative that appear to fuse together, encouraging a careful unwrapping and peeling apart to get at the heart of the story. Rejects, because, as the story does unfold, one realises that 'unfolds' is in fact a poor description of what is happening.

Brissett does seem to provide hints as to how one might approach *Elysium*, though they aren't as helpful as they might initially seem. Which is hardly surprising—why would an author want to give away everything at the beginning? Maybe because it's fun to hide something in plain view and wait for people to notice? Or not. But while I am interested in the way readers approach science fiction and fantasy novels, and the expectations they bring to them, I am also interested in the ways in which authors indirectly comment on readers' expectations, and it feels to me that to some extent at least, this is what Brissett is doing with *Elysium*.

Have I ever mentioned how much I dislike computer gobbledygook in a narrative?

I suspect I dislike it because I have read so many (mainly unpublished) novels in which the use of 'programming language' is a marker of 'science fiction'. Or indeed, 'near-future thriller', because the two are pretty similar, aren't they? (We will move rapidly past the would-be author who numbered their chapters in binary). My tolerance of this kind of thing is low, especially when too often the ideas being conveyed in the 'language' pass me by entirely. I'm a user, not a programmer. You may therefore imagine my joy at seeing the opening page of *Elysium*. I could feel whole areas of my brain closing down immediately, because, yes, like everyone else, I have my dislikes and my prejudices, and this is one of them. It took me a long time to get through Gwyneth Jones's *Escape Plans*, for that very reason.

This is how *Elysium* begins.

```
>>
>> open bridge
Connecting
*BRIDGE CONNECTED*
>>
>>
>> begin program
BRIDGE PROCESS: INITIATED 0000-00-00-00:00 (loc. 36)
```

But this is what comes next:

Floating high above the city, dipping and swooping through the valleys of cinderblocks and concrete, landing on the edge of a rooftop to look down upon the inhabitants below. Watching, seeing, learning. (loc. 43)

What is doing this? A drone seems reasonable, given we're already being programmed to think about computers. A flavour of *The Truman Show*, perhaps. But 'landing on the edge of a rooftop' sounds more like a bird. Unless they've got some unusually cool gadgetry in this fictional world, which might be the case. Either way, I can't help noticing that it is as though we're pulling the focus on this possibly non-existent camera, zooming in closer and closer to the street, until we encounter Adrianne, in a busy city, on her way to meet a friend for lunch. It's a human moment: she's been looking forward to this lunch all week. We forget about the techno-window dressing. This feels … real. Also, unreal. At least, if you think science fiction is all about the techno-window dressing, as many people do. We might, if we expect our SF to look like that, be asking 'what's with the woman doing nothing?'

So Much Depends on a Green Dot

For that matter, what's with the elk? And the owl? But especially the elk, because that comes first.

> Its antlers rose high upon its elegant head, spreading upwards like giant fingers into a crown as it strode nonchalantly along the bustling city street. Adrianne stopped to examine what she could so clearly see, yet everyone else seemed blind to it. (loc. 53)

How do we respond to the presence of this elk? Is it real? Is it a figment of Adrianne's imagination, a first hint of psychosis? At this stage it's difficult to know what to make of it. Being the reader I am, I tend to regard its appearance as evidence of some sort of fantastical or mythic intrusion into the world, so I am happy to see it as being both real and unreal simultaneously. This is a view I am going to have to revise extensively as the novel unfolds. I also have one slight problem with the elk. It reminds me terribly of the Glenfiddich stag advert, though in that instance while the stag seems to be perceived by everyone, the key to the advert's effect is that that its presence is acknowledged and thus legitimised by the Morgan Freeman lookalike, presumably because he's cool, drinks Glenfiddich, and can thus accept incredible things when they walk down his street.

I'd be inclined to suggest that the opening sequence of *Elysium* is asking something similar of us. How much of what we are seeing can we accept? It teases—is it SF? Is it fantasy? Is it a realist novel in disguise? But it is also, though we don't yet realise it, asking us another question, possibly two, the first being, why *can't* we have all these things in the one novel, and the second: why should it matter if they are all in there together?

Though one is tempted to immediately focus on discussing the ways in which gender and identity are (or are not) represented in *Elysium*, I think that is only part of the picture. The presentations of gender and identity in what, for the sake of argument I'll call a science fiction novel, are fascinating on their own terms, but what interests me is the way in which Brissett seems to be using them as a means of talking about science fiction itself. In her review of *Elysium* in March 2015's *Lightspeed* magazine, Amal El-Mohtar notes that the computer program at the heart of the narrative is:

> ...throwing up iteration after iteration of a single story, transforming it every time by changing the variables of gender, sexuality, location, and moment. In so doing, the novel throws into sharp relief our own social programming...

These iterations sound as echoes, but instead of becoming fainter with each repetition, they gain substance until we find ourselves at the heart of the shout that created them. The entire text is haunted by its sound, by a sense of its own lack of substance in the wake of it, reminding us of the fact that even now the universe reverberates with the faint echoes of the Big Bang, still perfusing our surroundings even millions of years after the event occurred. And I ask myself if something similar, on a shorter timescale obviously, is going on here, given that the further through the novel we move, the more overtly science-fictional it becomes.

It is as though Brissett is tracking the echo, or maybe it's a ripple, to its source, or to the centre, meaning that we're (perhaps accidentally) taking a tour of the ways in which science fiction has transformed itself. This is not to say that *Elysium* is arguing for a return to good old-fashioned 'genre' SF—quite the opposite. I would argue that *Elysium* as science fiction novel deliberately avoids foregrounding the 'big ideas'—alien invasion, generation starship, dystopia—that allegedly define SF. Instead, we have this staggeringly ordinary scene with a woman killing time in a street market, which could be anywhere.

> The sounds were a blending stream of conversations and sighs. The faces that passed here were from all over the world. Each a different shape and color. (loc. 75)

This is sensory overload, for Adrianne, it seems, and for me as the reader. Heat and cold, sun and shade, a perfume that 'was a mixture of sea breezes and powder' (loc. 75). It is that line about sea breezes and powder that does it for me, for some reason.

Whatever we as readers may feel about this scene, only one thing in it is strange to Adrianne:

> She looked up and saw a dot of green hovering in the blue sky. It hung there for a few moments, and then it was gone. (loc. 86)

What would I have made of that dot if *Elysium* had not begun with a piece of computer code? Would I have thought immediately, as I did, of a computer monitor that no longer worked, or a graphics card that was beginning to fail? Which in turn made me wonder if this street market was quite what it appeared to be. And as for that elk … But again, only Adrianne sees the green dot, so perhaps it is all in her head. The *** SYSTEM FAILURE *** comes as no surprise. Maybe it is meant not to be.

What strikes me too by this point is that the computer language actually makes sense. Rather than just letting my eye slide past it as I normally would, I find that the words are actually conveying something meaningful. Bridge. Crash. Delete. Cannot Open. Error. Especially Error. Only Bridge might seem contextually difficult, but if coupled with Connect, and Restarted, it reminds me of the ftp program I use to transmit large files to one of my clients, constantly connecting, closing, and connecting…And this, it will turn out, is significant.

*** SYSTEM FAILURE ***

I did wonder if we were perhaps in a revision of Joanna Russ's *The Female Man* (1975), with versions of the same identity in different worlds. Then at some point I noticed that phrases kept being repeated. 'released into sorrow' was the first to catch my attention, because it was unusual, but later whole paragraphs, sections, and characters began to resurface. I have been rereading *Beowulf* recently (the Seamus Heaney translation is very good), and thinking again about how orature is often structured around images, ideas, rote-learned passages that can be recited at suitable points, and indeed how the story itself is structured in certain ways to trigger that recitation.

All of which prompted me to ask: how much of *Elysium* is *story* and how much *plot*? It's a fine distinction, I admit, but is this a story about the author manipulating the reader, or is there another layer of 'reading' in here? Is it accidental artefact—created by the malfunctioning computer program, or that ftp program that can't quite mesh with the computer memorial? Is the observer actually receiving the story that Adrian, the computer whizz, wanted to tell?

History is written by the winners ... or at any rate, by those who escape ...

Adrian is the core of *Elysium*. Adrian, the omnicompetent man beloved of a certain kind of science fiction; the man with big ideas, and the back of an envelope on which to casually scribble them down. How are we meant to respond to this Adrian, this saviour of humanity, or at any rate, some of humanity ...

We are a long way into the novel before we reach its core story. By the time we find this Adrian, we've passed through many stories, or versions of stories, of people called Adrianne, Adrian, Antoine, Antoinette, Helen, Hector, and many combinations of relationship and friendship. Some stories are intensely domestic—like Adrianne's at the beginning, with only that green dot, displaced animals, and an inexplicable time shift to suggest the science-fictional element. But something has happened before the novel begins, and Antoine and dying Adrian, Adrianne frustrated by the living Helen to mourn the dead Antoinette, are living in worlds somehow changed. I might be reading for those changes—the games in which animals are set loose on one another—but at the same time I also enjoy the portrayal of the here and now of daily science-fictional life, rather than the usual heavy-handed allegory of survival in the ruins.

There is some of that to come, of course. As we slip past the simply domestic, past the muddled history in which the Roman Empire comes to the US and Adrianne becomes a Vestal Virgin, we reach two new threads of narrative: a post-apocalyptic world and the rescue from the hospital, the two braided and rebraided as different characters come to the fore. Stories are fast becoming tropes—after everything goes wrong, Antoine rescues Adrian from the hospital, and Hector comes too. They take refuge in a supermarket, as you do—but wait, when did Antoine and Adrian suddenly become so much younger? They take shelter in the subways until Antoine, now Adrian's father, vanishes, leaving Adrian, now the artist, to paint memorials all over the town. All of this seems oddly familiar, and not merely within the context of the novel. Similarly, Adrianne, holed up on the upper floors of a high-rise, waits for her father to come home. He has flown away to find food. She knows now that her wings are growing in, and she is afraid, not least of her father's reaction. Assuming he comes home, which is by no means a certainty.

Have you ever wondered what happens when you put down insect powder?

Do the ants or the cockroaches die tidily? Or do they change, mutate, transform horribly into something else, at a microscopic level?

Even this is familiar in some respects. Aliens come to Earth, find it inhabited, dust the place with something out of a galaxy-sized container to get rid of the vermin problem. Which is us. Humanity. Later, 'they', the aliens, will try to tell us it was because we attacked rather than talking, while 'we' will point out we thought 'they' were attacking us to begin with. Communication failed before it began. If there is a difference here from the usual scenario, it is that the white-skinned people are the ones who experience the appalling transformations, while the brown- and black-skinned peoples of the world are the ones who remain unchanged, the ones who begin to devise solutions. The ones who refuse the refugees who want to join them when they begin to create safe spaces.

Going underground. Building underground. Building cities underground. Deciding to leave Earth. Generation starships.

At this point, the story stabilises as Engineer Adrian builds his city. Engineer Adrian is also the basis for the memorial that is inscribed in the atmosphere, when everyone finally departs. I have no quarrel with that. However, I cannot help wondering what might have happened if it had been Engineer Adrianne who was scanned? Because insofar as we agree we are recapitulating a history of science fiction in this story, what doesn't seem to be acknowledged as yet is that everything we've experienced along the way emerges from the mind of a man. A man of colour, yes, but a man nonetheless, and a man possibly with a flair for the melodramatic.

What we have been fighting our way through is not a dispassionate historical account, however much we might want to see it as that. We are dealing with one man's experience, and possibly one man's hubris. In which case we might want to stop at this point and wonder whether Engineer Adrian hasn't bigged himself up just a little in his own memory. And whether his perspective isn't just a little skewed when it comes to recounting certain events. It would account, for example, for the excessive romanticism of the account of the loss of his wife, Antoinette. For that matter, it may go some way to dealing with the otherwise clumsily handled death of Helen, the trans woman nobly sacrificing herself for the sake of Adrian and his brother. I do wonder why, when everything else about this novel is so expertly handled, those two aspects of the story do seem clunky by comparison.

One might suggest that the type of science fiction we are dealing with at this point in the historical tour is inevitably going to include these kinds of ill-judged scenes as emotionally stunted men try to write about their emotions, and attempt to second-guess what is going on in the heads of those around them. And that may be so ... Except that a 'but' hovers, like that green dot, which is not a malfunction, I belatedly perceive, but a marker, the way in and out of what we finally learn are projections, immersive environments.

And having criticised the fact that the 'story' is a man's story, here is the mitigation. Perhaps it is not just Adrian's story that is memorialised. He was the prototype, yes, and not by his own choice, but perhaps everyone else's story has been preserved as well. The final portion of the novel is given over to Adrianne—by this time we must have noticed that it is almost always a version of Adrianne who has a sense that there might be something beyond the direct experience—the last of the actual survivors, who emerges into a world now populated by the aliens, the krestges, to update the memorial in the atmosphere one last time, an Eve of a sort, if you like.

Is that really a mitigation? I'm not sure. We might try for 'And it was all a dream' ... except, of course, it isn't.

And perhaps this is the truth that lies at the heart of this novel. There is no easy way out. If you follow the history, the visible history, the articulated history of science fiction, there is no other path that Brissett could have taken. To do otherwise is to tell a different story altogether, a secret history, and maybe that is worse, because then women become the creatures men don't see, and that reinforces a whole different strand of historical storytelling, one that forever relegates women to the edges of the story. Whereas, as Brissett shows, women do take centre stage, with ease, the moment a certain style of science fiction is put aside.

The Exhausting of the Author

We place such a burden on the author—the actual author—to account for everything. Too much of a burden, perhaps. Jennifer Marie Brissett has created this extraordinary, original text; this cunning survey of the ways in which science fiction is constructed, and what happens when the template is undermined, begins to disintegrate, how much better it becomes when it breaks free.

And still I want more. Or something slightly different. Or I see things in the text that maybe the author didn't, or didn't foreground, or left for the reader to discover, like a T in magic marker on a brick.

Of course, I do all of this because criticism is part of the process of reading. I could go all Barthesian and mutter about the necessity of the death of the author, but in this instance I shan't, not least because I know that half the reason this novel is so good is because it is working hard to bring together so many thoughts and ideas. To complain in detail about what isn't there is to burden the author with the requirement to fix absolutely everything through one novel, when that's clearly nonsensical. On the other hand, it perhaps indicates that we are—I am—hungry for novels that do more than reflexively support the status quo or churn out the same old dystopian product while claiming that it is something new and exciting, literary even, when it plainly is nothing of the sort. Our admiration squeezes the life out of the very thing we are delighted with by wanting it to be even better, and *Elysium* is already awesome.

And perhaps this is the critic's biggest dilemma. How to love something without crushing it to death with the weight of expectation and analysis, when true love can only be shown through expectation and analysis?

Europe in Autumn – Dave Hutchinson

The original *coureurs des bois* (the runners of the woods) were French-Canadian woodsmen who ventured into the North American interior, trading goods with the native peoples in return for furs, learning their languages and cultural practices, sometimes taking native wives. Early on, there was some official encouragement of this from the French, who claimed the territory needed men who could negotiate with the indigenous peoples, but as the authorities became more interested in matters of regulation and ownership, the *coureurs des bois*, unlicensed as they mostly were, pushed even deeper into the interior in an effort to circumvent the authorities' attempts to curb their operations.

They were explorers and adventurers, intensely romantic figures, often treated as outlaws, and some of them were probably crooks, though on occasion they could also be of use to the authorities. Above all, they were beholden to no one but themselves, careless of borders, able to travel swiftly and mostly unremarked, thanks to their skills as woodsmen.

The desire to explore the forbidden or the unknown, coupled with a need to pass through territory unobserved, permeates travelogues and spy stories. Explorers were almost by default spies as well: Richard Burton, the translator of *One Thousand and One Nights*, disguised himself in order to visit Mecca, while a number of Europeans disguised themselves in order to explore the Himalayan region, and the British government sent trained Indian surveyors into the region disguised as pandits in order to map the area. Such activities reached their literary apotheosis in Kipling's *Kim*, a novel that also popularised the term 'The Great Game'. Closer to home, closer in time, John le Carré's stories exemplify Cold War efforts to unobtrusively move information and people in and out of eastern Europe, across tightly monitored borders.

With the arrival of the European Union and the Schengen Agreement, with most of Europe's borders standing wide open, one might have supposed that crossing from one territory to another would become the easiest thing in the world, yet in the wake of 9/11 and the advent of the Global War on Terror, some borders have become ever more tightly controlled, governed by security operations that come perilously close to farce. And while in Western Europe, demands for regional autonomy have, for the most part, led nowhere, further east, the former Soviet Union and its satellite nations are still dividing into a series of ever-smaller sovereign territories, each demanding recognition as an independent nation. One only needs to look at the current situation in Ukraine to see how this might play out in the next few years, and to start wondering what that might mean for a Scottish bid for independence, the ramifications of which are already being discussed.

There has always been an underground trade in moving things, and sometimes people, secretly around the world. Even now, there still exist what are called Queen's Messengers, carrying documents too sensitive or too private to be committed even to diplomatic bags. Today on the radio I heard an interview with a man who carries donated stem cells from one hospital to another. Smuggling has always existed, although these days it's as likely to be people as cigarettes and alcohol that are being moved illegally. Journalist Glen Greenwald's partner, David Miranda, was arrested and questioned as he passed through Heathrow, under suspicion that he was carrying documents illegally acquired by Edward Snowden.

Europe in Autumn, Dave Hutchinson's new novel, takes this situation to its furthest logical extent. Autumnal Europe is one in which the European Union has pretty much collapsed, taking with it the open-border idealism of the Schengen Agreement. Instead, as one character observes, 'Europe sinks back into the eighteenth century' (p.18), fragmenting into a series of 'quasi-national states' or polities, some of them stable, others lasting as long as autumn leaves. 'I saw on the news last week that so far this year twelve new nations and sovereign states have come into being in Europe alone,' observes Dariusz. 'And most of them won't be here this time next year,' comments Rudi, who claims to have no opinion on the matter. 'I'm a cook,' he says. 'Not a politician' (p.17).

This new imposition of borders, this shifting lattice of grudge and allegiance, brings with it new problems. It's the same territory as before, only 'More frontiers. More red tape. More borders. More border *police*' (p.18), and more difficulty in moving things around. As a consequence, people like Dariusz— we might call them smugglers, crooks, gangsters; they might disagree with us—have to find new ways to transport things. The new *coureurs des bois* work much like their ancestors, except that they are shyer and rather more retiring. No one knows who they are, who runs them, or anything much else about them. They can be found when needed. When not needed, they slip quietly back into the woodwork. Anyone who has read le Carré will recognise what the coureurs are: an organisation of lamplighters, people who create legends, carry information; they facilitate. Indeed, there is more than a passing whiff of le Carré about the coureurs.

Rudi learns all this when he is recruited to their ranks. As a sort of favour to Max, his employer, and Dariusz, who runs the local protection racket and a few other things besides, Rudi carries an Estonian passport, which makes him rather more welcome in certain places than, say, Poles like Max and Dariusz. He has travelled into the city-state of Hindenberg to collect a message. His mission is successful and later Dariusz asks him, 'How would you like to do that kind of thing for a living?' (p.35). 'I'm a chef. For a living,' replies Rudi, though he finally agrees to be a coureur as a hobby. 'So long as it's a well-paid sort of a hobby'. In fact, it seems to be a remarkably well-paid sort of a hobby, so long as one doesn't ask questions.

And despite Rudi's regular reaffirmation of himself as a chef, he takes to the work. He's already served a long peripatetic apprenticeship, working his way through the restaurants of the Baltic states. He taught himself to cook as a child by watching English and Polish cookery shows, which in turn required him to teach himself English and Polish. He is utterly self-contained, a polity all of his own, within the city-state of a restaurant kitchen, so often presided over by a tyrant. He's already learned to observe, to blend in, to accommodate the foibles of others, and knows when to say nothing. He is punctilious and precise, and has an instinctive ability to sense when something is not quite right. Added to that, in appearance he is, by his own admission, 'not anything really' (p.19). In short, he is the pefect coureur.

But the suspicious reader might perhaps be wondering by now whether this set-up isn't a little too perfect. Rudi himself acknowledges that the whole thing 'smacked of cliché. Cloak and dagger, clandestine meetings on darkened streets in Central Europe' (p.29). Indeed, all it lacks for the cliché to be complete is a hint of zither music, but as Hutchinson is far too intelligent a writer to succumb to that sort of thing, one must and should conclude that he is up to something else. The question is, what? That the question is not easily answered is, I have to say, one of the several great joys of this novel for me.

Rudi's wry commentary on the new milieu in which he finds himself is a delight. There is a sly humour at work throughout the novel, manifest in *sotto voce* asides that leave the reader thinking 'did he really just says that?' and such miniature absurdities as the village-state run by fans of Günter Grass—'Rudi was vaguely sorry that Grassheim had been reabsorbed by the Pomeranian Republic [...] He really liked *The Tin Drum*' (p.27). However, Rudi's observations do raise some interesting points about what a reader might expect of a narrative that dresses itself in the costume of a spy novel, or indeed of an organisation that apparently models itself on a fiction. Should we read this as someone somewhere recognising that le Carré's fictional model of the Circus is so damn good they might as well put it to actual use, or is Hutchinson ever so gently pointing out that our perception of how the secret service works is shaped more by the fiction we read than the reality we can never experience, with the underlying possibility that they might just be the same? Or is all of this a distraction, a 'legend' that Hutchinson himself is fabricating, to draw our attention away from something else?

It is worth keeping that thought in mind as the story unfolds, though it is easy to be distracted not only by the descriptions of Rudi's apprenticeship as a coureur in which he learns his new tradecraft, but by the account of his apprenticeship as a chef. The two are remarkably similar in their way, and it's not too much of a stretch to consider them as a form of commentary on Hutchinson's own journey as a writer. He's been writing for a long time, having already published four collections of stories by the time he was twenty-one, and then spending many years as a journalist. I first encountered his stories in the mid-1980s and even then they seemed to me to have an indefinable 'rightness' about them, a quality that emerged from a combination of well-crafted writing and a good eye for a human story, practiced but not polished to inhuman perfection. His talents have matured beautifully in the last thirty or so years, and are fully on show in this novel, from the long opening sequence as Rudi and Max deal with a group of badly-behaved Hungarian gangsters, to the unexpected jump-cut as the story shifts forward to Rudi's being recruited to collect a message, all interlaced with Rudi's memories of his long and difficult apprenticeship in Max's own kitchen. It takes courage, but also confidence to commit to such a wilfully discursive narrative technique, but there is no trace of arrogance in Hutchinson's work. As Rudi cooks, so Hutchinson writes, and the story unfolds.

The pacing is also interesting. From the early chapters with their slow unfolding and wealth of detail, we move more rapidly through a series of missions which reveal the variety in the work that Rudi undertakes. He is still a chef even if he no longer cooks. He is good at what he does, he earns a decent living, he tries not to worry too much when things go wrong, though it is of course in the failures that the story lies. By this time, we might be tempted to dismiss the novel as a series of episodic adventures, with Rudi hopping across Europe under a number of aliases. They're very good adventures, no denying it, but a whole novel of this might eventually become … well, boring, even though Hutchinson has a neatly compressed way of showing how time passes.

Rudi's technical skills improve, the world changes, and so on, all without making a fetish out of the history or the tradecraft. Were this simply a comic caper, the narrative would demand that something go cataclysmically wrong, and indeed it does—insofar as finding the severed head of a man in a left-luggage locker is ever anything other than wrong—but because this novel was never just about the future of spying, when things go wrong, Rudi goes on furlough, and visits his family back in Estonia.

In terms of narrative structure, this might be regarded as a diversion from the main story, but within the terms of this novel, it fits perfectly. With Rudi's arrival in Estonia, the reader's attention turns more fully to the reasons why the coureurs are needed in the first place, and the complex politics of a post-EU Europe. Colonisation is by no means a new phenomenon—it has been a reality ever since humans plucked up enough courage to sail out of sight of land—but autumnal Europe has reached the stage where declaring independence might be the only way to protect, say, a national park, rather as if the National Trust were to attempt to turn the Lake District into a polity. This is precisely what Rudi's father seeks to do, only Rudi isn't there to see the resulting bloodbath as he is unexpectedly, inexplicably 'rescued' by British forces, and finds himself detained in London for no reason he can determine.

The London episode is the most enigmatic portion of the novel. If the rest of the narrative involves travel, movement, action, then this London sojourn seems most notable for its lack of incident. Rudi is not exactly imprisoned in a set of chambers somewhere off Fleet Street, but neither is he entirely free to leave. For his own part, he seems happy to lie low until a moment of epiphany reveals the way forward. It's an unexpected way, one that doesn't make much sense until a long time later, and it shifts the novel's dynamic entirely. Were Hutchinson not such a good craftsman, I'd be questioning this apparent longueur. Instead, I read it as the novel's hinge, the point where the narrative changes direction entirely, a necessary moment of reflection while Rudi considers what brought him thus far.

At this point, *Europe in Autumn* moves far beyond the conventional spy narratives of le Carré into altogether stranger territory, a universe akin to that of the Great Game, or even a pithier (a much, much pithier) version of Neal Stephenson's work, as Rudi and his team (he has a team now, just a small one) uncover the existence of an alternative world, an invisible territory that hides in plain sight, mapped by its discoverer, and vital for the coureurs to maintain their service. Except it turns out that the coureurs are rank amateurs, up against a far, far older network. At which point, the reader might start wondering, 'hang on, why didn't I notice that before?' To which the answer must surely be, because the author didn't want you to, and he is extremely good at what he does.

I am a sucker for a well-executed secret history, and equally so for a cartographic mystery, so this latter section of the novel more than adequately scratches a few of my literary itches. I can see that for some it might appear that the narrative has finally veered lethally off-piste. Yet I would draw their attention once again to the work of the original coureurs des bois, travelling into the unmapped interior of North America. Unmapped by the white incomers yes, but familiar terrain to its residents, the indigenous peoples, who mapped it through story and song, and considered the idea of 'ownership' to be utterly bizarre. Yes, each tribal band had its ancestral lands, confirmed through occupation and usage, but the western concept of sovereign territory was anathema to them. This is not to say that everyone could freely cross their land, but the underlying philosophy was not predicated on ownership.

The original coureurs formed a loose-knit company of their own as well as being part of a wider community linked by bonds of kinship rather than land. One might see Hutchinson's latter-day coureurs in a not dissimilar light. Some of them at least are in it for the money or to further criminal ends, but there is an underlying Schengen-inspired philosophy that sees the maintenance of open borders as a human right. But what if the coureurs have already long since been infiltrated by government departments, their studied neutrality nothing but a front? What if other players are involved as well?

If the situation was complex at the beginning of the novel, it's even more complicated by the end. The tantalising thought of a secret country with the concomitant prospect of free movement across Europe dangles enticingly before us, and yet there are clearly other consequences to consider. How might one defend that freedom other than by fiercely protecting those boundaries that are not boundaries in the conventional sense? Which are questions for the sequel that is hinted at, and which I very much hope will appear in due course.

For now, though, we have to be content with this first instalment and fortunately, it is the kind of novel that repays more than one reading. On the surface, *Europe in Autumn* is a novel pieced together from apparently meaningless Situations, each occurring in tiny, rigidly defined territories that refuse all but the barest connections with one another, other than that of lines drawn on a map. At a deeper level, it is an intensely layered narrative. Each revelation brings with it another layer of mystery, as though one is unpacking a set of nested boxes, with no centre in sight. This is a deceptive piece of work, and intricately layered. I like fiction that challenges as well as entertains, and this more than fits that bill. Which is why I shall be nominating *Europe in Autumn* for the BSFA and Hugo Awards next year, and hoping to see it on the Clarke shortlist, because, yes, it really is that good.

The Stone Boatmen by Sarah Tolmie

The brief biography of Sarah Tolmie that accompanies *The Stone Boatmen* suggests that the novel is in part derived from her fascination with the fourteenth-century poem *Piers Plowman*, by William Langland. *Piers Plowman* is a dream vision, a form popular in medieval writing, in which the author claims to have dreamed the story that is being presented. The dream narrative's primary characteristic is its necessary obliqueness: while dream images may be vividly realistic, they often conceal deeper meanings. Thus, a dream poem might explore a deeply personal experience, such as the death of a child (*Pearl*), an intense religious experience (*The Dream of the Rood*), or, as in the case of *Piers Plowman*, provide a history of Christianity and a powerful critique of the writer's own times. In each case, the dream structure functions as a protective distancing—this is the dream speaking, not the conscious human being—while its allegorical nature nonetheless enables the writer to say what's on his mind.

The influence of *Piers Plowman* on *The Stone Boatmen* may be oblique but is nonetheless pervasive. The novel is set in what might seem to be a dream world: a fluid landscape with no shape, no names, only the most basic of geographical features—sea, harbour, land, city. In the city—at this point it has no name—is a palace, and in that palace is a prince. It is a city that is built on elaborate ceremonies. As the novel opens, Prince Nerel, no-name, stripped of his own name at his accession to the throne five years earlier, awaits the annual feast of the Perihelion. During the feast, he will perform a series of baffling private ceremonies, while his public duties are undertaken by his *nerelkho*, a double chosen from among the men of the city, for whom these duties are presumably just as puzzling.

This year, however, things are to be different. While ordinarily the *nerelkho* might bear only a fleeting resemblance to Nerel, the majordomo has discovered Azul, one of the fisherfolk, who looks as though he could be Nerel's twin. It has frequently been noted that Nerel looks exactly like the stone boatmen in the harbour, a hundred mysterious statues of the ancestors leading out to sea, a circumstance that suggests his reign will be a fortunate one. For Azul, as a fisherman, such a resemblance is considered closer to a misfortune: his very name has been chosen to ward against potential disaster. That the Prince has an identical *nerelkho* is unprecedented, and suggests that strange currents have been sent in motion. And indeed, change is on its way, though not in the dramatic fashion that such a coincidence would imply.

While these generic trappings—the huge palace, the interminable, apparently meaningless ceremonies, the sense of the palace and city existing in a world of their own—might seem to hark back to Mervyn Peake's *Gormenghast*, the two novels are in fact very different. Peake's world has already reached the point of no return, its ceremonies long since emptied of genuine significance, and carried out by Lord Sepulchrave only because he has no alternative. By contrast, Nerel is alive to the potential of his ceremonies, even while he recognises that as yet he finds no personal significance in them. His very name, or lack of it, positions him as a blank tablet, awaiting some sort of revelation. And while Steerpike's irruption into the closed system that is Gormenghast merely hastens its inevitable decay, Azul's ceremonial introduction into palace life instead brings new possibilities into being.

While Nerel may be symbolically detached from his own identity during the Perihelion ceremonies, with Azul as his *nerelkho* he is finally able to understand in a more literal sense his ceremonial death and renewal, and to understand how this represents his dual identity as a public and private person. As a result, Nerel experiences a quiet transformation as he at last begins to find a sense of purpose, a sense of purpose that will, in unexpected ways, shape the rest of the story.

Titus Groan's epiphany can only be brought about by a sudden and violent expulsion from Gormenghast, followed by a wanderjahr during which he learns about the outside world. For Nerel and Azul, epiphany comes as a more gradual process in the form of connections made when least expected: not least when Azul, a working fisherman, instinctively recognises the functions of instruments left behind by the ancestors, instruments that Nerel has always assumed must have ritual rather than practical significance. At the same time, the presence of Azul enables Nerel to see his own role in the world more clearly:

> All along inside him he had borne this vastness, an interior copy of the world, which name came out and touched ends with the world he walked on. No name could compass it, for it meant everything, all things in one, from which no part could be distinguished. (p.15)

Excited by such revelations, and also by Azul's instinctive yet appropriate responses to palace ceremonies, drawn from the rituals of his own people—'He had been the man in whom the ritual came to life' (p.42)—Nerel determines to record the city's ceremonies, a project that irrevocably changes the relationship between the city and the palace. Nerel is transformed from a remote figure into a much-loved ruler, seen often around the city, gradually breaking down many of the barriers that previously existed between the two groups. In doing this, he literally embodies the idea of connection.

Nerel's exploration of the city's most important activities is all-encompassing, while throwing into sharp relief the many microcosms of which the city is composed. Yet when he attempts to give Azul a continuing role in palace life, Azul baulks at the idea, conscious of the gulf that remains between the two classes. It is only when he falls in love with the Lady Megarion that integration of a sort begins to occur. The gradual unfurling of this first section of the novel, its dream-like quality, reflects the caution of both city and palace, where change comes so slowly it is as if it isn't happening at all. Yet both Azul and Nerel realise that things must have been changing all along, albeit imperceptibly slowly.

Tolmie describes Azul and Nerel's growing friendship and its wider consequences with such delicacy and deftness it is impossible not to be drawn into their story, and that of their children. It is Mahar, Azul's son, who takes the next momentous step and decides to set sail in search of the Ancestors' original city, still talked about in children's stories. Mahar believes that the boatmen statues in the harbour point in the direction of this lost city, and sets about constructing a huge ocean-going vessel of a design so contentious he is thrown out of the boatbuilders' guild for attempting it. It is only through Nerel's intervention that the ship is completed at all, and everyone has misgivings about the voyage.

Mahar is, by his own admission, bored by the emphasis on ceremony and ritual in his own city. He is also acutely aware that he does not fully belong, either to the city or to the palace, and his determination to be a sailor and boatbuilder is a deliberately calculated expression of that uncertain status. It is also indicative of Mahar's future role as a different kind of bridge, one between the different cities of the Ancestors.

If the first section of the novel is almost hallucinatory in tone, then Mahar's portion of the story, while still short on concrete detail, is nonetheless marked by a new energy and sense of movement as he voyages forth. The smooth surface of life in the city is for the first time disturbed as the *Aphelion* moves away from the comforting familiarity of city life.

But the story Tolmie gives us is one of arrivals rather than of the journeys themselves. Mahar reaches first the city ruled over by the queen, Naran. This is the city where there is 'a word and a name for everything' (p.65), almost literally so, with words 'everywhere, engraved on every surface, above every doorway' (p.66). It is the public nature of words that delights Mahar, the way in which people 'spoke for themselves and not just in the forms of ritual' (p.71).

What Mahar begins to realise is that while the magic of words themselves is acknowledged, their function in communicating ideas has been forgotten. Inscribing the word on the object it represents has become more important than conveying the concept to others. Mahar notes that 'those scholars who knew the ancient works at all cared little about making things work and were bogged down in mazes of detail' (p.72). While information has undeniably been lost along the way, the implication seems to be that much of it survives. What has been lost is curiosity and the inclination to do anything with the contents of the libraries. This seems to be tied to the slow pace of life in each city. Mahar's sailors had hoped to discover a new way of being, but are disappointed to find Naran's city is not unlike their own. When they finally reach the legendary city of the Ancestors, ruled over by the bird-priests, they find the same again. Few people are resistant to change if it comes, but neither do they actively seek it out. The world seems held in a benign stasis. Not even the unexpected arrival of the *Aphelion* can immediately alter this. The ship and its crew are instead literally written into the city's discourse, covered in words in an elaborate ceremony before they sail on.

By this time, the reader will have realised that *The Stone Boatmen* itself is not quite what it initially seems. There is a temptation to read it simply as a particularly lyrical fantasy novel, one that is perhaps a little old-fashioned, even a little fey in places, in keeping with that dream vision. Yet it seems to me that Tolmie is deliberately challenging a very specific science-fictional trope, the one in which a novel's inhabitants become increasingly aware that their ancestors had skills and knowledge that they no longer possess. Usually, one exceptional person somehow manages to intuit all this, the inhabitants gladly recover all that knowledge in the blink of an eye, and their lives are instantly transformed for the better. When Mahar sails his remarkable vessel into the harbour of Naran's city, this should signal the moment when everything changes, but Tolmie's approach is more intriguing. There is no rapid transformation. Tolmie's novel is less bothered about these moments of epiphany, more concerned about the responsibilities such rediscovery brings with it. Increasingly, the characters come to wonder why the Ancestors decided to conceal their knowledge in the first place.

As Mahar and his companions come to realise, this was an entirely conscious decision on the part of Harel, the last king and the first bird-priest. The bird-priests are perhaps the most intriguing element of the novel. They practice a form of government based almost exclusively on the observation of the behaviour of the golden temple birds. It sounds absurd, yet, as Mahar sees, it is not what the birds tell the priests that is important so much as the way in which the priests learn to observe what the birds are doing. A similarly intense scrutiny is then applied to the problems of the inhabitants of the Ancestors' city. The close relationship between the bird-priests, led by Herodias, and the city folk is vastly different to that which exists between Nerel and his people at the beginning of the story, yet we see that Nerel, almost by accident, has begun of his own accord to create a similar arrangement, though for an entirely different reason.

Once links between the three cities are re-established, *The Stone Boatmen* shifts tempo, its meditative pace becoming much livelier, almost mercurial, reflecting the changes wrought by Mahar's marriage to Naran, and to the presence of Ahimsa, later called the Rose Poet, and her daughter, Fjorel. If Nerel, Azul, and Mahar are the initiators of a new desire for connection, then Fjorel and the Rose Poet represent a flowering of creative energies brought about by those connections. The circulation of ideas is as much an intellectual process as it is the exchange of actual technique. Fjorel in particular contributes a new understanding of the intentions of Harel, drawn from her own visions and from a strange telepathic connection she has forged with Maleki, one of the temple birds. The belief is that Maleki contains the spirit of Harel, though how he might have got there is unclear to everyone except the reader, and even that explanation depends on a particular reading of the novel.

And this is to barely scratch the surface of this narrative, which seems constantly to fold itself into new shapes in the reader's mind. Expectations are often wonderfully confounded. Tolmie plays with ideas of doubling and interconnectedness, but while twins recur as an important motif, they are never fetishised or assigned any mystical significance. She is fascinated too by the process of creativity, and much of the novel's central section is devoted to the Rose Poet's apprenticeship as a writer, the way in which she cunningly combines the old and the new, and at the heart of it, the palpable joy she takes in discovering her abilities.

The narrative itself is a complex structure—it is unsurprising perhaps that weaving plays a significant role in one portion of the novel—but it never overwhelms the story's unfolding. The reader is never forced to admire the 'cleverness' of the storytelling. Instead, one has a great sense of the harmonious interaction of the story's disparate parts. The narrative is never less than utterly compelling and absorbing, yet it mostly eschews high drama for a steady, even unfolding of events. It is in so many ways the complete antithesis of modern fantasy writing, a novel that deals with the intellectual problems of a world rather than battles or magic. Indeed, one way to read *The Stone Boatmen* is as an allegorical questioning of the assumptions that underlie so much modern genre writing.

It is a nourishing sort of book, the kind of novel where you want to make notes as you go, because it raises so many interesting questions. It is also a book that develops with each subsequent reading. I've now read it three times, and I'm still finding more to think about. This is not to suggest that it is entirely perfect. One might feel a slight unease at a certain binarism creeping in at times, as women intuit and men deal in the empirical, for all that women exert at least as much power as men. One might also suggest that Fjorel's dissemination of skills acquired from her visions becomes a little too much to accept at times, but Tolmie always manages to pull back just in time.

Whether or not *The Stone Boatmen* is but a dream remains for the reader to decide, but this I can say: this is a novel that will remain long in my memory, because of the quality of the storytelling and the ideas it explores. I cannot recall reading anything quite like it in recent years. It is perhaps a little early in the reading year to say this, but I feel sure already that it will be one of my favourite books of 2014.

AFTERWORD

Maureen by Jonathan McCalmont

Maureen Kincaid Speller was one of the most remarkable people I have ever known. I consider myself immeasurably richer for having known her and infinitely poorer for the knowledge that I will never see her again. She was unique.

I first met Maureen on one of three separate occasions. Memory rebels at any further attempts at ordering as I cannot remember a time when I was aware of her existence whilst not also being her friend. This is because Maureen didn't so much meet you as effortlessly envelope you in her social world. She was not one for tentatively moving up through the gears from polite smiles to small talk and then on to shared references ... No, she just reached out and included you in whichever conversation it was that she happened to be having. I may not be able to remember exactly when it was that Maureen and I first met but I am certain that the first thoughts I had about her in person were 'who the fuck is this madwoman and why is she talking to me?'

Maureen's casual but persistent inclusivity was unusual in that it came less from an extrovert's need to stage-manage conversations and more from a genuine desire for intellectual connection. Maureen would sometimes speak to me of her youth and I always got the impression that, prior to her relationship with Paul, the people in her life tended to view her love of books as a baffling and border-line embarrassing eccentricity rather like going to the shops clad in a beard of bees.

This lack of early support and encouragement seems to have cast a long shadow over Maureen's life. It left her feeling as though she were perpetually on the outside looking in, always hearing exciting conversations taking place in other rooms whilst not being allowed to participate. This sense of pre-emptive rejection meant that when Maureen Kincaid Speller included you in a conversation, it was not because she valued inclusivity as some kind of abstract liberal principle, but because she wanted to hear what you had to say as a person. More than anyone I have ever known, Maureen believed in the power of conversation and the ability of books to shrink the distances between human hearts. She never once took for granted either her connection to SFF or the connections she made with individual fans.

Maureen viewed herself as a critic. She treated criticism with the upmost seriousness and revelled in that identity even when she struggled to do much writing herself. Indeed, it is telling that two of her final contributions to the discussion of SFF include a lengthy piece about the challenge of engaging critically with a much-loved author and a podcast that was politely trying to clear a space for critical engagement in spaces that have, over time, come to view it with no small degree of suspicion.

A few years ago, Maureen was going through one of her periodic bouts of self-doubt. No longer able to see the value of her contributions to the field, she asked me where I thought her critical strengths lay and I, having been put on the spot, answered that I most valued her voice. At the time, this went down like a lead-balloon as I suspect she was looking to me for reassurance her that she had the requisite number of skill-points to unlock the 'Critic' prestige class. While Maureen may not have liked my answer, I continue to stand by it as the things that draw me back to Maureen's writing are her sensibility and her voice rather than her 'take' on any specific book or trend. Maureen viewed herself as a critic and it is only right that we should honour that self-image, but I believe that thinking of Maureen in terms of her contributions to criticism is to diminish both the scope of her intellect and the depth of her commitment to the conversation surrounding SFF.

Back when I was most active in SFF, people used to produce manifestos and series of blog-posts expanding their thoughts on criticism and the ways in which it differed from reviewing, and the kinds of unpaid PR work that have become increasingly common in book-adjacent spaces on social media. While there is, naturally, discourse to be had over power dynamics within SFF and who has the ability to speak in a disruptive manner in spaces that have come to be dominated by marketing and professionalised cliques, the point is that fandom is a set of social relations and social relations change. The window for certain forms of speech opens and closes with the passage of time and while Maureen seems to have felt most at home inhabiting the role of critic, she was other things as well. In fact, she was arguably one of the most adaptive thinkers in SFF commentary because she was willing to change and to follow the conversation.

Glancing at Maureen's page at the Internet Science Fiction Database, it is hard not to be impressed by the sheer scale of her commitment to writing about science fiction and fantasy. Most people who try their hands at reviewing often wind up burning out or migrating towards other areas, but Maureen started putting her work out there in the 1980s and continued producing work right up until this year. As someone whose critical career pre-dated the internet, the scale of Maureen's output also had physical implications. I remember visiting Paul and Maureen in Folkestone for the first time after being asked by the British Science Fiction Association to help put together a collection of her reviews. They pulled these huge stacks of zines off of shelves that were deeper than a man's arm and piled them all at my feet. At one point, Maureen flicked through a magazine with some hand-drawn cover art, harrumphed, peered over the round spectacles she favoured at the time, and fixed me with one of her fabled Hard Paddington Stares before instructing me that some of these pieces were going to need a vigorous edit if they were ever to see the light of day again.

At the time, I knew Maureen's work chiefly from its appearances online and in the magazines of the British Science Fiction Association but as soon as I started looking into her back-catalogue, I quickly realised that Maureen's engagement extended much further. I was lucky enough to know Maureen for more than fifteen years and before I had met her, she had already served on award juries, been a guest of honour at conventions, been responsible for convention programming, made the Hugo shortlist for Best Fan Writer, and administered the BSFA. I mention all of these things in the same breath because these were all honours and activities I understood as someone whose engagement with SFF post-dated the creation of online venues and spaces. The further back I looked, the more I realised that Maureen was an accomplished and celebrated contributor to SFF before online fandom was even a thing.

This is significant as, back in the noughties, a lot of older and more established fans were acutely hostile to the idea that publishing stuff online might be viewed in the same light as publishing stuff in the form of a fanzine. This may seem absurd in the current climate but a serious attempt was even made to restrict the Hugo fan-categories to material published in traditional zines. To her eternal credit, Maureen was not one of those fans ... she was simply delighted to discover that people were discussing books on the internet and so followed the conversation online. In fact, one of Maureen's more endearing traits was her desire to overcome whichever technological barrier stood between her and the conversation. For Maureen, there was no fundamental difference between mimeographed zines, academic journals, blogs, online magazines, Discord servers, or podcasts; they were all just different places to talk and if you wanted to participate in the conversation, you learned the technology and adapted your thinking.

It is in this sense of continuity between different venues and forms of conversation that Maureen's voice really rings out. If you are fortunate enough to read her more recent criticism or receive her editorial advice, you will find the same voice and sensibility that once graced the pages of traditional fanzines like *Bottled Lightning*, *Snufkin's Bum*, or *Steam Engine Time*. That voice was so distinctive and endearing that it not only won Maureen a Nova award for traditional fan-writing, it also helped her become the beneficiary of the 1999 Trans-Atlantic Fan Fund. Decades later, Maureen would still speak animatedly about the many experiences she had travelling the country and meeting American fans. She had even internalised regional American culinary discourse on a number of issues including what constitutes a proper 'barbecue'.

In the years that I knew her, Maureen tended to downplay the work she had done in non-critical fanzines because that whimsical and intensely personal style of fan-writing had fallen out of fashion in an SFF culture that was growing steadily more serious and commercialised. Whenever I asked to see her earlier writings, Maureen would adroitly change the subject, but when I did eventually track down copies of her non-critical work, I was delighted to find the exact same voice that was present in all of her criticism. A voice that was somehow always on the brink of both exasperation and child-like glee; the id of fandom's passion always held in check by the wry and erudite superego of someone who treated the act of writing with a sense of magisterial solemnity.

I called the collection of Maureen's early reviews ...*And Another Thing* because Maureen was someone who always had something more to say. There were times when starting a conversation with Maureen was like popping the cork on a bottle of champagne; it was as though her ideas had spent years maturing in an oaken cask beneath a French chateau only for them to force themselves out with such force that you could only stand clear and help mop up the spill. Maureen wrote the way she spoke; in long, looping sentences that moved effortlessly from one insightful observation to another, filling the room as quickly and efficiently as possible lest someone dare to try and shut her up. There was always more to say and more conversation to be had. Lunch at the Speller Kincaid household only ever ended when someone looked up and noticed that the sun had gone down.

Maureen's commitment to SFF and her desire for intellectual connection broke through all boundaries. When the energy began to ebb away from traditional fanzines and towards online publication, Maureen simply altered her methods and followed the conversation. When the energy began to ebb away from blogs, Maureen altered her methods again and drew more heavily upon her skills as both an editor and an administrator. Many recent arrivals into the orbit of SFF's institutions may know Maureen chiefly as the long-standing senior editor of the reviews department at *Strange Horizons* but Maureen's commitments extended to a number of other institutions including research bodies, journals, and small presses. Maureen's commitment to the conversation was such that she not only followed it wherever it went, she also rolled up her sleeves and did the work required to allow others to participate. SFF culture will miss Maureen because even when she wasn't participating in the conversation, she was helping to include, empower, and welcome others. The casual inclusivity that Maureen practiced in person was echoed at every level of her work.

Maureen will be missed for everything that she was and everything she did.

Afterword by Aishwarya Subramanian and Dan Hartland

Maureen would not want us to look backwards.

That's not to say she would have disapproved of this book—far from it. Among the last conversations she had with us was about how keen she was to collect her work into a single volume. This was not an ambition which she suddenly discovered only after her diagnosis in March of 2022. It was an objective she had pursued for some years—and, for reasons we could never understand but suspect were more to do with others than with her, had never quite managed to fulfil.

What do we mean when we say that this volume's posthumous publication says more about its context than its content? Only that Maureen never received the recognition during her lifetime that we think she—and her work—deserved. There are, we are sure, many reasons for this. In Nina's introduction to this volume, she writes of the sexism—overt and covert—that characterised and characterises the often chilly and sceptical reception received by the work of women critics. That was certainly part of her experience.

But so, too, we might suggest, was her refusal to rub along, her restlessness and forward thinking. As Jonathan McCalmont writes in his own essay in this volume, as early as the noughties Maureen had set herself apart from many of her generation by embracing online publication; she had a habit of very rapidly growing beyond groupthink and comforting verities. This quality made her a fiercely incisive—and important—critic. But it didn't always leave her comfortably in any camp, and—in publishing as in fandom—the clubbable tend to seek each other out.

Maureen wouldn't want us to look backwards, then, because she never did. That untiring forward momentum might be another reason she never got around to collecting her own work: what was the point, she might have groaned, when the *next* review, the *next* essay, the *next* critical breakthrough was always around the corner? SFF is full of old voices discussing old books—or new voices that strangely resemble the old ones discussing recent books that seem wearily familiar. Maureen would not have wanted to contribute to that.

But, as this volume shows, her work is not of the past merely because it happened to be written in it. What shines through in Maureen's criticism is an innovative spirit that inspected a book from unexpected angles, and in this way generated productive insights about not just the particular book or writer in question, but its genre or mode or form more widely. This gives her work a vitality that extends beyond the year in which it was written, which offers us tools with which to do something *today*. Criticism is a creative act, and Maureen was one of our most creative critics: never hidebound, never nostalgic; never satisfied, never certain.

One of the ways she achieved this remarkable elasticity was in her writerly voice. She did not adopt a Leavisite grandiosity or a performative precision. She was both frankly discursive and confidently tentative, writing in a style that was characterised by an apparent lightness which in turn enabled in fact a more robust and deeper penetration of a text, precisely because of its water-like transparency and flow. This does not mean she was *less* a critic—that somehow her eschewal of the tired old conventions of authority and gravitas made her something else. No, her insistence on impishness made her a *better* critic, a more contemporary critical voice than any of her peers. She pointed the way to more constructive, more open, more *dynamic* means of engaging with texts. She showed those of us who paid attention how to do better.

Some of this required her to stand back even from her own work—that work she never quite managed to collect herself, that work which we now see before us, between these covers, and can assess in the round. She was not above or shy about questioning it, or the frames within which it had been produced. She came to connect less with British SFF fandom than she once had in the 1980s and 1990s; she developed a scepticism about the very wisdom of taking award shortlists seriously, as she had in the 2000s; she applied postcolonial readings to her favourite writers and she was brave enough to find them wanting. She was always moving forwards. She saw that what was next was always worth engaging with, was always worth trying to make better, and that this sometimes required us to shed our selves. Criticism was how she developed new understandings; it was how she tried to show us the way.

When the three of us were appointed, in 2015, as Reviews Editors at *Strange Horizons*, we each knew each other somewhat, largely by reputation or through mutual friends or by reading each other's work. Maureen had considerably more experience in writing SF criticism than any of us, and in a magazine like *Strange Horizons*, which privileges the new and the emerging, in some ways this perhaps seemed from the outside as odd: had Maureen Kincaid Speller not already spent years at publications of every kind. We were taking over from Abigail Nussbaum, who had in turn inherited the department from Niall Harrison; Maureen belonged to a generation prior to the rest of us. Could she really lead this department into the future?

She could, and she did. As Senior Reviews Editor, she took the department further than it had ever been before in terms of its diversity, its radicalism, its professionalism. Within our first year, forty-four per cent of our reviews were by women; in our second, it was fifty-eight per cent, a just proportion that eludes so many other magazines and yet held until her final days with us. We published trans reviewers and reviewers of colour; we eventually adopted not just radical content but a radical structure, formalising the anarchistic tendency by which we'd always run the Reviews department and seeing it spread across the magazine as a whole. We curated engaged criticism for special issues which spotlighted trans and nonbinary SFF, Arabic SFF, Palestinian SFF, Brazilian SFF, SFF in translation … on and on. As a team, we saw four managing editorial regimes come and go; and, building on the foundations we inherited from our predecessors, we cobbled together a department which—we believe—is one of the best sources of SFF criticism available anywhere today. And we did it all under Maureen's leadership. We did it *because* of Maureen's leadership. We did it thanks to her unerring forward momentum.

None of this was new to Maureen's practice. While it's notable that of the forty-nine pieces Nina has collected for this volume, only two predate the turn of the millennium—and a full forty were produced after 2010—Maureen's work had always been characterised by an insistence on progress. Take her 1993 *Vector* piece, 'A Judge's Summary of the Clarke Award'. In it, she fulminates against a male critic's dismissal of a novel written by a woman as reading more like 'creative writing' than proper SF; she knowingly professes to be at a loss as to why the selection of that year's winning novel—also by a woman—by a majority vote rather than unanimity 'should be such a big deal'; and finally she needles the SFF cognoscenti-at-large which distrusted any fiction published from outside the genre ('if it looks like a duck … and is labelled a hen, it is still indubitably a duck'). This is entirely the Maureen we might recognise from her final piece, published in *Strange Horizons* in January 2022, in which we read, 'It is uncomfortable to be out of step with everyone else, and yet you have to say what you see'. Maureen was never afraid to do this—or, if she was, she was honest enough to proceed regardless.

These decades of truth-seeking are contained (though certainly not exhausted) within these covers. They add up to a formidable body of work which demands the attention of any serious critic of SFF because it is—possibly uniquely—untainted by the need to be accepted. Its only purpose was—is—to understand.

One might imagine that by 2015, Maureen, having already spent so long expanding our understanding of the genre, might have felt her work to be done. But in fact, she often remarked to both of us that she considered *Strange Horizons* to be the most important thing she would ever do. This left us blinking, since her work seemed to us so much wider and more vital than that: it encompassed her own criticism, published in its fullest form on her website, *Paper Knife*; her editing work for *Foundation* and elsewhere, which contributed so plainly to opinion-setting in the field; and her foundational work in the 1980s and 1990s which, whatever her later ambivalence about those spaces, created room within traditional fandom structures for women critics to be heard. In this context, her work alongside us was perhaps *an* important part of her long career; but *the* most important? What could she mean?

It came to be plain to us that she felt the best thing she could do—the most important thing she could do—was equip the next generation of critics and reviewers to do better than she felt her generation had done. This was not just a process of education; it was a task of construction. Her project, she believed, was through *Strange Horizons* to build the truly diverse, rigorous, innovative and exciting base of SFF critics that she knew the genre needed. She saw herself as—and she successfully became—the Gandalf of a new company, their inciting action, their first opportunity, and their finest finishing school. SFF suffered, she believed—and we agreed—from a critical community that was too white, too Anglo-American, too backward-looking, too insular. The reason she believed her work at *Strange Horizons* was the most important she would ever do was because she selflessly knew that her legacy would be not just what she wrote—but who she helped to write next.

In January of 2022, *Strange Horizons* published its first ever criticism special, a moment that Maureen had been instrumental in achieving. In the editorial for that issue, the three of us wrote, 'we trouble [...] boundaries where we can. Widening our sense of who gets to be part of the critical conversation, as well as what contexts and frameworks and forms of expression are available in engaging in that conversation, is a political choice'. It won't be any surprise to the reader of the work collected in *A Traveller in Time* that Maureen was the governing intelligence behind this statement of intent. If, in future years, we and *Strange Horizons* continue the tradition of an annual criticism special, it will be because of Maureen's foundational work; if, in future years, SFF criticism is more wide-ranging, more expansive, more *radical* than before, then Maureen would have played a large part in achieving that, too. And all of this was seeded in Maureen's very earliest work—*Strange Horizons* and her contributions to the future of SFF criticism weren't so much where Maureen ended up as they were the place she was always trying to reach.

Maureen's final full year at the helm of *SH*'s Reviews department was 2021. In that year, a quarter of all our reviews were by brand new writers; a similar proportion took as their subject debut works by authors new to the field, the language, or both. We had established a tradition of multi-person reviews which offered more than one perspective on a single text, roundtables which made explicit Maureen's view of criticism as a conversation; we insisted on placing comics and academic monographs side-by-side with gallery exhibitions and poetry. We wanted to do more. The department never stopped growing, expanding, or striving. Maureen was never settled, never self-satisfied, always looking forward. Her questions were always: what was next, what more could be done, what more space can we create?

To our knowledge, the only documented instance of Maureen Kincaid Speller agreeing with a Tory was on Theresa May's insistence upon the virtue of being a difficult woman. Maureen would want you to know that she was one, and that it was part of not just how she did criticism but also how she built critical spaces. Publishers received short shrift when in search of puff pieces; spec reviews that did not seem to have been tooled to a magazine's particular needs were spiked; figures in fandom, and the genre more widely, who let the side down or did not get onboard with what needed to be done were not given many chances to rectify their oversights. Maureen's work was not all hugs and bunnies; it couldn't be. Occasionally, too, she burned out, and one or other or both of us would cover while she was gone. She, of course, would do the same for us. She wouldn't want you to think that anything worthwhile is ever plain-sailing—or that any writer is somehow a saint.

But we nevertheless came to refer to ourselves as 'the gestalt', because on the questions that really mattered, we agreed. If one of us thought a review was worth commissioning, it was almost always true that the others did, too. If one of us thought a particular convention had put a clomping foot wrong, the others were similarly disapproving. And, most importantly, our opinions converged with predictable regularity on the subject of which were the bad books ... and which the good.

We were, though, always persuadable otherwise. That is the purpose of criticism, after all: to enhance our understanding, and in doing so, perhaps to change it. Maureen sought out reviewers who could help her see texts from new angles—and, crucially, help the genre see itself in new ways, too. 'Critical' is not 'negative'. As we wrote in our tribute to Maureen in the first issue of *Strange Horizons* to appear following her death, 'when we want to refer to positive commentary we are forced to add an adjective, writing of "constructive criticism"—[but] criticism is always constructive; the adjective is redundant'. In writing her own criticism, and in the way in which both that work and her editorial practice helped build a platform for others to join the conversation, Maureen sought to critique the genre—and sometimes its readers—in order to improve it. In order to improve us.

That work is ongoing, and is being undertaken in good part by writers who learned from Maureen: from reading her work, or from being edited by her, or from seeing the spaces she built. More than that, it will be undertaken in the future by writers who enter the genre because of work she did, who walk through doors she opened—sometimes through ones she built herself, sometimes through holes or cracks that she bashed out of unwilling stone. Many will not even know they do so; Maureen would not have cared. What she would have wanted was for the work to be good, and for the work to have impact. She would have wanted SFF to be better, to know itself more, to move forwards.

We now take that work on. We hope you will, too. Look back, of course—because as these pages have shown, writers now gone leave behind them wisdom. But look forward more: because the best of those writers—and Maureen Kincaid Speller was among the best of them—entrusted us with their work so that we might build on it. Time travels on; and always forwards.

Aishwarya Subramanian and Dan Hartland

December 2022.

Acknowledgements

So many thanks to Paul Kincaid, who embraced the idea for this project from the moment I first suggested it. Paul has given generously of his time and attention in the most tragic of circumstances, for which no words are enough. Thanks also to Dan Hartland, who has been exceptionally helpful and generous with his feedback and support, likewise to Aisha Subramanian and Jonathan McCalmont for their fine contributions to this volume. Thank you to Farah Mendlesohn, whose encouragement has meant a lot and whose crowdsourced biographical tribute to Maureen—now published in *Vector* #296—provided an invaluable checklist of significant dates. Thanks also to those of British fandom who assisted Farah in putting together that tribute. Thank you to Iain Clark, whose generosity allowed us to use his work 'Path' as the cover art for this volume—a more fitting image I could not imagine. Thanks to Leigh Kennedy, whose beautiful photograph of Maureen appears inside it. Huge, huge thanks and love to Francesca Barbini and her team at Luna Press Publishing, who came on board instantly and without whom this book would most likely not exist. Thanks to Chris, for his support throughout. And finally, thanks forever to Maureen Kincaid Speller, for her friendship, for her intelligence, for her inspiring conversation, for her presence in all our lives. We will think of you always.

Reference List

The articles in this volume, as presented, first appeared in the following publications and online venues:

2015. {and then} – a writing life beyond reviews. *Paper Knife* [blog] 19 July. Available at: <https://paperknife.wordpress.com/2015/07/19/and-then-a-writing-life-beyond-reviews/> [Accessed 19 April 2023].

2012. All right, have it your way – you saw a man with a raygun! *Paper Knife* [blog] 4 June. Available at: <https://paperknife.wordpress.com/2012/06/04/all-right-have-it-your-way-you-saw-a-man-with-a-raygun/> [Accessed 19 April 2023].

2014. Reading Margaret Atwood's *In Other Worlds: science fiction and the human imagination*. *Foundation*, 118 [online]. Available at: <https://fanac.org/fanzines/Foundation/Foundation118.pdf> [Accessed 19 April 2023].

1993. A Judge's Summary of the Clarke Award. *Vector*, 173, June.

2018. On wanting to be astonished by science fiction. *Paper Knife* [blog] 20 March. Available at: <https://paperknife.wordpress.com/2018/03/20/on-wanting-to-be-astonished-by-science-fiction/> [Accessed 20 April 2023].

2015. We Need To Talk About Dragons – John Mullan, George RR Martin, *Game of Thrones* and the triumph of fantasy fiction. *Paper Knife* [blog] 10 April. Available at : <https://paperknife.wordpress.com/2015/04/10/we-need-to-talk-about-dragons-john-mullan-george-rr-martin-game-of-thrones-and-the-triumph-of-fantasy-fiction/> [Accessed 20 April 2023].

2013. Making an Emotional Investment – surviving the announcement of the Hugo Award shortlists. *Paper Knife* [blog] 8 April. Available at: <https://paperknife.wordpress.com/2013/04/08/making-an-emotional-investment-surviving-the-announcement-of-the-hugo-award-shortlists/> [Accessed 20 April 2023].

2006. *Daughters of Earth*, edited by Justine Larbalestier. *Strange Horizons* [online]. Available at: < http://strangehorizons.com/non-fiction/reviews/daughters-of-earth-edited-by-justine-larbalestier/> [Accessed 20 April 2023].

2020. *Women's Weird 2: More Strange Stories by Women 1891–1937*, edited by Melissa Edmundson. *Strange Horizons* [online]. Available at: <http://strangehorizons.com/non-fiction/reviews/womens-weird-2-more-strange-stories-by-women-1891-1937-edited-by-melissa-edmundson/> [Accessed 20 April 2023].

2008. *Galactic Suburbia: Recovering Women's Science Fiction* by Lisa Yaszek. *Strange Horizons* [online]. Available at: <http://strangehorizons.com/non-fiction/reviews/galactic-suburbia-recovering-womens-science-fiction-by-lisa-yaszek/> [Accessed 20 April 2023].

2006. *James Tiptree Jr: the double life of Alice B. Sheldon* by Julie Phillips. *Interzone*, 205, Jul-Aug.

2017. *Love Beyond Body, Space & Time* edited by Hope Nicholson. *Strange Horizons* [online]. Available at: <http://strangehorizons.com/non-fiction/reviews/love-beyond-body-space-time-edited-by-hope-nicholson/> [Accessed 2- April 2023].

2014. They Are Not Ghosts: on the representation of the indigenous peoples of North America in science fiction and fantasy. *A Dribble of Ink* [online]. Available at: <https://aidanmoher.com/blog/tag/maureen-kincaid-speller/> [Accessed 20 April 2023].

2014. Reading *Motherhip: Tales from Afrofuturism and Beyond* edited by Bill Campbell and Edward Austin Hall, and *We See a Different Frontier* edited by Fabio Fernandez and Djibril al-Ayad. *Vector*, 276, Summer.

2013. *AfroSF: Science Fiction by African Writers* edited by Ivor W. Hartmann. Interzone, 245, March-April.

2016. *AfroSF* Volume 2 edited by Ivor W. Hartmann. *Strange Horizons* [online]. Available at: <http://strangehorizons.com/non-fiction/reviews/afrosfv2-edited-by-ivor-w-hartmann/> [Accessed 20 April 2023].

2010. *Quis Est Iste Qui Venit*. *Paper Knife* [blog] 28 December. Available at: <https://paperknife.wordpress.com/2010/12/28/quis-est-iste-qui-venit/> [Accessed 20 April 2023].

2005. England's Redemption: An Examination of Richard Cowper's Corlay Sequence. *Foundation*, 93, spring. Paper originally delivered as: 2001: A Celebration of British Science Fiction. Part of *2001: A Celebration of British Science Fiction*. Liverpool, Foresight Centre, University of Liverpool, UK, August 2001.

1987. *The Owl Service* TV series adapted for the screen by Alan Garner, directed by Peter Plummer. *Matrix*, 71, Aug-Sept.

2005. 'Fusion with a land rescued me': landscape and presence in the writings of Alan Garner. *Glasgow Worldcon*. Glasgow, SEC Glasgow, UK, August. Later published online at *SF Foundation*.

2012. *Boneland* by Alan Garner: preliminary notes. *Paper Knife* [blog] 2 September. Available at: <https://paperknife.wordpress.com/2012/09/02/boneland-by-alan-garner-preliminary-notes/> [Accessed 20 April 2023].

2018. *First Light: a celebration of Alan Garner* edited by Erica Wagner and *The Beauty Things* by Mark Edmonds and Alan Garner. *Strange Horizons* [online]. Available at: <http://strangehorizons.com/non-fiction/reviews/first-light-a-celebration-of-alan-garner-edited-by-erica-wagner-and-the-beauty-things-by-mark-edmonds-and-alan-garner/> [Accessed 21 April 2023].

2022. The Critic and the Clue: tracking Alan Garner's *Treacle Walker*. *Strange Horizons* [online]. Available at: <http://strangehorizons.com/non-fiction/the-critic-and-the-clue-tracking-alan-garners-treacle-walker/> [Accessed 21 April 2023].

2017. *A Field Guide to Reality* — Joanna Kavenna. *Anglia Ruskin Centre for SF&F* as part of the Shadow Clarke project [blog], 13 April. Available at: <http://csff-anglia.co.uk/clarke-shadow-jury/a-field-guide-to-reality-by-joanna-kavenna-a-review-by-maureen-kincaid-speller/> [Accessed 21 April 2023].

2012. Walking with Tolkien and Macfarlane. *Paper Knife* [blog] 28 December. Available at: <https://paperknife.wordpress.com/2012/12/28/walking-with-tolkien-and-macfarlane/> [Accessed 21 April 2023].

2021. Review: *Mothlight* by Adam Scovell. *Paper Knife* [blog] 24 August. Available at: <https://paperknife.wordpress.com/2021/08/24/review-mothlight-by-adam-scovell/> [Accessed 21 April 2023].

2014. Reading for the Future. *Paper Knife* [blog] 3 November. Available at: <https://paperknife.wordpress.com/2014/11/03/reading-for-the-future/> [Accessed 21 April 2023].

2017. *The Children of Green Knowe* and *A Traveller in Time* – a tale of two novels. *Paper Knife* [blog] 17 January. Available at: <https://paperknife.wordpress.com/2017/01/17/the-children-of-green-knowe-and-a-traveller-in-time-a-tale-of-two-novel/> [Accessed 21 April 2023].

'We were all monsters and bastards and we were beautiful' – Rachel Hartman's *Seraphina*. *Paper Knife* [blog] 11 May. Available at: <https://paperknife.wordpress.com/2013/05/11/we-were-all-monsters-and-bastards-and-we-were-beautiful-rachel-hartmans-seraphina/> [Accessed 21 April 2023].

2007. Reading *Diana Wynne Jones: Children's Literature and the Fantastic Tradition* by Farah Mendlesohn. *Science Fiction Studies*, 102, July.

2013. *More Than This* by Patrick Ness. *Strange Horizons* [online]. Available at: <http://strangehorizons.com/non-fiction/reviews/more-than-this-by-patrick-ness/> [Accessed 21 April 2023].

2017. 'Recordings alone aren't sufficient' – speaking *Arrival*. *Paper Knife* [blog] 9 January. Available at: <https://paperknife.wordpress.com/2017/01/09/recordings-alone-arent-sufficient-speaking-arrival/> [Accessed 21 April 2023].

2016. The View from G21: watching *Star Wars: The Force Awakens*. *Paper Knife* [blog] 17 January. Available at: <https://paperknife.wordpress.com/2016/01/17/the-view-from-g21-watching-star-wars-the-force-awakens/> [Accessed 21 April 2023].

2016. 'he had a remarkable gentleness and courtesy in his dealings with women'– the *Sherlock* Christmas special. *Paper Knife* [blog] 5 January. Available at: <https://paperknife.wordpress.com/2016/01/05/sherlock-christmas-special/> [Accessed 21 April 2023].

2012. *The Hobbit*, or Madly in All Directions. *Paper Knife* [blog] 27 December. Available at: <https://paperknife.wordpress.com/2012/12/27/the-hobbit-or-madly-in-all-directions/> [Accessed 21 April 2023].

2015. Watching *Hamlet* (dir. Lyndsey Turner 2015). *Paper Knife* [blog] 3 November. Available at: <https://paperknife.wordpress.com/2015/11/03/watching-hamlet-dir-turner-2015/> [Accessed 21 April 2023].

2013. Reading van Vogt's *Slan*. *Paper Knife* [blog] 5 January. Available at: <https://paperknife.wordpress.com/2013/01/05/reading-van-vogts-slan/> [Accessed 21 April 2023].

2012. The Weird – *The Dunwich Horror* – H. P. Lovecraft. *Paper Knife* [blog] 1 February. Available at: <https://paperknife.wordpress.com/2012/02/01/the-weird-the-dunwich-horror-h-p-lovecraft/> [Accessed 21 April 2023].

2012. *Embassytown* – China Mieville. *Paper Knife* [blog] 19 April. Available at: <https://paperknife.wordpress.com/2012/04/19/embassytown-china-mieville/> [Accessed 21 April 2023].

2012. *Osama* – Lavie Tidhar. *Paper Knife* [blog] 28 April. Available at: <https://paperknife.wordpress.com/2012/04/28/osama-lavie-tidhar/> [Accessed 21 April 2023].

2017. *Azanian Bridges* – Nick Wood. *Anglia Ruskin Centre for SF&F* as part of the Shadow Clarke project [blog], 16 May. Available at: <http://csff-anglia.co.uk/clarke-shadow-jury/azanian-bridges-by-nick-wood-a-review-by-maureen-kincaid-speller/> [Accessed 21 April 2023].

2015. *The Book of Phoenix* by Nnedi Okorafor. *Interzone*, 259, July-August.

2012. *The Testament of Jessie Lamb* – Jane Rogers. *Paper Knife* [blog] 25 April. Available at: <https://paperknife.wordpress.com/2012/04/25/the-testament-of-jessie-lamb-jane-rogers/> [Accessed 21 April 2023].

2012. *Gods Without Men* by Hari Kunzru. *Strange Horizons* [online]. Available at: <http://strangehorizons.com/non-fiction/reviews/gods-without-men-by-hari-kunzru/> [Accessed 21 April 2023].

2012. *By Light Alone* – Adam Roberts. *Paper Knife* [blog] 17 April. Available at: <https://paperknife.wordpress.com/2012/04/17/by-light-alone-adam-roberts/> [Accessed 21 April 2023].

2013. *Zone One* – Colson Whitehead. *Paper Knife* [blog] 31 March 31. Available at: <https://paperknife.wordpress.com/2013/03/31/zone-one-colson-whitehead/> [Accessed 21 April 2023].

2015. Reading *Elysium* by Jennifer Marie Brissett. *Paper Knife* [blog] 9 August. Available at: <https://paperknife.wordpress.com/2015/08/09/reading-elysium-by-jennifer-marie-brissett/> [Accessed 21 April 2023].

2014. *Europe in Autumn* – Dave Hutchinson. *Paper Knife* [blog] 25 May. Available at: <https://paperknife.wordpress.com/2014/05/25/europe-in-autumn-dave-hutchinson/> [Accessed 21 April 2023].

2014. *The Stone Boatmen* by Sarah Tolmie. *Strange Horizons* [online]. Available at: <http://strangehorizons.com/non-fiction/reviews/the-stone-boatmen-by-sarah-tolmie/> [Accessed 21 April 2023].

www.ingramcontent.com/pod-product-compliance
Lightning Source LLC
Chambersburg PA
CBHW070507120526
44590CB00013B/777